ACROSS
THE GOBI DESERT

Ting, Tsui, Hsü Ping-chang, Li, Haslund, Bergman, Dettmann, von Kaull, Hempel, Zimmermann, Hedin, Mühlenweg, Heyder, von Massenbach, Haude, Hummel, Norin, Söderbom, Lieberenz, Larson (Walz, Marschall von Bieberstein, Yüan, Huang, Ma, Chan, Liu, and Kung, not present)

MEMBERS OF THE EXPEDITION IN FRONT OF PERMANENT STATION No. 1

[frontispiece

ACROSS
THE GOBI DESERT

BY

SVEN HEDIN

WITH 114 ILLUSTRATIONS
AND THREE MAPS

GREENWOOD PRESS, PUBLISHERS
NEW YORK   1968

Translated from the German

by

H. J. CANT

First published in 1931

This edition published by special arrangement with
E. P. Dutton & Co., Inc. (New York) and
Routledge & Kegan Paul, Ltd. (London)

First Greenwood reprinting, 1968

LIBRARY OF CONGRESS catalogue card number: 68-23296

PRINTED IN THE UNITED STATES OF AMERICA

PREFACE

AGAIN in Asia after a forced interval of many years. And this time not alone, for the task that I have set before me for this expedition, the greatest of my life, encroaches to so great an extent on the most diverse spheres of knowledge, that it was natural that for the various departments we should take along with us younger specialists.

The expedition was to work with all the equipment of modern investigation, so I developed the plan of flying over those places in the desert that were inaccessible. In this I hoped that Germany would lend assistance. I appealed to Professor Hugo Junkers, by whom I met with the most lively interest. Later the Deutsche Luft Hansa declared themselves prepared to further our relations with the German flying circles. So we were accompanied by eight more Germans, all of whom were experienced in both the theoretical and practical sides of flying.

But in Urumchi we met with a serious check : the powerful governor of the province of Sin-kiang, Yang Tsêng-hsin, prohibited flying over his territory. Thereupon first of all the German fliers returned home, and in June I too left for Europe, above all in order to secure further means for continuing the expedition during succeeding years, and I sought the assistance of the Swedish State.

How the Chinese scholars and students came to the expedition is told in detail in the book. Here for the present I will only say how valuable and indispensable to me their co-operation became from month to month.

*   *   *   *   *

The first part of the great journey in Asia lies behind us, the march from Paotow to Urumchi across the Gobi Desert during the winter of 1927–8. Now I go on board the ship

v

that is to take me back to my comrades, who throughout these summer months have not allowed their scientific labours to cease. New tasks call me.

I have hesitated whether, so early as this, I ought to have published anything on the journey, for, at the moment, I have no time to gather together into a book my voluminous notes recorded day by day. So I have left this entirely to my publishers, as well as the choice of illustrations from the many hundreds of photographs taken by our diligent German photographer, Paul Lieberenz, who has also taken the film of this journey: "With Sven Hedin across the Deserts of Asia."

*   *   *   *   *

I cannot conclude without paying my debt of thanks to all who have helped me to realize my long-cherished desire to return to Asia, and moreover at the head of so large an expedition.

In this, especially the Germans. Never shall I forget the chivalrous conduct and the spirit of accommodation with which I was met on the part of the Germans. This occasion seems to me like a fairy-story and a dream, and will always be numbered among my dearest and most cherished memories. The co-operation with the leading figures of the Luft Hansa has at all times been marked by sincere trust and the utmost cordiality.

In as short a space as possible I must also express my warm thanks to the Swedish Minister, Oskar Ewerlöf, and Baron Carl Leijonhufvud, both of whom rendered me invaluable services during my stay in Peking and, later, during my journey; to Professor J. G. Andersson, who was my untiring adviser, and, moreover, drew with full hands out of the rich store of his Chinese experiences; to the head of the Geological Survey of China, Dr. Wong, Professor Dr. A. Grabau, and the great American explorer, Roy Chapman Andrews, for the goodwill and help that they accorded me; and finally, the "Opposition" in Peking, the Chinese scholars who, from being my opponents, became my friends and co-workers.

I also express my sincere and cordial thanks to every individual member of my staff, in which every man did his duty, all friction was banished, and nothing but good fellowship held sway. With such men as my Swedes, Germans, and Chinese, one can in the course of time open up to scientific study vast territories in Central Asia. The earnest and friendly co-operation between Europeans and Chinese was a source of real joy to me, and I held it to my advantage to have come into such close contact with representatives of the greatest and, in many respects, most interesting people of the earth.

With especial thanks do I remember my good old friend Fred Löwenadler, who as long ago as 1912 placed at my disposal a very generous contribution towards my " next journey."

An expression of thanks to my servants will presumably never reach them. Most excellent services were rendered us by the three archæological collectors, Chuang, Pai, and Chin. The Chinese and Mongols who were in our service all carried out their duties faithfully, and exceptions were rare.

Finally, I remember with sadness the faithful camels that without complaining carried us and our loads across the endless spaces, so many of which are lying for ever on the long, weary road across the Gobi Desert.

SVEN HEDIN.

STOCKHOLM, *August 7th*, 1928.

PREFACE TO THE ENGLISH EDITION

THE expedition [1] described in this volume was transformed into a purely Swedish and Chinese undertaking in the summer of 1928, when the Swedish Government granted me a subsidy of half a million crowns for two more years of work. In the autumn of 1930 our funds were exhausted, but by the generosity of the Swedish Government I was honoured with a new grant in the spring of 1931 sufficient to ensure the continuance of our Sino-Swedish exploration until the summer of 1933.

It is my first duty to express my deep and respectful gratitude to His Majesty the King of Sweden and his Government for the interest, sympathy, and generosity shown to me and the members of my staff, both Swedes and Chinese, and the three Germans, one Dane, and one Russian who belong to our Mission.

I also regard it as an especial privilege to express my sincere gratitude to His Royal Highness the Crown Prince of Sweden, who is our Patron and Protector, and supports us in every possible way.

It would take me too far to mention all the firms, societies, and private persons that have facilitated our undertaking by generous presents, both of money and outfit. In this connexion I shall only express my sincerest thanks to the British-American Tobacco Co. for their generosity in presenting us with the gigantic quantity of three hundred thousand cigarettes.

In the present volume the reader will become acquainted only with the first period of our personal experiences. If this volume arouses interest in the English-speaking world,

[1] Called in Chinese "The Scientific Expedition to the Northwestern Provinces," and in European languages, "The Sino-Swedish Expedition."

ix

I hope to publish a second one, which will take the reader to the actual situation in our Mission. It may even now be said, that all the scientific members of the expedition have made brilliant contributions to our knowledge of Central Asia. Never before have pilot balloons been sent up, in the very heart of Asia, to a height of 69,500 feet. Three hundred and fifty such balloons were sent up by our chief meteorologist, Dr. Waldemar Haude, who has also given instruction to a numerous staff of young Chinese students now busy as observers in the permanent meteorological stations we founded at Etsin-gol and in Chinese Turkestan.

For four years our chief geologist, Dr. Erik Norin, has explored the geology and orography of Chinese Turkestan and its surrounding mountains in a way and in a detail entirely unparalleled. At the same time he has studied the quaternary climatic changes of the Tarim basin, thus giving a definite and conclusive explanation of the desiccation of these regions. When, on February 20, 1928, I heard from natives in Turfan that the Tarim River had changed its bed and returned to its northern course in the Kum-darya, I sent Dr. Norin to make a map of the new river. This he did in the spring of 1928 and the spring of 1930, on the latter occasion accompanied by our Swedish astronomer, Dr. Nils Ambolt, who has made more careful astronomical observations than has ever before been the case in the history of these regions. Dr. Ambolt has also made very detailed observations of gravity, using the most modern Inwar-pendulums.

As Dr. Erik Norin had already made several journeys of geological survey both in Kashmir, Ladak, and Western Himalaya and in Shan-si, he was very pleased to extend his exploration to the whole of High Asia. It is no exaggeration to say that his results are epoch-making. On the subject of the Kuruk-tagh mountains he has written a very detailed monograph. The permo-carboniferous ice-age of Kuruk-tagh belongs to his important discoveries. He has also studied the quaternary ice-age and moraines in K'un-lun, and the post-glacial sea that filled most of Eastern Turkestan, and has left very beautiful beach-lines along its shores.

Professor P. L. Yuan, our chief Chinese geologist, has been in the field with us since the spring of 1927, and has done excellent exploration work in the fields of several sciences, geology, archæology, topography, etc. Amongst other things he has discovered, at the northern foot of the T'ien-shan, east of Urumchi, fossil dinosaurs in great numbers, probably belonging to a species hitherto unknown. At the present moment Prof. Yuan is on his way to Peking through the Gobi Desert bringing with him all his own and Dr. Norin's collections, and completing his work as he proceeds.

In the same way the young Chinese scholars, the archæologist, Hwang Wen-pi, and the palæontologist, Ting Tao Heng, have contributed most effectively to our results. For example, Mr. Hwang has made very important additional surveys of the lower part of the present Kum-darya and has found about 80 wooden slips with manuscripts from *circa* 80 B.C.

Our young Swedish archæologist, Folke Bergman, has collected about 50,000 implements, hammers, axes, arrows, etc., of neolithic type. Together with articles of the same nature collected by Prof. Yuan and Mr. Hwang, our collections from the stone age will now have reached the figure of over 100,000 specimens.

From June, 1930, until late spring, 1931, Mr. Bergman examined and mapped the whole region of Etsin-gol with its numerous watch-towers. His first discovery of MSS. on wooden slips, to the number of some 360 pieces, was made at Borotsonch, east of lower Etsin-gol. When he returned to Peking at the end of May, 1931, his collection of MSS. on wooden slips had increased to more than 10,000 pieces, all dating from at least 86 to 31 B.C., a few even earlier. This enormous collection will be carefully deciphered, translated, and published, by Professor Bernhard Karlgren, of Gothenburg, and Professors Liu Fu and Ma Heng of Peking. Within the walls of Kharakhoto, Mr. Bergman also discovered heaps of MSS. on paper, in six different languages, Uigur, Chinese, Mongolian, Hsi-hsia, Iranian, and a language probably hitherto unknown.

Our Swedish palæontologist, Dr. Birger Bohlin, well known for his work upon Sinanthropus pekinensis, has made many very important discoveries of fossil animals, the most interesting being perhaps fishes and insects of the carboniferous age which had been astonishingly well preserved through some hundred million years. This spring he has discovered, some days' journey to the west of Suchow, masses of palæolithic implements, together with fossil animals from the Late Tertiary or Early Quaternary period.

Our young Swedish palæontologist, Gerhard Bexell, has made a collection of many thousands of fossil plants in the Gobi Desert and in the Nan-shan Mountains. He has, like some other members of our party, suffered a good deal from bandits. On June 6th, 1931, he was plundered and robbed of everything he possessed, but continued his work as if nothing had happened, and we have been able, by the kind assistance of the Chinese, to send him a new outfit, instruments, arms, and money.

The surgeon of our Mission is Dr. David Hummel, who, besides carrying on his medical work, has made very large and valuable collections of plants, reptiles, fishes, and insects. He has also carried out several hundred anthropometrical measurements, a kind of work for which he was prepared by Dr. Paul Stevenson of the P.U.M.C. in Peking. During 1930, Dr. Hummel made a very fine journey through Szechuan and Kansu to Choni and Tebbu on the N.E. borderland of Tibet. He was accompanied by a young German, Mr. M. Bökenkamp, and by three Chinese students, who were of great assistance to him. During the earlier stages of our expedition, Mr. Georg Söderbom and Lieutenant Henning Haslund acted as his assistants. Except for this, these two gentlemen have had more to do with the commissariat and the large caravans of the different groups of the Mission.

Dr. Nils Hörner, one of our geologists, joined the expedition during the summer of 1929. He has done excellent work in Lang-shan, along the old beds of the Hwang-ho, in the Gobi Desert, along the Etsin-gol, in Nan-shan, and along the desert road to Lop-nor. His work is related to that of Dr. Norin and Dr. Bohlin, and he is accompanied by the young Chinese geodesist, Parker C. Chen, who has done brilliant work during very hard campaigns in the heart of the continent.

Professor Hsü Ping-chang is the leader and chief of the Chinese contingent of the Mission. During our different journeys he has studied the history and ethnology of the regions through which we have passed. He has always helped me and the other members of the expedition with the greatest generosity in dealing with questions of historical interest. This assistance was facilitated by the fact that Mr. Hwang brought with him from Peking some three camel-loads of ancient Chinese books.

A year ago Professor Hsü published in Peking an excellent volume describing the first year of our expedition. It ought to be translated into European languages, not only on account of its value, but also because it gives a very clear idea of what an unusually able and learned Chinese scholar thinks of collaboration with European scholars.

Georg Söderbom, born in Kwei-hwa the son of a Swedish missionary, has served the expedition from the very beginning. He has been meteorological observer at our Etsin-gol station. He has been assistant to Dr. Hummel, and brought us with motor-car through the deserts. He has also collected plants, reptiles, and birds, and been useful in every way.

The very able and experienced Dane, Mr. Friis-Johansen, has on different occasions accompanied Dr. Bohlin or Mr. Bexell, and taken splendid care of our camels.

Not belonging to the expedition but still in my service, is Dr. Gösta Montell, the chief of the ethnographical department. He has made very large ethnographical collections and supervised the building of a replica of the Golden Pavilion of the Temple of Potala in Jehol which, by the generosity of Mr. Vincent Bendix, is to be erected in Chicago next year. Another temple, in Tibetan style, is to be built in Stockholm. All the furnishings of both temples, as well as large collections of ethnographical objects, have been gathered most conscientiously by Dr.

Montell, who has also made several journeys in Mongolia, the Gobi, and North China. Mr. Georg Söderbom is now acting as his assistant.

In close relation with us is the famous sinologue and Keeper of the Far-Eastern collections of the Museum für Völkerkunde in Berlin, Professor Ferdinand Lessing, who, since July, 1930, has been living in the " Swedish House " in Peking, and takes part more especially in Dr. Montell's work. To us it is a great privilege to be so closely associated with Professor Lessing. Professor Lessing will be the author of several of the books on Lamaism and temple architecture we are going to publish.

There are certainly many other members of our expedition whom I have not yet mentioned; for example, all our faithful Chinese and Mongolian servants, and some assistants, such as the young Russian, Vorotnikoff, who is always with Dr. Ambolt; the Anglo-Russian, Dr. W. Etches, who is looking after our interests in Urumchi during our absence; and several young Chinese who are joining different groups of the expedition.

I should like to say a word of most hearty thanks to our Chinese collaborators, both in our Committee in Peking and in the field. Without their assistance and generosity our expedition would have been impossible. To all of us it has been most agreeable to collaborate with these distinguished Chinese scholars, all of whom are now our friends and comrades. I have never been able to understand the complaints of Europeans against the Chinese. In most cases I think the misunderstandings and differences are due much less to the Chinese than to the Europeans.

As far as our expedition is concerned, it is an agreeable duty for me to express my deep gratitude to the National Government of China for its great generosity to us, as well as to all the Chinese members of the expedition. If, by any chance, our Swedish collaboration with the Chinese should prove to be of any use in the promotion of science in China, we shall all be very happy indeed.

SVEN HEDIN.

STOCKHOLM, *July* 14*th*, 1931.

CONTENTS

b

CONTENTS

LIST OF ILLUSTRATIONS

LIST OF ILLUSTRATIONS

xviii

LIST OF ILLUSTRATIONS

LIST OF ILLUSTRATIONS

XX

LIST OF ILLUSTRATIONS

xxi

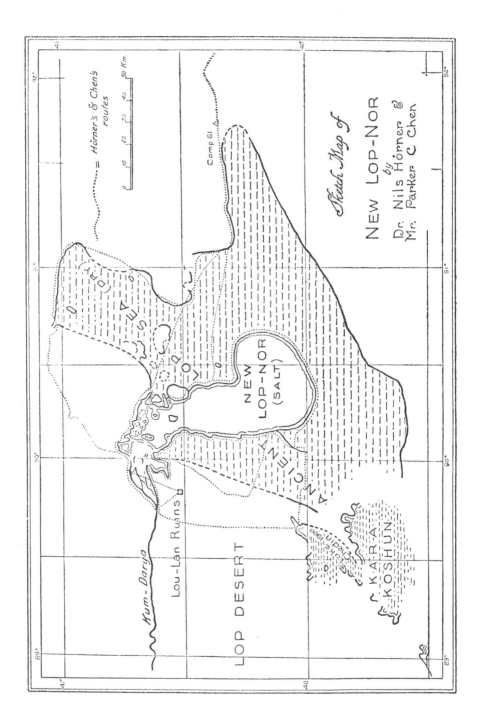

Sketch Map of
NEW LOP-NOR
by
Dr. Nils Hörner &
Mr. Parker C. Chen

ACROSS THE GOBI DESERT

I

AWAY AT LAST

A STRANGE time lay behind me, a period of ferment and transition in the history of China. I had watched attentively from a distance the tumult in Hankow, Shanghai, and Nanking. From my quiet peaceful room in the Legation Quarter of Peking I had followed day by day the shifting scenes in the confused chaos of wars and disputes between the various generals. I had myself been in the middle of a small storm-centre whose attack was directed against my expedition and threatened to frustrate my plans.

At last my last day in Peking had come. I had now only a single member of my staff left with me, the doctor of the expedition, Dr. David Hummel. I do not know which of the two of us on the 8th of May had most to do. We packed, and I went round and left my card at the Legations, English, American, and German, Danish, and Norwegian, that during the course of the winter and spring had shown me such great hospitality. I took my leave of Dr. V. K. Ting, Dr. W. H. Wong, and Dr. Grabau, the last of whom had promised to look after my interests in Peking during my absence, and finally I spent one pleasant hour more with the famous explorer of Mongolia, Roy Chapman Andrews, who had rendered me valuable services, not least in having sold me sixty-five well-tried camels that he was no longer using : he had decided, on account of the uncertain position, not to undertake during the coming summer a journey of discovery into Mongolia.

The last evening Dr. Hummel and I spent with the Swedish Minister, Oskar Ewerlöf. With energy, understanding, and tact, he had assisted me from the beginning in procuring, when it was necessary, the permission of the Chinese Government to undertake a great expedition in this time of unrest, and during the last weeks he had with the same skill and attachment helped me to pilot our undertaking past a number of dangerous hidden rocks that threatened to wreck us. But now we were victorious, were celebrating the evening with sparkling champagne, and were emptying our glasses to the health of the expedition and all those taking part in it.

The hour of deliverance draws near. On the morning of the 9th of May our luggage is placed down on the pavement in front of the Hôtel des Wagons-Lits; it is to be loaded on the motor-car that is coming from the bank and is bringing us a considerable part of our travelling-chest in silver. The car is late. The train leaves at 11.50. Thus we have only another three-quarters of an hour. The car drives up, and the luggage is placed on top. It is too heavy. A spring breaks. Other cars are sent for by telephone. I rush on in advance to the station by the Hsi Chih Mên, the north-west city gate of Peking. Here there is a crowd of Chinese: the five scholars and five students who are to take part in our peaceful campaign across Asia, most of the professors of the National University, and various members of the Board of Directors, the committee appointed to be our advocate and official protector during our journey of investigation.

An exciting half hour follows. The train runs in, and the carriage that has been placed at our disposal fills with our Chinese and their luggage. The station-master explains that he can only wait another ten minutes. It is already half past twelve, and the silver, our travelling-chest, is not here yet. I cannot hand over responsibility for all this money to Hummel alone: I must remain here and let the train go off. But this idea I regard very reluctantly. The Peking newspapers would then say that at the last moment insurmountable obstacles had been placed in my way. Some of my friends promise me that they will act as surety for the sending on of the silver. So I am inclined to go off without the luggage.

2

A cloud of dust whirls across the open square in front of the station and three or four cars rush up. "Hummel!" shouts the Swedish Minister. It is really our cars with the silver and the luggage. The splendid doctor has saved the situation. A crowd of coolies lend a hand and drag the heavy boxes into our carriage. When all is ready we bid farewell to Ewerlöf and our other friends, and the train begins to move. "Blessed be this hour," is my thought, "now begins the journey across the expanse of Asia."

Peking fades away behind us. The mountains that earlier seemed to form a dull, greyish-blue background to the stage stand out in more distinct colours. On both sides of the railway line there stretches away the wide alluvial plain with villages, huts, and grey walls, fields becoming green, arable land divided into plots of brownish grey, shady woods of poplars and willows. At the Nankow Pass there opens a natural portal that leads away into the mountain range. To the right the road runs off to the hallowed ground of the Ming Tombs, where the Emperor Yung Lo has been slumbering for five hundred years under his awe-inspiring tumulus.

Suddenly a dust-storm sweeps over the valley and wraps the whole surroundings in a thick haze. The old Wall that winds away over the mountains is lost to sight, and in our carriage everything becomes covered with yellow dust. But that does not spoil our holiday mood. All, not least the Chinese, are pleased to get away. What does it matter that the goods-van that the authorities have placed at our disposal is a former cattle-truck, in the middle of which and along whose sides narrow benches have been fixed, and in whose walls rectangular openings have been cut? Never has a first-class sleeping-carriage in Europe or America appeared more attractive to me than this dirty, dusty hovel. Hummel and I have established ourselves in the front part, where we make our tea and have our breakfast. Our immediate neighbours are the three archæological collectors who are soon to show their skill in hunting out prehistoric settlements.

In another group sits Professor Hsü Ping-chang engaged in conversation with two of his colleagues, whilst the students open their travelling-bags and take out their provisions, and the young photographer Kung makes the vain attempt to transfix on his plate a suitable stretch of the ramifications of the Great Wall in the narrow Nankow valley.

Not far away from us sits a man with strongly marked European features, in Western dress. His name is Li and he is a professor of geology. He has for that reason asked to be allowed to travel to Paotow in our special carriage with five of his students, and we are very pleased to have him with us : for he is amiable and good company and explains to his students and to us the geological formation of the valley. Hsü, the director of the Chinese staff of the expedition, and Li are welcome guests at our breakfast and dinner table.

We travel through places that I had passed through before, and the next day we arrive at Kuei-hua-chêng, the capital of the district of Sui-yüan, where we stop for twenty minutes and have the pleasure of meeting Dr. Erik Norin, our geologist, who is here purchasing Chinese provisions for our Chinese. Then on again, and hour after hour goes by. The plain stretches, uniform and dreary, to the south, where the Yellow River, the mighty Hwang Ho, gleams in two curves. Blossoming orchards lend colour and grace to the grey villages. In the north the low hills of the Yin-shan stretch away to the west as far as the eye can reach. Through the openings of the windows the sun sends in its warm rays to us. The Chinese are asleep, are smoking, or are drinking the tea that with them never ends, and we, two Swedes among seventeen sons of the Middle Kingdom, are discussing the vague unknown future and our great plans.

The sun goes down. In the distance Paotow emerges, the terminus of the most northerly of China's railways if one does not take the Manchurian railway into account. At 7.30 the train stops. At the station eight members of my German staff are awaiting us, among them Major Hempel, whom I have nominated as chief of staff, and Dr. Haude, who has charge of the meteorological observations and the wireless receiving-apparatus ; there is also

4

Camels passing through the streets

The entrance to our quarters

WE ARE DETAINED IN PAOTOW

[face p. 4

The provisions are packed in boxes . . .

. . . and loaded

PREPARATIONS IN PAOTOW

our Swedish archæologist, Folke Bergman, and the interpreter, H. Ssŭ, who is married to a German and speaks
fluently the mother tongue of his wife. Two policemen
are wanting to see our papers. Hummel and some of
the other principals escort the bullock-waggons that are
taking our treasure in silver to our farmstead that has
been rented since the past winter. The rest mount our
beautiful great camels and ride on to the city in advance.
In just a quarter of an hour we reach the south gate of
the city, and then, inside the city wall, have to go just as
far again to reach our farm. It is twilight, and, here and
there, the stalls of the traders in the market-streets are
lighting up their lamps. The dusty streets are still full
of life and are crowded with soldiers of the garrison that
Yen Hsi-shan, the governor of the province of Shansi,
has quartered in the city. Trumpets blare out ; the whole
place is full of soldiers. In the gateway of our farmstead
stands Larson, straddle-legged and in a commanding attitude, and he welcomes me and congratulates me on my
final triumph. I greet our servants, Chinese and Mongols,
and under the guidance of Larson and Baron von Massenbach I make a tour of our first headquarters on the road
to Central Asia. A narrow passage on the left, between
the cooking department and a larger room in which our
Chinese students are to live, leads to a small court-yard
where Larson has set up his tent, the front pole of which
flies the Swedish flag. Three rooms open on this court-
yard : a smaller one set aside for me, and two larger ones
to serve as club-room and dining-room.

On a second larger court-yard are situated the rooms
of all the other principals. Here are piled up hundreds
of boxes of provisions and stores, forming small hills.
It was nothing to get this enormous baggage to Paotow
in two goods-trucks, but it staggers one when one remem-
bers that these forty tons have to be carried by camels
across the belt of desert and day by day loaded and unloaded.

Crossing over a small hill we reach the third court-
yard where the camels we have so far bought are sheltered
and are given their fodder. Between these two court-

yards Dr. Haude has his meteorological observatory with all the delicate instruments that respond to the moods of the weather and of the winds.

While we are still making our tour of inspection the creaking of our silver-waggons can be heard, and the oxen drag their heavy burdens into the yard.

Not till 10 o'clock does a kitchen-boy go across the yards with a hand-bell, when we assemble in the dining-room for late supper. There is soup, fowl, and rice. We sit at two tables. Despite the absence of alcohol we are in joyful mood and high spirits. To those who had waited here for Dr. Hummel and myself since the 24th of March the time had become very long.

Some of our party had not yet joined us. Norin, known for his journeys of research in China and the Western Himalayas, was, as I mentioned before, in Kuei-hua-chêng, whence, reinforced by Major Walz and Baron Marschall von Bieberstein, he was to convey the newly-bought Chinese provisions on sixty camels to the agreed objective near the monastery of Beli-miao in Inner Mongolia. There two other members of the expedition were also to join the main caravan : the Dane Haslund-Christensen, whom I had taken into my service in Peking and who was to act as Larson's assistant, and our German cinemato-grapher, Lieberenz. Both these had received instructions to proceed to the Swedish mission-station of Hallun-ussu, 160 kilometres north of Kalgan, to take over the sixty-five camels that I had bought from Andrews.

Still, at our tables we were a large enough company for all that, and Professor Li was our guest of honour. All regretted that he was not able to accompany us. Over coffee I rapped on my cup and made a speech, in English for the benefit of the Chinese. I spoke of the tasks that awaited us, and how singular it was that we, in the midst of the civil war and seething unrest, were on the point of setting out towards the distant provinces of China, whilst all other Europeans were leaving the country and proceeding to the coast. All my white friends in Peking had viewed the co-operation with the Chinese scholars with doubts and misgivings. We would prove that the white and yellow races can live and work together very well, and that knowledge transcends political frontiers and the prejudices of the different races. Disturbing dissensions or short-sighted nationalism I did not intend to tolerate. In my caravan all would be friends, and the Chinese would enjoy the same rights as the Europeans. The Chinese, moreover, were in their own country, at home; we, on the other hand, were guests. I expected, therefore, that every man would do his duty; for, if all members of the expedition did their best, the results that we obtained would indeed contribute to the good of mankind. Finally I expressed a welcome to all present and the wish that we should all have a pleasant and successful journey.

Professor Hsü Ping-chang thereupon rose immediately and spoke in the same spirit on behalf of the Chinese. And then for a long time we continued sitting together.

It was long past midnight when I went to bed. I still lay awake a long time, lost in thought. Was it really true that I was at the head of the biggest scientific expedition that had ever set out for the centre of the greatest continent of the earth?

Nine days more had we to remain in Paotow, this frightful hole of 60,000 inhabitants and, for the time being, a garrison of some 30,000 men, this small city on the north bank of the Yellow River. Here I had in February, 1897, long before the time of the railway, spent several days, never to be forgotten, with the pleasant missionary family Helleberg from Stockholm, who were afterwards, like so many other Swedish missionaries, murdered during the Boxer rising. Nine whole days! Still there was nothing else for us to do. Before the negotiations in Peking had been brought to a satisfactory conclusion, I was not able to give Larson the order to buy the two hundred and fifty camels that we needed. And until these were bought we had to be content with hired camels. But the latter were pasturing on the mountain slopes at a distance of four days' journey from Paotow, and could not be at our disposal before the 18th of May. So we had again to possess our souls in patience.

7

We had, however, plenty to do, and so the days did not seem long to us. To the leader of a caravan of sixty men and about three hundred camels all come with their reports, requests, and complaints. Thousands upon thousands of things must be talked over and settled, so that everything may run smoothly and this moving town form an organic and harmonious entity. Nothing must be forgotten. I must check and confirm all the figures that are placed before me by Herr Mühlenweg, our paymaster, who has charge of the cash-box and the accounts. Already even now I see that we need more money. It will be demanded in Peking and must be entrusted to the missionary Svensson in Paotow. The interpreter, Ssŭ, is no longer required, and is replaced by Söderbom, the son of a missionary, who was born here and speaks Chinese quite as well as Swedish, and Mongolian besides.

The provisions are packed again, and in such a way that, when we encamp, in a particular box everything that one requires is found, and we are saved the trouble of opening more boxes. The members of the staff too are putting away their belongings. Major Zimmermann, who since the autumn has been my adjutant on the journey through Siberia and Manchuria, is my right hand in this, and knows exactly where to find everything.

In the large court-yard as in all the rooms of our house all are thus hard at work. Now and again small incidents provide us with a change. Thus we could once see from our roof how some twenty soldiers surrounded and searched a neighbouring house and captured and bound a thief.

From this roof we could see the Hwang Ho, which, coming from Odontala in north-eastern Tibet, flows through Kansu and the northern provinces, and in a mighty bend encircles the desert of the Ordos, in which I was once near being frozen to death.

One day all work in the court-yard was stopped by a torrential downpour that quickly turned to hail. Even the camels that were in the open were frightened. The hailstones were as large as hazel-nuts, half conical and half hemispherical. It became as cold as ice, after the temperature of 28 degrees we had previously had. When the rough

8

weather was over and all lay white in the court-yard, a
few of the younger members of the expedition amused
themselves with throwing snowballs, and chose as target
for their shooting practice the windows of their companions, which were made of paper pasted over wooden
frames. From inside the rooms came forth wild shouts
of anger and rage and aroused the greatest joy on the part
of those who were throwing and of the onlookers. Still
it was *our* house, and what did it matter that a few
paper window-panes were broken? We wanted very soon
to leave the farm behind us, which for most of us had for
so long a time been a prison. No-one would miss it,
and still less the swarms of bloodthirsty bugs that it
harboured.

Our court-yard, packed full with boxes, sacks, water-
containers, tent-baggage, and other articles, was too small
for it to have been possible for us to load hundreds of
camels there. We therefore hired an inn in front of the
north-west city gate and on the 16th of May began to
transfer there the four hundred and more packing-cases
and all the rest of the equipment. On the 18th of May the
two hundred and twenty camels arrived, whose hire cost
us 1,650 dollars, and the same day the last conveyances
left for the caravanserai, last of all the heavy silver-chests.
Accompanied by our doctor I paid my farewell visit to
the family of the missionary Svensson, who had been ever
friendly and ready to lend assistance, and at dusk went to
the caravanserai in whose court-yard our tents were erected
for the night. In an adjoining court-yard our two hundred
and thirty-two camels were sheltered.

The next day under the burning sun double ropes are
tied round all the loads. Then one has only to slip a stick
through two loops, to secure the boxes on the pack-saddles.
The court-yard is filled with life, excited and varied.
Policemen in black uniforms, foot-soldiers in greyish-blue
uniforms, and boys in rags, stroll about there among our
Chinese and Mongolian servants and caravan men. The
" paymaster," Herr Mühlenweg, makes the last payments,
the principals of the staff write postcards to their relatives,
tents are struck and like the sleeping-bags are rolled together

into longish bundles, the camels are led to water. It is our intention to set out as soon as the heat of the day has lessened. At 3 o'clock the bell rings that calls us to our meal. Scrambled eggs, pork, butter, bread, and tea are served on the boxes. We sit at our meal in various groups, and, at my "table," behave as if we sat on the Opera Terrace in Stockholm. A strong north-west wind is blowing, and the dust whirls round us. Then we seek the little shade that is to be found, resign ourselves to doing nothing, and wait, and finally find ourselves forced to remain yet another night here.

When I was awakened by Larson at 5 o'clock in the morning on the 20th of May, and walked out into the open, a wonderful animated scene presented itself before me. The sun had just risen. The camels were led in strings of five or ten to the long lines of packs, were easily and quickly loaded, and were then taken to the open space to the east of the caravanserai where the caravan was growing into a mighty army. One camel, which was carrying the instrumental equipment for one of the permanent stations that we intended to set up in Central Asia, threw off its precious load in the gateway of the inn, but fortunately nothing was broken. Outside are waiting also the thirty mounted foot-soldiers that the commanding officer in Paotow has appointed as our escort. They are wearing red-white bands on the left arm, are armed with rifles, and are riding small shaggy ponies. This special service is a pleasant and welcome change for them, and their jokes and laughter and their songs tell us that they are in the best humour.

The loading of the camels goes on without any break. One string after another is led out. Most of the animals are brown, but one or two are black. Just now they are on the point of losing their wool. It hangs on them in matted strands and tufts from head, sides, neck, and legs, and forms streamers in the wind. This spring dress is certainly not becoming. But that soon improves when the warm weather sets in and the camels have completely lost their winter coats.

Now the riding-camels of the Swedes and Germans are

coming out in long procession. Rifle-case, field-glasses and photographic apparatus in leather cases, saddle-bags of yellow leather containing hot-water bottles, light refreshments, note-books, pistols, and ammunition, as well as other things, make a clatter as they strike against the American and Mexican leather saddles, which are substantial and are splendid with their bright reflection.

I walk about between the growing columns. Now everything is all right, I think, and I return to the caravanserai, where I still find quite a number of boxes. Black pigs with hanging belly are roaming about between them, and are rooting up the ground, and the innkeeper's wife is hobbling round, surrounded by a crowd of shrieking, half-naked children, and is collecting camel-dung in a basket. The eight heavy silver-chests are just loaded on four strong camels, and then finally the thirty-eight hydrogen-cylinders come up, which require fifteen camels and are well packed in felt and straw matting, that they may not explode in the heat.

We can scarcely speak of *one* caravan. It is a whole series of caravans of five or ten camels stretched side by side. During all the years that I have spent in Asia I have seen innumerable caravans : my own, those of merchants from Arabia and Mesopotamia, going to Kansu and Mongolia, of pilgrims visiting the holy tombs, of the Shah of Persia in Elburz, and in the Great War the Turkish and Bavarian dromedary caravans between the hills of Judea and the Desert of Sinai. But, nevertheless, *this* caravan of mine seems to me the proudest that my eyes have ever gazed upon. It is a magnificent sight, an army on the march, full of colour, stout, and mighty. The sun has meanwhile risen above the mountains and lends colour to the picture, but the shadows are still long and ill defined on the ground, which is tinged with green.

Larson reports that the court-yard is empty and all the camels with their loads are outside on the plain. Everything is ready, we mount, and the caravan begins to move. Our learned Chinese do not use saddles, but seat themselves on their packs as on a throne. I myself, who am constantly busy with compass, watch, drawing-board, and note-book, as before have had my riding-camel tackled for me in a particularly snug and comfortable way. It carries on its sides my rolled-up tent and my bedding. Between these and the humps rugs, cloths, and skins are spread out, and I sit in the small hollow as in a bird's nest, and can vary my position and stretch my legs at will. And in order that I may not be in the slightest degree interrupted in my work by the gait of my camel, I have it led by the Mongol Mento, a trustworthy man who is riding a huge camel himself.

The body-guard of thirty riders whirls round us in a cloud of dust. With noiseless, crawling steps the camels in endless procession march slowly away up towards the first pass entering upon the northern hills. The foremost camel of the first section carries a Swedish flag. Behind us we lose sight of Paotow, the second of our cities of delay and trial.

My dream of many years has at last become a reality. We are on the way to Central Asia, to the zone of desert that extends across the whole of the Old World like an enormous dried-up river-bed. We are on the road to great tasks and mysterious adventures.

II

THROUGH THE PROMISED LAND OF ROBBER BANDS

INDEED, we are really on the way. We have set out on the first day's march of our endless journey across the great continent of Asia. I have taken my first sighting and have entered it on Chart No. 1. Many thousands of others will follow it, before the long route, with all its turns, undulations of country, hills, streams, ravines, and camping-places, is outlined, and its position on the map finally settled by means of the astronomical determinations that we shall carry out. We have laid down a first base-line of 150 metres in order to measure the length of the step of my riding-camel, by means of which I obtain the distance covered. No instrument can be more accurate. My excellent camel is unaware of the important rôle it is playing in the mapping of the line of march.

When ten sections of together a hundred and fifty camels have marched past me up towards the first pass, I follow on their track with Mento. In the monotonous, dull-yellow landscape, in which here and there the earth reflects a faint green light with the young grass of summer and of isolated hills of the steppe, but occasionally is almost entirely bare, the long, winding caravan affords a majestic, overpowering prospect. The foremost camels, which are almost lost to sight in the distance, show up like a string of fine black beads ; those immediately following are swinging along at a steady pace with their heavy burdens. On either side ride the soldiers, chatting and singing. When I turn round I can scarcely see the end of the mighty procession, which fills the whole landscape. The camels are not heard at all. Their light steps make no sound in the soft, dusty soil, like those of a cat. The only sounds

that one hears are the creaking of the wooden boxes rubbing
against the poles of the pack-saddles, the jarring and
rattling of the handles and locks on the iron-protected
chests, the screaming of a camel that has broken loose,
and finally the voices of the soldiers, of the Mongols, and
of the principals of the staff, and the rush of the north
wind.   But there is no tinkling sound of caravan-bells.
Probably it is found wiser to travel through the promised
land of robber bands as silently as possible.   But as soon
as we have our own camels, our bronze bells shall ring
out their melodies, immemorial and yet ever new, through
the desert.'

One sighting links up with another, and the road over
which we have travelled grows slowly on the chart.   On
our right and in front of us are low hills.   We travel
towards the north-west and follow the road that leads to
Patse-bulung and Wu-yüan and along which Fêng Yü-
hsiang, the " Christian General," has travelled in a motor-
car.   Till we reach these places, that is, for yet a few
more days, the telegraph-line keeps us company.   One
first experiences a feeling of real solitude when one has
seen the last telegraph-pole disappear behind one.

From time to time we pass through a wretched village
with old dilapidated mud huts and crumbling walls.   Some
appear to be uninhabited, since their unfortunate dwellers
were driven out by soldiers and robbers.   In others one
sees the inhabitants and their children in rags, and often
we catch sight of a peasant ploughing his field with an
iron plough drawn by two horses or black oxen.

Dust-spouts come flying over the plain like gloomy
spectres.   In their spiral progress the dust is drawn into
them and whirled upwards, while at the same time the
small cyclones move slowly forward.

At 12 o'clock our endless procession troops through the
village of Gunhuduk, whose inhabitants stand before their
huts and view the unaccustomed spectacle.   In the middle
of the village street lie the motors of two flying-machines
that have come to grief, silent witness to General Fêng's
campaign.   It is a curious sight, and one cannot blame
the camels for taking fright and even becoming unmanage-

able. Dettmann's camel makes such wild leaps that its rider falls head over heels to the ground and receives a nasty knock in the back. Heyder has as much as he can do to hold his camel in check, and tears open his hands on the halter and makes them bleed. But Dr. Hummel has to his hand in a special bag all that he requires, and promptly binds up all who have hurt themselves.

We are approaching the foot of the range of mountains in the north-west. At some distance to the left the presence of an irrigation-canal is indicated by a line of young willows to which its floods give water and life. In the west the monastery of Kundulung-sumo with its white façades is visible, a fairy castle in the desert. Only a few of the many lamas belonging to it are in residence at the moment; the others are acting as priests among the nomads in the north.

Before the gateway of a rectangular mud wall of a caravan enclosure the members of our body-guard have dismounted and have tethered their horses. They explain to us that this is the first camping-place, and advise us to bring our silver within the safe protection of the wall. But we prefer to set up our tents on the plain outside, where we can keep an eye on our goods and chattels and watch over them.

It is really marvellous with what rapidity and ease the Chinese servants free their camels of our loads. One after another, as they arrive, the various sections are led forward, the animals made to lie down, the poles drawn out of the two loops, and, in a trice, both boxes are on the ground, ready, next morning, after another manipulation just as simple, to occupy again their former position on the back of the camel. In half an hour all the two hundred and thirty-two camels are unloaded. The boxes are piled up in a rectangular space, and form a town in miniature, of houses and streets, in front of the tents, which are set up in the meantime by the principals of the staff. Mento and Matte Lama erect my cheerful dwelling, and furnish it with the boxes and bags that I require daily, and with carpet and bed. Each member of the staff has his light collapsible iron bed. I myself, however, discarded this structure here in the very first camp. During all my years in Asia I have only on one single occasion made use of a canopy-bed of wood, and that found its way into the camp fire after journeying a few days. It is probably only old " Asiatics " who regard it as a favour to come into the closest possible contact with Asiatic earth. So, too, does Larson, the "Duke of Mongolia," like best of all to lie on the ground. Dr. Hummel has followed our example, and I believe we shall leave quite a number of these canopy-beds behind us before we have advanced 500 *li* (1 *li* = 442 metres) towards the west. " Now the camels have less to drag along," Larson is in the habit of saying, whenever anything is thrown away or used up.

Here in camp by Kundulung-sumo there rose up for the first time the proud line of our blue Mongolian tents with their white ideographs and spiral ornamentation that are said to mean long life and immortality. As already stated, six members of the staff were still to join us, in spite of the fact that we had erected sixteen tents. In the centre of the row of tents, towering above all the others, was the tent that serves as our club-house, resplendent with its bright green. It is of English make and is double, for the tent proper is screened by a great awning that does not quite reach to the ground and forms in the front a sort of veranda. Inside, a table was built up with ordinary boards and trestles, and all round it were set the folding camp-stools.

At 5 o'clock the bell of the club-house was rung and called us to tea. The opening of the club-house tent was celebrated and it was praised by all. One found that it was worth the 200 Mexican dollars that Larson had paid for it. All were excited and in joyful mood. A Chinese merchant caravan came up and encamped in the court-yard of the caravanserai. It had followed on our heels for safety. From the west, probably from Uliasutai, a second caravan was heading towards us. So far it had come without mishap, and now it had only one more day's march to Paotow. One can imagine with what feelings it approaches its destination, after it has travelled four or five months through the wilderness.

16

Gathering

Forward to the north

AWAY AT LAST

The town of tents grows up

Our meteorologist, Dr. Haude, with his instrument-box

THE FIRST CAMP

[face p. 17

We had scarcely returned to our tents, when a sudden storm rose up from the north-west and passed over the camp like a lash. The weather side of my tent was stretched like a drum-skin, and the rest of the canvas fluttered and beat with the greatest violence. I sprang to my feet and gripped the foremost tent-pole, while stays and ropes threatened to snap. But to go outside to see what was happening was clearly impossible. One could not stand upright in this storm, and not a trace of the surroundings could be seen, not even the nearest tents. The air was full of sand and dust, the tent-flaps were banging and the fine dust was penetrating everywhere and covering everything that was exposed. Lighter objects, paper and charts, had to be thrown into the boxes as hastily as possible, that they might not fly away. Bergman's sun-helmet disappeared in the haze. Larson expressed the opinion that it had flown back to Paotow, but it was found again later between the pack boxes. After a few minutes the violent squall was over. It ceased as suddenly as it had appeared, and now we could inspect the damage that it had caused us. Four of the sixteen tents had been thrown to the ground. Among them the club-tent, whose outer awning was absolutely torn to pieces and was fluttering in the wind like a tattered banner. An amusing touch among these horrors of the devastation was provided by the picture that the helpless occupants of the blown-down tents presented. Out of the ruins of his dwelling rose up the stately form of the " Duke of Mongolia," as he sat on a box philosophizing, and meditating at which end he should begin to set up the tent again. At both other abodes of disaster the beds stood covered with dust and sand, and the occupiers were gathering together their scattered belongings.

After a light rain at dusk, the camels were led to their loads, and were to lie here and chew the cud the whole night. The camels are always brought into camp in the evening, not for fear of thieves who might possibly steal them, but because, unlike horses, they cannot see when they are out at pasture in the dark.

The last duty for the day was the apportioning of watches

for the night. Two Europeans and four men of the body-guard were chosen for this. The soldiers entreated us not to take ourselves any distance from the camp, for by so doing one might possibly be carried away, or shot on the return journey. The command was therefore issued that no-one was to be allowed to stay outside the bounds of the camp during the night.

When a man knows that he is awakened again in the early hours of the morning, he has no objection to lying down to sleep as early as 9 o'clock. To my own surprise I did not feel the least tiredness after this first day's march on our long road westward. I lay awake yet quite a while and reflected on the singularity of my fate. After an interval of nineteen years I was again on an expedition in Asia. On earlier occasions I had always set out on adventure alone. Now I was the leader of a staff of twenty-eight Europeans and Chinese. All were scholars or at any rate cultured men. Most of them had read my books. Now they were themselves keeping diaries and would in the course of time have opportunity to determine whether my accounts accorded with reality. Not one of them, not even Larson, Norin, and Yüan, who had travelled the most, had ever been in the heart of Asia, where I have spent some of my best years. Of the Europeans most had never set foot on the soil of Asia before, and the Chinese had only travelled within the frontiers of China proper. The road by Gashun-nor and Hami to Urumchi was unknown to all of us. I had purposely chosen a road and a region of which I was as yet ignorant. The first day's march already gave us a foretaste of coming days and months. On each new day's march we should be looking out towards the west over the boundless spaces where all was new for us and rather obscure for the whole world outside. We should keep our eyes well open when we were travelling the 2,100 kilometres that separated us from the capital of the province of Sin-kiang, Urumchi.

The desire and dream that for so many years had floated before me had at last been fulfilled. I lay on Asiatic soil, I heard the steps of the sentries round our tents, and listened to the roaring of the night wind above our camp.

It was a dream no longer, it was reality, and I had taken the first steps to carry out the greatest task that I have ever planned, that I have ever set before me.

When I was awakened at half-past four in the morning of the second day of the march, I had to rub my eyes before I could realize that I was really journeying again across old Asia, and that the whole continent lay open before me and my companions. What a proud and glorious feeling! The night had been rather cold; at 5 o'clock it was still only 8·8 degrees centigrade. I noticed nothing of the tiredness for which I had been prepared. Maybe my back was a trifle stiff; but that will become supple as time goes on.

On all sides there is calling, shouting, and commanding —in Swedish, German, Chinese, and Mongolian. Larson marches about like a field-marshal and superintends everything. The camels scream angrily and spit when the loads are placed on their pack-saddles and they are compelled to get up for a new day's march. Tents are struck, beds are rolled up, the kitchen is stowed away in its boxes, and again we enjoy the splendid spectacle of the mighty caravan setting itself in motion and making for near-lying hills.

Our way leads up the valley of the Kundulung-gol, where we wade across the murmuring stream, splashing about at our ease. In sheltered glens grow yellow wild roses and blue sword-flags and other flowers just in bloom, and here and there, where the valley broadens out, we pass over meadows and come across bullock-carts with creaking wheels. It is fresh and cool, and in the biting wind one is glad to have one's leather waistcoat. Professor Hsü Ping-chang has wrapped himself up in his ulster—all Chinese wear European sports clothing. One or two of them enthrone themselves in complete peace of mind on their packs and read. We halt at a bend, and let the endless procession march past us. One of the principals of the staff rides at the end of the caravan, and is responsible for seeing that nothing gets lost.

Near the village of Sabasa stand a number of bullock-carts and two of the pretty and useful vehicles commonly known as Peking carts, here used as a means of conveyance.

19

The upper part of Sabasa lay in ruins and was deserted. Here, right in the middle of the village street, stood three shrapnel as a reminder of Fêng's light field-artillery. The telegraph-line to Wu-yüan still keeps us company. It consists of three wires. The lowest hung in one place so low that we had to lift it up high with a pole, to prevent it from being damaged. The wreckage of two cars that have been looted also bears eloquent witness to Marshal Fêng's campaign in these parts. Some villages are completely deserted and ruined, but for all that one sees everywhere the marks of the plough. Others are carrying on their work, charming to behold amid the verdure of willows and elms in which they are hidden.

The valley is now broad and open. We pass along the left-hand side of it, where in pools of great length, extensions of the small stream, algæ are growing rank. Here stretch tender, sweet-smelling meadows—a splendid place for a camp. It was a paradise in this parched, yellowish grey, desolate land. But the vanguard is marching further on over barren undulations of country, and the paradise dies away like an apparition in a dream.

Some distance further on we reached the village of Wu-funtse. Here we intended to spend the night, the soldiers could get what they wanted, and above all we had here to change our escort. The camels were unloaded, and in a short time our town of tents grew up in a field before the village. As soon as the smoke began to come from the fire-place and the filter-apparatus was set in working order, the inhabitants of the village, wrapped up in their rags of red or dark blue, assembled round this curious spectacle. Our chief steward, von Kaull, rummaged about in the kitchen boxes and fetched out the preserves that were required for supper, as also butter, cakes, cheese, and English marmalade.

In the glow of the sun, already in the west, we photographed the thirty soldiers who were to return from here to Paotow. The new troop, twenty men strong, with red-yellow flag, and red-yellow bands on the left arm, was already on the spot. On the suggestion of the Chinese it was arranged that both sections should share in the guard duty for the night, the old section in the camp and the new one at a greater distance outside in the direction of the circle of hills that surrounded us. It was explained to me quite bluntly that the red-white and the red-yellow soldiers must have separate tasks allotted them, to prevent their coming to blows and stealing each other's arms. A small civil war in the middle of our camp—that would, indeed, have been exciting. The soldiers who were off duty rode into the village, there to spend the night.

I talked with our Chinese on the subject of the night duty, and they regarded it as quite natural and as a matter of course that they too should do their duty in this. They only desired that they might have an armed European with them, who could in case of necessity protect them against the dangers of the night and of the darkness. All four students immediately wanted to prove their watchfulness, and had their hours allotted them. Then, during the nights following, the Chinese scholars began their guard duty, and even their leader, Professor Hsü Ping-chang, insisted on not being left out. Of the Europeans only Larson and I are excused night duty, on account of our age. I wanted to exempt also Dr. Hummel and Dr. Haude, who have to work hard the whole day through, but they desired to have no advantage over the others in anything.

Darkness comes on, and the shadows of night fall upon the earth. The camels come from pasture, the night's guard duty begins. Friendly gleams of light break through from half-open tents. Everywhere can be heard the sounds of talking and laughing. From a mandolin come lively airs. All around us reigns the greatest quietness. Who could believe that we have just set foot upon one of the worst districts for robbers in northern China, and that we are in a region where the civil war may any day flare up anew ?

The next morning I had scarcely dressed, when I was told that the old escort was waiting to receive its dismissal from me. The soldiers had mounted and arranged them-selves in single file, and in front of them, also mounted, was their commander. Accompanied by most of the principals of the staff, who had among other things armed themselves with photographic apparatus, I went up in front, and in Chinese thanked them for their watchfulness and wished them a safe journey home. After they had received their allowance of 60 dollars, they wheeled round on their small ponies and galloped away in the direction of Paotow.

The new troop of twenty riders now entered our service. They had bright blue-grey uniforms like the previous soldiers, but instead of military caps they wore ordinary little round caps of silk. One of the men was carrying the red-yellow flag on his lance. All had secured their rifles to the pommel of the saddle, with the muzzle pointing downwards. Their small ponies were not very good, but in spite of that their riders did all they could to frighten our camels to death, as they approached our camp in a gallop, with clamour and uproar, rattling guns and bags, lively songs or wild cries.

We decamp. Two soldiers ride on in front, and in their company Dr. Haude, who himself leads the philosophically peaceful camel that is entrusted with two boxes that are particularly valuable and sensitive. One contains our chronometers, the other the instruments of the meteorological observatory that are required every day. For a change I too ride at the head of the procession, with Larson, Hummel, Bergman, and Dettmann. We form a group full of lively chatter. What I mean is that the *others* are talking and joking ; I myself must for ever keep my attention fixed on the road and the chart, and enter all observations in my note-book. We are on a wide plain, in the form of a longitudinal valley between two very flat ranges of mountains. Almost everywhere the land is cultivated with oats, mustard, or opium, or at any rate has been cultivated up to a short time before. By no means such a very long time ago this land was purely Mongolian, but Chinese colonists have purchased land for themselves for trifling sums, and coax the earth into yielding its harvest. A few Mongols, it is true, are still living here; but they are usually worsted in the struggle with the tenacious and industrious Chinese, who are acquainted with the secrets of agriculture. The latter acquire land, while the Mongols, who are nomads, are irresistibly pushed back to the north on the southern frontier of Outer Mongolia. So, before one's eyes, there is going on here a continuous migration of peoples, of exactly the same kind as I have observed further to the east on my motor-car journey through Mongolia in 1923. But in the region that we are now traversing, peaceful work has been hindered, or its life-blood has been completely drained away, by civil war and plundering robber bands. On the fields of the village of San-funtse a solitary peasant is walking behind his plough and his black oxen, and out of the ruined farmsteads of Sadyayu yawn only poverty and distress. Not a hen is to be seen, rarely a black pig, only a few haggard and hungry, ragged forms. But they do not beg, they only regard us with astonishment, not understanding why we are travelling in such numbers through the devastated land.

Still more of these small wasted villages lie on our way, which shows signs, however, of a really busy traffic. The fields of Örtenigo are irrigated by means of small canals, whose banks are planted with elms. In their uppermost branches there are the nests of magpies. It is refreshing to see water, and trees putting forth leaves.

Towards midday a strong north wind set in. In the bright-blue heaven in front of us in the north there floated a most peculiar formation of milk-white cloud, a vaulted bridge over the whole firmament from west to east, similar to arch-shaped northern lights, a symbolic triumphal arch through which we were to enter on this land that against other Europeans was as good as barred.

We were riding now in the middle of the caravan, which was preparing to make a halt on some fallow land beyond the village of Örtenigo. Several loads were already removed from the camels. But contrary to expectation the head of the caravan began to move on again, and all the columns followed, now in a cruel north-west wind. We had low mountains on either side, and it was impossible to perceive in which direction the land fell away. Only the nearest hills stood out in the turbid air. We continued our march for two hours more—two hours that we did not forget as quickly. The wind gathered strength and became troublesome. Skins, covers, and anything else that was loose on the camels, fluttered and banged about, and I had a fine task to prevent chart, bag, and compass from flying away from me. My camel is now the very last of the whole caravan. Larson and Bergman are travelling on foot by my side. Before us over the steppe, which is enveloped in a haze, the gloomy procession winds its way in ever more indistinct shades of colour, which finally are lost completely in the whirling dust. The foremost columns cannot be seen at all. But even in this light the scene is beautiful. The spirits of the air assemble against us, but for all that we go on, an army on the march, a wandering tribe, a vast host of men and animals on the way to a strange land. The wind whistles and howls round the loads, and on the camels and horses hang dense clouds of dust like grey tails of comets. We ride as through a surging river of whirling dust and sand. But here and there one sees local whirlwinds, dust-spouts that come dancing along over the steppe. I cannot recall to mind that I have ever before been near being thrown down or swept down from the camel that I was riding. But now I was very near it. From the north-west there rapidly whirled along towards us a yellowish-grey dust-spout, at the bottom dark brown and constricted, a small raging typhoon or tornado of miniature proportions. The other dust-spouts passed by us, sometimes in front of us, sometimes in the wake of the caravan. But this one appeared to have been particularly intended for us, and with irresistible force made straight for the end of the procession.

" Hold on to your hat," shouted Larson to me, at the same time throwing himself on the ground.

At the very same instant the whirlwind passed over my camel and the next four in front of me. I threw myself with all my might over to the weather side and held on tight to the ropes of the load. The whirlwind struck us like a lash. If I had not held on fast I should certainly have been swept to the ground. The camel's whole load rocked and was near slipping, for the animal, the load, and I, formed a splendid target for the wind. The whole bag and baggage was very near going overboard. The camel staggered, took fright, and, like its comrades, swerved to the lee side. Small stones and sand were hailing on my tropical helmet and my hands, making the latter smart. But everything was over after a second or two. The dust-spout continued its mysterious journey over the steppe. It might have measured 15 metres in diameter. It was a peculiar, a remarkable, sight. One must, however, feel such a rascal against one's own body before one develops proper respect for him and his kind. The other members of the caravan hadn't noticed the least thing.

It is indeed no pleasure to ride in such weather, and the very reverse of easy, at the same time from the back of a swaying camel, to map out a route on a chart. But when we turned round the next spur of hill, we saw to our joy that the columns were coming to a halt one after the other and were pitching the camp quite near the little village of Nobo-deen, which, in the number of its inhabitants, could in no way compare with our wandering town. As soon as my tent was erected the Swedes came in to me, and regaled themselves with tea, cakes, butter, and marmalade. We laughed and chatted, and felt extremely comfortable, while the storm outside raged and howled. The strength of the wind was 18 metres per second, and the temperature was at 6 o'clock only 12 degrees above freezing-point. The sun one only saw as a faint disk.

After supper Major Hempel and Professor Hsü came, in order to speak with me about the night-watch. The Chinese had had long consultations how they ought to act in the event of a sudden attack. Some of them had been for the idea that they should creep out of their tents and lie still on the ground, since they were not armed and therefore could not participate in the defence; for a band of robbers would certainly make targets of the tents. Hempel advised them to remain calmly in their tents and not to rush out, for they might easily be shot in mistake in the darkness and confusion.

Our body-guard had complained to Professor Hsü that it had insufficient ammunition, and had therefore asked for some of our cartridges. Hsü, however, thought it best if the soldiers had as little ammunition as possible, and therefore in reply had told them that our cartridges would be too large for their rifles.

The four students were to-day to keep watch again, as well as six men of our guard, one at each corner of the town of tents and two on patrol. Every two hours the sentries were to be relieved. We decided too that two of the Germans should share in the watch. They had been in the War, vigilance was in their blood, and they could, in the event of a sudden attack, gauge the position with far greater reliability than the Chinese. We were thus quite securely guarded and watched over.

But the night passed away—to the accompaniment of the howling of the storm and the many-voiced chorus of the wind—without any incident, and when the sun rose and gave a red colour to the flying dust we had no loss of men or goods to deplore, neither had our tents been shot through with any bullets.

III

OUR CARAVANS ASSEMBLE IN MONGOLIA

THE village of Nobo-deen has a coal-pit of its own, but the coal is rather poor, and, when we moved on on the 23rd of May, the inhabitants of the village hurried up with baskets and sacks to collect the camel-dung, and also the wool, which they twist into cords and ropes.

Again we witnessed the imposing spectacle of the mighty caravan growing up out of the camp, which at the same time disappeared from the earth. The stately camels stood loaded in close groups in the gleam of the rising sun. A magnificent picture, their bodies, brightly lit up on one side, stood out against their shadows like an immense sculpture in stone.

The long procession moves in a north-westerly direction towards the nearest hills. We move into these low mountains and climb upwards in a narrow, winding ravine —a bed of sand between stony hills, where, here and there, there are outcrops of crystalline schist and granite. The soldiers at the head of the caravan are of the opinion that this ravine was *made* for a sudden attack and is dangerous, and therefore ask that some of our riflemen may ride on ahead. But our men will not let their rest be disturbed. Our laundry-boy lies asleep on his camel, and two of our students will soon be nodding too on their animals' swaying backs.

The heaven is a glorious blue, the wind almost cold. At a bend in the valley stands a well with a stone trough for thirsty animals. On the north side of a little pass a broken-down stone wall, extending quite a distance, is to be seen on the hills to the left of the road—a defence-work from times of old. At the entrance to the pass a small heap of stones is raised up ; pious travellers here lay down

a stone for the spirits of the mountain, as a thank-offering
for their having come so far safe and sound. A second
pass that we cross is 1,700 metres high, and then the road
goes down to the inn of Niu-chang-wang. The name
"Cow's-Gut Bend" is not amiss: the valley grows
narrower here and is bounded at times by precipitous
mountain sides. The erosion terraces are 3 metres high.
Among the hills one hears the cooing of rock-doves and
clucking of partridges; a bullock-cart that we meet,
loaded with skins, sings its creaking song.

The valley broadens out again and the country becomes
flat and open. At the foot of the last mountains lies the
village of Yagar-chigo or Yagarin-gol. Near the village
of Hung-watzŭ-kung-yung we set up the camp. It takes
less time with every day, for all know what they have to
do.

Every morning shortly after four o'clock we are awakened by Larson's loud cry of "Fall in!" The Chinese
do not know what the words mean, but all have a laugh
when they hear the "Duke's" command. But Larson
shows no mercy. One must get up at once to be ready
for breakfast. After that, a long interval follows while the
tents are struck and everything is packed. Then, if one is
so inclined, one can in some suitable place snatch a further
short sleep. But, so far as I myself am concerned, I can
affirm that I have been wide awake all the time, with the
confused noise, of shouting Mongols and Chinese, and
screaming camels, that surrounds me on all sides. At
home in Stockholm I go to bed at four o'clock in the
morning. Here I get up at this time. But anything can
be done if only one is used to it, and here, moreover,
I lie down to sleep at nine o'clock in the evening.

The country that we are now crossing is slightly undulating. But no matter how flat the undulations are, one
has an almost endless view from their crests. It is, of
course, always the caravan that dominates the scene. I
am riding in the middle again. From my elevated observation point it appears as if I had the greater part of the
caravan in front of me, and yet I count eight more long
columns behind, leaving out of account isolated camel-

28

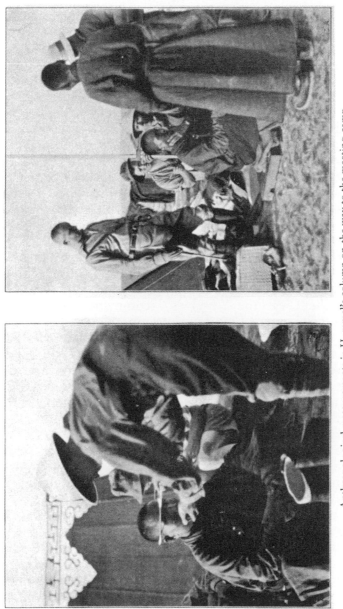

Anthropological measurements in Hummel's column on the way to the meeting-camp

WORK BEGINS

The winter wool gradually falls off

Chinese of the Neighbourhood buy wool from us

IN THE NEIGHBOURHOOD OF HUTYERTU-GOL

riders and the soldiers riding on either side on brown or black horses.

After we have crossed over a few more flat land-waves the land becomes almost completely level. Marks of the plough are still frequently to be seen, and here and there a little village. Near one of them stands a quite simple votive altar with a statue of Buddha scarcely half a metre high. Then we approach a village with round towers and battlements, resembling a fortress. The Mongols call it Hacho, the Chinese Hachao-tang. We march on, however, and do not halt till some time later, near the little village of Bayin-buluk, " the bountiful spring," where we set up the camp on an inviting meadow.

Here, we are 1,585 metres above sea level. Chinese colonists have been in this region for as long as six decades, and the Mongols have retreated to the north.

On the 25th of May we approached the northernmost frontiers of the civilized territory that has been conquered by the Chinese settlers. On the other side of this frontier stretch the boundless spaces of Mongolia. Larson and his Mongols are longing for them, but we others, too, are looking forward with pleasure to the time when we shall leave behind us the last furrows of Chinese ploughs and come out into the wild, untouched desert borderland, the home of nomads and antelopes.

The ground is now more furrowed again. On the crest of a ridge of hill over which our road leads Larson and a few of the others have stood still. In the north a broad plain is to be seen, bounded right away in the distance by low eminences. The " Duke of Mongolia " takes off his hat and cries, " That is my country ! " Indeed, he is at home there !

By a little watercourse, Abogayin-gol, containing but little water, we set up the camp. It was yet early in the day. Some had a little nap, to fill out the time till dinner ; others had discovered a herd of thirty antelopes and went hunting.

In the twilight, when we sat down to supper, the camels came from pasture ; like shadowy ghosts they crept with soft steps to their loads. Bergman, enthroned upon a box, to the accompaniment of a lute sang old Swedish songs out into the listening steppe, over which in times of old Jenghiz Khan with his mounted hosts rode along. To-night Hummel and von Kaull are to keep watch. They are armed with pistols and powerful electric lamps, which on our body-guard have made a greater impression than our weapons, since they are regarded as magic forces.

Early next morning our escort received payment of the remainder of its money, and also a gratuity since we were parting company. They swung themselves up on their horses and arranged themselves in rank and file, and I dismissed them, as with their predecessors, with a simple " *Hsieh, hsieh, i lu ping an!* Thank you, thank you, a peaceful journey!" They saluted, threw their little ponies round, and trotted off.

Matte Lama, whom Larson had dispatched to keep a look-out for Norin and his caravan, had not yet returned.

At 7 o'clock we moved off and travelled over ground that was agreeably soft and covered with short grass. On a dry erosion furrow two wolves ran along and leered at us. Larson on his own account stalked after them and levelled his gun: not one of us believed that he would hit, for the distance was far too great. The shot reported, and one wolf fell. There was general rejoicing, the Chinese were overwhelmed, and we regretted that the " body-guard " had not witnessed this master-shot. Some of our men hurried off to view the four-legged robber for themselves. He leapt to his feet, showed them his teeth, and snarled. A pistol-shot gave him the finishing stroke. The distance from which Larson had killed him amounted to 520 metres, and the skilled shot was known from that time as " Wolf " Larson. A weasel and a fox were seen, too, in this neighbourhood, and the ground was often undermined with the burrows of field-voles. The wolf is quite common in Mongolia ; he is the antelopes' cruellest enemy. On the other hand, he seldom becomes dangerous to man.

At the usual time, on the morning of the 27th of May, the tents were struck, and the camels waited to be loaded. But just then it was reported that the grey horse belonging to the leader of the caravan had made off in the night, and that all the Chinese camel-drivers had set out to make search for the runaway. We had the day before come past a herd of three hundred mares that were pasturing here in order to be sold later in Kalgan, and it was now believed that the horse might have betaken himself off to this well-stocked harem. But he was not there, and the time slipped by. Heyder and Hummel went hunting, and Larson killed a she-wolf that had bravely remained with its cubs. After an hour Heyder returned with his first antelope. From that time scarcely a day passed without his shooting one or two of these beautiful fleet-footed animals with the long, slender horns. He provided the kitchen with a constant supply of fresh meat, and so liberally, indeed, that one grew tired of game and longed for roast mutton. But in the region where we were one could not buy sheep, and therefore Heyder's skill proved especially useful to us.

When the camels were again being left to pasture, we saw that the prospects of an early departure were very uncertain, and then when, in honour of a wild turkey-cock that Larson had killed, the kitchen fire was being lighted, it became clear to us that the day was lost. Our town of tents grew up again on the same spot, and the day came to an end.

On the 28th of May we decided to transfer the camp only a bare hour's journey further to the north, to a point a short distance up stream along the same small water-course on which we had camped yesterday and the day before, known as Hutyertu-gol, "the soda river." Its water is clear, and full of small fish, frogs, and water-weeds. On account of its good pasturage and fresh water, the spot was better suited to be our headquarters for a lengthy period. For a lengthy period? Indeed, in this camp, No. VIII, we had now to remain several weeks.

And why this long interruption in our advance so happily begun? Why did we not rather proceed with our journey further, so far that we might feel ourselves quite secure against sudden attacks by robbers?

It was because we had to buy camels. Till now, we, our

31

equipment, and our stores, had been carried by hired camels. I had, of course, not known to what conclusion the long negotiations in Peking would lead, and had no desire to purchase two hundred and seventy camels, to be compelled later, perhaps, to sell them off again at a loss. So this purchase, on which the whole Expedition depended, had to be made up now. Larson had already sent out in various directions his trustworthy Kalgan Mongols, but it might be some time before they returned and brought us information. We had therefore to bear patiently and wait.

Camp VIII had still the attraction of newness, and we found it enchanting : open water is not very common in this part of Mongolia, and on the excellent pasturage our own camels could eat their fill to their hearts' content, and store up energy for the hardships that awaited them on the road to Gashun-nor.

With our first lunch in this fixed camp a buoyant mood accordingly prevailed. And I had scarcely sought out my tent, when Larson appeared and reported that on a small ridge of hill in the north two Europeans were standing photographing the camp. They had one Mongol and four camels with them : it could be no other than Haslund and Lieberenz. In spite of wind and turbid air, up there Lieberenz was taking his film, and then they approached, were cordially received, and delivered their report, a performance that was filmed in its turn. The sixty-five camels belonging to Andrews were safe, in defiance of all threatening dangers, and, on the way, Lieberenz had had opportunity of taking a number of beautiful and unusual films : Mongolian princes and princesses in all their splendour, as well as their daily life in tent villages and yourts.

At 4 o'clock new rejoicing was heard along the street of tents. " What is the matter ? " I asked. " Norin's caravan," was the answer. In fact, there he came on foot at the head of his column, and, although he had only fifty-one camels instead of sixty, the procession looked really splendid. He had thus carried out his commission in Kuei-hua-chêng brilliantly, in spite of robbers and camel-thieves. I went to meet him. He was quite a distance in front of the others, and, with his long hair and flowing beard, looked like a savage, but he was sunburnt, alert, and cheerful.

Shortly afterwards the others reached us. Walz, a picture of strength and energy ; Marschall von Bieberstein, sitting bent up on his riding-animal, and, when he had dismounted, supporting himself on a stick, like an old man : his camel on an occasion had become unruly and had thrown him, whereby the poor man had received an awful blow in the back. We were delighted to see them all again after a separation of several days, and they were all the more welcome as they brought with them the new Swedish member of the Expedition, Herr Söderbom, the linguist son of a missionary from Kuei-hua-chêng. He was appointed our chief steward and undertook responsibility for the kitchen and provisions.

While the new loads were being piled up in a place specially for them, the six new members had their dinner. We now consisted of eighteen Europeans and ten Chinese. When our companions had refreshed themselves, they started to tell of their experiences and adventures, and it was really a rushing torrent of news.

The town of tents also grew. We had left gaps in the street of tents for the airy dwellings of the new-comers. Now we numbered twenty-one tents. It was really almost a genuine town in the wilderness. Norin brought with him a Mongolian spear with head and horse-hair tassel. It was fastened to the front pole of my dwelling, and the Swedish flag fluttered from it over our camp.

After our meal we visited and returned visits. The Swedes and Haslund, who, although a Dane, is reckoned with the Swedes, assembled in Larson's tent, and Haslund showed us a temple banner, a prayer-wheel, a drum made out of two human skulls, and other things that he had obtained possession of, and which he offered to the Expedition.

In my tent, Norin then showed me the excellent chart of the territory of Beli-miao, 80 *li* eastward from here, that he had drawn up, and which, in the next weeks, he will extend and complete, and I showed him my map of the route, the fifteen sheets of the road from Paotow to Hutyertu-gol.

We took late supper by the light of lamps, and we now noticed already that we had not only got a new chief steward but also a new, skilled cook, Norin's servant. Our former chief cook, who is as snub-nosed as von Marschall's little pug-dog from Peking, had been removed from his position, and was now shutting himself up in the servants' tent, sulking, and inveighing against the Europeans.

We were in the best humour. For the first time we had assembled in full muster at the club-tent tables. We had made our arrangements so carefully that all three caravans, from Hallun-ussu (north of Kalgan), Kuei-hua-chêng, and Paotow, had reached their objective on the very same day !

IV

" THE TOWN OF NATIONS "

THE 29th of May was our first rest-day in our fixed
camp on Hutyertu-gol, in which, whether we liked
it or not, we had to remain for nearly the whole of two
months. But necessity was stronger than our desire : it
takes time to buy two hundred camels.

We knew that, and it had too a decisive influence on
the organization of our life and work and on the disposi-
tion of our town of tents. I had already the day before
discussed and settled the organization of the camp with
Hempel. It had to some extent settled itself.

With the never-ceasing wind that prevailed in early
summer, the tents could not be arranged in a cluster, for
all the dust that is stirred up by those walking on the
weather side sweeps across the tents on the lee. We
decided to set up all the tents in a single long straight
line. Larson firmly insisted on our having the entrances
to the south like the Mongols : he said we should be
laughed at if we allowed our tent-openings to face in any
other direction.

Between the tents and the street stand the packing-
cases, in long rows or piled up one on top of another.
The camp is magnificent, and presents an impressive sight
if one views it from the neighbouring hills in the south,
whose spirits, from ancient times propitiated by some *obo*
or other, have now been disturbed in so unexpected a
manner by a moving town.

The reader may, perhaps, believe that it must be a
difficult task to be the leader of an expedition of eighteen
whites, ten yellow men, and thirty-four servants. I had
certainly no experience in such a matter, for I had previously always travelled alone. But I have found that it

35

is absolutely nothing; it is the simplest thing that one can imagine, if all the participants are intelligent, scholarly men, filled with enthusiasm for their task. How many youths and men in their best years there are who would most ardently have desired to take part in our journey across this mighty continent, which now more than ever is attracting the attention of the whole world! To be able to see Asia with one's own eyes just at this time is a good fortune and an attraction verily to be envied. With us no wearying military discipline holds sway. If anyone wishes to go hunting, he simply saddles one of the five horses that we have hired of our Mongolian neighbours, and towards evening comes home bringing with him one or two antelopes. If everyone does his duty no strict orders are necessary, and the discipline that otherwise must be maintained by constant overseeing, regulations, and penalties, is with us the most natural and matter-of-course thing in the world; it would occur to no-one to act against orders.

We are here in the middle of the small district of Inner Mongolia bearing the name of Mingan-Jasak, and called by the Chinese Mao-ming-an. The chieftain of this district lives about 50 *li* to the north of us. Immediately after our arrival he sent an officer and three soldiers into our camp to find out who we were and what we wanted. They had heard the shots of our guns and were glad that we had put an end to three wolves. The chief's deputy explained that we were free to do as we liked; only we might not dig in the earth, since by so doing we might disturb the spirits of the earth and of the hills, and we were asked, above all, to leave in peace the hills bearing an " obo " at their summit. The next day I sent Herr Walz and Dr. Yüan, to pay our return visit to the great lord. They found an amiable old Mongol, who put an immense number of questions and wanted to know everything, and finally explained that he intended to visit us in his own person. Two days later a senior colonel visited us in his name, wearing large spectacles, a picturesque dress of dark blue material, a silver sword-belt, and weapons. He and his soldiers were entertained with tea and tobacco, and were filmed as we sat in conversation in the entrance of the club-tent.

As I mentioned before, our fixed camp is situated 1,570 metres above sea level. For Tibetan conditions this is no altitude; in Tibet proper one cannot descend so low anywhere. But for Sweden, just as for Germany 1,570 metres is quite considerable. And when one crosses the belt of steppe and desert of Central Asia, this figure is not bad either. In any case, mountain climate prevails here. Although we are writing in the middle of June, the temperature has not risen above 27 degrees in the shade, and we were greatly astonished when the thermometer one night fell to 1 degree. Two nights later we even had 2 degrees of frost. But when for once it happens to be calm during the day-time, one has 38 degrees in the tent, and even in the open air one can feel the sun's rays burn. We are all, white as well as yellow, tanned by the sun, with the exception perhaps of a few Chinese who avail themselves of the large fashionable red sunshades of their native country. The climate is thus ideal. We are in a real mountain health-resort, where we find it so pleasant that we cannot wish to better it ourselves. Only between 11 and 5 o'clock in the day can one speak of a noticeable heat, yet never burdensome. As soon as the sun has gone down it becomes cold. The direct rays of the sun, which in denser, lower strata of air are to a large extent absorbed, here beat on us with far greater power. But, indeed, the wind is nearly always blowing, and from all directions. We have already had wind strengths of more than 20 second-metres, and in this continuous, fresh, cooling breeze there is no need, in truth, for one to complain of heat. One day, when it was completely calm, Ming fetched water out of the stream and poured it out round my tent; that produced an agreeable coolness. But I have nothing against the heat; I have frozen more than enough in the course of my life. Nevertheless, I feared that as time went on we should get more of a good thing than we liked.

Of the scientific staff the Swedes are in the majority. Dr. Erik Norin is our geologist, and is at present occupied

37

in drawing up a map of the neighbourhood of our fixed camp to the scale of 1 to 50,000. Dr. David Hummel, our doctor, has to treat not only the ailments and infirmities of ourselves and our servants, but also those of many wandering Mongols and Chinese. The state of health in the camp is so excellent, however, that he has much time over for his botanical and zoological collections, which grow quickly. Whenever opportunity offers he also takes anthropological measurements after the excellent scheme and the instructions that Dr. Stevenson of the Rockefeller Institute in Peking has given to him and a few Germans. Some of our principals are being instructed by him in this subject. Archæology is entrusted to Folke Bergman, who devotes himself to his task with great zeal, in spite of the fact that, in accordance with the decisions arrived at in Peking, the finds fall to China. Nevertheless, I cherish the well-founded hope that the Chinese will, with true high-mindedness, resign to me the duplicates, which would not make them poorer and yet would well make me or, to be more exact, the Eastern-Asiatic Collections in Stockholm, considerably richer. I myself am drawing a map of our line of march, and, moreover, according to the same methods that I have employed before on my long journeys this way and that across Asia. Naturally I am also keeping a diary and am collecting material for the geographical and topographical description of the country.

You should see Larson, that youth 57 years old from Tillberga in Västmanland in Sweden, who has spent 34 years in Mongolia and has travelled about there this way and that more than any other white man in the world, and to whose eyes the tears rise when he beholds the Swedish flag in front of my tent. You ought to see him when he comes striding along Marco-Polo Street, slowly and surely, his hands behind his back, a friendly smile about his lips. He comes, then, upright and proud, and throws scrutinizing glances over the camp to convince himself that everything is in order and all is well.

Nothing escapes his attention, he is present everywhere, and he knows everything that takes place in our town. He is a living newspaper and reports to me all the news of the day. With his cap in his hand he steps under my veranda, and always says, in his broadest Västmanlandish, "Excuse my troubling you." But he never troubles me: he is always welcome, is my right hand, and I consult him on all questions, big as well as small. He seats himself on the box to the right of my writing-table, and twiddles his fingers round his cap as he makes his report. How should I manage without him? He has the camels and the Mongols under him, and without them we could get nowhere.

Larson thoroughly enjoys this journey. He is in his element. It is a pleasure to see a man who is so positively in his right place and who walks about with the glance and air of the expert, regards his work, and sees that it is good. He says: "During the long years that I have spent in Mongolia it has always been my dream to take part in a real expedition, but I have never ventured to hope to participate in anything so imposing as this." And at the same time he has taken part in Andrews' and several other expeditions.

I owe Larson the greatest of thanks. During the difficult times in Peking he has often been my support and made easy my battles for me. In the darkest hours he always remained calm—the same as I. Larson cannot forget himself, he cannot say an unfriendly word, he is always cheerful and friendly. He would not lose his self-control for an instant, for he knows too well that he who cannot control *himself* will never be able to control others. His friendly and pleasant manner of expressing his opinion or giving orders is the whole secret of the esteem and respect that he enjoys with all of us. Even the German ex-officers willingly place themselves under him, when questions of moment are involved. In our daily life all are the best of friends and laugh and joke together, particularly at the dinner table. But woe betide him who attempts to tread on Larson's foot or to suggest anything that is not good for the camels, as an unnecessary excursion, too long marches for one day, the getting of new coolies, or the like! Larson does not get angry or shout. With the softest voice in the world he just explains quite simply that nothing will be done in the matter. And there he stands all the time with legs wide apart, his hands in his trousers pockets, his cap cocked on his head, and his face carrying a friendly smile. In the face of this calm, collected manner of commanding, no-one ventures to say a word. The proposer becomes dumb and with that the matter ends. It is as simple as that to bring men under the spell of his will. But that is a power that very few possess. The first requirement for it is self-command, the second is knowledge of men; and then, also, come charity and a sense of justice. Larson possesses all these qualities; with such a man as chief of staff one could conquer the world.

His right hand is Haslund, formerly employed with the British-American Tobacco Company, a particularly alert, capable, and enthusiastic young man, who proved what he can do, when he brought Andrews' camels into headquarters. Söderbom, who is only 22 years old, is a "special number." He is totally different from other men; for, when he arrived here, he had no other clothes with him than those he carried on his back, no bed, no fur, and no other luggage than a tooth-brush. An uncommonly wise man, I said to myself. How much simpler it is to ride across Asia without luggage than to drag 40,000 kilograms with one as we are doing! Söderbom was, however, fitted out, and received a brand-new suit, and finally looked like a servant on an estate in his Sunday best. He is unshakably calm in every emergency, is afraid of neither robbers nor wolves, and understands exceedingly well how to deal with our self-conscious cooks.

Of the Germans, first of all is Dr. Haude to be mentioned. He is our meteorologist and has a thorough grasp of his science and its subsidiary sciences. Besides, he is quite a wonderful fellow, loved and esteemed by us all, not least the Chinese. When he is not to be seen in his meteorological observatory, he is either on the top of some hill taking observations of wind and temperature, or is letting up a pilot balloon, which happens twice a day. The time he has over he makes use of for calculations and notes. In his various occupations he has several

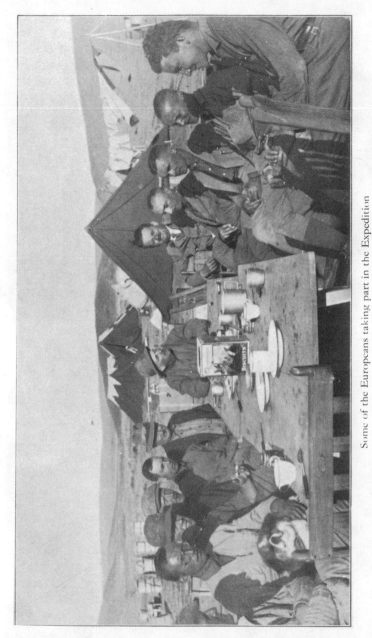

Some of the Europeans taking part in the Expedition

(From left to right, Walz, Haude, Haslund, Söderbom, Hummel, Larson, Hedin, von Marschall, Hempel, Heyder, von Kaull, Mühlenweg)

IN THE NEIGHBOURHOOD OF HUTYERTU-GOL

[face p. 40

Left, Dr. Yüan ; right, Professor Hsü Ping-chang

The students, Li, Ma, Liu, and Tsui, in front of their tent

CHINESE MEMBERS OF THE EXPEDITION

[face p. 41

assistants, Germans as well as Chinese. To the meteorological observations the four Chinese students bring an astonishingly great interest.

Herr Dettmann has been a naval officer. He has the astronomical instruments and observations to attend to and renders assistance to Dr. Haude with the wireless time-determinations. He is, besides, a skilled amateur painter and—on less serious occasions—an incomparable joker. His mandolin is particularly popular.

Herr Lieberenz is our film-operator and first photographer, and as soon as any interesting subject or events present themselves, he falls upon them, armed with his cinema-camera or one of the ordinary kind, like the falcon on its prey. He has travelled with Dr. Heck in Abyssinia and has experienced many unusual adventures.

Herr Heyder, a retired major, is my chief of staff. He maintains order in the camp, passes on my orders, decides the night-watches, has messages and reports to deliver, and so on. Herr Mühlenweg looks after the money matters and accounts, and in his tent has the silver-chests from which he makes all the payments. Herr Walz and Herr Zimmermann are Dr. Haude's permanent assistants. Baron von Massenbach and Baron Marschall von Bieberstein look after the baggage, and know, just as Herr Mühlenweg does, what are contained in all the four hundred boxes, of which they keep exact lists and detailed inventories. Heyder is our hunter and master-shot, and Herr von Kaull is employed in everything.

Professor Hsü is the leader and chief of the ten Chinese scholars and students who, whether I desired it or not, were commissioned, in accordance with the demands of the new Nationalist era, to take part in my Expedition, and thereby, at least formally, to place it under Chinese supervision.

Hsü is his family name (" hsing "), Ping-chang his first name (" ming "); but Professor Hsü has besides, like other Chinese, still another first name (" tzǔ "), in his case meaning " Morning Redness," that only his friends use.

Professor Hsü was born in 1888 in the village of Jênho in Southern Honan, near the border of the province of Hupeh. When he was 17 years old he left his parents' house and went to Peking to study. In 1913 he proceeded to Paris, where he studied philosophy for six years at the Sorbonne. When he returned from France he obtained an appointment as teacher of the French language and of the history of Chinese literature in Kaifêng, the capital of the province of Honan. In 1921 he became Professor of the History of European Philosophy in the National University. His salary at first amounted to 220 dollars a month, but rose subsequently to 280. For 2 years the professors have only received the half of their salaries and probably still less. They have to look for additional occupations, and have, for example, to teach in schools and deliver lectures, in order to be able to support themselves and their families. Since they are always engaged in this way, they have no time left over to follow up the advances of their subjects, and the life of learning and its development suffer accordingly, while the civil wars of the various generals swallow up enormous sums, civil wars that only serve selfish ends, lay waste the country, and unsettle its industrious inhabitants and break their spirit.

Hsü is no blind nationalist, and is not in the least affected by any hatred for foreigners. He is enthusiastic for the freedom and the right of self-determination of peoples, and in no way desires to put restraints on Mongols and Tibetans in favour of China, when they prefer to go their own ways and can get on alone. But it is his desire that the treasures of art and antiquity that have been found by foreigners on Chinese soil shall be placed under ban of export and annexed for all time to the museums and collections within China's own boundaries.

One beautiful day in the beginning of the winter I came to Peking, and it gradually became known that I contemplated undertaking a great expedition into the interior. " Aha ! " thought the leading men of the new age in the sphere of research and mental culture, " here is a new bird of prey, which wants to plunder and carry

off the treasures that are concealed in our earth." Thereupon there blazed up the opposition to my undertaking,
and Professor Hsü was one of my keenest opponents.
But when after negotiations lasting almost two months
we finally came to an agreement that, among many others,
contained the stipulation that ten Chinese scholars and
students should accompany me, Professor Hsü was chosen
as their leader and director. I welcomed the choice with
the greatest satisfaction; for during our long, difficult
negotiations I had got to know Hsü as a particularly
moderate, unassuming, and amiable man. And now,
after I have travelled with him without the shade of a
discord or the echo of a false note disturbing the harmony
that reigns in our camp, I cannot but be glad to have gained
as fellow-traveller a man who stands at the very top of
the civilization of his country, reigns supreme over the
history, literature, and philosophy of his fatherland, and
in addition has not merely a superficial knowledge of
European life and thought.

Professor Yüan Fu-li, who signs himself Ph. L. Yüan and
is called Hsi-yüan by his friends, was born in Peking in
1893. He studied geology and archæology in America.
Here with us Yüan proves himself eager and versatile.
He has as good an eye for neolithic settlements as for
geological problems and topographical surveys. His
knowledge in these subjects is sound and meets all European requirements. He finds it a pleasure to show us
Europeans his finds and to explain their significance.
With my Swedish co-workers Norin and Bergman he is
on the best of terms, and there is no question of jealousy
or disputes on account of the division of work. To him
as to the two others all that matters is to achieve the
greatest possible results for the good of European as well
as of Chinese research.

The second archæologist who is accompanying us is
named Huang Wên-pi. He is 33 years old and was
born in Hupeh, in the little town of Han-chuan-hsien to
the west of Hankow. After he had obtained his doctorate
he went to the Sinological Institute, under the direction
of Professor Shên. Like his colleagues he assisted in the

arrangement of archæological exhibitions, and thereby acquired a great interest in the investigation of antiquity. When he heard that a number of Chinese scholars were to join my expedition, he applied to the committee that had to select the participants and to lay down the conditions, and asked to be allowed to travel with us.

Our fourth Chinese scholar is named Ting Tao-hêng, and comes of a very distinguished family in Chih-chin-hsien in the province of Kweichow, south of the Yangtze. He is 28 years old.

The fifth and last bears the name of Chan Fan-shun, and was born 35 years ago in the town of Wu-yüan-hsien in Southern Anhwei. After the conclusion of his studies he returned to his home province and settled down in the capital, Anking, on the north bank of the Yangtze Kiang, in the gardens where cherries, apricots, pears, and mulberries ripen, and where the "River's Temple of Welcome," Ying-chiang-szŭ, is famous for its beauty and its pagoda, and for the same reason draws many believers to worship Buddha.

The four Chinese scholars and their leader, Hsü Ping-chang, were thus born in five different provinces—namely, Chihli, Honan, Hupeh, Kweichow, and Anhwei. Strictly speaking they represent five different peoples, for as far as nature, climate, population, and language are concerned, the provinces of China differ greatly from each other.

The first and most important condition that the Opposition in Peking laid down in their negotiations with me amounted to this, that several scholars and five students should take part in my expedition. When, however, the men in question were chosen, we let the matter rest at four students and in place of the fifth substituted a young photographer, who was above all to be at the disposal of Herr Yüan and Herr Huang for the photographing of geological and archæological objects. The number four was settled upon for the additional reason that I had explained that it was my intention to establish four permanent meteorological stations in the interior of the continent, and the Chinese Government had proposed to take over the stations and staff them with Chinese meteorologists, after the termination of the Expedition. So it was decided that one student should be assigned to each station, in order to receive for at least a year German guidance and German instruction in the art of meteorological observation. Then in the agreement of the 26th of April there was inserted the amendment that the stations should not be handed over to the Government but to the committee, the " Board of Directors," that has to represent the interests of the Expedition in Peking. The care and development of the stations by Chinese and without assistance from Europeans became thereby a question of the future, on the significance of which from the standpoint of pioneering I shall have occasion to say a few words later.

It was thus by no means a whim of the " Federation of Scientific Institutions of China " to present me with the condition that I should take four students with me. It was on the contrary an act of wisdom and foresight, which now, after I have become acquainted with the students, I have all reason to be thankful for, for it proves that the Scientific Federation in Peking was serious when, in place of the Government, it took over the responsibility for the future care of the stations. Now that my plans are in the course of events assuming a more and more settled form, and are transforming themselves into reality with the useful modifications that the situation may prescribe in certain particular eventualities, I should sooner be inclined to regret that we have not eight students with us instead of the four ; for it is to be desired that each Chinese director of a station has an assistant or substitute to stand by him after the German meteorologists have withdrawn. Now there is a gap that requires filling up.

The National University in Peking has its own journal. In this as in the publications of other institutions and seminaries there appeared a short account of my projected expedition and the notice that students of the mathematical and physical sciences—of meteorology especially—were free to offer their names as participants. The applicants would undergo an examination, and there would also be taken into consideration their knowledge of English or French.

Thirty students of mathematics and physics applied; there was even a young girl student among them. Before her name was accepted, her parents were asked whether they gave their assent to her accompanying me on the lonely roads across Asia. What their answer was I do not know. Either the answer was to forbid it, or else the young lady failed in the examination. Anyhow, she is not with us.

The examiners were our friend Professor Yüan and the Professor of Mathematics, Li. The thirty young people were first of all examined in languages, and then by Yüan in mathematics and physics. To each of them eight questions were put, and Yüan found that eight examinees satisfied the requirements. These underwent a new examination by Professor Li, after the doctors had examined them and declared them fit and well. Only with one of the eight men, Ma, had the medical examination an objection to make : his pulse was too quick ; but when he was declared fit by Dr. Dipper of the German Hospital, he too was admitted to the last, deciding examination. Of the eight candidates the four best were chosen, and one of them was Ma. The others are named Liu, Tsui, and Li.

Of the students three are from Chihli and one from Shantung.

Of our ten Chinese there is now only one more missing, Kung Yüan-tsung, the photographer. He thus forms a section to himself.

Kung is at present living with Professor Hsü Ping-chang. The four students have a large handsome tent, in which the beds are placed near the outside, and in the middle their boxes full of books and clothes, which serve as table. From time to time I visit them for a while and converse with them. They are always cheerful and friendly, and the slightest anecdote or the least joke makes them laugh uncontrollably. In their tent order and comfort reigns. On the improvised tables stand candles and lamps, and cigarettes and odds and ends lie between piles of books and note-blocks.

Meteorological manuals are always to hand, and one can see that they are used.

One receives the definite impression that the students that have passed the examination have approached their new task with the resolve to serve science and to bring credit to their country.

One can imagine what a Babylonish confusion of speech must prevail in such a motley caravan. At my table I usually have Larson, Haude, Lieberenz, and Yüan on my right, and Hummel, Hsü Ping-chang, and Hempel on my left. So we speak Swedish and German, French with Hsü, and English with Yüan, and the two last-mentioned among themselves Chinese. But when Haslund sits down beside us, with us Swedes he of course speaks Danish. Larson speaks Chinese with Hsü, and when the caravan men come with questions gives his orders in the Mongolian language. With von Kaull I sometimes for a change converse in the Russian language; for he was born in St. Petersburg. That makes already eight languages. In Hami and then in Eastern Turkistan there must be added Eastern Turkish as ninth language, and there I shall outdo all the others. Thus one has in this wandering Babel rich opportunity for practising European and Asiatic languages. The most splendid thing for me is, precisely, to speak Swedish; for in former days I have tramped about in Asia for years without ever having opportunity for a single Swedish word.

47

V

ONE OF THE CHIEF TASKS OF OUR EXPEDITION : METEOROLOGICAL OBSERVATIONS

IT is a matter of common knowledge that every civilized state grants considerable sums for meteorological stations, and we know too that these sacrifices are not made to no purpose, for the weather-service promotes the general welfare. Upon the weather, above everything, depend farming, forestry, the utilization of water-power, and sea and aerial navigation, and it would probably be impossible to state in figures how many human lives, sea vessels, and valuable cargoes have already been saved up to now through weather-forecast and storm-signals. How important meteorology is for the utilization of the water-power of a country may be inferred from the fact that in recent years several large power-stations have established their own weather-stations, because the public stations were not sufficient.

In the Northern hemisphere of the earth there are at the present time numerous meteorological observatories that make their observations daily on internationally accepted principles. Europe especially is richly provided ; Sweden possesses forty-one, Germany many hundreds, of first, second, and third rank. North America and Africa also have their stations, and in the same way observations are carried out daily on many ships. From a number of different points these arrive every few hours at the central office where the meteorologists form their forecasts.

It is only Asia that is still badly neglected in this respect. If one enters all the existing observatories on a map of the Northern hemisphere, Central Asia, which forms an enormously great part of the continental mass, presents an unbroken empty expanse. One has, indeed, in Urga, Udi,

Uliasutai, and Urumchi, made continuous, if indeed insufficient, investigations, and for the belt of desert as well as for Tibet there are my observations over many years, of especial importance those that I have carried out in fixed quarters, e.g. at Yangiköl, Charkhlik, and Mandarlik. But after all, our knowledge only rests on widely disconnected evidence. From it one can, it is true, get in broad lines a general idea of the characteristic features of the continental climate and a general idea of the working of the meteorological elements; one knows also the terribly violent storms at Hami—I have myself experienced many of the bigger raging storms from the east-north-east in the Lop-nor desert; one can also theoretically define the circumstances of their formation and from the practical point of view explain the result of their working—yet what do we know after all of their causes and character? Nothing.

To the original plan of my journey, which I am now putting into execution, there belongs as an important part the filling up of the empty expanse that spans the immeasurable spaces of Central Asia. With this the last gap in the network of meteorological stations in the Northern hemisphere would at last disappear, and many puzzling problems relating to the climatological and meteorological conditions of this hemisphere would find their solution. Secondly, we should be able to perform a service for China of incalculable significance, for a system of warnings of approaching dust-storms, which do great damage to the agriculture of China, could be put into operation. The permanent stations that I intend to set up in Central Asia will, if my plan succeeds and meets with adequate support from the Chinese authorities, play the same part on *land* as the storm-signal stations introduced by the Jesuits in Sikawei do on the coast.

One sees from this that the work of our meteorologist, Dr. Waldemar Haude, will bring about a revolution in meteorology and climatology, and that its results will find a prominent place in all new handbooks dealing with the subject. In truth, the task of Dr. Haude and his co-workers is of such great and wide significance, that our big and expensive expedition would even prove itself fully justified if, when we returned home, we had no other results to show.

Dr. Haude's observatory was ready on the very day on which we set up our tents on the Hutyertu-gol. It consists of a cubical wooden shed with protecting roof and lattice walls, through which the wind can move freely while no ray of sun penetrates. The shed rests on four posts, high enough to shut out any influence due to the heating or cooling of the ground. A few steps lead up to it, so that one can read off at convenience the instruments that have been set up. The whole thing is moored in all four directions with strong ropes, and never once have the most violent storms been able to shake the observatory. In the open at various altitudes protected minimum thermometers are to be found, fixed horizontally in tightened clamps, and on the ground lie insolation thermometers, as well as other sensitive instruments.

Dr. Haude's sanctum forms, as it were, a suburb for him on the outer edge of our camp town. His tent is filled with instrument-boxes, which are loaded with aneroids, cooking-thermometers, tools, and all sorts of curious apparatus. Before the entrance of the tent a veranda made of canvas has been put up, and in front of that stand other instrument-boxes, more or less unpacked or quite untouched. The full boxes contain complete sets of equipment for each one of the projected stations.

If one wants to go into Dr. Haude's suburb after dark, and does not exactly know one's way about there, one must be careful. For he has erected two metal masts, 10 metres in height and at a distance of 40 metres apart, for our wireless station, and outwards from these, 1 to 2 feet above the ground, run three metal wires, snares that one must avoid. I will take this opportunity to mention that we also possess a wireless station, which is under von Kaull's direction. Of course we cannot *send* with it. The difficult thing about our dry-batteries is, above all, that the current ceases after four minutes. One must, therefore, have luck and a quick perceptive faculty, if one is to hear Nauen, Cavite, or some other station. Dryness and heat are the worst enemies of the batteries and of ourselves. If I am not mistaken, Andrews has had in this respect just the same unpleasant experiences, as he tells us in his book, *On the Trail of Ancient Man*. He set up a wireless station in a motor-car, but could hear nothing either. Possibly our unpleasant experiences are to be attributed to climatic causes that cannot be eliminated with the means that rest at our disposal. Naturally we have no desire to be kept well posted up with the course of world events—we feel it rather a release to escape from all news of the outer world—but we should have liked to pick up the time-signals from Nauen, Bordeaux, Cavite, or Batavia, in order in this way to fix the degrees of longitude with certainty and for nothing.

If one looks up Dr. Haude in his sanctum, one mostly finds him—provided he is not just reading instruments or letting up a pilot balloon—absorbed in figures, formulæ, and tables, or else occupied with Herr Walz and Herr Zimmermann—who assist him and calculate the paths of the balloons—in dictating observations and calculations. The interior of Dr. Haude's tent impresses one as exceedingly learned and " weather-proof." He himself is one of the most charming and amiable men I have ever met. He does not belong to those scholars that lie over their knowledge like dragons over their golden treasures. It occasions him pleasure, on the contrary, to explain his researches to others. The listeners run the risk, with his interesting and clear expositions, of becoming meteorologists themselves.

In Dr. Haude's observatory, at the internationally agreed-upon hours, that is to say at 7, 2, and 9, o'clock, observations are made daily, and in every fixed camp every two hours in addition throughout day and night. In the night this work is entrusted to the watches, which are on duty from 9–1 and 1–5. They have to examine, above all, the mass of clouds and the direction of the wind, for Dr. Haude attaches far greater value to these elements than to the temperature curve, from whose appearance one can, indeed, also get a similar idea. With the series of observations that were taken for a year in Urga, Kalgan,

Udi, Uliasutai, and Urumchi, one paid too little attention to the clouds and winds; we thus have here particularly important work before us.

For the superintendence of temperature, and of the pressure and humidity of the air, there have been set up in our meteorological observatory a thermograph, a barograph, and a hygrograph. To the altitude, form, and direction of motion, of the clouds Dr. Haude devotes an especial interest; he has taken a big series of unusually beautiful photographs of different types of clouds. The velocity of the wind is measured in the camp as well as at the top of a hill, 26 metres in height; its maximum lay as yet between 28 and 30 second-metres, thus a wind strength of 11 on the Beaufort scale or a rough storm. Here, indeed, wind almost always prevails. It rises at 8 o'clock in the morning, increases in strength till noon, and drops towards 6 o'clock or a little later. In the night it is usually completely calm and clear. If rain falls, it evaporates for the most part before it reaches the surface of the earth. The density of precipitation increases up to the rainy season. And what does it become then? Well, of that we know nothing, and it is that, indeed, along with much else, that we want to know.

Dr. Haude believes he can determine, by means of his researches, whether something could not be done in the future for the reclamation and utilization of the land, and whether a planting of forests would be possible; by this means the land would mount in value to an unprecedented degree. It may be, however, that the Mongolian steppe is too severely limited by unfavourable climate for it to be possible to subdue it.

Another problem to whose solution we hope to be able to bring important contributions is the drying up of the country. For Central Asia is unquestionably facing a period of dryness. Almost all the lakes are sinking and diminishing in extent. For the elucidation of these questions we shall acquire excellent material on Gashun-nor. Definite conclusions one will not be able to form till after some decades. But by means of our exact observations, which one will have to repeat in the future in order

The daily pilot balloon rises

The observatory in the neighbourhood of Hutyertu-gol

METEOROLOGICAL OBSERVATIONS : ONE OF THE EXPEDITION'S GREAT TASKS

Camp cooking-stove of the Chinese

Camp cooking-holes of the Mongols

IN THE NEIGHBOURHOOD OF HUTYERTU-GOL

[*face p.* 53

to obtain material for comparison, we are laying the foundation for them.

Dr. Haude makes in addition very careful and delicate observations of the insolation, the sun's radiation, and of the nocturnal radiation from the earth. The stratification of the air over the surface of the earth by night has often been observed by him already, as in Paotow. Now he has also his series from the border of Mongolia, and the work rests neither in the camps nor on the march. Dr. Haude is delighted whenever we are forced to remain still. He employs the time for work, and obtains homogeneous and continuous material that he can relate to that of other countries.

There will probably not be, at least in Europe, a meteorological observatory that is engaged in more thorough and less interrupted investigations of the movements of the aerial ocean than the aeronautical observatory in Lindenberg near Berlin, where pilot balloons and kites rise in the air daily. This establishment was founded by Assmann, the inventor of the aspiration psychrometer, the apparatus for the determination of the true humidity of the air, and was taken over in the year 1912 by Hergesell, who employed pilot balloons in Strassburg for the exploration of the atmosphere as early as from 1900 to 1906. In Germany all the larger stations and observatories now send up pilot balloons. Sweden has three stations, Finland one near Helsingfors. The weather-service in Stockholm receives every day reports from about twenty pilot-balloon stations at various places in Europe. In China up to the present only a few balloon ascents are said to have taken place. Neither in India does one appear to avail oneself of this method of research to any extent worth mentioning. So too in this respect does the whole of Central Asia form an enormous *terra incognita*. This being so, one can imagine what it will mean for the science of the movements of the air currents at heights up to 15,000 metres and more, to learn about the atmospheric conditions over Central Asia by means of Dr. Haude's investigations with pilot balloons during a whole year. Our expedition will not only present to science the whole of the extensive material relating to the conditions on the surface of the earth, but at the same time will in addition extend the knowledge of the movements of the air currents up to 15,000 metres.

The pilot balloons should disclose to us along what lines the interchange of air takes place between the Pole and the Equator over the greatest land mass of the earth. They should also reveal to us how far into Asia the changeable weather that we are accustomed to in Europe extends, or in other words, how far towards the east Europe's areas of high and low pressure reach. How far is Asia's annual heating and cooling perceptible in a *vertical* direction? How high up in summer do the air currents go that travel at the surface of the earth from the sea to the land, and in the higher regions from the land to the sea? And how high up does the reverse condition of winter prevail, when the air flows over the surface of the earth from the cooled land to the sea, and above these currents, in higher regions, an interchange in the opposite direction takes place?

It is our intention to find the answers to these and other similar questions. If we succeed in this, as we have every reason to hope we shall, it will be possible to establish laws of very great importance for the circulation of the atmosphere.

By means of the pilot balloons one ascertains, not only the direction of the wind in the higher regions, but also changes in the distribution of the pressure of the air at various heights above the earth, and if there were a sufficiently large number of stations, one would then even be able to draw isobar maps for the separate layers, which would appear quite different from those for the surface of the earth. With the help of pilot balloons we can get an idea of the appearance of these, as yet, non-existent maps.

The mean height that was reached amounts to 7,500 metres above sea level, and the greatest up to the present 14,700 metres. The pilot balloons that one sends up from ships are considerably larger than ours. We have three different kinds, but even our largest are too small to be

[1] On a later occasion 21,200 m.

clearly observed above a height of 15,000 metres. They are made of the best yellow or red rubber, and, so far as the yellow ones are concerned, are almost transparent. They have a diameter of about three-quarters of a metre or of 120 centimetres. The former kind are 30 grammes in weight, and must be able to carry 90 grammes before they are allowed to go up ; the larger ones, with a weight of 110 grammes, must bear a weight of 325 grammes. The small ones have a speed of ascent of 150 metres a minute, the large ones 250. In ten minutes the latter thus reach a height of 2,500 metres above our camp, which is situated 1,595 metres above sea level.

As early as the autumn of 1925, when I was drawing up the original scheme of this expedition, the setting up of four permanent meteorological stations in the heart of Asia seemed to me a task of the very greatest scientific importance. In spite of the greater and lesser modifications that this first scheme underwent, under the pressure of circumstances in the course of the following year and in the winter of 1926 to 1927, I always kept to the idea and intention of founding these four stations. I have already shown of what immense importance these stations may become for our knowledge of the climatic and meteorological conditions of the Northern hemisphere, and what they mean for China in respect of practical matters and forecasting.

When the Swedish Minister, Ewerlöf, and I were negotiating at the end of November and the beginning of December, 1926, with the Chinese Government of that time, concerning the sanctioning of my expedition, I also volunteered to hand over later, after their European staffs had carried out series of observations over at least a year, the meteorological stations, together with the whole of their instrumental equipment, as a present to the Chinese Government, on the assumption that, after the termination of the expedition and the departure of the European staffs, the Chinese would maintain the upkeep of the stations with properly trained staffs, and would carry out my plans throughout coming years ; for only in the future, when the series of observations extended over tens of years,

would the true value of the stations and their advantage
to China show up in the right light. The meteorological
elements in distinctly continental regions—and especially
in the heart of Asia—are on the whole fairly settled, and
series of observations of rather more than a year are even
so soon, therefore, of great importance. But series over
many years, which make possible the fixing of reasonable
mean values, would raise the rank of these scientific observations and put them in a line with the most valuable on
the earth.

The Chinese Government offered courteous thanks for
my offer, but what on earth was the Government to do
with my stations after my staff and I had left them? Govern-
ments seldom dispose of the information that one needs
in order to be able to judge of the weather conditions on
the earth.

But when the opposition had raised its storm against
my expedition that at first appeared irreconcilable, and
then when, after a series of meetings, we had come nearer
and nearer together and had discussed the various problems
and practical questions and finally the conditions on which
Chinese scholarship believed it to be possible to open the
portals of Central Asia to me, then, indeed, did the stations
too find the attention that they deserved.

The men who had previously been my opponents
became now my allies, in respect of the scheme to set up
permanent stations, as well as of the idea and intention
to take them over in the future and keep them going.
That this was not merely hollow pretence and fine words
with which the scholars wished to save their faces, may
be concluded from the demand they made to me, to take
the four Chinese students with me, whose business it
should be, in each case, to join one of the four stations.

Station 1 is to be set up on Etsin-gol, Station 2 in Hami.
In Urumchi we establish Station 3. This town becomes
our headquarters for some time. The principal caravan
moves afterwards across the Lop-nor desert to Charkhlik
or Cherchen, in order there to set up Station 4.

That the Chinese are really taking an interest in my
scheme may be concluded from the fact that, even before

my departure from Peking, the central observatory asked me to give Stations 2 and 3 instructions to send a telegraphic weather-report every day to Peking, naturally at China's expense. I was gladly prepared to comply with this request.

Above Station 4, at a height of at least 3,000 metres, we erect, for a period of at least some months, a mountain station on the edge of the Kun-lun range, at which observations are carried out at the same time, in order to provide Dr. Haude with material for the investigation, how during the different seasons the temperature decreases and increases with the height, and how high up the dust-storms reach, with the deposit of loess-forming dust that the wind carries with it. For the mountain station we cannot spare more than one European, so the rest of the staff has to consist of natives.

During my delay in Peking I also thought how desirable it would be to set up a Station 5 on the Khotan-darya, at about the point where I encountered the river after my ill-fated march across the desert in the April and May of 1895. Dr. Haude is of the opinion that such a station would be of particularly great importance, for it would give us a clear idea of the temperature, the sand-storms, and the rest of the weather conditions, in the middle of an absolute desert. It would also be exceedingly valuable to obtain a detailed description of the quantity of water in the Khotan-darya and of its pulsations during the summer. When I reached the river-bed on the 5th of May, 1895, I found it dry. Only at great distances apart did I discover small pools of water, which, if they are sufficiently deep, hold out throughout the whole summer. The pool that saved my life was found 11 years later by the English archæologist Sir Aurel Stein, who sent me a photograph of the "God-given lake." For guide he had my servant Kasim. Herdsmen in the wood reported that the whole bed fills with water at the beginning of June, but that the quantity of water decreases even after a month and a half, finally in the autumn to stop altogether. Where eddies form in the stream and hollow out the bottom, frozen pools of water remain over the whole winter; but these shrink up in the spring, and in May the river-bed is as dry as it can ever be. I should consider it an advantage to obtain a picture of the life and of the sleep of death of the river in the various months of the year, and of its triumphant battle right up to the present day against the sandy desert. Such a knowledge can only be acquired through continuous observations on the spot during a whole year. Therefore the temptation is very strong to add yet a fifth station to the four planned.

To the members of our wandering town that have to remain behind at the stations, it will not be exactly easy and pleasant to part for ever from our great, splendid caravan and its gay, varied life, and I fear it will be with a feeling of loneliness and sadness that they will see us others go away to meet with new vicissitudes and adventures, whilst they themselves are facing a whole year of monotonous captivity. We are, sometimes, already now discussing the question of the distribution of the staffs at the several stations, and the difficult thing about it is that all would prefer to come to the last station, in order to lose as little as possible of our long journey. The worst off in this respect are those that remain on Etsin-gol, for their separation from the main caravan takes place first. But when they learn their fate, I shall not conceal from them the fact that Gashun-nor and its surrounding country are probably the most interesting region that we shall touch upon on the whole journey. If I myself had to stay for a year at one of the projected stations, I should choose Gashun-nor and in the second place the Khotan-darya. Which of the three towns, Hami, Urumchi, or Cherchen, would become my place of residence, should the occasion arise, could be immaterial to me; for all three lack the stillness and Sunday peacefulness of the desert. But wherever one is, one has inexhaustible opportunities to study the surface of the earth and its life as well as the life and activity of mankind.

Professor J. G. Andersson at the beginning of the winter made the suggestion to me that the staffs of the stations should, as often as ever they could, not let the opportunity escape them to undertake anthropometric measurements.

We applied therefore to Dr. Paul H. Stevenson at the Anatomical Institution of the Peking Union Medical College.   Dr. Stevenson and Dr. Black took a great interest in our scheme, and the former gave a course of instruction in anthropometry to the principals that were kept in view for the stations, and even wrote for them a short pamphlet with the title, " An Introduction to Anthropometry on the March, specially compiled for the Sino-Swedish Expedition to Central Asia."   This little work is quite excellent as a guide to anthropometric measurements and is illustrated with photographs and drawings.   Dr. Stevenson has informed me personally how difficult it is to induce the different races to allow themselves to be measured.   But two of our principals, the Swede Söderbom and the Dane Haslund, have already shown themselves to be especially ingenious intermediaries and interpreters, at the measurements that our doctor, Dr. Hummel, has up to the present carried out, and they will shortly be able to work independently.

VI

WE SEPARATE INTO THREE COLUMNS

MONGOLIAN soil detains us. A month has already passed away since we set up our tents on Hutyertu-gol. We cannot understand what has become of the time. Of boredom we know nothing, everyone is working, something new happens every day, we devise schemes, and are kept in constant suspense by the waiting and longing for the departure. We are waiting for the camels.

Our camel-buyers are availing themselves of various traders and intermediaries who have connexions with rich Mongols in Outer Mongolia, many of whom own herds of a thousand animals. A few days ago two of our Mongols came back and reported that they had bought a hundred first-rate camels for 100 Mexican dollars each. But the various owners wanted to have the silver first, before they handed over their animals—the times were bad, and one could never know what kind of people they were, with whom one was having business dealings.

Therefore, before we had seen anything at all of these camels, we had to count out 10,000 silver dollars (more than £1,000) and hand the sum over to our agents.

The paying out was quite a romantic spectacle. The sun went down as red as a berry and poured out its light over the slumbering steppe, the cool of evening came creeping along over the ground, and one or another put on his fur. As if for the last course, the mountains of silver were being piled up in front of the club-tent. There lay the piles of dollars in long rows, one thousand alongside another. And by the side stood the hardened Mongols and the crafty Chinese, waiting and counting, and cramming the silver into bags, which were then packed in small wooden boxes, to be, the next morning, conveyed under the protection of von Massenbach and Mühlenweg to the owners of the camels.

On the 16th of June the first new camels reached us. They were big, plump, and beautiful. It was an especial pleasure for me, to inspect, under the guidance and with the explanations of Larson and his Mongols, the twenty-four animals. Their humps were fat, firm, and conical, and therefore stood erect. The animals had already for the most part lost their winter wool, and consequently appeared bare. Above our heads Dr. Haude's pilot balloon was just mounting upwards and stood out glistening like a diamond against the background of a turquoise-blue heaven. The two Mongols, strangers to us, that the new members of the caravan had brought into our camp were fine, hardy, weather-tanned types of their race, famous from the times of Jenghiz Khan. It was amusing to observe them when the balloon rose in the air. They stood there speechless and stared after the bright ball till it could only be seen with the field-glass.

At the present time we possess two hundred camels, although only a hundred and four are in the camp. According to a recent enumeration and weighing of the baggage, we require two hundred and ninety-four camels, a number that we intend by repacking to bring down to two hundred and seventy. Sixty-three of them serve as riding-animals for us and our servants. A camel becomes free every third day, and on our arrival in Hami a large number will go without loads. If we lay out 15,000 dollars in gold for two hundred and seventy camels, one must not forget that the camels represent a live capital that can at any time be converted into money, at a profit or loss, according to supply and demand.

Shortly before sunset I paid the camels one more visit. Some stood there erect and dignified, others lay and chewed the cud, and the red ball of the sun was reflected in their sparkling brown eyes, that they shone like the rubies from Badakshan.

All around reigned silence. In the silver light of the moon the tents throw deep-black shadows. I remain standing in front of my dwelling and regard the white bands that decorate the tents. They are not lifeless decorative designs, but have a deep meaning. In the two bottom corners on each side is to be seen the ideograph *shou*, which signifies " long life." In the middle of the face of the tent the same sign is to be found once more, stylized in the form of a circle. This is surrounded by the five bats, *fu*, with outstretched wings, whose signs signify " bliss." On both sides float heavy stylized clouds.

It may appear venturesome to send out into the unknown a crowd of hard-bitten Mongols with 10,000 silver dollars, and one cannot but become finally somewhat anxious, when one day after another goes by without our Mongols sending any news. The period of eighteen days that I had given von Kaull, Söderbom, and Haslund, for the execution of their orders in Paotow, Kuei-hua-chêng, Peking, and Tientsin, has now already been overstepped by four days and of them too we have heard nothing. But we have heard a rumour from wandering Chinese, that the Kuo-min-tang has raised its flag in Paotow and that Chang Tso-lin is dictator in Peking. If these reports, which we cannot verify, are true, it was not to be wondered at if the Peking-Paotow railway line was closed to all other travellers but the military. Our people may also have had the misfortune to be cut off from us. But if they had already left Kuei-hua-chêng with their silver and the rest of their baggage and had been surprised by robbers on the way here, news of it would certainly have penetrated to Beli-miao and into our headquarters.

On Sunday, the 26th of June, we had in the town of nations a real popular festival. A strange company had come into our camp : four or five men with three women and half a dozen dirty children. They explained that they were a touring theatrical troupe and had looked us up to show us some samples of their art. Some of us believed they were cleverly disguised spies of a robber band, and in this case they played their part really well. For why should a company of players stray up here into the desert places of Mongolia, when they have the whole of China at their disposal ? But perhaps competition is so strong that it even pays to entertain the Mongols. Such adventurers have nothing to fear from robbers ; it would not pay to rob them, and presumably the bandits too need some diversion from time to time.

The troupe settled down close by the tents of our servants, and after they had been entertained with food and tea, the ladies began to pick off each other's vermin and effect a relentless massacre. Dr. Hummel was of the opinion that this respectable business must take place some-where else, not here, where we ran the risk of possibly picking up typhus-carrying lice, and I asked Yüan to send the company away and assign them somewhere to live on the other side of the river, so that the vermin could not get into our tents without getting wet feet.

At the usual hour the tea-bell rang and we gathered at the tables of the club-tent. Usually afternoon tea is unceremonious and does not detain us long. But it is never missed ; at 5 o'clock one is thirsty after the heat of the day and wants to have tea. To-day, however, we remained sitting longer than usual. For the wandering troupe wanted now to be seen. Under the awning of the club-tent and along the table in front of the entrance chairs and benches were arranged in rows, and we took our places. In the middle of the open space, enclosed by packing-cases and provision sacks, in the south along Marco-Polo Street, as we call the free passage in front of the tents, the actors fitted up their open-air stage. An empty case was placed there, and the orchestra established itself on two chairs, two travelling musicians, of whom one played the flute and the other operated a stringed instrument.

The actors were still in our servants' tent, in order to dress and make up. The spectators gradually collected. Alongside and on the packing-cases sat the Mongols and our other servants. The open-air stalls were taken. If these actors were spies in disguise, then the number of inhabitants of the wandering town must have inspired them with respect.

Now they came on the stage. There were two men, but one played a female rôle and had a woman's face by nature. He wore a woman's wig and ornaments like those the Chinese women wear. The other had made himself up round the eyes a dead white and wore a long black moustache. They knew their parts well. Singing and screaming and bawling, they poured forth unintelligible words, while the music played and put forth its strength. I asked Hsü and Yüan if they could follow, but they explained that they only understood a word here and there. But that the piece dealt with love was clear. " How old are you ? " he asked, and she gave a pert answer. The piece was divided into four acts and the two lovers quarrelled throughout the whole time. It was a consolation to us that even the Chinese could not make more of it than such punning disputes about words. It would certainly have been a really amusing reading to go over the whole text of this wonderful play. One may perhaps believe that it must become monotonous when two people in love tease and make sport of each other right through four acts. But that is not the case at all. It is not a dialogue in which two stand facing each other and speak like ordinary people, but our actors jumped and danced about the whole time, struck each other on the forehead with fans, making a smacking sound, or from a kind of long rattle made of hard wood produced rhythmic creaking sounds. They made leaps like acrobats, crouched down like cats, made grimaces, and raised a real Red Indian yell. Without doubt they said really frivolous things, but their movements were not offensive, their mimicry was excellent, and from it the Chinese spectators derived great fun. The music was not bad. It had the monotonous rhythm of the Asiatic art of music, to which I for my part shall not become tired of listening. In the whole of Asia from west to east I have listened to its notes and to this bewitching lulling music have dreamed of rosier times. It stills the restlessness of the heart and leads the thoughts to rest ; one understands that the flute of the snake-charmer subdues the cobra.

When the play was over and actors and musicians had received their reward, they went their way and the spectators dispersed. We had had at all events something like a popular entertainment in our town.

On this day Dr. Haude read 32·2 degrees Celsius, the

Dicky's foster-father and foster-mother

Camels cost money, and cash silver dollars at that

In the Neighbourhood of Hutyertu-gol

[face p. 64

Chinese actors demonstrate their art

Dried camel-dung is in demand as fuel

IN THE NEIGHBOURHOOD OF HUTYERTU-GOL

[*face p.* 65

highest temperature up to the present that we had had in headquarters. During the night the thermometer only fell to 14·8 degrees, a temperature that seemed to us uncommonly warm and brought to life a species of small brown beetle. Round my lamp I counted over six hundred, which swarmed here and there in close battalions and ran this way and that over my paper whilst I wrote. When we have only a few degrees above zero they are not to be seen, and I can devote myself in peace to my note-books and letters.

On the 28th of June there came two Mongols with four good camels that they wanted to sell in our camp. We bought them for 90 dollars each, and with them a black dog that they brought with them.

The 30th of June brought us a glad surprise. Just as we were sitting down to dinner, one of our Mongols appeared and reported to Larson that a herd of camels was approaching. We hurried out with field-glasses. Two of our Mongols that we had sent out to the north-east were driving the herd towards our camp, they themselves riding on camels. They came travelling along at a quick pace over the steppe. When they were quite near, the animals took fright at the tents, and set off in wild flight away from them, making for the north again in a great bend and enveloped in clouds of whirling dust. But the riders soon succeeded in becoming master of them, and they again approached the little stream and forded it with leaps attended by plunging and splashing. Then Larson and I inspected the forty-two arrivals; they were fat and well and gave the impression of being able to withstand a summer's march to Urumchi.

When in the evening the whole cavalry brigade of our camels returned from pasture, they had thus received a considerable reinforcement, and it was a pleasure to watch the proud walk of the splendid animals. A second spectacle was presented to us by the sunset. It was quite different from those of the last four weeks. The red colour was completely absent. The western heaven was covered with small, elongated, bluish grey, silver-edged clouds. Behind one of them the sun was concealed. Then it could be seen again for an instant, but only to be plunged in a bed of blue-black clouds. This dark wall already extended upwards to the zenith and approached us nearer and nearer. A calm as never before lay over the whole region ; a burning candle would not have made the least flicker. But that was the calm before the storm. One could see that a terribly rough storm was approaching. Angry spirits of the air were on campaign towards the east. All hurried into their tents. One could hear powerful hammer blows that were driving in new strengthening pegs all round the tents. When the first gusts of wind reached us, full of its dust, I packed away with all haste all light objects that were lying about, such as charts, books, notes, articles of clothing, and so on. There was the hurricane already above us, a dust-storm of the first magnitude, which so blew inwards the weather sides of the tents, that they threatened to split every minute. All of a sudden it was pitch black. It howled and roared all round us ; one could only hear the voice of the storm. It raged for more than two hours.

It was still quite early in the morning on the 1st of July when I was awakened in order to be present at the departure of a small, very carefully organized caravan that is under the command of Dr. Norin. To his column belong Messrs. Heyder, von Massenbach, Bergman, and Ting, as well as Collector Chin, two coolies, two Mongols, and a cook. They are taking with them six weeks' provisions and three tents.

Regarding the task that they are to carry out, the state of affairs is as follows :

When Norin returned to headquarters ten days ago, he laid a plan before us, the object of which was to carry out a more thorough cartographical survey of the road to Gashun-nor than we had at first intended. The original plan only provided for the simple mapping of just the route of the march as I have been accustomed to do it from of old, in addition to which Norin and Yüan were to survey certain regions with reference to the survey of this route, according to the time that we could sacrifice for this and the importance of the areas in respect of geology and archæology. Small charts of exclusive archæological

66

interest were to be drawn by Bergman and Huang. On the whole the map of our road would in this case have been only a line, with small extensions here and there.

Now came Norin with his great proposal, and I hardly need to especially emphasize that I assented with delight. He will triangulate the whole road right to Gashun-nor. We thereby acquire a continuous system of triangles, whose angles between special heaps of stones and fixed points are measured with the theodolite, and whose sides have a length of between 10 and 15 kilometres. The principal axis of the system of triangles follows the caravan road to Gashun-nor. The measurement of the triangles is entrusted to Herr Heyder, who himself rides from one fixed point to another, while the trustworthy coolie Wang-kuei has to go on foot and carry the precious theodolite.

Norin himself fills up the area inside the triangles with topographical particulars, and in this depends on the fixed points. His assistant in this work is von Massenbach, who surveys all watercourses and well-defined paths through the valleys. Both use plane-tables for this work, and Norin even has time still to spare for his geological observations and for geological mapping. Heyder and also von Massenbach had as officers gone through courses of topography ; they were therefore no longer beginners when Norin showed them, on several practice excursions in the neighbourhood of the camp, what it was they were concerned with. They were full of enthusiasm for the undertaking and the tasks that were assigned to them, and looked forward with pleasure to being able, in this department too, to contribute to the results of the expedition.

As usual we discussed this scheme of map-making with the Chinese management and with it met with cordial approval and the keenest interest. Whereas Norin's section is keeping in general about 20 kilometres to the right or north of the main caravan, the Chinese made the proposal to form a topographical column of their own that is to march to the left, that is to say to the south, of the main body and keep at a distance of about 10 kilometres. We shall thus move forward in three, in the main, parallel columns, the northern under Norin's command, the middle

67

one, the main body, under my leadership, and the southern under Yüan's. Yüan sets out from here on the 3rd of July, accompanied by the archæologist Huang, Collectors Chuang and Pai, a cook, two coolies, and two Mongols. He is taking with him provisions for four weeks and requires fifteen camels.

The northern section in which Bergman, assisted by Chin, is looking after the interests of archæology and Ting of palæontology, has the most difficult part of the work to perform, since the angle measurements require the greatest accuracy; it therefore set out on its forward march as early as the 1st of July. Yüan's troop has a better chance of being able to keep the same pace as the main caravan, but nevertheless sets out on its journey on the 3rd of July in order to get a little start, especially as Yüan hopes to find opportunity too, along with the topographical work, to make archæological and palæontological finds and investigations, which take up their time.

Naturally both side columns will always keep in touch with the principal troop; communication is maintained by Mongolian couriers, riding on swift-footed camels. Of such racers we have several—some were filmed by Lieberenz yesterday, and in this it was shown that one of them could not be overtaken by a horse in full gallop.

Water and pasture lands will as usual determine the camping-places. Therefore it is possible that two or perhaps all three columns will spend the night at one time or another at the same spring or watercourse. At other times we are independent of each other. This much, however, is quite certain, that all three sections will meet at least once, that is when we have travelled half the journey, at a monastery known as Shande-miao. The troop that arrives there first, in all probability the main caravan, has to await the arrival of the other two. The camels must rest there a few days, while the topographers compare their labours and bring them into relation with each other. Then, if all has gone well and the result is satisfactory, the mapping is to be continued in the same way right to Gashun-nor and is to form the framework of the system of triangles.

VII

THE LAST DAYS ON HUTYERTU-GOL

OUR life flows on uniformly but pleasantly, and that, during the height of summer in Mongolia and at so considerable an altitude, is indeed not to be expected otherwise. I have previously named 1,570 as the figure for the altitude of our fixed camp, but it was based on an observation of the pressure of the air over a period of only two weeks. Now, after more than five weeks, we have determined 1,595 as the mean value with a possibility of error of 60 metres above or below. A more certain value will not be obtained until after our observations have been compared with those of other stations in Asia.

On the 8th of July some Mongols were sighted, approaching the camp with a herd of camels. There were nineteen splendid animals from the north, which increased our camel caravan to two hundred and twenty.

Two Chinese brothers came and offered us for 5 dollars an antelope kid about eight days old. Larson warned us against taking it; for if we did so, we should be inundated with young antelopes from every side. The poor little animal was given lukewarm milk, and we nursed and cared for it as well as we could. Wrapped up in coverings, it is now lying in front of my tent, and I really don't know what I am to do with it. If I knew where its mother is, I would take it out to her; but the steppe is big and the antelopes are as fleet as shadows of clouds gliding along over the surface of the earth. The Mongols have a particular name for them: they call them "Larson's sheep." Friend Larson is indeed Duke of Mongolia, and the antelopes belong to him.

To our zoological garden belongs also a small, neat, elegant kangaroo-mouse or jerboa, which Dr. Hummel

keeps in a large empty box and has already almost tamed.
On the floor of the box there is an open cage with a large
pad of wadding. In this the jerboa every day makes its
bed. In bowls it is given water, rice, and bread, and
always has a heap of buttercups, whose petals seem to be
its favourite dish. It is most charming when it sits upon
its disproportionately-large, strongly-developed hind-legs
and with its small, stunted forelegs and paws holds the
petals to its mouth. It is greyish brown, has very large
thin ears, and big brown eyes. It is a nocturnal animal
and becomes lively and wide awake as soon as the sun has
gone down. Dr. Hummel has indeed captured it during
the night-watch. When the mouse moves freely on the
ground, it only uses its hind-legs and keeps its body almost
erect. Its tail, which is long and powerful and ends in a
white tuft of hair provided with a black transverse stripe,
then serves it also as support. Dr. Hummel is on a footing of great confidence with it. He takes it out of its
cage and lets it walk about on his shoulders and arms. It
shows no trace of fear or shyness and is extremely interested in everything. But its menu is curious and is not
confined only to vegetables. One day Dr. Hummel was
of the opinion that it might need company, and put a
frog out of the stream in its water-basin. In the morning the frog had been eaten up, right up to the head.
Another occurrence, which for some time put the jerboa
out of favour in the camp, was its devouring the two tiny
frail, helpless young that it gave birth to in its wadding
nest. It allowed them to live for a few days, but appeared
to take very little interest in its offspring, for it trod care-
lessly on them and let them lie by themselves and squeak.
I explained that its apparent voracity might rather be a
touch of heroism, in that it wanted to secure its young
against an uncertain future in captivity.

The day has, however, also brought us a real sensation.
The Mongols who brought camels reported that three days
previously on the caravan road between Beli-miao and
Kuei-hua-chêng they had met a Chinese caravan; the
leader of the caravan had related that when they had been
in Kuei-hua-chêng three days before, they had seen Euro-

peans, who were buying camels there. More the Chinese had not known. We have come to the conclusion that at the moment it is almost unthinkable that any other Europeans are buying camels in Kuei-hua-chêng than our envoys von Kaull, Söderbom, and Haslund. Spirits are therefore high in the camp, and we hope that our party is out of danger and that in a few days we can shake off the fetters of our long captivity.

When seven days over the calculated time had elapsed, doubts even rose with the, at other times, always imperturbable Larson. In the middle of the night, at half-past twelve, he and Dr. Hummel came into my tent, where I was still up writing. Larson made the proposal to send one of our best Mongols to Kuei-hua-chêng with a letter from me to the Belgian doctor, Dr. Kaisin, in which I should ask if and when our people had left the city, and if they had not left it, what the reason was for their delay.

The 9th of July went by like all other days. In the evening, after Dr. Hummel and I had fed the young antelope and had arranged its bed, we were standing chatting in front of the doctor's tent under the red-cross flag, when Larson, with both arms waving about in the air, came running up—he who is usually always so calm. He was calling and shouting, but we did not as yet understand what he wanted.

" What's the matter, what's the matter ? " we asked.

" They are coming, the whole caravan is coming."

" Where then ? "

" There, over the hills in the north-east."

Sure enough, their camels could be seen there, dark forms in the advancing twilight. We hurried towards the stream to the place where the road crosses it. There they came, copper-coloured like American Indians, covered with dust, in tatters, ungroomed. They looked like real highwaymen. But they were well and in good spirits and their camels were quiet and well cared for. Five they had bought in Kuei-hua-chêng at a price between 105 and 120 Mexican dollars.

What a commotion there was in the camp ! The three were the heroes of the hour. They were the centre of a

real public meeting. They were besieged with questions
from all sides ; von Kaull approached me, struck his heels
together, raised his hand to his cap, and reported that
the caravan had carried out all orders, and had presented
itself in headquarters without losses. I bid him and the
two others welcome and thanked them.

" Have you the mail from Paotow and Peking with
you ? "

" Yes, the whole of it."

" Have you received the money ? "

" Yes, all has gone well ; the whole amount is there,
allowing for the cost of the journey, the camels, and
commission."

" Are you hungry ? "

" Yes, fearfully."

The cooks received the necessary orders, and in a trice
the food was ready. Meanwhile the camels were unloaded
and the mail was unpacked. Everyone received his share ;
whole heaps of newspapers lay stacked up.

On the 15th of July Larson comes to me in the tent
and makes the following report : " We have now two
hundred and thirty-seven camels. We have bought two
hundred and forty, but two have died and one has run
away. Up to now we have paid 21,286·90 Mexican dollars, that is to say, on an average, 88 Mexican dollars for
each animal. That the average price is so low, we have for
the most part to thank Andrews. Of our two hundred
and thirty-seven camels twenty-six are in Norin's column
and fifteen in Yüan's. The loads at headquarters require
altogether a hundred and ninety-five camels, and in addition
we require twenty-seven riding-camels. Sixteen riding-
camels for the Mongolian caravan men have been reckoned
in with the hundred and ninety-five. We still need, then,
at the most only thirty, and these I expect precisely
to-morrow."

" When, in your opinion, can the caravan be ready for
departure ? "

" At the latest, on the 20th of July."

" How many camels do you believe will hold out as far as
Urumchi ? "

"All of them. I have lived 34 years in Mongolia, but I have never seen such a multitude of magnificent, first-rate camels. At first they will be difficult and stubborn, but after that they will soon calm down."

I had hoped to be able to send along with the last courier, who is leaving at 4 o'clock in the morning on the 17th of July and is taking with him our mail and two boxes full of archæological finds, a letter dealing with the information concerning Gashun-nor that one is able to find in the annals of the earlier Han dynasty, that is to say from the last two centuries before the birth of Christ. The archæologist Huang, a very scholarly man, has with him six boxes of old Chinese literature, which can be of very great use to the archæologists. Among these books are also the annals of the earlier Han dynasty ; Professor Hsü has at my request read through them. On the way to Gashun-nor Hsü will translate for me the nine different passages in the annals where the region of the lakes and Etsin-gol are mentioned. The annals are the work of Pan Piao, his sons Pan Ku and Pan Chao, and his daughter Pan Chao. The book is thus the work of a family. How important it is for us to have at hand Chinese sources in which we can find how it appeared in earlier times in the regions through which we are passing ! Instead of Gashun-nor and Sokho-nor the earlier Han annals mention only *one* lake, the Kuien-hai. They also know a district Kuien-chêng, whilst the name of the town Kuien-hsien does not appear until during the third and fourth centuries after Christ. We allowed that to persuade us—for even without having seen the lakes it sounds probable—that they, just as the case is with Lop-nor too, were connected in the earlier Han period, and formed a single larger lake, and that the bipartition, the same as there, is probably caused by the advancing desiccation and does not take place till a later period.

In the fourth century before Christ there were in China seven kingdoms. The three northernmost of them, Yen, Chao, and Chin, bordered on Mongolia. Our archæologist Huang has been occupied for some time with investigating and following up the ruins of a very old wall that lies

50 *li* to the south of Beli-miao and runs towards the west south of our headquarters.   On our way towards Shande-miao and to Gashun-nor we shall cross it.   Huang has in a letter to Professor Hsü given expression to the conjecture, that this wall is the great wall that the three above-named kingdoms set up, each for itself and independent of the others, as a protection against the Mongols.   I do not yet know what clues Huang has found in his books, and in actuality, for his opinion, but Professor Hsü has the impression that it may involve an important historical discovery.

I have in passing touched upon these episodes in order to give an idea what an advantage and what a significance the co-operation with Chinese scholars can have for an expedition on Chinese soil.   If I had travelled alone or only with Europeans, I should have had, at best, to turn to European sinologists after my return home, in order to get information concerning the historical events that were enacted on Gashun-nor 2,100 years ago.   Now I have, not only the sources, but also the scholars who can interpret them for me, here with me on the spot, and I can immediately learn what I want to know.

One will now perhaps understand me when I say that the Chinese staff is an invaluable accretion of worth to my expedition.

It is now two weeks since the northern column under Dr. Norin's leadership departed.   Up to now communication between us has not been broken off, and the mounted Mongolian couriers have not only carried our letters to and fro, but have also taken to Norin the things that his section needed.   In a letter of the 3rd of July he writes :

" The sacred mountain of Bayin Bogdo (' Rich God ') merits its name ; the whole of the south side is pure ore, iron and manganese.   The ore-bearing horizon stretches right up to the monastery of Tsagan-obo-sumo and I have cartographically surveyed it.   Bergman was the first to find it."

Under the date of the 5th of July Bergman reports :

" I have to report to you the gratifying information, that Chin has discovered quite close to our earlier camp a magnificent stone-age settlement. It proved to be my richest site up to the present; not less than 1,450 objects have we collected during the two days and a half that we stayed there. The material consists for the most part of very beautifully worked scrapers and stones, of which some have an axe-like appearance. Nor is pottery lacking, but it shows no ornamentation, and therefore gives no precise clue for a determination of the period. If potsherds had not been found there, one might, to judge from a part of the artefacts, very probably think of the older stone age. It is possible that the place already began to be inhabited in the palæolithic age and was afterwards inhabited further on in the stone age. On that, however, I should not like to express myself with certainty, before I have had opportunity to study the whole of the stone-age material from Mongolia that has been discovered before. I drew a map of the district to the scale of 1 to 2,000. I am as pleased with it as I am with the site. As you will understand, I am greatly delighted with Chin's discovery, and, to encourage him, have promised him 25 Mexican dollars. . . ."

On the 8th of July Norin writes from Tsagan-obo-sumo :

"Our work has up to the present turned out satisfactory. I have two new sheets ready, just as extensive as the earlier ones, and Heyder has a splendid network of triangles that extends another 60 *li* further towards the west. Since it now looks as if you will still remain for a while on Hutyertu-gol, we are not in such a hurry. Bergman is still discovering new sites and is exceedingly satisfied."

One will understand what a joy it occasions me to receive such reports, and to hear that the various tasks are progressing well. The Chinese too always keep me well posted up and show me their finds. Thus Professor Yüan writes on the 11th of July :

"DEAR DR. HEDIN,—
I am at a distance of only 18 kilometres from the main camp. Pai [one of the three collectors] has found stone implements and fossilized bones in the neighbourhood. That was the reason why we have gone so far to the north, 3 kilometres to the north of the main road. I am doing my best with the topography. To-morrow we are moving towards the south,

on the top of the ridge of hill that with the field-glass you can probably see from your camp. Further to the west there is another region of streams, across which I shall march quickly, in order to reach the mountain to the west of it. . . ."

Huang can only write Chinese and sends in his reports to Professor Hsü, who never forgets to inform me of their contents. In the same way I tell Hsü of the reports that I receive. The news of the iron-ore pleased him especially —we have already dreamed of a railway from Paotow to Bayin Bogdo, and have reckoned up millions in profits for China.

After new dry-batteries had arrived from Peking, our wireless receiving-station acquired new life. Its masts had up to now stood there rather aimlessly, staring towards the stars. Now on the very first evening I received the report : " We can now hear Nauen quite well." I hurried to Haude's tent and found him and von Kaull lying on the carpet with the phones on their ears. They had just heard the midday time-signal from Nauen, that is to say 1 o'clock by Central European time, corresponding to 12 o'clock Greenwich time. With us it was about 8 o'clock in the evening. I was given one of the sets of phones and heard the ticking very distinctly. It made a powerful impression upon us to hear this message from Berlin. Had our batteries been strong enough, we could have picked up the news from all over the world and could have spoken daily with our relatives. I had originally thought of taking with me a complete wireless installation, but that came up against difficulties and would have been an amusement all too expensive. The only thing that we have wanted is the longitudes, and them we get through the Nauen time-signals.

The eleven Germans of my expedition prove altogether splendid. With such men one can achieve what one will. During the critical period of waiting in Peking, there were those who wanted to urge me to send some of the Germans home again, and it seemed as if that would become necessary. But I held out, and threw no-one overboard. Only Major von Dewall journeyed home,

[face p. 76

At last we have got together the required number of camels

IN THE NEIGHBOURHOOD OF HUTYERTU-GOL.

Larson, the " Wolf-killer "

Marschall, Li, and Zimmermann, remain behind at the observatory

DEPARTURE FROM HUTYERTU-GOL

[face p. 77

but of his own accord and for private reasons; he was missed, and his loss was lamented, by all of us.

Without Germany and China this great expedition would never have come about. In Germany I found understanding, interest, and sympathy for my plan, and in Germany I found generous patrons. On the other hand, if I had refused to work together with Chinese, the whole undertaking would have been set aside, and I should have had to give it up and could have set out on the journey home.

In the afternoon of the 16th of July the archæologist Huang returned with his small caravan of ten horses, and a few minutes later, in the company of Professor Hsü, came into my tent to make his report. He had ridden approximately 40 *li* to the south right up to the great wall, and had followed it up in both directions for a stretch of 20 *li*. From the statements in the old books that he carried with him, and the investigations that he carried out on the spot, he drew certain conclusions, for the probability of which he alone is responsible. According to his view there are three distinct sections of wall, which were built in the fourth century before Christ, and connected up into a continuous wall in the third century by the Chin dynasty. Of this there is now only very little still in existence. It makes itself known as a rounded-off earth embankment that only rises up a few feet above the surface of the ground. Here and there Huang found pieces of burnt bricks, but for the rest the wall appears to have consisted of a framework of wood with a filling of straw and clay. It was extraordinarily thick, and on its outer, that is to say its north side, was accompanied by a ditch. At a distance of one *li* from the village Huang has discovered a town of the earlier Han period. Of houses and streets there was nothing more to be seen, but the city wall could be made out clearly and it was easy to establish where the west gate had been situated. The peasants in Cha-sha-miao know quite well of the existence of this town and call it Chung-ku-liao. Here Huang found a number of baked bricks with zigzag ornamentation, specimens of which he brought away with him. The

77

old town lay at the northern foot of the Yin-shan, the
" Female Mountain " ; Yang-shan, the " Male Mountain,"
is a range of hills further to the north. Huang was so
pleased with his finds, that he is already planning a complete expedition in this region, when our peaceful campaign has come to an end.

In truth, this 16th of July was not a bad day. We had
at last got together the requisite number of camels, Huang
had made most promising discoveries, and shortly before
sunset, just as Larson and I were inspecting the camels,
Hummel came galloping along Marco-Polo Street on
his grey horse, rode up to me, and reported as follows :

" The expedition to Beli-miao has successfully concluded its task and is on its way home. We have taken
1,100 metres of film of the temple festivals, have made
half a dozen anthropometric measurements and blood-
tests, and have bought seven first-rate camels."

" Excellent ! When are the others coming ? "

" At midnight."

" Have you got wet ? "

" Yes, soaked to the skin ; at isolated places in valleys
and hollows the animals waded right up to their knees in
water."

" Are you hungry ? "

" As hungry as a wolf."

The signal was given to the cooks, and our family
doctor and staff surgeon had a square meal set before
him, but he was so eager to tell of all the wonderful things
that he had seen, that the food got cold and I was obliged
to keep on reminding him, with the words : " Eat up,
lad."

At midnight in the streaming light of the moon Lieberenz and Haslund arrived with the camels, and in the
main street two new tents were set up. All three were as
happy as sand-boys. Lieberenz was quite enthusiastic
over his films, which surpassed all his expectations.

Then, the next morning, Hummel and Haslund made
me their detailed report. Their story was so interesting
that I will not omit it here. It was as follows :

On the sixteenth day of the seventh month of the current

" year of the hare," *tola-yil*, the festival of Maidar, or
Maitreya, is celebrated. It lasts three days and fell this
year on the 13th to the 15th of July. The abbot of the
monastery goes by the name of Chiren Lama. The
monks highest in rank after him bore the titles Da Lama
and Dung Khörö. In the monastery there is also a " god "
—a *gigen*, incarnation, corresponding to the *rinpoche* of the
Tibetans. His name is Jolros Lama. He received our
party with the greatest hospitality, and they lived in his
house, where the young prince Dumuro Namchil was
also a guest. The chieftain of the district, Dakhan Beli
Wang, had of course also arrived for the festival. During
the last military expeditions in this region Beli-miao had
been laid waste and burnt down by the Chinese, and had
now in the course of a decade been rebuilt. The new house
of the *gigen* had been erected in the Chinese style, and
the timber was sacred wood from Bogdo Kuren, that is to
say Urga.

The hall of the library with the heavy sacred books on
firm shelves ; colonnades ; court-yards and balconies—
all was as in Tibet. When Hummel described the monastery I could see it before my eyes : there were the same
pictures that I had beheld in Tashi-lunpo and countless
other monasteries in the holy land of Lamaism.

In the way of the door opening on the court-yard for the
festive performances the orchestra, with its huge trumpets,
drums, and cymbals, had taken up its position. Along
the walls and on the balconies sat the people of rank and
opposite them, on cushions, the women. Two yellow
lamas with masks and skirts, which hung like fringes, enter
the arena and perform figures and dances. An amusing
clownish figure is known as Tsagan Obogen, " the white
old man," who is considered as the father of the yellow
masks. A scripture is unrolled, and one reads aloud
from the teachings of Maidar, the coming Buddha, the
Messiah. From the left appears a crowd of high lamas
with yellow hats. They establish themselves in the court-
yard and bring offerings. Thereupon they arrange themselves into a procession, with music at the head. The
grand lama walks along under a canopy, and behind him

79

soldiers carry an image of Maidar, who sits in a kiosk-like sedan-chair, and images of his disciples. They are followed by numerous masks. The procession leaves the monastery, encamps in the open on the plain, takes tea and refreshments, and then makes a circular tour round the sanctuary. On each side, corresponding to the four quarters of the heavens, they make a short halt. Having returned to the monastery, they say prayers in the presence of countless pilgrims and of all the distinguished guests.

On the 14th of July the festival reached its culminating point. At 10 o'clock in the morning the deep-sounding blasts of sea-conchs and trumpets resounded from the roofs of the temple, and were joined by the ringing of bells. In the court-yard for the festive performances the faithful again assembled in their places, according to rank and dignity, and now the exorcism dance began. The lamas marched in, two by two, as masks, representing skeletons, stags, wild animals, and other things—exactly as in Tibet. They danced and presented their ceremonies, and the music accompanied the play. There was also dancing on a balcony. Lieberenz was so pushed and jostled by the inquisitive crowd, that he made his escape on a low column, from which place he could keep his cinema-camera busy. An important item of the ceremonies consisted in lamas carrying a large triangular piece of paper, which was held over the heads of the crowd and had the property of drawing to itself all evil and all sin. Then all went out on the plain and established themselves in a semicircle. A fire was lighted, and the paper was thrown in, and consumed, with everything that was dark and all that was evil, by the flames. Another special item on the programme was the appearance of two men possessed of demons. Evil spirits are driven into them by two lamas, and they then become as if actually possessed. Their faces swell up and become red, their eyes protrude almost out of their sockets, foam stands on their mouths, they are in a state of hysterical derangement or uncontrollable ecstasy. They are positively dangerous. Our party had been warned not to come too near them, for both were armed with spears and swords, which they brandished blindly about and thrust in all directions. They also shot with bows, and, indeed, not only in the air, but also horizontally, and could hit and wound anyone who had the misfortune to sit in the line of fire. On one occasion they threw with stones at Lieberenz, when he was standing taking his film on a roof.

The 15th of July was celebrated with new dances, plays, humorous sketches, and the appearance of magicians in high hats. The sacred books were spread out, and the crowd worshipped them and covered them with *haddiks*, those long thin bands or little narrow pieces of silk that form holy gifts and offerings and congratulatory objects. One even carried little children here and bent them down over the sacred books.

By noon the festival was already over; the crowds of pilgrims scattered and went their way. As Hummel tells us, they all wore their best clothes, the women silver ornaments, head-bands, ear-rings, and necklaces, bracelets, and rings. The yellow, red, green, and blue colours were faded and softened down, and were beautifully worked. The whole was an unforgettable and magnificent scene.

It was fortunate for our party that they were guests of the " god " and lived in his house. For that reason no-one ventured to touch them. Immediately on their arrival in Beli-miao they paid their visit to the chieftain Dakhan Beli Wang. He was friendly and in a mood for joking, and at the same time received other visitors too, who brought him presents, apricots, sweetmeats, confectionery, and *haddiks*.

On the first day of the festival, receptions had also taken place at the house of Jolros Lama, who sat on his throne in the throne-room and blessed innumerable pilgrims. All presented him with gifts. The *gigen* gave them his blessing by means of a yellow book with which he touched their heads. The seven-year-old Khambo Lama (in Tibetan, Kanpo Lama), who appeared before the " god " with the others, Jolros Lama lifted up and set down beside him on the throne, that he might fondle him and talk to him—a charming, unforgettable picture, since both were unusually noble and aristocratic types.

Hummel, Lieberenz, and Haslund were received with the greatest friendliness, and special orders were issued for their safety. Even if the honour of being sprinkled with the consecrated water out of the sacred vessels in which one dips peacock's feathers did not fall to their lot, they were yet given all the care and attention that one can expect from a courteous host. They made to the temple a present of 50 dollars and to the holy monks a series of small trifles such as alarum-clocks, knives, and other things. When they took their leave of the *gigen*, he asked them for prints of the photographs that they had taken in the monastery, and promised them that he would give us a letter of recommendation that would be valid and of use to us further to the west. We are therefore going to send off a special messenger to him, who will take him the desired pictures and other presents and at the same time fetch the passport promised by the " god."

I have spoken of our camels and have quoted Larson's remark that he had never yet seen together such a splendid stock of first-rate animals. Yesterday he caused general amusement at supper, when he recounted that I had found during the inspection of the camels that if one looks at a standing camel from behind, its body forms an oval that stands vertical; but, he said, with many of our animals the oval lay horizontal. They are so fat. Their bellies are plump and distended like balloons. They are only much too well nourished and filled out. I have never, indeed, heard that pack-camels that in a few days are to start out on a desert journey of more than 2,000 kilometres have to *fast* for three days. But with our animals this is now necessary. Yesterday, to-day, and to-morrow, about a hundred of our fattest camels are lying tied up in the camp, in order to undergo a very necessary thinning cure.

Larson has confided to me that he has passed a sleepless night, and, what is worse, that the Mongols cannot sleep peacefully—from open concern and anxiety how it will be with the camels. If camels, as at present ours, had no other occupation for seven whole weeks than to eat at pasture and put on fat, they become high-spirited and rebellious and have a liking for neck-breaking tricks. As their flanks are so round, pack-saddles and loads will not, with the swaying movement, remain on as they should and preserve a balance. It needs only a load to roll off, nay, the wind need only blow a rider's sun-helmet from his head, and the nearest camels become completely crazy and unmanageable and run at full career into the steppe. That sets them off, and all the others follow. No box, no flour-bag, remains there on the pack-saddle; *everything* is thrown off, the boxes are smashed, and their contents are scattered on the ground. And, what is the worst thing of all, having become quite free of their loads, the camels continue their wild flight for hours before they calm down. After such a mutiny of destruction one may need several days to gather everything up, mend the boxes, and pack afresh.

We do not forget, of course, any of the precautionary measures that must be taken. One of these is to make the strongest animals go rather hungry. Another, to let the great caravan march in several sections at a distance of about 100 metres, in order to localize the catastrophe and prevent infection. A third, which is now just being put to the test in the country surrounding the camp, is to pick out the fastest among our camels, which are then ridden, on the march, by young, alert Mongols, who overtake the runaways and compel them to halt. In any case the departure becomes really exciting. Since I have neither time nor inclination to expose myself to the risk of a broken arm or leg, I have given Larson instructions to select for me a camel that is calm and cool-headed. The choice has fallen upon an eighteen-year-old female camel, a giantess, black, peaceable, and elegant. I can stroke her over the eyes and nose, without her taking the least notice. If one attempts this with other camels, they spit, and before one knows what is happening, one has a glaucous-coloured mess on the clothes or in the face, the appearance of which reminds one of gooseberries and cream. But my old camel has good manners and knows how to behave herself. The Mongol that sold her to us along with several others declared at first that he would not part company with her; for she had carried his son to Chi-nan-fu and back, without blinking when she passed through the noisy street of the blacksmiths in this city. But when Larson told him that I should ride the animal to Hami and Urumchi, the owner changed his mind:

"If the great chief himself wants to ride her, I will hand her over willingly."

When from my "writing-table" I in these days let my glance stray over our wandering town, I am quite melancholy. Everywhere there is packing; boxes are being dragged hither and thither; envelopes and scraps of paper are flying about—everything points to the departure.

Very painful to me is the parting with the little antelope. It runs about here in complete freedom, and from time to time comes to my tent to visit me. It pries into everything, and even sniffs at Hami, our dog, who returns its obtrusiveness with contempt.

To the chieftain of the district, who has made no claim for any compensation, we make, in thanks for all the juicy grass that our camels have eaten on his territory, a present of 100 dollars and various small articles. Numerous other inhabitants of the district, Mongols as well as Chinese, receive payment and rewards for services that they have rendered us, and Mühlenweg's paymaster's office has plenty to do.

Meanwhile, the 19th of July, our last day on the " Soda River," has dawned. Everywhere travelling mood prevails, all the camels were in the camp by 1 o'clock, and the whole day was spent in placing the pack-saddles on them. On the left cheek they all bear the initial letter of my family name, an H, branded in. Lieberenz wanted to film them to-day in all their growing splendour, but it is raining hard and is dark and rather cold.

We are already in the midst of the heat of summer that I had feared because of its suffocating heat. At 1 o'clock we had to-day 18 degrees, a pleasant temperature in itself, which one finds rather cold, however, when it is windy and is raining. Up to the present no heat has as yet bothered us. We have frozen sooner. When once we are safe and sound with our camels on Gashun-nor, then the worst is over. We reckon two months to reach the lake, for we are making short daily marches, on account of cartographical work.

Dr. Haude is exceedingly anxious that throughout the whole of July meteorological observations shall be carried out here on Hutyertu-gol, and he has urgently begged me to make this possible. That can be done without too great a difficulty either. Whilst we others are setting out with the great caravan to-morrow, Zimmermann, von Marschall, Liu, and a Mongol, are remaining on here until the 31st of July. The "observatory," too, is still to remain standing, and the observations are being continued as heretofore. Haude thereby gets two whole months and their meteorological mean values for comparison with the series of observations of other Asiatic stations, which advantage he regards as very important.

Those remaining behind will probably feel rather lonely when we have gone from them and Marco-Polo Street has been robbed of the picturesque outlines of the blue tents. But as consolation they are allowed to keep the little antelope.

We thus have a start of twelve days. Zimmermann's small caravan of nine camels will then make long daily marches, in order to overtake us, possibly at the monastery of Shande-miao, or on the way between this and Gashun-nor.

I was still in doubt yesterday whether it is wise and proper to leave such a small section behind on Hutyertu-gol. The chieftain of the district had explained to Larson that as long as the whole caravan had been situated here, there would have been nothing to fear; for no-one would venture to attack a camp inhabited by so many Europeans; but peace and security did not reign in the land here, and for those remaining behind he could assume no responsibility. He would, of course, warn them if he heard anything, and he was prepared, with pleasure, to provide them with a guard of Mongols.

A journey across Asia is at the present day always attended with dangers, and if one intended to try and

avoid them always and at all times, one might just as well
stay at home.   But I do not believe that it is as dangerous
as it sounds.

Human calculations often meet with disappointment.
In agreement with Larson I had fixed the 20th of July as
the day for marching off.

But the sky was covered with thick clouds, it was raw
and windy, and the weather looked very threatening.
Immediately after we had risen from our, as we believed,
last lunch on Hutyertu-gol, it began to rain.   I should
never have thought that a *rain* in these regions could
mean a hindrance on our journey.   Indeed, we had lately
complained of drought.   What would become of the
summer grass if the ground received no moisture ?   We
were longing for rain.   Larson had asked Haude, who
knew his way about with the weather, to see that the
heaven opened its sluice-gates and watered the grass.
Now it began to rain at last.   It rained quite fast.   But
it took its time, before the dry ground had become so
wet that the earth remained sticking to the soles of one's
shoes if one walked about outside.   In the course of the
afternoon the rain became heavier ; it beat and pattered
on the drenched tent-cloths.   The boxes containing the
heavy baggage, provisions and thousands of other things,
were already standing there in pairs and tied round with
ropes, and were only waiting to be loaded on the camels.
It was to be feared that wheaten flour, sugar, and other
easily affected goods, would spoil.   The Mongols had left
their work and had gone into their large tent to drink tea.
They do not like to work in the pouring rain.   But now
Larson came and sent them out.   All the boxes of provisions had to be brought together again and covered with
tent-cloths.

Hour after hour went by.   The ground was now completely soaked.   It splashed and flopped about under one's
feet.   In all hollows stood puddles.   From my veranda
streams of water ran down, which formed little lakes in
front of the tent.   It dripped and trickled and ran everywhere.   No living being could be seen outside.   All sat
in the tent and occupied themselves, one with this thing,

another with that. Larson came to me, after a new inspection, and reported that a departure the next day was not to be thought of, for the pack-saddles and their covers and ropes were quite soaked. If we had already been on the march for some time, that would not have been so dangerous. But now the camels were much too well fed, much too lively, and half wild. If one were to load them now, the ropes would then become loose with the gradual drying. The loads would slip off, and it only needed *one* load to do that, and the other camels would bolt and throw off their loads. Wet covers also rot easily and chafe in consequence of the heat that is developed ; for the flanks of the camels, after they have lost their wool, are now more sensitive than in winter and spring.

I therefore gave the order : we are still remaining in camp on the 20th of July. The members of the staff resumed their occupations, and even the wireless station was set up again. The rest of the day passed with sunshine and wind.

On the evening of the 20th of July it was clear to us that we should not be able to set out before the 22nd of July. The covers for the packs were only dry on the surface, but inside still wet. And, in truth, we needed this additional day too, the 21st of July, to put everything in order again.

The territories that border on our district in the west have the names of Dondur-gun-hushe, Barun-gun-hushe, and Dyun-gun-hushe, " Territory of the Middle, of the Western, and of the Eastern Duke." *Gun*, " duke," is the title that Larson has received from the Mongols in Urga. This region is not exactly held in good repute for hospitality towards strangers. There in the year 1900 were murdered certain Swedish missionaries of the Scandinavian Mongolian Mission—namely, Sjöberg, Seeberg (a Swedish-American), the sisters Hilda and Clara Andersson, and Miss Lund, presumably by order of the Boxers. During last year the Middle Duke seized four Russian motor-cars loaded with ammunition. Fêng Yü-hsiang, who was at that time carrying on war here in the region, sent a detachment of two hundred men to win the cars back, but it is said to have turned out unpleasant for the soldiers.

Now the 21st of July too is drawing to its close. We have just had our afternoon tea. All the camels are in the camp. The whole day was necessary in order to place the pack-saddles on them, but now the work is done. There was work again with the boxes too. All of them had to be tied up afresh after the ropes had dried. The huge quantity of baggage has again been spread out, so that all the boxes stand in pairs at some distance from each other, in order to be ready for loading early in the morning. It looks peculiar. One can scarcely find one's way about. The whole scene gives the impression as if we were on a campaign. I keep on walking along between the lines of camels lying and standing. Real roads and streets run out between their ranks. The characteristic smell of camels, which is not exactly fragrant but which one no longer thinks about when one is always living among camels, fills the air. The whole wide surface where the camels are spending the night, and where the long ropes are stretched out to which the thin nose-cords are fastened, is covered with a thick layer of camel-dung, which for a long time to come will furnish the Mongolian villagers of the region with fuel.

Right in the midst of all this activity comes a courier from Norin and Bergman with the order to deliver letters and to return again forthwith. He brings good and longed-for news of Norin's column, which to the north of the caravan road is making for Gashun-nor.

Norin writes :

" Our work has made good progress, and we are all getting on excellently. Since Söderbom joined us the work has gone considerably easier, since now during the marches I am not obliged to remain with the caravan. But we are eager to hear when you contemplate starting out and what length of daily marches you will make. To-day we are stopping here, to put our maps and diaries in order, but to-morrow we are moving on."

On the same day Bergman writes :

The silken banner, six metres in height, with the image of the god Maidar, in front of the main temple

THE MAIDAR FESTIVAL IN BELI-MIAO

[*face p.* 88

A picturesque cart filled with camel-dung is unloaded

A wall-painting in the house of a high lama

BELI-MIAO

[*face p.* 89

" Since my last letter I have made fourteen new stone-age finds ; most of them not very rich, but still sufficient to establish a settlement. In all, I have twenty-eight sites. I am now beginning to get so exacting that I look for at least one site a day. Later, I am sorry to say, I shall not be able to have such good results, since Norin intends to march every day, and I am only really able to do proper work during rest-days ; but in spite of this I am convinced that even with the new order of the day I shall discover quite a number of beautiful objects. When once we have reached Gashun-nor, then the really big discoveries will come."

Since I have just heard again to-day of the state of unsafety in the western regions, I breathed a sigh of relief when I read news like this of the columns that have separated from us, which, indeed, are rather small and weak. I shall be in some anxiety concerning Zimmermann, von Marschall, and Liu, who are remaining behind, but they laugh about it and take the matter very calmly.

VIII

REVOLT OF THE CAMELS

THE 22nd of July dawned at last. Punctually at 5 o'clock I was awakened by Larson.

The morning had just begun to grow light, but in my tent it was so dark that I had difficulty in finding my way about without a light. Ming brought the large wash-basin full of warm water and arranged my clothes and my things for washing with, and I was ready in less time than usual, for I longed to get out. The great day had arrived. I felt that it would be a day that I and all the others would not forget for the whole of our lives. We were now setting out on the journey with our own splendid camels, no longer with hired ones as from Paotow. The town of our camp was filled with bustle and shouting. Larson gave his orders, and the camels screamed with rage when the heavy boxes were raised on their backs. One could hear eager conversations, questions and answers in all possible languages : Mongolian and Chinese, Swedish and German, Danish and English. It was a departure in great style, as if a small army was setting out on a campaign through a strange land.

I packed the two hand-cases of mine that are always in my tent and contain the things that I require every day : diaries, writing-materials, maps, magnetic compasses, sets of compasses for drawing, two changes of clean under-clothing, a few books of reference, my mother's Bible and hymn-book, and many other things.

At a quarter to six we all sat down at the breakfast table—for the last time on Hutyertu-gol. Larson was calmness and unconcern itself and was pleased to get on the move. Now at last the hour had arrived when he was to assume the supreme command over my first caravan. He was even ready before the others, and hastened outside.

" Is everything in order ? " he asked the Mongol Mären, a magnificent type resembling an American Indian.

" Yes, all the camels are loaded."

" Have you counted them ? "

" Exactly a hundred and fifty are going with us ; ninety-eight are still remaining here."

" Good-bye," Larson called out to us as he went forward to the head of the caravan, in order to conduct the first group on foot. The second was led by Mühlenweg. No other Europeans went with them. Larson had only eleven Mongols with him, much too small a number for so many animals. But we who were remaining behind and were not to march off before another two hours required four Mongols ; two were with Norin's column and two with Yüan's.

Punctually at 6 o'clock Larson disappeared behind the hill that was crowned with the *obo*. He led a string of twenty camels. The other three groups, each of about fifty camels, followed. Now the last went past the hill too, and then up the Hutyertu-gol to the west. In this direction the undulations of country are so flat that at 7.15 with the field-glass I could still see the three sections very distinctly ; indeed, the last could still be made out at half past seven, as a dark line in the bright sea-green. What a relief to know that they are on the way ! Indeed, we had no need to foster any misgiving whatever : Larson was with them. And if, in fact, one or other of the loads was thrown off, it wouldn't matter : its whole pack would consist of provisions, the heavier personal equipment of the staff, and the silver-chests, all of which were things that were not susceptible to injury.

Meanwhile, our tents were taken down, beds and blankets were rolled up, the camels were led to their loads, the kitchen was packed away, and we were waiting patiently to be able to leave. Dr. Haude flew pilot balloon No. 78. It rose as high as 8,000 metres, where it disappeared in a cloud. A strong wind was blowing from the south, the sky was clear, and we were burnt by the blazing heat of the sun. But the drowsy mood was the peace before the storm.

Suddenly the Mongols cried out : " Larson's camels ! " and pointed in the steppe towards the north-west. Now life came into our Mongols ; they threw themselves on their swift riding-camels and dashed at a tearing pace towards the north-east, in order to get in the way of the nine camels that were running away in full career towards the east. One of them still had its load on its back, and two others their pack-saddles ; the others had thrown off everything.

It was not difficult to understand what had happened. The nine camels had become frightened, had broken loose, and had run away in wild flight. Further away in the background on the hills Dr. Hummel descried in addition fifteen other camels, which stood out against the horizon and were running towards the north as if mad. So the misadventure was not confined only to a few; we had indeed already seen a seventh of the caravan.

One of Larson's Mongols came galloping up at full tilt and rode into the camp without dismounting.

"What has happened ? " I asked. He only made circular movements with his arms, shook his head, and shouted :

"Everything is topsy-turvy "; and then rode away again at a gallop.

It was twenty minutes past eight. We waited for a messenger from Larson. Dr. Hummel, Dettmann, and I, went on the *obo* hill and directed our glasses towards the west. At a distance of 2 kilometres about fifty camels were pasturing, but they belonged to a Chinese merchant. Far away in the west a series of bright points could be seen, obviously thrown-off loads, as well as darker stripes, probably camels from Larson's column. On the elevation to the left in the south-west a white camel ran with boxes on its back, closely followed by one of our Mongols on a riding-camel. It was overtaken and secured. The Mongol led it towards our camp, which lay nearest. The camel was stubborn and did not want to follow, and Dettmann and Hummel hurried down to help the Mongol to unload the animal and bring it to the camp. From the north-east came the nine that we had caught sight of first of all. I went down and had a look at the runaways. The white camel had on the left side rubbed the skin off its thighs and belly on sharp edges of the boxes and was bleeding. Of course, the boxes are by no means designed for such a speed as that. If the camel walks slowly, then naturally its body does not come into contact with the load. There were also a few of the nine bleeding and badly used.

Walz, who in the meantime had galloped to the scene of the disaster, came back and brought us particulars.

"It looks terrible," he said. "Everything is lying thrown about on the ground, jumbled up in confusion, and over a hundred camels are missing."

"And what does Larson say?"

"He asks for two buckets of water, and thinks that the caravan must be reorganized in the new camp."

At 1 o'clock, at lunch, I gave the order that *all* who were not tied by special work were to go out into the open country and help the Mongols to look for camels and thrown-off loads.

"What does this occurrence mean to us?" someone asked.

"The loss of an interval of two weeks, the loss of a number of camels, and, possibly, that Mühlenweg's silver-chests are on the way to Outer Mongolia, where they and the animals carrying them will be stolen."

Immediately after Walz's return I had sent von Marschall and Hempel to Larson. Marschall soon returned and reported that the new camping-place looked like a battle-field—awful. Larson was there with two Mongols.

Whilst I had been on the top of the hill, my tent had been set up again. That was, of course, well meant, but it was unnecessary, for, immediately after lunch, I set out, accompanied by Hummel, on my journey to the new camp. I took with me only a sheaf of maps, a compass, a pencil, a note-book, and cigarettes. Before we went we said good-bye to the little antelope. Just as we were examining the badly wounded white camel, the antelope, as delicate and fragile as a porcelain figure, came near the great animal. The camel, which was still snorting nervously and excitedly with expanded nostrils, was frightened by the antelope and kicked out with one of its hind-legs. With the enormous force that there is in such a kick the antelope would have flown like a tiny ball right up to the tents. But the kick missed its mark and just went above the careless little creature's head, and we drove it as quickly as possible out of the place of danger.

Walz's riding-camel was standing by the others, tied to a sack of rice, but not with the nose-cord but with the halter. For some reason or other it took fright and ran bucking most wildly into the midst of the other camels. The sack of rice flew hither and thither like a feather pillow. Then it ran about among the last tents and wrought havoc there. Finally, it threw itself again among the tied-up camels and made them unruly. Luckily it was at last captured and securely bound.

Now we turned our steps towards the scene of the disaster. Even on this occasion I sketched in the route of the march on the map.

Not far from the crossing-place we reached the herd of camels belonging to the Chinese merchant. I was busy with my chart and was not thinking of the herd, but it struck Hummel that a few of the animals were carrying pack-saddles. We therefore halted and looked into the matter. The Chinese herdsman assisted us and indicated to us six camels that did not belong to his master. They all bore the branded H on the left cheek. We tied them together. Hummel led them and we were pleased in anticipation that we were not coming to Larson with empty hands. We also brought with us something else for him, two wooden buckets full of cold water from the spring near Camp VIII.

The steppe was desolate, but along the stream the grass gleamed fresh and green. We approached the fateful place. The distance was only 4·17 kilometres, and for that we needed fifty-nine minutes with the usual rate of marching. It was thus a very short day's march, but eventful and disastrous.

Long before we had reached the scene of the disaster we found the steppe strewn with saddle-covers, which lay about, isolated, twisted one in another, or entangled in ropes. Each pack-saddle consists of six covers, which are placed together before, between, and behind the humps, and tightly compressed longitudinally by two poles, whose ends are tied together with strings. At a longer or shorter distance from our road lay boxes and sacks, trunks, table-tops, tent-poles, and chairs, in a terrible state of confusion. The place where the panic had broken out, however, the new camping-place, formed the culminating point. One thought instinctively of war. The same aspect had been presented by commissariat columns in France or Galicia that had run into heavy artillery fire on the military roads and been annihilated. With us only the mutilated horses were lacking; in place of them we had wounded camels. About fifty were already standing together again, with their nose-cords tied to boxes that were lying about. I was astonished that comparatively few of the boxes had split open; a few bore blood-stains. Larson came to meet us, calm as ever, but depressed. He stammered something about the destruction of Jerusalem, about Poltava, and Waterloo, and finally expressed his feelings with a simple:

" I am terribly thirsty."

" Wait a minute; here comes Charlie."

The camel had to lie down, the buckets were placed on the ground, and Larson was given a good cup of cold water. I don't know how much he drank, for all three of us drank. Water is a splendid drink, especially when one is thirsty, and in these dry regions in summer one is always thirsty.

Then Larson began to tell his story. He had noticed from the first instant that the camels were seething with unrest. They were nervous, stared towards the horizon, and made quick movements with their heads. But they set out. The caravan moved slowly forward. They frequently halted, to see whether the loads were balanced. The three sections kept a certain distance apart, until they were at a distance of 3 kilometres from Camp VIII. Now Larson divided them into five groups, which marched much too near each other и d in parallel formation rather than in single file. They crossed the dry bed of the stream and then moved slightly towards the west on the plain along its right bank. Here Larson saw that it would be an impossible task to keep the camels quiet any longer, and he decided to rest and encamp.

But he was now with the whole caravan in a hollow, through which the stream flows, and thought of the danger of flooding in the event of a heavy rain falling. He had only to lead the caravan 200 metres further, to reach an easy, secure slope. Had he remained in the hollow, then no accident would have happened. But now his misfortune was such, that just in this short stretch, a camel, the last of one of the strings, broke loose and ran by the side of its companions towards the front.

It soon began to increase its pace. Its boxes were jolted up and down, and their contents rattled. The animal took fright and bolted. The camels in the adjoining strings fell foul of each other and became frightened too and ran away in full gallop, at the same time dragging all the others with them. There arose a terrible confusion. If they had run in an unbroken troop towards the west, the mounted Mongols would then have been able to overtake and stop them. But they first ran round in a circle a few times. Most of them frisked and jumped in order to get rid of their loads, which fell down to left and right and flew about like match-boxes. There was rumbling and crashing as when a house collapses ; a deafening noise filled the air. It was dangerous to be in the middle of this whirling tumult.

Larson was on foot. He held his string with his left hand, and in his right the nose-cord of the wild camel that was carrying my large Stockholm trunks. The animals tugged at the rope, reared up, and threatened to tread him underfoot. But in his right hand he had also his Mongolian camel-whip with a handle like a knotty stick. With this he struck the enraged animals, without mercy and with all his strength, on the middle of the sensitive nose, where the plug is pierced through the cartilage. They became stupefied with the pain and calmed down. He held his own string in check and also the camel that was carrying my boxes. Quiet, I grant, they were not, but they stayed, and if they assumed an appearance of bolting they got one on the nose again. Larson's string numbered about twenty camels. He hoped to be able to hold all of them, but then a fleeing string of camels came rushing on from the side and broke Larson's string right in two, so that he had only seven left. The others ran away in wild gallop.

Mühlenweg fought bravely, and Larson admired his strength and presence of mind. His only fault was that he wanted to save too many. He held two strings in the one hand, but when he attempted, with the other, to secure and stop the third string as it rushed by, the first two broke loose with bleeding noses and ran in different directions as if possessed, when they threw down their boxes or dragged them along the ground behind them by the ropes, until they became loose and remained lying on the ground whilst the animals rushed on. But Mühlenweg was not beaten yet. He was riding a fleet-footed racer and, swift as an arrow, hurried after the fugitives, overtook some, hit them on the nose, seized them by the rope, and led them to the place of the accident, where he fastened their nose-cords to heavy boxes. Thereupon, he rushed after the next fugitive, and each time brought back a new prisoner. But the field was soon empty, and his raids became more and more prolonged. Larson says that Mühlenweg on this day performed marvels. He saved a large part of the caravan, yet if one wanted to learn anything about it from the man himself, he only smiled and asserted that he hadn't been able to do much.

The Mongol Mären also proved splendid. He mastered six camels. Only thirteen of the hundred and fifty animals could be held back. All the others disappeared like chaff before the wind. Larson recounted that he had seen how a great camel, with the two boxes on its back that weighed their 220 kilos, jumped over the stream like an antelope. He had once been in Mongolia with a caravan of a hundred camels loaded with skins and wool, and these camels had started a similar rebellion. He had also countless times witnessed smaller mishaps, but a revolt similar to that of the 22nd of July, when *all* the camels went completely mad, he could never have imagined.

H

The Mongols had marked out the camel that had started the wild dance. It was to be humbled; with heavy loads they would drive the devil out of it. It was to learn to behave itself. The Mongols asserted, moreover, that the catastrophe had its origin, not at all in the fact that the camels were too fat and too well fed and had rested too much, or that they had become frightened, but it was a perfectly natural consequence of their own neglect, in not sacrificing to the spirits of the locality on the sacred *obo* that was raised near our earlier camp. I begged them to offer by all means as much as ever they could, in order that we might be exempted from sacrifices, which I should have to pay in the form of runaway camels and lost boxes.

It was 4 o'clock before Larson had finished his account. He affirmed that he simply could not describe what he had witnessed on this steppe a few hours before, which now was like a battle-field.

Haude, von Kaull, and Lieberenz, by degrees also joined us. They had found boxes and covers a long way off, and specified to Larson in which direction he should send out the Mongols. Lieberenz was in despair that he had not set out with Larson. Larson told him categorically that such a spectacle on the film would have been unique in the whole world and worth fifty times more than what it would have cost. But, he added considerately and consolingly, Lieberenz would find on the way to Gashunnor, not one opportunity, but ten or twenty more. And I tried to console him with telling him that if he had been present at the affray, he would certainly have been ground to pieces and his cinema-camera all smashed up.

The three principals wandered back to Camp VIII, and Hummel accompanied them. Larson and I remained alone with a few Mongols, and while my splendid caravan leader gave orders or received reports, I stretched myself out on a camel-cover and fell asleep.

When after an hour I awoke, in Camp IX all was quiet. Larson was standing with his penetrating field-glass, on the hill to the west of the camp, and besides him there was only to be seen one Mongol with a straw hat, who was receiving the pieces of wreckage that now and then arrived. I asked Larson if any important things were missing.

" Yes, two silver-chests containing 4,000 dollars. We are making a special search for them, but so far without success. Mühlenweg has just left to look for them."

" Does he know roughly in which direction the camel that was carrying them made off ? "

" No, of that he has no idea. The whole thing was one turmoil ; it was impossible to keep one's eyes on a particular camel."

" What shall we do if the money has gone ? If robbers or thieves find the boxes, we shall never again see a sign of them. Four thousand dollars is too big a loss for our funds."

" Oh, we shall get all right as far as Hami with what we still have. But we shan't rest till we have found the lost money again. One box that we have here was split right open, but luckily the silver hadn't rolled out."

" Well, let it turn out now as it will, I am not sending a messenger out a second time to fetch money from Peking. We must just be sparing, until we are in Hami. Then thirty of our camels will go without loads. These we will sell to dealers, and then we shall get to Urumchi all right."

At a distance of scarcely fifteen paces from the place where I sat and entered my observations, eight captured camels were standing with their nose-cords tied fast to boxes. The animals were nervous, restless, and excited. Usually so quiet and almost motionless, they were still quite unruly from their wild flight and did not stand still for a second. They kept circling round the boxes, pulled at the ropes, and would with the greatest joy have galloped along after their comrades that had disappeared. They snorted and spit through their wide-open nostrils ; their eyes, usually so soft and dreamy, burnt like red-hot coals and were bloodshot. All at once my hard white sun-helmet flew from my head and rolled noisily right among them. Then they became quite crazy, stood up on their hind-legs, threw their necks about, and jumped round and over the boxes. The hat was in jeopardy, but came safely through this purgatory, and continued to roll on the other side until it was stopped by a box. I went up to the camels and spoke friendly and soothing words to them, and the dance round the boxes gradually stopped.

About 7 o'clock a Mongol approached with fifteen camels. Some had loads on their backs. We made them lie down, freed them of their loads, and one after the other tied them fast to boxes.

" Hurray ! " shouted Larson. " Here are the missing money-chests."

" Splendid ! Then we are saved, and need not sell any camels before we reach Hami. It is immaterial now what else is lost ; we shall now leave for the west as soon as possible."

Half an hour later two mounted Mongols again appeared on the hill ; they were leading a string of twenty camels, all with loads that had been picked up here and there in the surrounding country.

" Here is my and Haude's baggage," shouted Larson.

" How many camels have we now ? "

" With those that have been taken into Camp VIII, roughly a hundred. About fifty are still missing."

" We shall probably have to wait here two days while the search continues. But I have no desire to stay here longer. If it comes to the worst, we can stand a loss. The riders must go on foot."

At sunset we received visits from the old camp. Between Camp VIII and Camp IX there was constant coming and going ; sometimes picked-up articles of baggage were brought into the old camp, if the place where they were found lay nearer to this than to the new one. And, of course, we had always to know what was still missing and how many camels had been brought in. Hempel walked about and wrote down the numbers of the boxes that were with us ; he knew exactly what numbers were missing. The next day he compared his lists with von Marschall's books.

Among the visitors was also Huang. I asked him if he had anything missing. Yes, one of the six boxes that contained his precious Chinese library. He took the matter philosophically and was to outward appearance

The orchestra

Two curious masks

THE MAIDAR FESTIVAL IN BELI-MIAO

[face p. 100

The Mongol king Beling Wang among the spectators at the temple-festival

The " living god " Jolros Lama in the praying-seat

BELI-MIAO

[face p. 101

unconcerned, but he went out alone into the steppe and searched until the sun went down.

Finally, Professor Hsü appeared too, with two students. He was astounded when he saw the horrors of the devastation, and was surprised that we were so calm and were able to joke.

In the twilight came Hummel and Ming, two Mongols, and a few pack-camels, and brought our and Larson's tents and sleeping-sacks, as well as a part of the kitchen.

It was quite clear to us that we had still to remain here at least three or four days, for the excited camels needed as long as that to calm down. Many of them had not worked for as long as a whole year, and so it was not to be wondered at that they became mad under our boxes. But worse was that Larson wanted to have more men for the great caravan. He wanted to engage ten Chinese as help for the Mongols. In the evening, therefore, messengers were sent into the villages.

In the evening we were all tired. The Mongols that were not out the whole night searching slept with the tied-up camels, in order to be at hand immediately, if they became troublesome. But the animals kept rather quiet and still; they too were probably tired.

Such a spectacle as we had witnessed in the course of the day is in itself quite interesting. It is a sort of mass psychosis: one camel becomes frightened or feels an irresistible need to stretch its long muscular legs in order to get rid of the heavy boxes. It bolts and throws off its load. The camels that are in its vicinity become infected, and before they have come to think the matter over for themselves or know why, they bolt. All the others become infected, without exception, and within ten or fifteen minutes the whole caravan is split up, all discipline has disappeared, and the animals are scattered like chaff before the wind. Thus, it is just as it is at a public meeting, where a forcible and energetic popular speaker takes everyone present along with him like a herd of sheep or camels. They have no time to think over or consider the reason, but still they follow him: for he has initiative and speaks with convincing force. *What* he has said is quite unimportant. If the

camels understood that they themselves suffer injury if
they bolt and chafe their flanks and thighs sore on sharp-
edged boxes, they would then perhaps leave the instigator
to run alone. But they don't think : they just let themselves be dragged away with it.

In it there also lies something of defiance, rebellion, and
revolution. If camels could really think, one could believe
that they rebelled against the yoke of bondage that has
been placed on their backs. They decide to follow the
leader that shows them how the yoke is thrown off. They
throw our precious boxes on the ground—that is battle
against the oppressor. To the men they scream : " If you
wish to have your goods on Gashun-nor, then drag them
there yourselves. We have no longer any inclination to
be your slaves. The sole return that you have given us
for our trouble is that you leave us for half-days to pasture
on the steppe. But this privilege we can procure by ourselves after we have got away from you and your cruel
whips. Well then, long live freedom, and to hell with
the baggage ! "

And with that an electric spark goes through the whole
herd. They have muscles as if made of steel, they fly away
over the steppe, and throw off the cases as if they were
empty cardboard boxes. But these boxes are made of
wood and in fact weigh more than 100 kilos each. Some
are so securely tied on that they keep on during the wild
chase. But perhaps the load slides to one side. Then the
box in question hangs below the covers of the pack-saddle,
and the camel's thighs rub and chafe on the sharp edges
with every step. But the animal knows nothing of that ;
of its wounds bleeding it notices nothing ; it is, indeed,
out of its mind, quite stupid—it is, indeed, participating
in bringing about revolution, and what does it matter then,
that it is bleeding from a few places where the skin has
been rubbed off ?

The 23rd of July went by with the search for the runaways. This morning, the 24th of July, several small
caravans again reached us from our earlier fixed quarters,
among others eighteen camels with Haude's hydrogen-
cylinders. I was eager to know how it would go with

these long torpedoes that for camels have so unaccustomed a form and, moreover, are heavier than loads usually are. I therefore went up on the hill above the camp and observed the caravan with the field-glass. It approached quite slowly and quietly, reached the camp, and deposited its dangerous loads on a meadow at a proper distance from the tents. Only the tent used in filling the balloons was erected in its immediate neighbourhood.

The camels cause us anxiety and claim our whole interest, and I suspect it will also remain so in the future. Of the rascal that ran away the day before yesterday after the great catastrophe and dashed towards the west, and of which there was a rumour yesterday that it had been captured and was fastened to a Mongolian tent, we have heard nothing more. The rumour was false: it was not a camel, but only a *canard*. Mongols have reported to-day that the camel has been seen in several places as it ran, first in a western and then in a north-eastern direction. One of our Mongols has taken up the chase.

Of two other runaways one has completely disappeared. The other has been seen in various places and has already been running now for more than forty-eight hours without stopping. Two of our scouts returned this evening and reported that it had run to the north and was now certainly 300 *li* from here on the road to the Republic of Mongolia. No-one had seen it pasture; it only ran on and on. It had become quite mad. This sort of animal I have already made the acquaintance of before. They are hopelessly lost. They do not stop before they fall down dead stricken with heart-failure. There is something impressively mysterious about such animals. They traverse the immense distances of the steppe as if it were nothing. They are like spectral forms, a sort of Flying Dutchman among the ships of the desert—but they go aground. With soft, quick steps they hurry in dark nights past the nomads' towns of tents. Riders and nomads see them glide quickly along over the steppe. All know how it stands with them; no-one tries to catch them; one knows that it is impossible. Such animals are bewitched and are not to be made use of for the service of man. They are lost for ever and must die.

This evening a census was arranged in the city of the camels. Walz, von Kaull, Mühlenweg, Larson, and Haslund, have done the counting, Mären and Gombo likewise. Eleven enumerations gave two hundred and thirty-three camels in our camp. To that are added ten in Camp VIII, two that are on reconnaissance journeys, and forty-one with Norin and Yüan; hence we have altogether two hundred and eighty-six camels. There were thus three missing, one of which we still hope to find. But we can manage quite well without them. As they were quite mad, it was perhaps the best that we got rid of them in good time.

Of the ten Chinese that we have enrolled, in order that they may help us on the way to Shande-miao, four have put in an appearance this evening. They are farmers, but understand too how to deal with camels. Since the bands of robbers make the land unsafe, the peasants regard it as useless to till the soil, and are therefore delighted to get work. I am glad that we can render a service to each other. With ten more drivers we can control the camels. When a month is up, the camels will certainly have become docile.

With the engaging of the Chinese camel-drivers we have, of course, also ten more mouths that will live on our stores. Fortunately Norin bought a large quantity of Chinese flour in Kuei-hua-chêng, and in Shande-miao we can again get more of it. The whole catastrophe of the day before yesterday thus costs us 350 dollars, and it could have been much worse.

It is now half past ten, and it is beginning to rain. Outside it is pitch dark. Now and then one can hear a camel screaming. It just sounded now as if they all screamed at once, and since the Mongols also began to scream and shout, I believed a new revolution had broken out, this time without loads. But then it became still again. The watchers who are outside in the open have no need to freeze. Last night we had 17 degrees as the lowest temperature. To-day's maximum was something over 30 degrees.

The rain is now beating gaily on my tent. To-night I shall certainly dream of the camel that runs on and on, in rain and sunshine, day and night, as if it was being driven by the evil spirits of the steppe or by its own longing for an unknown fairyland in the north.

Since the 25th of July life in the camp has again pursued its accustomed uniform course, as if nothing unusual had happened.

Camp IX lies somewhat higher than Camp VIII. It is probably due to this circumstance that the time-signals from Nauen can be heard with extraordinary clearness, considerably better than before. To erect the wireless station and its masts is quite a simple matter. Haude, von Kaull, Dettmann, and the Chinese students, are ready with it in an hour. In places where we remain longer than a day the wireless station is always set up, and if we make rather long marches at a stretch, we set up our masts even if we only stay for a night. In this way we always know the time and the longitudes.

The northern column under Norin has sent us no news for a few days, but I suppose it is moving slowly and surely towards the west. From the southern column under Yüan I have on the contrary just received a long letter in which, among other things, he reports that he has found a volcano, whose circular slopes he is mapping. The place is called Getsik.

From a letter from Bergman it appears that he and his collector Chin with the northern column have also made rich finds. As the archæologist Huang is accompanying our principal caravan, I hope that this or that find will be made also with us, although we are marching faster than the other two sections. Presumably the neolithic settlements will be found further to the west along the whole road right up to Gashun-nor, but will fall off on the road to Hami, where we cross a belt of absolutely barren desert with dunes, almost 200 kilometres in breadth. If in the more recent stone age the same climatic conditions as now prevailed there, finds of importance are not to be expected. But the interior of the continent is meeting with greater and greater dryness, and it is possible that several thousand years ago the Gobi was not such a desert as in our days. In any case our archæologists will keep their eyes open there too.

However, everything is quiet in the Shipka pass. Dr. Hummel now and then has a few patients, for the most part Mongols. Larson or Haslund acts as interpreter. Larson came just now with one of our camel-drivers, and I heard how he said to Hummel: "This man here has a boil on his abdomen. Don't cut him too deep, for I shall need him to-morrow."

The weather is curious to-day. Yesterday we had a maximum temperature of nearly 33 degrees, and in the night only 11 degrees. To-day at 5 o'clock in the afternoon we had only 16·7 degrees and at 7 o'clock 15 degrees, together with a half gale from the north and heaped-up threatening clouds, which travel along at a height of only 80 metres above the earth. Bayin Bogdo and other small hills are enveloped in clouds. It strikes us quite cold, and we have leather waistcoats on; and the end of July! It is as if the autumn had already begun and we had escaped the suffocating heat of summer. If anyone found it too warm, I used to say: "In a few months you will wish these days back again."

This evening all the camels returned home earlier than usual. On the spirits of unrest that are to move on with Larson to-morrow or the next day were placed the pack-saddles. We treat it as the last time; Larson is marching on ahead and is choosing the camping-place, that is, if he is lucky. The camels are anything but quiet. But with time they will become tame. We have now engaged eight Chinese camel-drivers, and two more are coming to-morrow. The order of marching is as follows: Larson and the Chinese lead the separate sections and the Mongols ride to the left and to the right, two with each section, in order to be immediately at hand and to intervene at the first indication of an insurrection. All the men are armed with short sticks. "We shall fight the camels," declares Larson, "we shall beat them tame yet." The camel is a real antique conveyance that must be lubricated with cudgel-oil so that it shall not go too fast. If they are too fat and plump they bolt; if they are too thin they don't go at all. Then they are led to pasture, to feed up and get fat and then bolt again. The camel is not as sweet-tempered as is believed. At least a hundred and fifty of our animals are quite wild. But, as stated, we shall in time instil behaviour into them.

One may be of the opinion that our advance proceeds much too slowly. But we are in no hurry; we are no Marathon runners, and the slower we march the better opportunity have the archæologists to work, and our other results too become richer. If we march quickly our results become poor and our archæologists have no time to dig and to search. In the one case we gain results, in the other case time. However we do it, we always gain something. But we have not come here to gain time, but to sacrifice time to exploration on the soil of Asia. And therefore every day is a gain. We have set no time limits to our activities, and the whole continent lies open before us.

On the 29th of July Larson woke me with the words: " Doctor, we are soon starting out now." I had asked him to inform me, so that I could view the departure that was in all probability pregnant with the possibility of disaster. The weather was splendid. The thermometer indicated 3 degrees below zero. Veils of mist filled all the hollows between the elevations of country. Earth and grass were wet with the morning dew. Then the sun rose and dispersed the mist. There was not a breath of air.

The camels stood there already loaded—the same camels and the same boxes that a week before had experienced the great catastrophe. Larson had a hundred and fifty-one camels in ten strings, and with them thirteen Mongols, seven Chinese, two servants, and also Mühlenweg and Lieberenz, who was already waiting to film the next revolt among the camels.

The first strings set themselves in march towards the west; the others followed at suitable distances, and at 6.15 the last moved away. Scarcely 1 kilometre from our camp one string became rather crazy and began to run. But the Mongols came dashing behind them swift as an arrow on their fleet-footed camels and forced them to stop, before the others had yet become infected with the unrest. The danger was on this occasion averted, and the mighty procession slowly departed with its yellow boxes.

Reassured I returned to my " writing-table " and wrote letters to my relatives and to a few friends. It was the last post—perhaps for half a year. If on the way to Gashun-nor and towards Hami we met with caravans that were making for Kuei-hua-chêng or Paotow, we could send letters by their leaders. We had left 20 dollars behind with the postmaster of Paotow and 30 dollars with his colleague of Kuei-hua-chêng, with the request to hand over to such a messenger 5 dollars as remuneration and to provide our correspondence with postage stamps. But we might come across no caravans at all. Of that we knew nothing. In any case to-day was the last certain opportunity for sending letters. It grew, too, into a regular parcel of letters that Hummel was to take into our earlier camp, where Zimmermann, von Marschall, Liu, the antelope, and the eagle, were staying as before.

But just as Hummel was giving the order to his riding-camel, von Marschall came on a visit, drank tea with us, reported that in Camp VIII all was well, and took our last letters along with him when he set out on his way back. He went on foot, and for a long time we could still see his magnificent form on the steppe. With that the last bonds were severed that had kept us up to now in communication with civilization. We were now cut off from the rest of the world in all seriousness, and could receive no other information from it than the Nauen time-signals.

In the evening we received a gratifying message from Larson. Two of his Mongols came riding up and handed me a slip of paper, on which was written :

" DEAR HEDIN,—
We are at a distance of 25 kilometres from your camp. The journey has gone excellently. Lieberenz had no work to do. Try to start out early, so that you have the day before you. There has been a lot of rain here, and it is glorious. Many greetings."

Thank God ! All had thus gone well, and we should now no more be held up by unmanageable camels. We were therefore as happy as could be.

IX

COUNCIL OF WAR IN CAMP XIII

THE next morning, on the 30th of July, I was awakened by Ming at 5.15 and quickly got ready. It was so warm that one did not require any particular top clothing, but I put on two leather waistcoats for safety. The sky appeared quite threatening : everywhere heaped-up, dark, low-hanging clouds. It took up a considerable time before everything was in order, and not till shortly before 7 o'clock did the first section march off. The other groups followed at fixed intervals. Finally I myself started out with Mento. As usual I had made myself extremely comfortable on my enormous female camel, which has been christened " the Lady of the Camellias."

The " Lady of the Camellias " on account of her huge size takes longer steps than the other camels that I had ridden before. In the seven trial rides that I made yesterday she needed on an average a hundred and fifty steps for the base line 150 metres in length. Her steps are thus usually 1 metre in length. At the same time she needed on an average two minutes two seconds for the stretch of road of 150 metres. On to-day's march the mean rate of travel of a whole series of time measurements was one minute fifty-five seconds for 150 metres. The rate of marching was very uniform, since we were not interrupted by our own caravans. My riding-camel consequently covered 4,695 metres an hour, and the whole stretch that we traversed to-day amounted to 24·6 kilometres.

Our way led—as mostly in these districts—over extremely flat undulations of the ground. Often one only noticed them from the fact that in the hollows the circle of vision contracted, while on the crests the view broadened out. It would, of course, have reached still further, if the masses of clouds had not hung so low and more distant elevations did not disappear in the mist.

At the very beginning of our march we came through an extremely flat depression with a flat bottom and short new grass. The ground here was crossed by regular fissures, which showed that the water of heavy downpours of rain had streamed here and then dried up.

At 9 o'clock the first drops of rain fell, and soon the most beautiful steady rain poured down on us and took from us the view over the boundless expanses. I hung over me a Mongolian cover or, more correctly, sackcloth that Mento had on his saddle, and so protected from the shower-bath my leather waistcoat, my white summer breeches, gaiters, and laced shoes. But the rain gradually penetrated through everything.

After an hour all the paths shone like winding silver bands, and here and there streams and pools sparkled. The whole ground was soaked, and splashed and squelched under the steps of the camels. Where it consisted of fine yellow clay it was treacherously slippery. Our riding-animals slipped and slithered, and on my elevated seat I was prepared at the next instant to sit below in the mud. In many places the clay was mixed with sand or gravel; there the camels went securely again. We crossed a road with wheel-ruts, in which water was standing.

After we had crossed a newly-formed stream full of dark-yellow rain-water, we came on a real road and travelled in a direction west-south-west. The rain still kept drizzling down. It splashes and patters, and everything is dripping and trickling, and I notice how the water penetrates through my clothes and cools my body. To draw on the usual sheaf of maps is impossible; I enter my notes and my route in a small note-book, which is completely soaked. On the glass disk of my compass there splashes a pattering drum-fire. In the bowl-shaped bird's nest in which I crouch, the water collects from all sides. It seemed to me as if I had already sat wet enough, but not till it began to splash about in my nest did I notice that I was taking a regular hip-bath. The water was lukewarm; I myself had contributed towards warming it. When I then drew up the left leg in order to stretch out the right instead, the waves rose between my legs, just as in a leaky boat. I did not, of course, have a ladle by me. With every step that the " Lady of the Camellias " took, the water splashed forward and back again. That I might perhaps drown was, however, not to be feared ; for from the top rim of my bath a small torrent led down to a fold in the sheepskin that lay on the neck of the camel. And what need had I for a ladle ? I took my handkerchief, dipped it in the broth, held it over the side and wrung it out, and continued this proceeding until the hip-bath was empty. The lower half of my body had not been more saturated, indeed, since my earliest childhood.

In the next depression innumerable pools had formed. In spite of the wet, everywhere large black beetles were to be seen, taking their walks. They seem to love the rain, for they were more numerous than ever. But they indeed wore splendid black rain-coats, their wing-covers, to which the drops of water did not cling. Dr. Hummel observed the love-making of one such tiny couple. He interrupted their happiness when he set a small unmarried male against them. Then the lover attacked his rival, and the battle was so fierce, that one could hear how it cracked in their bones and jaws with the bites. That is found in the best of families, but one would think that the beetles could leave off fighting over their women when it is *raining*.

At half past eleven the rain slackened to such an extent that I could light myself a cigarette and also offer one to Mento. But before we had taken the last draws, the rain became heavier again, and hissed on the cigarettes and put them out. My bath filled afresh. From the crest of an undulation of country I could see Bagha-nor, the " Small Lake," in the south-west as through a glass partition, and in the north-west the monastery of Dagin-sume. In the hollow in which we then descended a herd of horses was pasturing in quite thick, high grass of the most beautiful shade of the green of springtime. On level stretches the whole ground shone with pools of water. It was as if one was riding through a swamp. The camel slipped continually, and one had hard work to keep one's balance.

Mento's camel shied at every skeleton on the road. Here very many " ships of the desert " had run aground.

To the right of the road in several places the yourts and herds of Mongolian nomads were to be seen. Not a few times we started wild ducks. Of other game we saw nothing.

At half past twelve it began to pour in torrents. Then every attempt to shelter was in vain; I really couldn't become wetter than I was already. But my note-book! It wasn't easy later to get the leaves apart, and some notes and lines I could only make out from the marks of the pencil on the other side, which was slightly raised there.

At last Camp X, Chenda-men, rose up before us, with the tents of Larson, Mühlenweg, and Lieberenz. Our stately Swedish caravan-bashi, who looked in his long blue coat like a country inspector of police from the middle of last century, came smiling to meet me, and asked me ironically if I had got wet. "O no, not dangerously. But now watch while the Lady of the Camellias kneels down." I raised my legs, and from my hip-bath a waterfall streamed over the neck of the kneeling camel. Larson laughed himself double and put his hands to his sides. But he and Mento then took my things and carried them into Larson's tent, where I stripped to the skin and put on fresh clothing from head to foot. Then I drank tea and had breakfast, which I enjoyed, while the rain continued to beat on the tents, if now, indeed, less strongly than before.

All the earthly belongings of ourselves and the camels were so dripping wet that we required a day for drying. The 31st of July was, moreover, a Sunday, and the sun shone and warm winds blew. Between the tents ropes were stretched, and all hung their trousers, blouses, shirts, underclothes, and bedding, out to dry.

Larson had already told us on the Saturday, that approximately 1 kilometre from our camp at the foot of the mountains there were several graves, and Huang and Professor Hsü, who were very interested in the matter, had immediately set out thither in the company of Hummel and a few Germans. In the evening, when I had already lain down to read, Hsü came into my tent and asked me

The arrested malefactors with the thrown-off loads

They are subdued with difficulty

REVOLT OF THE CAMELS

[*face p.* 112

Resaddling the camels

REVOLT OF THE CAMELS

[face p. 113

if I had any objection to his proposal that Huang should remain here and excavate one of the graves. No, not at all; I should be delighted if he found anything. Yes, but it might be that he needed several days for it, three at least; might he then stay here so long? Yes, of course. He had only to follow our track, and could probably so arrange it that he joined Zimmermann, Marschall, and Liu, who were, in fact, setting out from Camp VIII on the 1st of August.

On the Sunday, however, Mongols of the neighbourhood appeared in our camp and complained that our Chinese were violating the peace of their graves. I do not know whether the Chinese will on this account allow themselves to be disturbed in their work. There are about a dozen graves. They are distinguished by stones, which form a quadrilateral with sides 2 or 3 metres long, and stones also lie inside this quadrilateral. If these graves are as deep as those that Koslov opened in the neighbourhood of Urga, three days will not go far. In any case we are not permitting ourselves to be delayed on this account.

After supper I visited the cemetery with Hummel. One grave, the largest, was 8 metres long and 5 metres broad; another 6 by 4 metres. In the former one could see clearly that the stones of the outer border, which measured up to 1 metre in diameter, were slabs that had been set up vertically and enclosed like a fence the inner surface of the quadrilateral, where isolated stones lay. Huang, whom we met here, informed us that here he had found five graves and in another place ten. We now betook ourselves there, and saw, among others, a row of vertical stone slabs, twenty-two in number, with long distances, measuring several metres, between them. Was it perhaps the grave of a chieftain? The place lay a quarter of an hour's distance from the camp. The journey back in the evening light was glorious. Hummel caught fifteen new kinds of grasshoppers.

To-day, on the 1st of August, we have put our clocks back an hour.

It was thus 5.15 when Larson, accompanied by Lieberenz, Mühlenweg, and his Mongols and Chinese, set out with the hundred and fifty rebellious camels. The animals appeared quite subdued and quiet, as they slowly moved away towards the west-south-west. It was a glorious day : not a tiny cloud was in the heaven; there was not a breath of air. Dew lay on the grass.

Hempel and Hummel again measured off the base line, 150 metres in length. My camel covered the stretch to-day in a hundred and fifty-four steps and required two minutes and one second for it.

When I set out on the road with Mento at half past six, the other sections, too, were ready for marching off. Haude was just letting up balloon No. 87, which reached a height of almost 9,000 metres above the surface of the earth. Lastly the section with the hydrogen-cylinders set out.

We followed the great caravan road and approached the little range of hills, where we again left the graves to their centuries-old peace. The Chinese had respected the wish of the Mongols yesterday and had left the graves untouched. The Mongols had maintained that Norin's column had taken a stone away from the *obo* on the hill, and that the result had been that one man had been taken ill and three sheep had died. The latter might be true, but stones had not been taken away by Norin.

The land slowly rose towards the ridge of hills, and the ground became more stony. In the chain of hills a door, as it were, opens, and one does not go over a pass. The landscape is without variety, but there is something imposing, impressive, in these endless expanses and these flat undulations of country where a day's march is as a drop in the ocean. One goes on and on, and yet the country remains unaltered, the same monotonous nature.

At 7 o'clock Mühlenweg came back at a gallop. I asked him what was the matter. A whole string of camels, twenty, had revolted; some had thrown off their loads. The camels of the front detachment were generally rather nervous; Larson wanted therefore a few more of our Mongols to help him. Mühlenweg rode back to the camp, while Mento and I continued our journey towards the west.

A quarter of an hour later Haslund with two Mongols

came therefore on screaming camels at a quick trot, in order to hasten to Larson's assistance, and called out to me : "Larson has trouble with the camels." He had given the order to the sections behind us, to force all the animals to lie down and be tied fast, if escaping camels raced up to them, so that they should not run off as well. Two more Mongols, one on a camel and the other on horseback, galloped past. It is just like the scene when the fire-brigade rushes through the streets to put out a fire. What had really happened was not quite clear. Had all the camels bolted again ? Should we again have to halt and search through the whole region, as on the 22nd of July ?

We were now between low ranges of hills. Here and there a few isolated miniature mountains rose up. To the left a shepherd drove a small flock of sheep.

We rode on and on, without catching sight of anything unusual. According to what we had been told, the scene should have been enacted 3 kilometres in front of us. We covered 3 kilometres, but saw nothing. I was in the greatest suspense and was only waiting to meet runaway animals that had thrown off their loads. But everything remained quiet. On a plain between the low hills a herd of thirty-five oxen was pasturing on the young grass.

We now caught sight of Larson's last section. We moved forward far more quickly than it and slowly drew nearer to it. Behind me at a great distance went one of our strings ; its camels were screaming the whole time. At 8 o'clock a Mongol rode past us again at a gallop. It began to get warm, the sun burnt one's back, and I took off my thick leather waistcoat.

Then we met one of the Mongols that had hurried to Larson's assistance ; he went on foot and was leading his camel. We asked him for news, and learned that all was in order now and that Larson had continued his journey. Splendid ! We could then be at ease—no further delays and losses of time and camels.

At half past eight we approached the last string of Larson's caravan. When we were as yet scarcely 10 metres distant from it, we heard wild cries and saw how the string opened out and broke up and the camels ran to right and left. The loads of the pack flew on the ground with thuds and crashing. We stopped a moment and asked ourselves whether we ought not to dismount, to help to catch the animals that were fleeing towards us, so that our riding-camels might not become infected and throw us off. But the fugitives were quickly caught by two riders. We rode on. On the road boxes, poles, and chairs, and the covers of the pack-saddles, lay strewn about. Haslund, who had remained with this section, told me that four camels had struck. The animal that was carrying the table-tops and chairs for the club-tent had become frightened by the rattling of its load and had broken out, and had infected three of its neighbours. It took a good quarter of an hour to load the animals again.

After a while we could see the next section of Larson's column, which was, however, still a good distance away. The road was like three or four parallel foot-paths, but the traffic seemed to be insignificant, for grass grew on the little elevations between them. We came not seldom, however, past skeletons and skulls of fallen camels. They were in various stages of disintegration through the agency of wind, rain, and burning summer sun. Our riding-camels scented them, quickened their steps, and made little detours. Life and death, the eternal round. The living foresaw, perhaps, that this fate awaits them when they are no longer able to carry the heavy burdens of man.

Leading his riding-camel, one of our servants came to meet us. He had been sent back as not being needed; that was a good sign. Here and there on the sides stony ranges of hills extended.

To the right an irregular black hill formed of primary rock rose up. The ground was quite thickly overgrown with low mugwort (*Artemisia*), between the small bushes of which one blade of grass and another peeped out, but the mugwort dominated the country-side. The road ran along between two exceedingly flat elevations that usually rose above the steppe between them to a height of about 10 metres.

A sign of traffic at last! Two poor Chinese farmers were leading a camel that was carrying their goods and chattels. We again crossed a small threshold of earth and had now a free view to the west and south-west. The low hills on the sides withdrew. To the right, not far from the road, a bed made by erosion could be seen, that has cut away a hill. There there is water, said Mento. At 9.40 we crossed a dry furrow a few metres deep and about 10 metres broad, probably the continuation of the one just mentioned. On its sides the grass was unusually thick.

Twenty minutes later we again crossed a furrow. It carried water, which flowed to the south; it therefore cannot be the continuation of the previous one. On its right, west bank, stood walls of unburnt clay and also a yourt. On a slope further above, Larson had halted with his caravan. The camels were just being unloaded. As usual my caravan-bashi came to meet me and invited me into his tent, where I was served with tea and was even offered chocolate. Larson told me that a string of twenty camels had meant to run away, but luckily had been held. Only two animals had thrown off their loads and run off. But one was caught by one of our Mongols on horseback, and the other by a nomad who by chance was sitting by the road looking on.

The various sections approached one after another, and my tent grew up again. Two hours later Haude and the instrument-boxes arrived; then the gas-cylinders under the direction of Walz, von Kaull, and two students. The camels had to remain lying or standing for three hours by their loads. It is bound to hurt their backs, if they go straight to pasture. They could, of course, go hungry a little to cool down—until the wildness was driven out of them.

Camp XI lies on the little watercourse of Honnen-chaggan-chollä, " the white stone of the sheep," or, more correctly, Honnen-chaggan-chollo-gol, which flows southward to the Mören-gol, the " river," or Hattun-gol, the " river of the princess," that is, the Yellow River, the Hwang Ho.

Here there is a toll-station, where one has to pay an impost on all camels that are allowed to go to east or west. The five Chinese that live here are all here solely on account of the toll. A few nomads, too, live in the neighbourhood. Near Chagga-hata-gol stood a town of tents.

We are now in the small district of Jugun(-hushe). There adjoins it in the west the district of Dondurgun (-hushe), which is said to extend right up to Shande-miao. " If you don't make longer marches than to-day, then you will need a month to reach Shande-miao," declared one of the Mongols of the place. But that was an exaggeration, even if we have not covered to-day more than 16·2 kilo-metres. We have still 30–40 *li* to go to reach the water-course of Chagga-gol. From Camp XI no special road leads to the Yellow River ; one can go where one will.

In winter not much snow falls here. This year, however, it had snowed for twice as long a time as most years, more plentifully than usual. The worst heat was now over, so we were told. Most caravans travel in winter. Further to the west robbers had made themselves evident, but the district was now quiet. The wolf is not common here, but probably further in the north. Antelopes are found, but not the argali sheep and not the wild ass.

Now, at 4 o'clock, the air is so calm and still that the flag hangs limp on the spear-shaft, which during the day is extremely rare.

Dr. Hummel has observed, that those large black beetles that were so amorous during rainy weather are to-day everywhere lying about dead. Some had still a spark of life in them, but lay on their backs breathing their last. The dead were in every case males. The females had presum-ably crept into the earth, to give in due time life to the next generation. The fate of the males is really pitiable. Why do they not remain bachelors ? Or perhaps there are these too, who are not willing for the sake of love to go to their death with the next rainy weather. It is with them as with Heine's Mahomet and the men of his tribe, " who die, if they love."

In the afternoon one of Norin's Mongols came and brought us a letter that Norin had written the day before in the camp of Bukheute-sume :

"We are now situated approximately 25 *li* to the west of the monastery of Burkhanten-sume at the foot of the range of mountains, and intend to wait here for the main caravan, if it isn't too long. Recently we have already asked ourselves whether anything has happened to you ; we have been expecting you since the 26th of July. Some days ago we sent a Mongol down the road to Liu-ta-kou, but nothing had been heard of you there.

Our provisions are now almost completely exhausted ; sugar and butter already for several days. If it will be two days before you arrive here, we should be grateful if our Mongol could bring us the following when he comes : a tin of sugar, two jars of butter, a pot of marmalade, and a box of oatmeal. If it will be longer than two days before you can be here, then be so kind as to send us correspondingly larger amounts.—However, all is well here. The work has gone according to programme, and has brought much that is interesting to light. Two camels have scabies badly, and it is to be feared that they will also infect the others. We should be obliged if our Mongol could bring some medicine with him. Söderbom says that sulphur and tar is good, but Larson certainly knows what is best.—We are looking forward to meeting again shortly. Our camp is visible from the road roughly 6 *li* to the north. Hearty greetings.

Yours truly,

NORIN, BERGMAN, & SÖDERBOM."

Chinese settlers who come up into this region must, so Hsü tells me, pay about 20 dollars in Sui-yüan and 1 dollar to the Mongolian chief of the district. But with irrigation it is bad here. It is so dry this year that almost famine prevails. On the Yellow River between Paotow and Wu-yüan it is different, for there one can provide the fields with water in abundance. There the grass on the virgin soil is so high, that horses and cattle that are pasturing cannot be seen. Mingan-Jasak extends right down to Wu-yüan on the Hwang Ho. In our region the corn is now twice as dear as two months ago.

When Larson woke me on the 3rd of August, he explained that a Mongol must ride to Yüan. I therefore wrote to Yüan and informed him of our next plans, that we intended gradually to increase our rate of marching, and that I hoped soon to see him and his column with us.

In the south-south-west of this region dwell several

Chinese colonists, who cultivate rye, wheat, peas, and other crops. They leave their families in China and remain here for some time, to return afterwards to their home country with skins, wool, and the like. They are exclusively dependent on the rain, for irrigation is impossible. The stream by our camp has this year carried no flood water. But during last year it flooded three times after heavy downpours of rain. The perseverance of the Chinese farmers is marvellous. Their battle with the freaks of the weather seems almost hopeless, but they fight untiringly and finally win.

The caravan road that we continue to follow on the 3rd of August is so dead and deserted that one is quite surprised when one meets a Mongol on a camel and two Chinese soldiers on horseback armed with rifles. We salute and in riding past ask the usual questions. Still more interesting is it to cross an erosion furrow cut out 4 metres in depth, with open pools of water in a bend. On its bank is situated the small Chinese settlement of Ta-shih-to, called Buttun-chillo by the Mongols. Here two Chinese are engaged in building a mud house.

The ground is traversed by innumerable canyon-like furrows, only a few metres deep but everywhere with vertical walls. They unite to form a main furrow to the north of our road. Alongside one such depression two Chinese are to be seen, ploughing the virgin soil with oxen. The road now runs along on the edge of the furrow, which is bordered in the north by a series of hills in strong relief. In its bed grass is growing. It is evidently a long time since the rain-water sought for itself an outlet here.

By Ja-cha-sa-go a small Chinese merchant caravan has taken a rest in the valley. Round its tents bales of goods with camel's hair, straw matting, and ropes, are arranged in a line. A little further on we ride past Haude and Dettmann, and are delighted with the charming spectacle, how the camels with the instrument-boxes walk along as innocent and well-behaved as lambs. We cross the furrow, on the bottom of which a few pools of water are standing and on whose banks the grass is unusually thick. We follow the bed and cross it again and again. Sometimes it is dry, sometimes covered with several puddles. The depression stands out more and more clearly as a valley between hills that are often cut vertical by a strong erosion.

It is hot, it is true, but the warmth does not bother me in the least. At 1 o'clock we have 27·9 degrees in the shade. A flock of sheep is pasturing in the valley, guarded by a shepherd and five snappish black dogs. Half an hour later we reach the small Chinese settlement of Tso-huan-tai-tei-ho, a solitary farm-stead enclosed by a mud wall. Its inhabitants kindly give us the information that we ask for.

For an hour more we follow the bed of the valley, which winds away between dark, sharply cut rocky walls, and finally, at a bend, we go up on its right bank. Here can be seen numerous traces of camping-places and remains of hearths, some of which are built of stones, while others are dug in the earth. It is obvious that this spot is frequently used as a resting-place for caravans and travellers. Those travellers who are going towards the west, here find good water for the last time for a considerable period, and those going towards the east like to stop here to drink, after they have left the thirsty stretch behind them.

Further towards the west the hills recede, and the country again opens out to the slightly undulating, endless expanses. The ground is hard and overgrown with mugwort. Shortly before 5 o'clock it begins to rain, and a violent north-west storm bursts forth. Hummel comes rushing up and offers me his rain-coat; he himself has a leather waistcoat. I must obey the order of the doctor and I do so willingly. We stop and wait. After a while the Mongol Matte appears, who has been talking to a shepherd and has learned that there is a spring in the neighbourhood. We ride for another hour to the west and south-west and reach it also. With heavy rain, rolling thunder, and flashing lightning, Matte and Mento put up my tent.

We have covered 40·6 kilometres. In the twilight the various sections arrive in rotation. It is already pitch dark, when we hear shouts and cries in the distance: the last column is approaching. Some of our men go to meet it, to lead it to the camp. Only Larson and his large caravan are still missing. He has, so we learn, made a halt far to the east of us in a dry furrow. But we also look about in vain for Dr. Hummel. In the belief that we intended to camp near the monastery of Burkhanten-sume mentioned by Norin, he had proceeded thither. Not till late in the evening did he reach us and share in our supper, which consisted of corned beef and green peas, and bread and butter. He had found the monastery uninhabited, and had lain down on a veranda, and had slept through the worst rain in the company of a white cat.

Somewhat stiff in the back from the 40-kilometre ride of the day before, I got up on the 4th of August at half past seven to begin a really eventful day. The camp that we were making for to-day has the number XIII, my lucky number. Where it would be situated no-one knew. We only knew that we should now pass by no more Chinese peasant settlers, and that we had now reached regions that are inhabited by Mongolian nomads. Everywhere, we had thus to be able to find water, and could interrupt the day's march as we felt inclined.

Larson with the wild camels and the huge baggage had spent the night 30 *li* to the east of us. They therefore did not reach our Camp XII till shortly before 7 o'clock, thirsty and hungry, and had a good breakfast, while their camels waited with their loads on their backs. Larson and his principals certainly found it rather mean, that I did not inform them yesterday, when I led the procession for a change for once, that we should make so long a march. But of that even I myself had not the least knowledge when we set out, and after they had quenched their thirst in our camp, they forgot that they had had to set out on the road in the morning without breakfast, and themselves laughed about their misfortune. I also consoled them by indicating that I myself had once gone thirsty for seven whole days, and that a little hardship and privation only did the body good. It was, moreover, not at all impossible that they would experience still harder days.

Then they continued their journey, and I put on my clothes, ate my breakfast, groats, eggs, and tea, and made myself ready for marching. Hempel and the student Tsui as usual measured off the base line for me, Mento and

Ming took down my tent and packed my things, the " Lady of the Camellias " was loaded with them, I climbed up into my high seat, and at half past nine left the Abderenten-gol, as the watercourse in the neighbourhood of Camp XII was called. In the north-north-east the monastery of Bur-khanten-sume could be seen at a distance of 3 or 4 kilometres.

The road consisted of seventeen paths that ran side by side and were separated from each other by low, narrow green strips. The whole day long the road was excellently suited for motor traffic, far better than on the previous day, when we had to get over a few rather difficult places between an approach to a chain of mountains and a pre-cipitous erosion-furrow. With a view to an eventual motor journey I always make notes, too, on the character of road and country. We continue our journey to the west-north-west, on paths where it would be a pleasure to travel with a motor-car. Cars can travel on the whole stretch from Kalgan right up to here ; up to now we have found no obstacles whatever.

In the west endless perspectives open out. It is as if one came out on the open sea. The eye roams unhindered to the west. One receives an impression of mighty Asia and of its boundless expanses. Only in the south-west and west-south-west can higher elevations be seen in the blue-fading distance. The country is without variety, but one does not grow tired of it ; it is always equally beautiful. It is a positive pleasure to traverse with the eyes these enormous distances from the high observation post on the camel.

At half past one we cross a furrow 280 metres broad with several damp depressions. To the right on the steppe, near at hand there are horses pasturing, and further off at the foot of the range of mountains stand three yourts. The country is now so flat, in all directions, that no undulations of the ground stand out.

A large flock of sheep proves that we are in a land of nomads. A furrow 15 metres broad was yesterday still full of rushing rain-water. The clayey mud on the bottom is still shining with moisture. Its right erosion-terrace is 4 metres high. The whole country, which here extremely slowly falls away from the foot of the range of mountains, has been washed over with rain-water yesterday, which has formed on the road innumerable deltas with lagoons. The ground even now is wet almost everywhere. It must have poured here terribly.

At the foot of the mountain range we can again see two yourts, and shortly before 3 o'clock we catch sight of Norin's camp with its four tents. We steer thither. Söderbom hurries to meet us and invites me to drink a cup of tea with them. Larson, Hummel, Mühlenweg, and Lieberenz, are already there also. I willingly consent to the little break. Heyder, Bergman, and Massenbach, welcome me and invite me to take a seat on Norin's camp-chair. They have laid Norin's table that he has taken with him on all his journeys, and they now set before me coffee, tea, marmalade, bread, and milk. We chat and smoke and tell each other of our experiences and work. We have not seen each other, indeed, since the 1st of July.

In front of the tent of the three Swedes waved the Swedish flag ; in front of the tent of Heyder and Massenbach the German flag. In the third tent Ting and Chin lived ; in the fourth the servants.

Norin himself unfortunately was not at home. We sat there for an hour and a half, and decided that Norin's column should move over to us the next morning. Larson's section had gone on. I asked him where he intended to camp. On the stream. And how far is it yet before one reaches that ? At the most about 10 *li*. Larson already left Norin's camp an hour before me, in order to overtake his section again and be present when it put up the camp. I still stayed and chatted ; it was too comfortable here. Then I said good-bye to them and invited them to share in our supper. To Camp XIII it was, indeed, only a stone's throw. They could thus return again to their camp in the evening and to-morrow move over to us with bag and baggage.

Accompanied only by Mento, I continue my ride. To the right there rises up in the opening of a valley the little monastery of Shiretin-gondyur-sume. The whole region is a pure alluvial land with traces of off-flowing rain-water.

Through inhospitable country

Skeletons of fallen camels mark the way

THE DESERT MARCH

[*face p.* 124

An old woman pilgrim makes tea

SHANDE-MIAO

The steppe is sometimes like a swamp. Everywhere stand pools and puddles. For the horny feet of the camels it is exceedingly soft and slippery. To the right we have low mountains the whole time, from which the rain-water empties itself into its lowland bowl. Elevations between these are already dry again and without fissures. To our left stretches the endless steppe. But in the west-south-west and south lie in the far distance somewhat higher elevations. After we have travelled past a small flat spur of hill to the right of the road, we can see at the foot of the mountain range three yourts, and on the plain to the left two yourts in one place and four in another, and at a distance of 10 *li* a small monastery.

The sun goes down with a red glow. At half past seven we at last reach Halle-Utayin-gol, a genuine broad erosion-furrow, which seems to come from a far distance and which is crossed in serpentine courses by two streams. Our thoughtless camel-drivers are just making the camels lie down to unload them. We call to them that they are to go on a bit further, up on the hills of the slope on the right bank, which rises up at the most 10 metres above the bed. There stand two yourts, and a tent that probably belongs to travelling merchants.

The sun has set, it has become dusk, and now the darkness comes on. Mento gets my tent ready on the top of a hill. From up here I have a view over the channel of the stream and towards the east in the direction from which we have come.

It is already dark when Dettmann and Haude lead their camels to us. In the distance shouts can be heard again and again. It is Walz and Kaull's section approaching. Suddenly wild cries and uproar are heard on the steppe. Several men are shouting at the same time ; it is noteworthy that the camels seem to be quieted by these piercing yells. It was clear that a revolt had broken out again. One could hear the crashing of boxes that fell upon the ground. But soon the shouts died away again and confined themselves to the accustomed volume, for someone or other is always shouting. Meanwhile it has become quite dark, and Larson sends some of his Mongols down to show the new-comers the way. The shouts come nearer and nearer and cross the channel of the stream. The first section climbs up the slope ; the second follows. They are the animals with the provision boxes and many other things. Finally all the camels are up with us, lie down, and are freed of their loads. Then at last it becomes quiet.

Thus did the various sections of our column assemble in Camp XIII. But the expedition was still split up and scattered. Why Zimmermann and von Marschall had sent no news of themselves we did not know. Yüan, too, was still far behind us, but had provisions for a month and also money. Norin was in his camp, and 10 *li* away to the east Haslund's camels had mutinied, which, however, were usually so quiet. How it looked there, we did not know. In Camp XIII everything was now to be organized afresh. Therefore we decided in the evening to remain here the next day.

The singular thing about this beginning of our long march to Urumchi is that neither I nor Larson decides its movement and progress, but the camels. And with full powers too. When they want to have a rest-day, they throw off their loads and run away. Then they know for certain that they will have it free the next day. But for us it is terrible and uncomfortable to be in this way at the mercy of the arbitrary action of the animals. If one rides, as I am accustomed to do, so that I have some sections in front of me and some behind, I do not know what is happening to them. The wild ones always go first of all, and if I overtake them on the road, I can see that everything is in order. But the mutiny may break out after I have left them behind me. The camels are admittedly our helpers and carry our baggage to the west, but they are also a pack of four-footed rebels that at any instant may cause us new losses and delays.

In consequence of this it is difficult at the moment to fix the rate of marching. We must first subdue the camels with the help of the loads, until they become quiet and well-behaved and we have them in our power.

At the moment only my column was on the spot, but it comprised, indeed, the greater part of the caravan, Larson with the provisions, Haude with the instruments, most of the Chinese, and much else. Some sections had arrived in the twilight; others when it was dark. The tents lay therefore scattered about in picturesque disorder, and the walls made by the provision boxes stood in our immediate neighbourhood, for the round hill offered quite a limited space. For the club-tent there was no place at hand. Our meals were like improvised picnics. We took breakfast under a roof formed out of saddle-poles and covers of pack-saddles. Dinner and supper were served on the boxes that stood near the kitchen: we got mutton, cabbage, radishes, and brown beans.

The day was warm, 33 degrees in the shade; the lowest temperature during the night had been 16 degrees.

I sent a courier to Norin with the order to transfer his camp and his whole column to us in Camp XIII. But the day slipped by without our seeing or hearing anything of them. We suspected that they were looking for runaway camels. Towards evening I therefore sent out a second messenger with the order that, in case they were on the way to us, they were not to go through the bush-covered steppe in the darkness, since in this unaccustomed region the camels might go off their heads.

At 1 o'clock in the night, when I had already been asleep a few hours, I heard how Norin was asking Larson, whose tent is always by the side of mine, whether I was asleep. "No, not at all," I answered; "just come in." Then they both came into my tent and remained sitting with me for two hours. As Norin informed us, they had tramped about looking for the missing camels and had not returned till 6 o'clock. But my letter was an order, and they had therefore immediately packed up their camp and had set out at 8 o'clock, when the twilight was already getting rather advanced. Then, on the way, they had received my second note and had then encamped on the edge of the bush-covered steppe, while Norin had gone on in the dark night on foot.

He was quite enthusiastic concerning the tasks that had claimed him and his men for more than a month. I was of the opinion that he was in need of sleep, but no, he must give an account of everything : how splendid Heyder's triangular survey was ; how conscientiously Massenbach mapped all the valleys and courses of streams ; how Bergman hunted out one stone-age settlement after another ; how Ting patiently tested the rock ; and how he himself, Norin, was delighted with his map, which put forth one leaf after another. I probably need not say that he had in me a very attentive and interested listener. At intervals we found amusement in Larson, who had been awakened in his sweetest slumber and in his haste had only put on his blue jacket—over his nightshirt, which was just as short. But finally I sent them both to bed, and Norin found accommodation in Larson's tent.

Early in the morning I was awakened for the second time, but now by screaming camels, the driving in of tent-pegs, and eager voices. Norin's column had arrived, and I hurried to get into my clothes.

The whole day was taken up by a series of important conferences. The first lasted several hours and took place in Norin's large tent, where he lived along with Bergman and Söderbom. For an old chart hand like me it was a real artistic treat to look at Heyder's three enormous sheets with the intricate system of triangles of all possible shapes and sizes. As fixed points Heyder had utilized every *obo* that was found in the region and formed on commanding peaks and heights a point that was clearly visible in the far distance with the theodolite. Where there was no *obo* a heap of stones often 2 metres in height was set up. Between these points the angles were measured and measured again. The whole had grown into a close network of triangles, which only needed two points astronomically fixed, for it then to be possible for it to be entered at the right place in the network of latitudes and longitudes. From Heyder's system of triangles Norin could obtain, where and when he wanted, new base-lines for his own detailed map and for Massenbach's measurements.

We sat for hours in Norin's splendid tent, in which the beds of the three Swedes stood near the outer edge and a table between the tent-poles served as table. Here the maps were spread out sheet by sheet. On the ground lay carpets in bright cheerful colours, and on them we sat round the table. We discussed, compared, and measured with the compasses. I showed my maps of the road to Camp XIII, and Haude and Dettman reported on the astronomically fixed points. Norin's charts were masterly with their contours and their geological colouring. He explained the geological formation of the whole region, a subject to which I shall return later. Finally Massenbach showed his cartographical surveys of the valley paths and erosion-furrows and how they fitted in with Norin's map and Heyder's triangular system. It was a pleasure to see how enthusiastic our companions were concerning their work, and with what suspense they awaited its continuation. So indeed it ought to be in a scientific expedition. Every member who has any scientific tasks to carry out ought to go to his work with pleasure and eagerness. And so it is with us. I never have to give a reminder of anything. I have rather to put the brake on, so that they don't over-exert themselves. In this respect I am particularly anxious regarding Norin, for he would like nothing better, one might almost say, than to embrace the whole of Central Asia, and he denies himself sufficient rest.

In the evening, news came from Zimmermann and Marschall that they were camping 15 *li* to the east of us. The messenger took with him the order, that they should present themselves at headquarters in Camp XIII with all possible speed.

At the spot where we were now, in the Han period a smallish settlement had obviously been situated, perhaps a fort or a station on a military road. Here lay an enormous number of potsherds and bricks, and a small, built-up platform resembling an altar, which was excavated by Huang and Chuang. It was surrounded by several hundred bricks bent at an angle. A coin of the period of the Han dynasty was also found. The Chinese were very interested in these finds and dug in several places simultaneously.

Finally I gave Larson the order to continue the march the next morning with his usual caravan and the wild camels. In the evening a messenger came from Larson with the news that he had covered 40 *li*, and that all had gone well. He intended to continue the journey in the direction of the monastery of Shande-miao, or Bayin-shandai-sumo, as the Mongols call it.

At 2 o'clock Zimmermann and Marschall arrived with their caravan of twelve camels. With both of them and with the student Liu it was going excellently. They had visited the monasteries in the neighbourhood of Norin's camp and carried sprigs of wild elm in their hats. The little antelope had made the journey with them in a sedan-chair, a padded box. It, too, was gay and well, and on the long road to Camp XIII had not suffered the least injury.

An hour later Yüan came riding up alone on a camel, and with him and Professor Hsü I had a longish discussion. He was very satisfied with his results and showed Norin, Heyder, and me his well-executed and beautifully drawn maps, which were now so far advanced that they could be combined with those of Norin and Massenbach and then fixed by means of Heyder's system of triangles. We sat together a long time talking about topography.

Later, we again had a second discussion with Yüan concerning his wishes and plans on Gashun-nor. For our stay on the " salt lake " I developed a programme that contained the following different tasks :

1. The drawing of a map of Gashun-nor and Sokho-nor with old shore-lines and general configuration.

2. Archæological investigations round the lakes.

3. An expedition into the desert to the west of Gashun-nor, where, according to the history of the earlier Han, there must be an old town that is 600 years older than Lou-lan.

4. Cartographical surveys of the lower course and of the tributaries of the delta òf the Etsin-gol.

5. Archæological investigations along the river.

6. According to circumstances a visit to the " Black Town," Khara-khoto, which was discovered by Koslov in the year 1909. Excavations were not to be undertaken there, since Koslov, so I have heard, has the intention of returning there, and since he naturally has the prior right to it. Moreover, I prefer completely new tasks. Neither

Koslov nor Stein has devoted any attention worth mentioning to prehistoric archæology on the river and the lakes, and *this* task has the attraction of newness and is sufficient for our archæologists.

Norin expressed the desire to be given task No. 1. Yüan had no particular wish and declared he was willing to take charge of whatever might be entrusted to him. Huang, as an historical archæologist, wanted most of all to have task No. 3. We agreed to make a suitable division of labour between Bergman and Yüan, as soon as we had reached the lake.

Until late into the night we had all sorts of consultations and discussions. Professor Hsü sat with me until 11 o'clock, and then came Dr. Haude and remained till half past twelve. Following that, I sat in Hummel's tent with Norin till half-past one; this night my sleep did not amount to much, for the next morning my column was to continue its journey to the west.

From Camp XIII our ways separated for some considerable time. Norin, Heyder, Bergman, von Massenbach, and Ting, were to go on with their work, and march more slowly than we. Yüan was to accelerate his labours and in seven, at the most nine, weeks reach Gashun-nor. Huang and the collector Chuang were, in accordance with their own desire, to remain here another three to four days and continue their excavations. All the other members of the staff were to accompany me on the road to the west.

X

TO THE MONASTERY OF SHANDE-MIAO

ON account of the long discussions during the night we did not set out on the 9th of August till 8 o'clock. With a Chinese merchant who lived here in a tent, we left behind provisions for three weeks for Norin and his column, and just as much for Yüan and the southern column. Huang was given provisions for ten days. Norin had twenty-nine camels, Yüan seventeen, and Huang five. I myself had sixty-seven; the rest were with Larson.

We rode at a quick pace over the flat land-waves of the steppe, which stretched between two low ridges of hill. On both sides are drainage furrows, which began suddenly in the middle of the steppe, and, what is more, immediately with vertical slopes. The little monastery of Enger-sumo and a few yourts we left to the north. Here and there herds of cattle were pasturing. Before us in the west low mountains fading away into blue were to be seen in the distance. A short distance from the road an old man was sitting alone spinning. We asked him the name of the place. It was called Honger-ava, and a monastery that lay at the foot of the range of mountains in the south-west, he gave the name of Dityis-sumo. To the right of the road an isolated mountain rose up, which had the form of a sarcophagus and on its summit bore a rather large *obo*.

Here the wild leek grew in abundance; the whole region smelt of them, especially after the last rain. The camels like to eat them; their breath, always bad without them, smells, after a solid meal of them, still more un-pleasant than usual. At the edge of the furrow of Hon-gerin-gol, which carried running water, we halted and put

132

up my tent, which I always have with me. I am thus independent of the caravan and can set out and can camp when it pleases me. I rode at a faster rate than the caravan, and had to wait quite an hour before it arrived.

The next morning we awoke with pouring rain and again resigned ourselves to getting soaked on the way. The steppe was now covered with innumerable hemispherical hills of vegetation of half a metre in diameter. The roots of the plants of the steppe bind earth and sand and produce this peculiar bumpy type of country, which further to the west is widely spread and would often obstruct travelling by motor-car.

We keep on riding past skulls and skeletons of fallen camels. They are milestones, as it were, on the long road of life and death of the caravans across Asia.

Haslund and Serat come riding up, to inform us that the spring of Hashat is situated close by here. They find it, and we go off there. The caravan slowly approaches, and the camp grows up in the accustomed arrangement. In the evening we have streaming moonlight. The highest temperature to-day had been only 27 degrees ; the lowest of the night before 13 degrees. The Mongolian summer is treating us really very gently.

On the 11th of August with a glaring clear sky it was already warm at 8 o'clock. The wind blew gloriously at our backs, on which the sun burnt. We crossed a belt of low hills and elevations of land ; on the highest rising stood an *obo*. Directly by the side of this votive token that was dedicated to the spirits of the mountain lay a dead camel. The fallen martyr had assumed the usual attitude of death : head and neck strongly bent over towards the back. Much more than the skeleton was no longer left of it, but its horny feet, which for some decades had trodden the desert roads of Asia, were well preserved. It was as if the dying camel had gone up to the holy place to seek help, but just by the token of stones it had been struck by the wrath of the spirits and had ended its wandering.

A little further on, the caravan road divides. The right road goes to the north, to Da Kuren or Urga ; the left, which we are following, leads to the monastery of Shande-miao.

Across a plain confined by hills we make for a rocky portal in the west, where a small chain of mountains rises up. There all the furrows of the region unite. We reach the narrow valley, in which the grass is growing thickly on the banks of a stream soon drying up. The mountains slope steeply, in part vertically, down to the bottom of the valley. We who for months have seen only plains found this scenery enchanting, and I gave the order to set up the camp. The tents were set up in the grass.

We wake up the next morning with pouring rain, and ask ourselves if we shall succeed in getting out of our ravine before it fills with water. The stream, however, only rises very slightly, and after a short march the valley opens into a wide plain.

In the north-west lies the monastery of Bombin-sumo. It used to number nine hundred lamas, who owned several thousand camels. Now it is only inhabited by about twenty monks, who are as poor as church mice and complain of the bad times and of the continuing drought. The Chinese are more industrious. They use their life and their time for work, not for temple service and the gabbling of meaningless prayers.

Our road then leads again towards the north-west through a barren narrow valley. Waste, and strewn with boulders of all sizes, it yet makes a picturesque impression in its solitude and wildness. In the natural hollow of a stone slab rain-water had collected; here twenty camels stood drinking. They had no herdsman with them, and looked like following us.

The valley ascended to open free plateaux, where ten antelopes ran away over the ground in light, springy jumps. We crossed a ledge of granite, and again had one of those endless distant views before us.

We rode on a little farther, reached a lonely spring, and here set up my tent.

I fear that this description has a certain resemblance to Xenophon's classic account of the " Retreat of the Ten Thousand," in so far as it becomes monotonous, and at the same time I do not even speak of how many parasangs we have covered each day. I will therefore mention that we in general cover 20 or 30 kilometres daily, occasionally 40. One is always dependent on water and pasturage. Up to the present we have suffered neither scarcity of the one nor of the other.

The morning of the 13th of August was cold, overcast, and dark. Is the autumn perchance drawing near already? Oh no, we have yet many warm days in front of us, before the wild elms lose their leaves. The wind blows from the east. From that quarter, from the sea, comes the rain. The chains of mountains in the south are called Khara-narin-ula, and are named by the Chinese the Lang-shan, the "wolf mountains." They lie to the north of the great bend of the Hwang Ho.

In the distance there appears a caravan that is approaching us. It draws nearer and becomes larger. Five Chinese are leading ten camels, which without doubt are loaded with opium. They march past us.

A fresh wind is blowing; it rustles more melancholy than usual in the grass of the steppe. One can hear strange sounds when gusts of wind sweep past at various distances. Sometimes one starts, believing that someone has called one by name. One turns round, but no living being is to be seen. We have already outstripped all the others a long time ago.

Then we again ride past a smugglers' station. Here rest the opium caravans from Ning-hsia and Wang-yeh-fu. They travel 100 *li* daily, which they cover in two stages, in the morning and in the evening. To be able to make marches of 55 kilometres their camels must be well cared for, and under the straw matting in front of the tents corn lies piled up. The caravan men have rifles and Mauser pistols and can protect themselves against robbers.

Dalai-buluk is a spring, which according to its name ought to be as large as the sea (*dalai*). In the neighbourhood of this modest stream we come past a new opium station. Then we meet a friendly and good-humoured Chinaman, who is driving a herd of a hundred camels. He tells us that Larson is 10 *li* in front of us.

We continue our journey and soon espy in front of us a village of seven yourts and immediately behind them Larson's tents. The place is called Khara-tologoi, the "black head." The main caravan was now together again.

The next morning Larson is already on his legs before 4 o'clock and is moving out into the steppe with his great column. We order our life more comfortably, and let the sun rise before we follow his track between irregular ranges of mountains past opium tents and herds of pasturing camels and oxen. In honour of Sunday and the hundredth balloon, after the burden of the day the flagstaff is erected in front of my tent. Usually the Swedish flag flies from my front tent-pole. The club-tent, however, we did not set up, but had our supper on straw mats by the kitchen. As we sat there with crossed legs in front of our plates and dishes, Dicky came jumping up and stepped right in the middle of the brown beans. It is indeed well that the camels are not so familiar, I thought, and heaved a sigh of relief.

The next day, the 15th of August, was for me a memorable anniversary. Forty-two years had now gone by since I set out for Asia for the first time. And still the great continent held me captive. Although a lifetime lay between to-day and then, I remembered that day clearly and distinctly. How slowly the last hours passed for me! My father read a psalm out aloud from the hymn-book and said a prayer for my welfare and a happy re-union. With courage and fortitude my mother concealed her anxiety concerning the uncertain separation. And then I travelled across the Baltic Sea to Russia and Western Asia.

Now, 42 years later, I was again on my travels, this time in Chinese or Inner Mongolia, and was riding on a gigantic camel past Tsaghan-obo, "the white votive token," on the endlessly long road across the very heart of Asia. Over the steppe crossed by dry ravines and bordered by bare hills, even to-day we went on towards the west.

The antelope Dicky is the darling of all. Probably

View of the monastery from a ravine

SHANDE-MIAO

[*face p.* 136

Burial-place, of lamas of high rank, known as " sovurgas "

SHANDE-MIAO

[face p. 137

never has an animal been so looked after and nursed and stroked as it has been. It makes the daily journey in its padded sedan-chair, which is carried by a quiet camel; and scarcely is the box on the ground when it hops out and looks for von Marschall, who has undertaken to keep the milk-bottle in readiness. It still drinks the milk through the rubber teat just like a suckling. But to-day the unfortunate thing happened, that in its eagerness it even swallowed the teat. The whole staff was seized with the greatest apprehension, but Dr. Hummel reassured us. Dicky's small droppings were then examined for an interval of a whole week, but the teat never came to light again. Dicky could not be better, however, than was the case after this unusual titbit. A wag made the suggestion that we should give it, too, the balloons that Dr. Haude burst during the filling.

On the 16th of August we again had an unbounded view from one of those insignificant undulations of the ground, and at last in the west-south-west caught sight of the Shande-miao that we longed for, which is said to mark approximately the half of the road between Kuei-hua-chêng and Gashun-nor.

The village consists of two parts, that of the traders with nine yourts and that of the monks, the monastery. We rode past the yourts, where only one man and a few dogs were to be seen. Here, according to the agreement, we were to leave provisions behind for Norin and Yüan.

Through a ravine the road went up to a rising, where Larson had erected his camp. Here the new town of tents gradually rose up. Directly after 3 o'clock the wind increased to a full storm. The fine dust penetrates through the tent-cloth, and inside the tent everything becomes covered with fine sand. Bed, carpet, boxes, and bags—everything becomes covered with a yellow layer, and the water for washing with looks like pea-soup. Of the surroundings nothing is to be seen. All is yellow whirling dust; even the nearest tents disappear. The wind reached a strength of 24 second-metres. The temperature rose only to 23 degrees. As Haude said, the storm went to a height of 500 metres above the surface of the earth.

From Paotow we had covered 473·7 kilometres, and we had still 420 kilometres to Etsin-gol. We had been told that Shande-miao was a toll-station, where one had to pay 5 dollars for every box. Having arrived there, we heard nothing, however, of a toll, and did not pay even a cent. We were given, on the contrary, the good advice not to keep too far to the north on the march to the west, since if we did we might run into the hands of the nosy tax-gatherers of the Mongolian Republic. The republican toll-station lay only 120 *li* farther to the north.

Near Shande-miao we had to make a halt of two days, to rest, allow the animals to pasture, repack our baggage, and sort out the boxes that had to be left behind for the last two columns. The place was not amiss. From the Chinese tradesmen one could even get candles and matches and a series of other odds and ends. We were here rather more than 1,700 metres above the sea; the temperature fell in the night to 6 degrees above zero. Thus the climate was good. The first day we partly used to clean our things after the sand-storm. Everything had to be beaten and aired. Larson, von Marschall, and Haslund, settled the question of the provisions. Four of the Chinese engaged in Camp IX were dismissed, and two new ones were taken into service in their place. On the 19th of August Larson was to decamp and go on ahead of us. I heard also how he woke his people at 4 o'clock in the morning, but nothing came of the departure, since two camels were missing. One was found in the course of the day. The other had disappeared and remained lost. The next day we were overtaken by the small caravan of the archæologist Huang. He had remained four more days in Camp XIII and had found seventy objects of copper, mostly arrow-heads, a hundred and seventy of iron, and twenty of bone, as well as coins of the period of the earlier Han. He also told us that, since we had parted, Bergman had discovered a first-class site and had found several hundred objects, probably of the older Stone Age, such as axes, curved stone knives, and other things.

Haude, just like myself, was longing to set up Station 1 on Gashun-nor as early as possible, and he therefore asked to be allowed to set out with his staff and his instruments together with Larson, who was to begin his march on the 22nd of August. The previous evening we decided in favour of this course, and our column therefore lost Haude, Dettmann, von Kaull, and Li, finally Huang too, who had asked to be allowed to join Larson, for the most promising field of work was calling him. In the evening all were with me in the tent saying good-bye. It was clear to us that we should not see each other again until we met on Gashun-nor.

In Camp XXI near Shande-miao my column experienced still a second loss, even if only for a few days. We had heard from the traders of the place that by journeying for two days one could reach the bend of the Yellow River. In the night of the 20th to the 21st of August I lay awake busy with new plans, and came to the conclusion that it would be valuable to re-establish a cartographical connexion with the great bend of the Hwang Ho. In the morning I gave Larson the order to get together a small light caravan, and elaborated to Hempel and Zimmermann the tasks that I had appointed for them. They were to ride to the nearest Belgian mission station, gather information there, and make a map of the road. I asked Professor Hsü to send two students along with them as interpreters. Liu and Ma were chosen for this. In the afternoon of the 21st of August the small light caravan started out. When it had gone away, there came doubts, however, to my mind for having sent so small a section into regions that were said to belong to the most popular fields of activity of the bands of robbers. What should we do if anything happened to our party and it did not return? The next day Larson set out on his journey, and took with him six of the war-experienced Germans.

Now my expedition was thoroughly scattered, the distribution being as follows : with me there only remained one Swede, one German, one Dane, and two Chinese—namely, Hummel, von Marschall, Haslund, Hsü Ping-chang, and Tsui. The column that had pushed forward the farthest consisted of Larson and six Germans, Walz, Lieberenz, Mühlenweg, Haude, Dettmann, and von Kaull, as well as two Chinese, Huang and Li. Norin had with him two Swedes, two Germans, and a Chinese—namely, Bergman, Söderbom, Heyder, von Massenbach, and Ting. Finally, Yüan had in his section only two Chinese, Chan and Kung. It is plain that an expedition that is in this way divided into five columns, achieves greater results than when all march as one. Each of the small sections is more independent and can move more easily.

While the caravan was being reorganized in this way, I lay ill in Shande-miao and unfit for active service. I had suffered an attack of my old gall-stone malady and in accordance with all the rules of the art of medicine was treated with morphia and other wonderful remedies by our physician in ordinary, Dr. Hummel. The anxious doctor even moved me over into von Marschall's tent, which was larger, and gave the order that I must lie on a real bed provided with sheets, a luxury I had not known since leaving Paotow. At my head on both sides a box was set up, and thus I had two bed-side tables—for medicine, tea, water, books, maps, and other odds and ends.

When Larson had gone away on the 22nd of August, the great peace descended upon us and it became quiet and still. Only rarely did a visit interrupt us. A high lama came from the monastery in order to show his sympathy with me, and, the same as another, who possessed the dignity of a knight, was entertained in my tent. The amiable and courteous Professor Hsü appeared three times daily at my sick-bed, and sometimes remained with me an hour or two. When I was alone I usually read.

We were still in the district of Dondurgun, whose chief was a despotic lord hostile to foreigners. He even had the lives of three Swedish missionaries on his conscience. He had left us unmolested, although we paid him no other attention than to dispatch to him Professor Hsü's and my visiting-card. We had only some few more daily journeys in his realm to cover. Then we entered Alashan, which I had crossed in my youth. To its prince or *wang-yeh* in Wang-yeh-fu, Hsü had a letter of introduction.

Fortunately my state of health improved, and on the 26th of August we decided to move our camp into the immediate neighbourhood of the monastery. The monks asked us not to erect our tents on the mountain above the sanctuary, but below in the sandy valley. There Mento and I conveyed my tent, and we were ready when the others came up between the hills. The view towards the monastery town in the north was not amiss. Its various temple buildings and dormitories, about fifty in number, lay like an amphitheatre on the slope.

After we had had our tea, Hsü, Haslund, Serat, Mento, and I went to the monastery, to pay a return visit to the lama who had come to see me. He was not at home just then, but, as pastor, was visiting the nomads of the region. We were therefore conducted to the abbot himself. He was a little old man with a round skull and shrunken features, and sat with crossed legs in his little well-furnished cell, surrounded by a whole host of gods in brass and colours.

Our greeting he did not return. He only looked at us astonished and bewildered and only seemed to want to be rid of us again. After we had gazed awhile at the old man, we therefore withdrew.

We went up to the main temple on the top of the hill, where stood also a neat row of *chortens*. A lama proceeded thither and put a light to incense in a metal vessel in front of the entrance, whereupon he took a seat on a cushion at the right end of the temple hall. Before him on a red-lacquer table he had the holy scriptures, from which he read aloud with a chanting rhythm, while from time to time he beat together the cymbals that he had in his lap and belaboured a hanging drum with a stick shaped like a swan's neck, which was held vertically and to whose end a ball was fixed. Sometimes he rang a little bell that stood on the table, where also the *dorje* or thunderbolt and other ritual objects were not lacking. All this took place in order to turn away the wrath of the gods provoked by our unwelcome visit.

141

The ceiling of the longish temple hall rested on four red-lacquer pillars, between which hung four unusually large and beautiful *tankas*, banner-like religious paintings. The end walls were decorated with paintings in red frames, while the back wall was occupied with book-shelves for the sacred writings of the *Kanjur* and some beautiful images of Buddha in glass cupboards. In the middle of the room there was raised up a *chorten* or, as the Mongols call it, *sovurga*, of the accustomed Tibetan kind. On the altar table stood brass vessels and incense-bowls, and before its centre hung a canopy of woven material.

Then we wandered through narrow alleys between white walls, over natural steps of a dark crystalline rock interspersed with veins of quartz, across court-yards and open spaces—exactly as in Tibetan temples and monasteries. The style of architecture is Tibetan, even if several roofs with front mouldings, carvings, and paintings are Chinese. Bayin-shandai-sumo lies picturesquely between its hills. At its foot lies a narrow valley. From the spring at its bottom the water was drawn up with a scoop of sackcloth and poured into a wooden trough. A few animals were just standing there drinking, a few horses, an ass, and a splendid camel, which latter belonged to a blue-coated Mongol from Kuku-nor. The whole was a beautiful picture in the warm red glow of the sunset, with steel-blue threatening storm-clouds in the north. Numerous monks visited our camp and wandered round in amazement between our tents. In dirty, hip-red togas, which left free their copper-coloured arms, they sat there and stared with open mouths, filled with astonishment at everything they saw. Our dogs had much to do to keep an eye on riders, wanderers, and dogs of the monastery. During the night we had to keep Dicky locked up, for he has an heroic tendency to throw himself with contempt for death right in the midst of the turmoil of battle with every fight among the dogs.

At last the small caravan had returned safe and sound from its excursion to the Yellow River. We remained sitting in my tent till midnight, and the two Germans told how it had fared with them and their Chinese and

Mongolian fellow-travellers. We studied the maps, particularly a large sheet of the bend of the Hwang Ho that they had obtained from the missionary Rodts. It was 57 kilometres in a straight line to his station in San-tao-chiao; with the bends in the road they had actually travelled much farther. For the march back they had chosen a more westerly route. During the next days they worked out their map in detail, and I bestowed praise and thanks upon them for their thorough work, which was a valuable addition to our geographical and cartographical results.

In detail they recounted as follows: They had ridden on the 21st of August with their little troop to the south-east and south, towards the Khara-narin range, which showed up a little from the north and resembled rather an open plateau broken by valleys. In the south its peaks rose scarcely perceptible above the horizon. From the hilly country the road went down slowly to the entrance to a valley, where a Mongolian sentry asked for particulars of their intentions. The country was very sandy; the dunes had piled themselves up to a height of 10 and 20 metres. A few old houses stood there uninhabited; they had obviously been left on account of the sand.

The narrow valley was shut in by black, bare rocks. The twilight was already changing into darkness when they occupied their first camp by the spring of Du-su-loän, whose stream after as short a distance as 10 metres dries up in the sand. A Mongolian yourt and a tent had been set up near the spring.

The following day they crossed a pass in a south-easterly direction. Up above on the crest stood an *obo* —Dabatoi-obo—with a Tibetan inscription carved in wood. The north slope is steep, but the south slope on the contrary falls away slowly; one would have expected just the opposite. The valley that led down did not lack a romantic beauty, shut in between bare rocks and with a scanty growth of plants, even adorned here and there with a tree. It bends off to the east.

Winding, narrow, and hemmed in between steep-rising mountain-sides, which on the right or south side had a height of 250 metres, the valley descends to the plain of the Hwang Ho. On the heights at its sides here and there old defence constructions and walls are to be seen. It is so narrow that its little stream covers the greater part of the bed of the valley, and one rides in water. Its entrance opens to the south-east. On the south side of the end of the valley there is a fortress wall 1·20 metres high and 30 metres broad. From the entrance to the valley one has a wide distant prospect over the valley of the Yellow River.

The two Germans rode on to the east over the heap of debris at the foot of the range and over small dunes and finally reached the first settlement, where the sand-dunes end and the land is more overgrown. After they had crossed a first canal, at that time dry, they camped at a place that was called Sain-nor. Here were found three settlements, and at some distance there could be seen several more. Wheat, millet, hemp, melons, potatoes, cucumbers, beans, cabbages, and other vegetables, were cultivated, as well as maize. For the right of cultivation the settlers had to pay taxes both to the Mongols and to the authorities in Sui-yüan. In the region are found antelopes and hares, pheasants and partridges, foxes and wolves. Vultures, swans, wild ducks, and geese are very common. The camel, ass, sheep, and goat are the domestic animals. In January the temperature falls to 20 and 30 degrees below zero, yet winter does not bring much snow. In March the sand-storms begin, which come from the west. The Hwang Ho is frozen up from December to March. Navigation on the river is carried on from April to November. For this rafts are used, which are borne by a hundred sheepskins filled with air. The fish of the Hwang Ho are most easily caught in the canals. Turtles are also found.

The Chinese traders have established themselves at the foot of the mountain range, where the canals run along. On these water-ways are carried flour, corn, coal, and such other things as are exchanged for skins and wool from Mongolia.

Our section's reconnaissance party crossed one of the

larger canals, which ran from the south-west to the north-east. It was 15 metres broad and 1·60 metres deep, and its water had a rate of flow of 1·5 metres per second. It stretched right to the foot of the mountain range, where 200 years ago the Hwang Ho had its course, which accounts for the many ruins of forts and walls. The river then moved its bed more and more to the south. With their tenacious perseverance in utilizing the soil, the Chinese colonists with enormous rapidity are spreading in this direction too. Already now one can count here only one Mongol to a hundred Chinese.

On the 23rd of August the road went to the east. They had to take a circuitous route round several canals, which were only 1 metre broad and half a metre deep and had banks about 30 centimetres high at their sides. The settlements became more and more numerous. They also passed by some barracks with the blue and white flag of the Kuo-min-tang.

To the right of the road there stretched a long sand-dune 10 metres high, at the eastern end of which they reached the monastery of Meling-miao. It is 200 years old and numbers a hundred and thirty lamas. Beyond that they had to cross a canal 15 metres broad, the Yang-ya-ho-tzǔ, on a ferry that is pulled across with a rope. It took up an hour and a half to get the camels across, which only with difficulty could be made to board the vessel.

On the other bank lay the village of San-tao-chiao with 400 inhabitants and some barracks with a company of a hundred soldiers, former robbers. Their leader is Wang-ying, of whom we had already heard in Paotow and who at the present time was said to live in Wu-yüan.

The canal runs from the south-south-west to the north-north-east and is 180 *li* in length. It was built throughout a period of generations by members of the Yang family and bears their name. A beginning was made with the construction a hundred years ago, and in 1917 it was finished. The Yang family is domiciled in the village of Yang-kuei, which is situated 30 *li* further to the south. In the eastern part of San-tao-chiao there is found the

Belgian mission station, surrounded by a wall 3 metres high, with, at the gate, watch-tower, loop-holes, and a trench—just like a fortress. In the four-year-old station our people were hospitably received and accommodated by Father Hilaire Rodts. He had not returned from Ning-hsia till three days ago, whither he had proceeded on account of the unsafety of the neighbourhood around. As he told them, San-tao-chiao had had much to suffer through robbers and requisitioning soldiers. From the eight-metre-high tower at the gate, one had a vast outlook in all directions, particularly towards the Lang-shan and other mountains in the north. In the east-north-east the little town of Shan-pa-tang was to be seen, which has 7,000 inhabitants, a garrison, and a Belgian station. In this part of China there are thirteen Belgian mission stations.

To the present bed of the Hwang Ho it is 90 *li*.

Father Rodts told them that the earthquake which on the 23rd of May of this year had visited Liang-chou, Ku-lang-chên, and other places in the province of Kansu, had taken toll of between thirty and fifty thousand human lives.

The commandant of the place was a courteous officer, who paid his visit to the strangers, and accompanied them to the ferry when on the 24th of August they set out on their return journey. The first day's march coincided with the last stretch of the outward journey; then they kept farther to the west and went past the monastery of Nar-sumo. They travelled along at the foot of the mountain range, and told how the old bed of the Hwang Ho can only just be made out indistinctly. After they had wheeled round a projecting headland, they climbed up-hill in a north-westerly direction in a narrow valley with a brook.

In this valley, which is called Budung-mao-to and is full of sand-dunes, they rode the next day to the north. At one place it is obstructed by a dune 40 metres high, in part overgrown, and they required more than forty minutes to get over this obstruction with the camels. The last part of the way again coincided with the outward journey. People that were settled in the valley they did not see, but they met some rather small caravans with altogether a hundred and forty camels, which were loaded with sheep's wool.

The Major's camels were tired after their forced march to the bend of the Hwang Ho and needed a few days' relaxation and pasture. I therefore stayed another two days near Shande-miao. Hempel's and Zimmermann's tent resembled a drawing-office; their packing-cases, which served as tables, were covered with maps, diaries, drawing-compasses, magnetic compasses, and rulers, and they themselves worked day and night. I wished to see their report before we left the monastery. It was, indeed, ready in time, and brought out the fact that San-tao-chiao lay 57·9 kilometres in a direction south 56 degrees east from our Camp XXI. It surprised me that the old bed of the Yellow River was so near to us, and that it ran along at the immediate foot of the mountain range. The river now flows at a considerable distance from the Khara-narin-ula. The shifting of its bed has thus taken place in the direction of north to south. One must wonder, therefore, that the water of the irrigation canals can flow at all from the south-south-west to the north-north-east.

XI

ON THE CAMELS' ROAD OF AFFLICTION

ON the 29th of August we were at last able to start out. Our road went uphill in the furrow in which we had camped, and led us for the whole of the day almost exactly to the south. We had to make in this direction a detour of several days' duration, in order to avoid the waterless sandy desert that stretches westward from Shande-miao. Before us rose the Khara-narin-ula with its low dark ridges. The dunes, between which the caravan moved along, were sometimes held together by vegetation, sometimes bare and, in this case, built up in the form of shields and crescents, pyramids, and backs of dolphins. The landscape strongly recalls the transition belts between steppe and desert in Eastern Turkestan. Between two high dunes we finally caught sight of the lake of Hoburin-nor in a flat depression. Here we put up our tents. Properly speaking there were two small ponds, one with fresh water, the other with water containing soda. The depression was surrounded on all sides by quite high and almost completely barren sand-dunes. Two of them, which Zimmermann measured, were 12·5 and 18 metres in height. This landscape was quite a new sight to most of the principals of the staff.

The next day we steered straight in among the sand-dunes. But it was only a narrow belt, and the scenery changed all of a sudden, for the sand stopped and level ground with hillocks in the steppe began again. To our right we could see the high sand, against whose yellow wandering hills the green of the sparse growth of plants contrasted bright and powerful. If we had chosen the straight road across the waterless sand, we could only have used fast camels that carried light loads and were

The dwelling of a lama

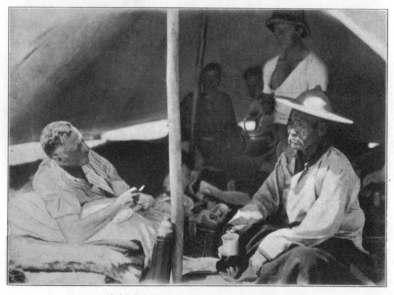

A high lama on a visit to Sven Hedin

SHANDE-MIAO

[*face p.* 148

A small temple : view of the interior

SHANDE-MIAO

[face p. 149

willing to cover their 100 *li* a day. That is impossible with a caravan.

When we again moved towards the west on the last day of August, we had on our left a sharply-bounded field of sand, while the belt of sand on our right became narrower and narrower and at last ceased altogether.

The Song of the Volga Boatmen resounded in my ears. Yet with us it was the camels that had to slave with their heavy loads on their backs. Kilometre after kilometre we made our way deeper and deeper into the great continent.

In cool, glorious weather our camels on the 1st of September were pushing forward towards the west. The high sand in the south, lit up by the sun, offered a splendid picture. We went along on the banks of two small lakes that were almost dried up, the " lakes of the white grass," Tsaghan-derisun-nor, and met a Mongolian caravan bringing corn from Wang-yeh-fu. The men were as happy as sand-boys, for they were on their way home, and joked gaily with Mento. Near Bayin-motto, the " abundant trees," an enterprising trader had built a mud hut, where now a large Chinese merchant caravan was resting on its long road to Gu-chan-tzŭ (Guchen). Here grew a hundred scattered wild elms.

Then the monastery of Tukhomin-sumo with its white houses and temples rose up. At the foot of the hill on which it is situated, we set up our camp. The monastery is small, but neat and in a good state of preservation. There is also a toll-station here, which demands a tax of 28 cents for each camel. To ask this tax of us was not even considered. As we learnt, in the previous year round about twelve thousand camels had passed through; but during this year in consequence of civil war and brigandage the traffic had greatly decreased. The caravans going to the west carry with them woven materials, tea, and provisions, whilst those travelling eastward carry wool, skins, furs, carpets, and raisins and other dried fruits.

The following day we rode along between hills and reached an extremely flat undulation of the ground, which nevertheless offered us from its crest an imposing distant prospect. The landscape was constantly changing. The *saksauls*, among which we came finally, were splendid and dark green. After our caravan had almost lost itself in this forest of *saksauls*, we spent the night near the spring of Shene-ussu, " the new water."

Larson was still moving on in front with the provision caravan, and it was questionable whether we should over-take him again this side of Gashun-nor and Etsin-gol. His camping-places were always easy to recognize. Such was the case near Tsagan-derisu, where we camped on the 3rd of September after a gloomy day. At 4 o'clock, when it was still dark, we were awakened, and before 6 o'clock the caravan set out again. Then I got up and ate my breakfast as the sun rose, while Hempel and Liu measured off the base-line by which I test the length of my riding-camel's step every day in the various tracts of country. At the same time Mento took down my tent, packed my things, and then in the customary way arranged my " crow's-nest " between the humps of my ambling camel.

We had not yet gone far in the furrowed territory when we met a picturesque caravan of fifteen Chinese, men, women, and children, with a dozen camels on the road from Cheng-fan, where they had intended to seek pos-sibilities of living. They had, however, found occupied all ground and land capable of being cultivated, and were now returning with bag and baggage to their old dwelling-places on the northern bend of the Hwang Ho. A small boy went at the head of the procession. Ragged, dirty, poor, with little children in their arms, the women sat on their bundles and bales, while the men went on foot. Three copper bells were ringing as for a funeral.

The surface of the moon can scarcely be more desolate than the land we are now crossing—barren, parched, only rarely a stunted hillock of vegetation. The spring near which our Camp XXIX rises has a fair amount of water, but the pasturage is very thin. Here all the pack-saddles are taken off, and the camels, which show signs of rubbing sore, are treated with ointment. One of them is sickly, goes without a load, and is fed on flour and butter.

On the 5th of September the weather is clear and calm,

but at first cool, the landscape flat and desolate, and our march monotonous. We look up in astonishment when a Mongol on an ass comes to meet us. Aha, it is Sonning Gibsh of course. He stops, dismounts, greets us in a cheerful and friendly manner, and hands me a letter from Larson. Our caravan-bashi informs me that he is leaving behind eleven thin camels without loads, which must rest and pasture and can then be brought along by Norin. Apart from that, all is well in his section, and all are hale and hearty. Here in this region Sonning Gibsh had stayed behind with six camels. One of them had died in the meantime, and another was sickly. The other five were grazing a little further to the west in the care of a Chinaman.

Our camp near Argalin-ussu was situated in the neighbourhood of a Chinese settlement, which consisted of a mud hut, a yourt, and a court-yard enclosed by dry bushes of the steppe. We visited the owner, who dwelt here with seven other men. He was cheerful and contented. In an outer room the stock of flour was piled up, and from a bar fixed to the ceiling hung two sides of mutton. The living-room had a *kang*, which is heated in winter and where now a tea-pot was simmering over a small fire. Here we settled down. One wall was decorated with four landscape pictures. In another picture we admired a horse, painted in Chinese ink, which turned its head at a really breakneck angle and coquettishly raised two legs high in the air. The text informed us that it was "a horse of noble and beautiful form." The decoration of the room showed that even a simple uneducated Chinaman has a certain yearning after beauty and comfort.

When Hsü asked his compatriot if he did not find the life year by year in this desert solitude hard and wretched, the latter replied, smiling philosophically : " But it seems one must do something to support oneself." To Wang-yeh-fu, which is quite simply called Yamên, " the court house," he reckoned it seven days' journey, and to the frontier of Outer Mongolia four.

Late in the evening Sonning Gibsh came with four of Larson's tired camels. When we continued our march the next morning, he remained behind with Haslund and

Bato, the "squad leader" of the Mongols of my caravan. Haslund was given the order to try at any price to get rid of the nine camels that were left behind. They would otherwise only become a burden to us, and neither could Norin's column, perhaps tired already, be encumbered with them.

Our road led to-day between hills towards the north-west. The "Lady of the Camellias" had been called for service. She was in excellent health, but her horny feet were worn down, and she had to be spared. The new camel that I rode had a pleasant tread, but was headstrong and took it ill when it was not allowed to go with its companions.

In our camp near Ulan-tologoi, the "red head," Haslund and Bato again joined us, with four beautiful new camels, which they had exchanged, with a deposit of 28½ dollars, for four of our animals that were unfit for service. Five of Larson's invalids thus remained behind for the present in the care of Sonning Gibsh and one of our Chinese.

The spring by which we camped was surrounded by blood-red hills. The sun went down as in melting gold, and the edges of the light thin clouds shone in a wreath of light. When they had disappeared, the horizon flamed as if with the reflection of burning steppe. In this wonderful light the camels came to drink, red-like figures of terra-cotta. In the deepening twilight the brilliant colour became more and more subdued.

Not far from our camping-place near Ulan-tologoi (No. XXXI) we came across the tracks made by the wheels of three motor-cars—a quite unusual and surprising sight in these desert regions. As we learned later from Larson, he and his forward detachment had reached Ulan-tologoi at the same time as the cars. He even knew one of the drivers from Urga. For it was from there that they came, and were making for Ning-hsia, in order to fetch fifteen Russian instructors who had served in Fêng Yü-hsiang's army and were now to return home. Our party spent a pleasant evening with the Russians, who invited Lieberenz to travel a little way with them with his cinema-camera.

So Lieberenz went on a motor-car excursion of 50 *li* and had an opportunity of filming a motor-car that was stuck fast in the sand and had to be made free with spades.

On the 7th of September our road led through a pronounced valley, a drainage furrow between low steep hills. Here and there a stately wild elm was again to be seen. The road ran along exactly underneath one of them, and for an instant one could listen to the rustling of its top and enjoy the shadow of its thick canopy of leaves. That was gloriously refreshing, and, moreover, the play of the wind in the foliage sounded like a rushing waterfall, a greeting from a far land. But the moment was quickly over, and we went on in the burning heat of the sun.

The road left the valley, took a turning to the left into a side furrow, and climbed up to a pass. From the entrance to the pass a ravine, a real valley of death, led down to the plain. Here in one place lay the skeletons of ten camels.

Day by day we move towards the west, and we are always the centre of a boundless desert. There is almost no growth of vegetation, no water for the day, no living thing; on one single occasion only, a lizard darts past. We camp near the spring of Shara-holus, " the yellow reeds." It would not be easy to find this little hollow in the ground, if its position were not indicated by a heap of stones. This pyramid was crowned with the skull of a camel with stones in its gaping mouth. It looked hideous, ironical, full of hate, cruel. It was symbolical, a warning figure at the entrance to this realm where one abandons all hope. Human beings get through sure enough, but the camels are doomed to death.

To-day we had a maximum of 30·8 degrees, yesterday 25.3, and the day before 24.8. The minimum of the last nights was 5·5 and 9·5 degrees above zero. During the day, in consequence of the strong insolation, the heat is burning. One counts the hours till evening, which comes as a deliverer and a friend. How should we have fared if we had set out on the march two months earlier? Good powers, too, have assisted us here. In *everything* we have had unusually good luck.

The evening was wonderfully cool, but the moonlight

icy cold—the impression of death borne by the landscape is thereby strengthened still more. No sound broke the silence. One could hear the slow breathing of the camels and the beat of one's own heart.

On the following day the sky was thickly covered with clouds, and the south wind blew with unusual strength. We moved along a chain of low hills on our left and crossed a pass, whose spirits were put in a conciliatory mood by two *obos*. Then we again came among dunes, and the sand flew in our eyes. In winter with drifting snow this road must be hopeless. The heaps of stones that are erected here and there—whether it be for the benefit of travellers or of spirits—are very necessary. We ride past a dead camel. It was one from Larson's column. It had collapsed in the middle of the march and now lay there in the usual position of death, all four legs stretched out and its neck bent back so that the head touches the front hump. It appeared quite fresh and untouched; indeed, only one day had passed by since it had suffered its martyr's death. Yet three big vultures were keeping watch over it. My camel showed fright. It looked on the sacrifice with sadness. It was a friend, a fellow-traveller, one of its own. It had done its duty and could follow us no longer. When the vultures have finished their work, its skeleton will bleach in the sun.

On a black hill stand two *obos* again. From afar they look as big as tents. In the turbid air one is deceived regarding their proportions.

On the 10th of September, too, I again rode on ahead with Mento. The whole sky was covered with clouds, and we did not notice much of the usual heat of the day. We travelled through a narrow ravine between dark mountains covered with sand, and now and again came past an *obo* made out of dry wood in the form of a pile of arms. Here are to be found only dunes and small mountains, and tamarisks up to a height of 5 metres. We also had to cross a wall of dunes across the valley, on the other side of which my camel stumbled and almost stood on its head, but without throwing me off. The scenery is constantly changing—it is not as it is on the great steppes, where one can ride for days without the landscape changing to any extent worth mentioning. A gap in the mountain range to the right is filled up with mighty dunes. Many stretches are completely barren; others are enlivened by beautiful tamarisks. We leave the spring of Shara-holuste to the right and a little farther on a bed full of stagnant, brackish water.

On ground of a gravelly nature, the learned, industrious Huang went about seeking for remains of the older Stone Age, of which he had already found quite a number. He showed us in which direction we had to steer to reach Larson's camp, which lay in the neighbourhood. First of all we had, of course, to cross through a labyrinth of dunes and over troublesome sandy risings. In the hollows between them grew reeds, *holus*, often quite thickly.

The tent village of our vanguard now stood out clearly, one white and several blue tents, lying picturesquely in the yellow sand. When we had approached nearer, Larson and Haude hurried to meet us, cheering and waving their caps. They had been not a little surprised when they saw me appear between the dunes; for they had not expected us so soon. Led by them, I marched into the camp, where Walz, Lieberenz, Dettmann, Mühlenweg, von Kaull, and our servants, greeted us cheerfully.

At supper, which had just been served in Lieberenz's tent, there was no end to the questions asked; we had, indeed, not seen each other since the 22nd of August, and to-day was the 10th of September. Travelling the same road as we, Larson had had five rest-days between Shande-miao and Camp XXXV near Shara-holuste, on account of the tired camels; we had not even had one. He had reached this camp yesterday at 12 o'clock noon, and had intended to continue his journey in the evening. But by that time a Chinaman had dug a well, which gave such plentiful and good water that he remained here, particularly as the reeds in the neighbourhood offered excellent pasturage.

Altogether Larson had had to leave eleven camels behind, but had bought four new ones for 240 dollars. Fifteen camels were now to be withdrawn from the vanguard and slowly brought on afterwards by Matte. Their loads, however, they were to keep. Larson needed one more camel-driver, and since we had more than sufficient, we transferred to him an oldish Chinaman whom the Mongols called Obogon, "the old man." We had taken him into our service near Shande-miao. On the march he usually went on foot and led a string of pack-camels, and in the camp he acted as handy-man. He was always the first on his legs in the morning, by about 3 o'clock, and gathered fuel and made a fire in the kitchen. He did his work thoroughly, and no fault whatever had been found. In the monastery we had given him 18 dollars to buy a fur and other articles of clothing.

A number of other changes in addition were decided upon. Since leaving Shande-miao, Haude, Dettmann, and von Kaull, the "balloon party," had been attached to Larson's column. They had found, however, that it was impracticable for them to march with the vanguard, which made itself ready to march at half-past four in the morning, while the daily pilot balloon could not be let up till 7 o'clock, when it was bright. They therefore had to wait every morning a few hours after Larson's departure. For this reason they asked to be allowed to join my section again, which naturally was willingly granted them. Huang also joined us, since he wanted to undertake further researches near Camp XXXV. Thus Larson lost eight men here, and his caravan became lighter.

My riding-animal, too, was changed for another and taken over by Larson; I received in its place a large splendid camel that we had bought in Beli-miao. I rode it for a trial in the evening and found its manner of walking quite pleasant.

Not till 10 o'clock in the evening did my section's advance riders reach us, and a short time later my caravan marched into the camp. It was a splendid picture, how the great camels marched calm and majestic past my tent in the light of the full moon and threw long dark shadows on the sand. New tents quickly grew up beside our airy dwellings, and for one night the camp town again had its old ample dimensions.

As one could not fail to recognize, the caravan moved more easily when it did not march as an army division, where the various sections obstructed the road for each other. It was better, too, to have the heavy provisions-column in front of one, and the working group behind. Therefore we arrived at the decision that Larson should first go to Ohyrin-ussu next morning and then continue his journey, quite independent of us, across the sandy desert to Etsin-gol, the river that empties itself into Gashun-nor and Sokho-nor. I myself intended to rest for a day in Camp XXXV, to allow my camels to pasture and rest. We also intended to set up our wireless masts, in order to obtain a determination of the longitude, and Dr. Hummel thought of investigating the flora of the sand. We had marched for thirteen days without having a rest-day, and were all in need of rest and sleep.

XII

A THIEF-HUNT IN THE DESERT

WHEN Larson set out on his march at half-past five on the 11th of September, he wanted to take Obogon with him. One inquired after him and shouted for him, but he was not to be found. He is probably out in the country collecting fuel for the kitchen fire, one thought. The great caravan could not be delayed because of one man, but set out.

A short time later Mento noticed that my new riding-camel was missing. Haslund immediately counted the camels and ascertained that, besides, the best animal that we possessed had disappeared. Now one began to smell a rat and called the camp. No-one had seen Obogon or could give information concerning him. But Wang, the Chinese principals' servant, recounted that he had woke up at about 2 o'clock in the night with someone tinkering about with the provision boxes, which are always placed near the kitchen. He had shouted "Who's there?" from his tent, and Obogon had answered that it was he, who wanted to light a fire in the kitchen. Since this was nothing unusual, Wang, not suspecting anything wrong, had dropped off to sleep again.

The provision boxes were now investigated, and the cook Wu was able to say immediately that since yesterday evening one bag of rice, one bag of flour, and so much tea and sugar had been lost. Five dollars of his own had disappeared. Besides, there was also a riding-saddle missing. The thief had obviously loaded the stolen goods in the night between 2 and 3 o'clock on the two best camels of our caravan and had ridden off. He knew his way about well in the region, and had been several times to Etsin-gol. Not one of us knew the secret paths and the

158

conditions of the country. Obogon had no doubt imagined, that out of joy over the reunion we should stay up till late in the night chatting, and should thoroughly have our sleep out next morning. He probably believed, therefore, that he would get a secure start. He did not know that the previous evening he had been assigned to Larson's column.

Now Haslund took the pursuit in hand, since I was still asleep. With the Mongols Bato, Mento, Serat, and Matte, he set out with five riding-camels to look for the fugitive's trail. But all the other Mongols also rode with him. They raged like furious hunting-dogs that are being set on big game. They had indeed received their pay for looking after the camels, and bore the responsibility for them. If the camels were stolen it was to their discredit. The Mongols love the camel, and God be merciful to him who does it any harm! In Mongolia camel-thieves are reckoned the greatest scoundrels that one can ever imagine. A camel-thief who is caught is beaten to death or shot without mercy. When now on stepping out of my tent I learnt that the four best and most gallant of our Mongols had gone in search under the orders of Haslund, who was himself like a raging tiger, I was almost frightened with the thought that they would find and shoot down the rascal. At no price did I want the expedition to be stained with human blood. All the same, I was furious about this piece of villainy and felt that the sinner deserved an appropriate punishment.

Haslund was meanwhile on the way with his troop. It is not easy to find the trail of two camels in a place where over two hundred camels have walked about for a few days. After much seeking, they had, however, found it; it led to the south up into the high barren sand. It was windy and the footprints became indistinct. Serat and Matte continued the pursuit in the direction towards the south, but Haslund and the others, who had the suspicion that the rogue had gone off to our earlier camp, Otakhoi, in order from there to flee farther towards the east, decided to ride thither. Their way led therefore past our present camp, and at 9 o'clock I heard them leave again on reconnaissance. Late in the afternoon they returned with empty hands. They had been to our previous camp but had found not a trace of the thief and the camels.

In the afternoon light rain fell, and in the evening there presented itself to us one of the most glorious sights I have ever seen. It was quite dark, and in the south, west, and north floated thick masses of clouds. Between these there were flashes of lightning to and fro so close on each other, that it was impossible to count them, for there were many flashes in a second. They had the form of clefts, rents, and zigzag lines, and lit up in whole areas. It was as bright as in the middle of the day, blinding, exciting astonishment, confusing. The fire in the heavens reached right up to the zenith.

The next morning we had already furnished a special troop that was to pursue the thief—or had we even to deal with a whole band of robbers?—when all of a sudden Mento rushed up, out of breath, and shouted:

" They are coming."

" Who ? " I asked.

" Serat and Matte."

" Alone ? "

" No. They have the thief and the stolen camels with them."

We hurried out. All who were in the camp wanted to see the triumphal procession of the Mongols. I stood in solitary majesty at the entrance of my tent.

Between the dunes in the south came three men and four camels. Serat and Matte each led two camels, and between them walked the culprit with a rope round his neck, whose ends were held by the two Mongols. His hands were bound to his back ; he walked in a stooping posture and with dragging steps. It looked as if they were on the way to the place of execution or at least to the court.

They made straight for my tent. Here Obogon threw himself at my feet in the sand.

" You're a fine fellow," I said. He only shook his head and looked thoroughly miserable.

Sven Hedin on " Lady of the Camellias," engaged in mapping the route

Mongols looking for the road

IN THE SANDY DESERT

[*face p.* 160

The caravan on the march

IN THE SANDY DESERT

[face p. 161

" Take him to the kitchen department and keep a close watch on him."

He was tied to a heavy box. Since the Mongols had the suspicion that he would make off at the first suitable opportunity, two iron foot-chains that could only be opened with a key were put on him. He was now in safe custody.

When we went into the kitchen department for dinner, I paid a visit to the poor straying member of our caravan, who sat there huddled up in his new fur, and gave orders for his ropes and irons to be taken off during the day and for water and food to be given him. At his request he was also allowed a few cigarettes. And when one of the Mongols gave him a few blows on the back, I forbade any sort of ill-treatment.

Then I had a conversation with Professor Hsü, and handed over the whole affair to him. I assured him that after I had got the two camels back, the man did not interest me in the least, and, as far as I was concerned, I did not demand that he should be punished. But I did not want him to be set free on the road we had come, for then he could steal camels from Norin or Yüan. Hsü was of the opinion that law and justice ought to take their course, and it would not be right simply to let him go. That might be of unfavourable influence on the others. He must be delivered up to the court in Mamu on Etsin-gol, where he would certainly be sentenced to imprisonment. So we first of all decided to take the unfortunate Obogon with us to Etsin-gol. How it fares with him there we shall see in the course of time.

After Serat and Matte, who had been on their legs for more than thirty hours at a stretch, had thoroughly slept off their tiredness, they were called into my tent to give their account of what happened.

It was really absorbing to listen to them. The thief had several advantages on his side : four hours' start and the two best camels of the whole caravan, in addition to which he had known the region for a long time. Finally, the fresh wind helped him to obliterate his tracks. It was therefore difficult, and took up much time, to trace them. On their rather tired riding-camels the two Mongols had none too good a chance of overtaking the fugitive and diminishing the distance between him and them. It could be taken for granted that he would ride for as long a time and as quickly as the strength of the camels permitted, and that, after all traces had been blown away, he would rest in some ravine that was accessible with difficulty. He had, of course, to reckon with the fact that his action would soon be discovered, and he knew the Mongols well enough to know that his life was not worth very much if they overtook him.

Behind three high dunes the trail disappeared in the sand, and the scouts spread out in different directions to look for it. After a while Serat discovered it in a depression and called Matte to him, whereupon they followed it full 40 *li* to the east. It ran in terrible sand up hill and down dale, to right and to left, and one could clearly see that the thief had chosen his way with full intention. He had kept as much as possible on the slopes of the dunes that were most exposed to the wind and where the impressions of the camels' horny feet quickly disappeared. The pursuers soon recognized this trick, and organized their search accordingly.

The trail now turned away to the south and then to the east and ran straight up to a rocky mountain-top, which towered up out of the sand and was higher than the dunes. Here all impressions in the sand again disappeared. Matte searched in a westerly direction; Serat explored in a circle, and soon discovered that the thief had made a loop, to lead his pursuers astray. In two places he had dismounted and gone back on foot to obliterate the camels' footprints with his hands. The rediscovered trail went to the north-east, but soon disappeared afresh when the sand ended and hard gravelly soil began, which led to one of the low ridges of hill usual in this region.

After eager search in all directions, they found that the fugitive had made for a field of low dunes, where his road could then clearly be seen 15 *li* away. Suddenly the two pulled up their camels. In a hollow between two dunes they spied the thief; he sat resting on the ground, was partaking of the stolen bag of provisions, and was winding his foot-bandages anew. The two stolen camels were pasturing in the immediate neighbourhood. The distance was scarcely 1 kilometre, 1 *li* and a half. Serat rode straight on, and drove his camel on at the fastest pace. On the way he had to cross a depression that was bordered by a high dune, so that for a time he could not see the thief and his camels, and when he reached the rising and had a free view, the fugitive had already left his resting-place and had continued his flight. The Mongols were persuaded, however, that he had not seen them yet. He soon appeared again in front of them, as he rode with every possible strange cunning device. They tried to bring their riding-animals to a quicker pace, but the latter found no pleasure in running quickly in the sand which gave way under their steps, and screamed angrily —as is the way with camels. Thereby the thief was warned; he smelt a rat and quickened his pace. When a high dune hid him for a time, the Mongols faithfully followed the trail and did not venture to take any short cuts. They could not even see him from the crest of the dune. That they were near him was evident; but the country is crossed with dunes as well as with rocky mountain-tops and hills. They now went forward along two different paths, in the hope of being able to tackle him from two sides. In the depression in which the spring of Orta-buluk, " the long spring," is situated, Serat caught sight of him. He had crept into the high reeds to hide. Serat's camel had unfortunately become tired, and lay down just at the critical moment. When the rider wanted to get it on its legs again it screamed out, and the thief was warned for the second time. He immediately mounted and rode on. Serat sent a rifle-shot after him, but intentionally too high, for he was afraid otherwise of wounding the camel. The thief took no notice of it but rode straight on, and Serat left his tired riding-animal behind and tried to overtake him running.

From a rocky hill he sent three more shots after the fugitive. Matte had also dismounted, but when he reached Serat's camel he mounted it and also got it really on its feet and in a trot. He gained ground, and the thief considered it wisest to let go the second camel which he drew along after him tied to a rope—the camel that Larson had chosen as riding-animal for me. Thereby having become more free to move, he could ride faster, so that the Mongols already feared that he would get away from them. Serat therefore aimed at his head. The bullet must have whistled by close to his ear.

They were now at a distance of little more than 100 metres from the fugitive, and Matte shouted to him at the top of his voice : " If you don't stop this instant, you will be shot."

Then the rogue gave up the game as lost, dismounted, and waited for his pursuers. When these had reached him he gave Serat the nose-cord of the stolen camel and said sulkily : " Now you have the two camels again ; now you can let me go home."

Instead of this he got a taste of the camel-whip, where-upon he fell on his knees and begged for mercy. Serat wanted to shoot him, but Matte, who is a lama, held his comrade back. He thought the culprit ought to be led before me and receive his sentence from me ; they were, of course, my camels that he had stolen. Moreover, Matte confessed that they had both been like bloodthirsty tigers ; quite out of breath and tired, he had completely forgotten that he was a lama, and he too felt a desire to kill the prisoner. But then he had suggested : " We must first rest a while and recover our breath." They finally agreed to let the fellow live. Had the camels been their property, they would have shot him down like a dog. Matte, who believed that a whole band of robbers was also in the game, declared to me, that if just at this moment a head had appeared over a dune, they would have shot the culprit down, to be rid of at least *one* enemy.

Meanwhile, as luck would have it, it had reached 4 o'clock in the afternoon, and the place where they were lay about 50 kilometres to the south-east of our camp. After they had bound the malefactor, they took the stolen property out of his saddle-bag and settled down to eat some food and drink some water. The prisoner, who

164

was quite tightly tied up, asked and begged for water but did not get a drop.

At half-past four they started on the journey back, all on foot. The thief had ropes round his neck and hands. He kept on throwing himself on the ground and saying that he was finishing and wanted to die. But that had only been shamming, the Mongols asserted. He was a cunning rogue and hadn't thought of dying at all ; he only wanted to remain alive and steal camels from honest people. When Larson heard of it, he thought the Mongols ought to have left the thief lying in the sand—he would have gone there, indeed, by himself of his own free will. I was glad, however, that they had taken him with them ; for otherwise he would have tried the same trick with Norin's or Yüan's column.

When it got dark they still continued their march a good step farther, so that no-one could see where they camped—if they really had to do with a whole band. They dug for water in vain, and their own supply was at an end. The pasturage, on the other hand, was good, and the camels were allowed to graze freely in the neighbourhood. The prisoner lay on the ground, tightly bound. He declared the ropes cut into his wrists, and asked for his bonds to be loosened somewhat. Since Matte too interceded for him, Serat relented and bound the ropes somewhat looser.

Tiredness now gradually made its influence felt, and one after the other the Mongols fell asleep.

But the one that did not sleep was the thief. He made use of the opportunity, to gnaw with his teeth through the ropes binding his hands, and while his watchers slept crept away as softly as a cat in the dark night. By chance Serat woke up and saw that the prisoner's place was empty. He gave the alarm and immediately hurried on his track. Matte was wise enough to run straight to the depression, and, sure enough, there he came across the fugitive. Since the latter now saw himself caught for the second time and probably believed that he would now certainly be shot, he decided to risk a fight to the death, quickly threw off his fur, and attacked his opponent. Matte admitted later, that he had been frightened at that moment by the wild look of the man, who was determined on anything. He was barely able to call to Serat, when the old man attacked him. To Matte, too, it was clear that life was at stake. He summoned all his muscular strength and his nimbleness, and with his right fist gave the fellow a blow right in the middle of his face, before the latter had yet struck him. The thief fell back stunned, and it was now easy to overpower him.

When they returned to their camping-place, they discovered that the stolen saddle was missing. They asked the prisoner where he had put it, but he declared he knew nothing about it. Blows assisted his memory ; he confessed that he had put the saddle on the slope of a near hill. His plan was, to creep to the camels, take the best, saddle it behind the dune, and flee under cover of night.

It had meanwhile reached half-past three in the morning. The Mongols tied the old man now so tightly, that his hands swelled up blue. Since they noticed that during an unguarded moment he again tried to gnaw through his ropes, they bound his hands to his back and also tied his legs together in addition. Furthermore, they kept a watchful eye on him.

With the grey of morning they again started on their journey. The prisoner groaned and moaned, declaring he was near dying, but got a good beating. "In the night, when you tried to steal the camel and make off again, you weren't near dying, you rascal."

The two Mongols told quite frankly how furious they had been and how the old man's second attempt at flight had increased their rage still more. In one place the trail showed that he had ridden together with a rider on horse-back for a distance. He denied this and again had the camel-whip. On the march back Serat and Matte entertained their prisoner by describing for him the punishment that awaited him in the camp. They told him that the only favour that would be granted him was that he would be allowed to select the place where he would have to dig his own grave. It was therefore not to be wondered at, that the poor wretch appeared quite exhausted, when the Mongols solemnly marched into the camp leading him between them—like a captured lynx—by a rope round his neck.

The first thing that they did, after they had got him in safe custody near the kitchen, was to take out the provisions that he had stolen, and scatter them over the dunes in the strong wind. The bags they tore into shreds; a stolen spoon they broke into small pieces. No-one would eat or use the stolen goods.

When Serat and Matte had made their report, I thanked them for their services and made each of them a present of 50 dollars. Bato and Mento, who had also used all their efforts to secure the thief, each received 25 dollars.

XIII

BY THE " ISLAND OF FABLE " TO THE " BLACK TOWN "

ON the 12th of September, at midday, a whirling sand-storm rose up from the north-west, and the flying sand whizzed and swept along over the desert. The strength of the wind amounted to 19 second-metres. A yellowish-grey fog floated above the horizon, which could only be made out indistinct and hazy. I sat for a long time with Professor Hsü on the crest of a high dune, observing the travel of the small, thin waves over its surface.

The stolen camels and their pursuers were tired after their wild hunt of almost 200 *li*; Serat and Matte asked for a further rest-day in Camp XXXV, where we had such good pasturage.

In consequence of the delay to which we had been forced by the bold action of the thief, the distance between us and Larson's section increased more and more, and we had to resign ourselves to not overtaking him till we reached Etsin-gol. Haslund therefore took stock of our provisions, and found that we had too little of many articles of food, especially rice and macaroni. To remedy this deficiency, I sent Hempel and Zimmermann with the Mongol Lobsang after Larson. They were to have the required provisions handed over to them and remain and wait for us at the place where they had overtaken the vanguard.

Just as Haude was sending up his balloon in the sky the next morning, which disappeared at a height of 8,400 metres in a layer of mist, I set out with Mento on my new riding-camel towards the north-west, keeping at an acute angle with the jagged mountain chain. We crossed in all directions between dunes and scattered tamarisks, before we reached the crest of a small rising in the ground adorned with an *obo*. From this elevation we had a very wide view towards the north, where on the blue-fading horizon in the distance quite flat land-waves became visible, resembling the surf of the ocean. In the south stretched the sea of sand with its mighty yellow billows.

The spring of Ohyrin-ussu, "the cattle water," by which we camped was closed in on all sides by the desert. In the east two flat sand-covered elevations towered up. The pasturage for the camels was scanty, but the water was unusually good.

On the morning of the 15th of September Matte and a Chinaman, who stayed behind with Larson's fifteen tired camels and their loads, said good-bye to me. We too left a camel behind that showed signs of fatigue. Matte had orders to follow us with his troop at a slow pace, and in places with good pasturage to stay one or two days. Our order of marching is as usual. Haslund leaves with the main caravan before sunrise, in order to reach the next spring before the heat of the day becomes burdensome. I myself with Mento set out on our journey an hour later, and Haude comes as soon as his pilot balloon is lost to sight.

The landscape through which we march is, with all its cheerless solitude and poverty, one of the most magnificent that I know in Asia. It is full of defiance and pride. With its stiff features it contemptuously looks on us as passing vermin that have ventured upon its paralysing, fearful meanness. We regard its might and greatness and its gigantic proportions with respect. But we too are defiant: we are going to master this majestic desert and bring low its pride. We are enemies. The desert wants to annihilate our camels, and, in its insatiable hunger, line the caravan road with skulls and skeletons. The desert wants to take all water from us, but we crawl patiently from one water-hole to another. When in the evening or in the night one lies in one's tent listening to the silence of the darkness and the solitude, then one feels secure—one has everything with one that one needs— but in reality one is resting on uncertain ground. One is quite dependent on the camels, the " ships of the desert," which have carried us into the forbidden land and without which we could not get out again alive. On their health and their well-being depends everything. If they collapse we are lost—like people on board a ship that suffers shipwreck.

Over the 16th of September hung something of the mystical, of legend, of infinity, a feeling that did not belong to every day. We again went a step further into the enormous Gobi Desert and reached—a real oasis.

For a space of two hours we have made for two short, dark lines on the western horizon. They gradually become larger, and we soon see that they are two woods of thickly-leaved trees with high, mighty trunks. They lie quite close alongside each other, and the gap between them is a narrow avenue. We had not had such a view since we left Peking. I could scarcely believe my eyes. Trees, high, living trees, in this boundless desert! Was it an illusion or a dream? Or could it really be true? I could scarcely have been more astonished, if suddenly, cleaving the blue expanses of the sea of desert in the north, a monster of the sea had appeared before me.

The little wood on the left consisted of fifty, that on the right of about a hundred and fifty trees. On the western edge of the larger wood the tents were set up in the cool, refreshing shade. The camp was not arranged as it usually was. The tents lay in a circle, and in the middle there was a small open space between the trees. Here a fire was to be lit in the evening. My tent was set up beneath an enormous poplar, so that I could enjoy as long as possible the cool shade of its thickly-leaved top.

We felt as if we had landed on the island of fable of the Phœnix, and the shortness of the delightful period of rest made us enjoy the fleeting hours with all the greater comfort and impressed this day all the more strongly on our memory.

The little oasis, in which several springs give precious water, bears the name of Olon-toroi, " many poplars." I immediately recognized again my old friends from the forests on the Tarim and the Khotan-darya, the wild

Asiatic poplar with the round thickly-leaved top, *Populus diversifolia*, the " unequal-leaved poplar," obviously so called because its new annual growths bear narrow, lancet-shaped leaves, while the older branches have heart-shaped leaves with a toothed edge.

What strikes one immediately, is that both little forests have such sharp edges. They form, together, as it were, an island in the sea of the desert. Not a single tree crosses the border. It is as if drawn with fire. All the poplars are old. Not a single young tree is to be seen. There seems to be no hope of continuation of life for this splendid forest, for wandering camels would not leave a single new shoot alone. Most of the trees are at the height of their splendour and beauty. A few are advanced in years, and are only just keeping alive. A few trunks have lost their royal crowns, but bear fresh growths with lancet-shaped leaves where they have been broken off. A few are dead but still have their roots in the ground. The storm had torn out a few withered trunks ; they lay on the ground like fallen heroes. The highest living trees were 18 to 20 metres high. Between their trunks and under their thick crowns one walked as if through the cloisters and under the arches of a Gothic cathedral.

We had landed with the ships of the desert on our great journey on the shore of an atoll, where, in the shade of the palms, clear cold water awaited us. My first thought was, to remain here for several days and thoroughly enjoy this small earthly paradise. Between the poplars grew thick reeds, and on my round I regarded with pleasure the camels and their splendid appetites. With their pliant, fleshy lips they dispatch into their mouths one juicy tuft after another of fresh green reeds, tear off with ease the tough stalks, grind the mouthful a few times between their strong teeth, and swallow it down, in order to take a fresh mouthful, which in half a minute goes the same way, to be softened with mucus and gastric juice, worked up, and mixed, before the chewing of the cud begins in the night. One of the greatest pleasures that one has on a long, trying desert journey is to see the camels at pasture, especially at such a delightful spot as Olon-toroi.

The day drew to its close, and the sun went down in the western sea. On the open space between the tents a mighty pyre rose up, whose body consisted of three immense logs of the sawn-up trunk of a poplar; they formed a pyramid, whose interior was filled up with dry branches and twigs. When it became dark, we settled down in a circle round the pyre, whose wood was devoured with raging quickness and furious avidity by the flames.

It was already half-past one in the afternoon, when I again left the poplar wood on the 17th of September, in order to continue my journey towards the west, sometimes through tamarisks, sometimes across barren sandy plains, sometimes by a small open spring with brackish water, here and there even again past an island of luxuriant grass.

On my next day's march I had a guide for a change, an old gouty Mongol, who rode before us on his own camel and, for a reward of 6 dollars, had promised to show us the way to Etsin-gol.

In the north-north-west low mountains stand out in the distance. To the left the high sand rises up in yellow hills. We meet a Mongol, who is leading eight camels loaded with wool. Tamarisks grow on the sandy ground, and dead, withered trunks and branches of this tenacious shrub lie about everywhere, twisted and distorted as if with cramp; they resemble Chinese dragons.

A little group of poplars looks charming between high tamarisks on sandy soil bound together by their roots. September-flies and swarming midges bother us, and our camels are irritable and restless.

Near Shara-bulung lies a Mongolian *ael*, a tent village. A spring in the neighbourhood has been surrounded with a rectangular wall and thus formed into a bath. In another spring horses are standing to get cool, right up to their bellies in the water. At the spring of Such we set up our camp for the night.

On the 21st of September we had our Camp XLII in the neighbourhood of the spring of Shardyakh, " the yellow tamarisk." Here a caravan-dog, which had attached itself to us a short time before and had received the name

The malefactor is brought in . . .

. . . and sentenced

A CAMEL-THIEF

[*face p.* 172

Sand-storms sweep the tents from the ground

Laborious digging results in a few bowls of salt water

IN THE SANDY DESERT

[*face p.* 173

of Hoilok after a Mongolian hero, called forth a lively and amusing exchange of opinion. A pack-camel had run off during the march and had been caught again an hour later. Professor Hsü and Dr. Hummel were of the opinion that Hoilok had frightened the animal; they had heard from the collector Chuang that the dog had bitten it in the hind leg. Marschall, Haslund, and I, took Hoilok's part, and declared that a caravan-dog *never* bites a camel. We agreed to have the camel officially medically examined. When we came to the camels' camping-place, we found Hoilok lying right amongst them, as, according to the testimony of the Mongols, he was accustomed to doing every night, to protect them against dangers. The camel really had a wound in the ankle-joint of the left hind leg, and our opponents already believed the game won. But, unfortunately, the Mongols asserted that the animal already had this wound on Hutyertu-gol. To Professor Hsü it appeared quite natural that the dog, which was hungry, should want to have fresh meat. I threw out the suggestion, that it had perhaps been Chuang that had bitten the camel. On the following day Hoilok disappeared without a trace, and we who had defended him saw in this a proof that he had regarded us as ungrateful, and no longer wanted to have anything to do with people who accused him of cruelty towards the camels, while he always sought to guard and defend them.

On the 22nd of September we do not start out till the afternoon. Our way leads through high barren sand-dunes. As we pass along in the shade of an immense dune, on whose crest rides the sun, there is heard in the distance, deep-sounding and awe-inspiring, the ringing of bells. It approaches and becomes louder. A first string of twenty camels shows up in sharp outlines against the sun. They swing slowly to the right and throw endlessly long shadows on the sand. Quiet and dignified like a funeral procession the caravan marches by. On the first camel rides a well-dressed merchant. We exchange the customary greetings and questions: "*Ni tsung na-li lai? Ni wang na-li chü?*" "Where have you come from? Where are you going to?" The caravan numbers a hundred camels and thirty men. They come from Guchen. Some are sitting in screened litters and look out between the curtains. They greet us and put the same questions. The last string of the long procession has larger and smaller bells. It sounds indescribably beautiful and solemn, as the tones slowly die away behind us on the road to Kuei-hua-chêng. The sun is submerged and the shadows of the dunes disappear in the twilight.

Shortly afterwards we reach the spring of Shubung-buluk. The whole western horizon burns and glows with a magic light between the branches of the tamarisks. We collect fuel and light a great fire, in order to show our party the direction. They reach us in the darkness. A new chime approaches : a second section of the great caravan. But now it is so dark that their camels appear like phantoms in the pale light of the stars.

In the neighbourhood of our camp lay a small " lake," Shavugin-nor, approximately 20 square metres in area and 10 centimetres deep : a spring pool. Here on a dune a shepherd lama was sitting, who sold us a sheep and a goat.

Across the soft sand of dunes and between tamarisks, on the 23rd of September we rode on towards the west. The country kept like this throughout almost the whole of the day, until we went into camp near the spring of Sochein-yakh. Here too a caravan of a hundred camels from Guchen came past us. It is manifest that the caravan traffic of the autumn has begun and that most of the caravans come from Guchen, a town which for trade seems to be of greater importance than Urumchi.

We approach Borosonch—at last a name that is found in Stieler's atlas. The ground is in some places hard and flat, in others covered with small dunes, and finally we cross a belt of more difficult sand-dunes, where one rocks to and fro on one's camel when it climbs up the slope or slides down.

To the immediate west of our camp there rose up out of the plain a hill approximately 35 metres in height, which some of us climbed the following morning, in order to inspect the fort which crowned it, and which, according to Huang, dated from the Han period. Numerous pot-sherds, a few specimens of which we took away with us, and the remains of a fire-place were to be seen.

Between scattered trees, whose leaves showed signs of the yellow of autumn, the road now went to the west-north-west. We camped near the spring of Sokhoän-hutuk, whose water tasted bad and smelt of sulphuretted hydrogen. The day's march of the 26th of September led over a few very low pass risings. The country was almost completely barren ; we only crossed two narrow tracts with tamarisks.

Near the spring of Sharhully we separated. We had reached our camping-place to time and knew that not far away lay Khara-khoto, the thirteenth-century town that Koslov discovered in 1909. All were curious to see it, and in various groups all the principals of the staff walked or rode over to it. Last of all von Marschall and the students Liu and Tsui left, with the camels and the things that they required for the night camp. Only Haslund and I spent the night near Sharhully, where the Mongols and the greater part of the caravan camped. Early next morning we followed the tracks of the others.

At 7 o'clock a bitterly cold west wind was blowing. The country was monotonous. We rode across several narrow hard plateaux, which fell away steeply on both sides but only rose up a few metres above the rest of the ground. Each of them had one or two *obos*. At the foot of the first grew a splendid wood of poplars and tamarisks. On the plateaux the ground was barren and covered with fine rubble. We came past three old watch-towers, which stood in a line.

Now there opened the beautiful and, with all its deso-lation, impressive view over the south and west city-wall of Khara-khoto with its rows of projecting towers, and over the mosque before its south-west corner. Not far from the latter stood the tents of our party. Most of our people were roaming about in the city, making drawings, or taking photographs. I myself climbed up on the wall and made a few rapid sketches. The city-wall has kept almost undamaged. Only on the east side and the west side has it gates. It forms an irregular quadrilateral, whose sides were measured by the students. The south side was 425 metres long, the west 357, the north 445, and the east 405. In the interior were found remains of buildings and houses. On the outer as on the inner side of the city-wall sand-dunes had piled themselves up, reaching right up to the battlement, and inside the west gate a solitary dune rose up, just at the spot where, for six hundred years, strong winds have swept through the open gate.

To describe this city is a matter for archæologists. That has already been undertaken by Koslov, who has written a book on Khara-khoto, and by Aurel Stein, and, more superficially, by Langdon Warner. This city is without doubt the Etzina of Marco Polo, a name which we meet with again in the A-tsi-na of the Chinese and the Etsin-gol of the Mongols. To-day the place is known as Khara-khoto, "the Black Town," but is said to be also called Batu-Yanyün-khoto, "the city of the hero general." Professor Hsü has his own views concerning the part that Khara-khoto has played in the past, and bases his conclusions on the study of the historical works that he and Huang have with them. Perhaps I shall come back to this again later. My old town of Lou-lan is more than a thousand years older than Khara-khoto. Lou-lan had already been sleeping in the desert for a thousand years when Marco Polo visited Etzina.

I only spent two hours and a half in Khara-khoto, and my old friend Pyotr Kusmich Koslov need not fear that I have cast nets in his fishing preserves. Not even Huang had a desire to stay here; all were longing for untouched fields of work on Etsin-gol and its lakes.

When I continued my journey at 2 o'clock in the afternoon, the road went to the north-west and soon led between two enormous hills of vegetation, forming, as it were, a doorway into a real labyrinth of such hills, through whose lanes and ravines our path twisted. Living as well as dead tamarisks were to be found in abundance. Some of them were 6 to 7 metres in height, like real trees. The ground consisted in part of bright loam with wind-furrows, in part of hard rubble. Between two dunes, bound together by roots, grew a wood of young poplars. The hills of vegetation had the same form as the dome of the mosque near Khara-khoto and a height of up to 8 or 10 metres.

The country then became more open and the distances between the domes of vegetation greater; we left the last islands behind us and put out again into the open sea. The loamy soil was furrowed by the hollowing-out action of the wind—just as in the Lop Desert; but the furrows were here still quite flat.

Camp XLVIII lay in the middle of the desolate plain, which was flat and hard and covered with innumerable trunks of a dead forest. This too recalls the old Lop-nor and the desert surrounding Lou-lan. But there is one great difference. For, there, numerous dead trees still have their roots in the ground, while the dead forest to the west of Khara-khoto consists without exception of fallen and rootless trees. The whole surrounding plain resembles a battle-field after a bloody combat, on which the fallen are lying about in confusion. Presumably this forest was still in existence in the thirteenth century and died out later owing to lack of water.

Not far from the " Black Town " we came past a ruin, which had possibly been an advanced defence-work.

From the folds of the tent in which Hummel and Haslund lived, in the camp there crept out a yellow scorpion. It was the first of its kind that we had seen, and was added to our collections.

The three last pilot balloons of Dr. Haude's had risen to 12,900, 12,700, and 10,800 metres.

XIV

A PASTORAL CAMP

THE 28th of September was the great day on which we were to reach Etsin-gol, on which Larson had already been for five days. At 5 o'clock Haslund set out with the caravan on the march; at 7 o'clock I followed. The road went to the north-north-west, between high hemispherical hills of vegetation. To the left two *sovurgas* or *chortens* and the ruins of a house were to be seen, and to our right a little further on five *chortens*.

Finally in the north-west a cheerful picture appears: the forest of poplars on Etsin-gol. Soon we have reached it and are riding between and under shady poplars, half of whose foliage already bears the yellow colour of autumn. By the sides of a dried-up river-bed, where flocks of sheep are pasturing, the forest is thicker.

Now open water gleams between the trees. That is the river. No, only a small side branch, quite shallow and only about 20 metres across. Some time later we are on the main stream, and Bato comes to meet us to show us the ford. He rides on in front and we follow, first my guide, then Mento, and last of all I myself. Our camels hesitate somewhat in face of the great water, but Bato's riding-camel has already crossed the river twice and has no fear, but seems on the contrary to like the bath. Our desert camels, which have probably never yet seen so much water in their lives, follow their leader, cautiously groping with their forefeet and splashing into the river, whose water is as thick and yellow as pea-soup. The greatest depth is almost 1 metre and the width is 212 paces. The rate of flow is quite considerable.

On the other, the left or west bank, I am received by Larson, joyfully shouting hurray and waving his hat, who then leads us to our new fixed camp. We cross between unusually high hills of sand, which were bound together by tamarisks, cypress-like *sukhai*-bushes, and other plants, and we also have two barren dunes to cross. Before us rises the poplar forest ; it is already becoming yellow, but green still prevails. We ride to the south through a first wood of thickly-leaved trees and see before us an open plain forming the bank, at whose outermost edge by the river the Swedish flag flies from a pole 7 metres in height.

The whole scene was an idyll, the most charming camp that we had ever moved into, so rich to overflowing in everything that we could wish for and desire, that the memory of the island of fable of the Phœnix faded away behind us in the distance. There, there were only two hundred poplars and waving fields of reeds ; here, we had whole forests, grass and reeds as high as a man, and dry fire-wood from the withered tree-trunks that could last for years. And, above all, here we had something that the little oasis was quite lacking in, a great river that flowed past our tents.

I was moved with feelings of joy and thankfulness, scarcely to be expressed in words, when I surveyed this camp which now was to become my headquarters for a month. In front of us we had a glorious time of relaxa-tion and work, behind us the long road of more than 1,000 kilometres from Paotow through wildernesses and deserts. The first great stage of our journey of discovery had been covered, and we could draw breath for a while.

The first thing that I did was, accompanied by Larson, to look in at all the various tents of the Mongols and of the Chinese servants. We had scarcely finished our round, when Ming sounded the midday bell ; the principals of the staff turned their steps towards the club-tent ; it had been set up a little in front of the outskirts of the forest, and was bathed in sunlight. The heat in the interior was almost unbearable. Only five of our camp-stools had withstood the 1,000 kilometres, and a few table-tops had been sacrificed, so that only five of us enjoyed the hot-house atmosphere in the club-tent. The rest of us ate our meal standing, by a few packing-cases, which had been set up in the open beneath thickly-leaved poplars; here a refreshing coolness prevailed. Although the autumn was approaching, the reign of summer was not yet quite broken. If it seemed to us here at the end of September warmer than at the end of July on Hutyertu-gol, that was due, in no small degree, to the fact that we had descended to an elevation of only 900 metres.

In the afternoon most of us bathed in the river and swam in the strong current that swept along our shore close by headquarters. Marschall had climbed up on a mud-bank about 30 metres from the steep slope of the shore, and called his pet, the little antelope Dicky, to follow him. Without hesitating for an instant the animal, which had never yet seen a river or swum in water in its life, went out into the stream and swam over to its lord and master.

Long before we came to Etsin-gol, it seemed obvious to me that I must thoroughly investigate the lower course of the river, and the two lakes into which it empties itself. Over table I therefore commissioned Larson to build a boat; how, I did not care. He calmly replied that that was quite easy, especially if one hollowed out one or two trees into canoes. He already knew exactly what the vessel must look like, and guaranteed that it would carry me to the lakes. The ship-building was begun the following morning.

We also busied ourselves with several other schemes, and a whole series of smaller lines of inquiry were discussed. A fair amount of time, indeed, was at our disposal: Norin's and Yüan's columns could, under the most favourable circumstances, not join us till the middle of October. Probably they would be late, just as we were, and we could not continue our march towards the west, before we knew how it had fared with them. Not till after their arrival would it be possible for us to draw up the programme for the near future, for the various fields of work must be apportioned in a way satisfactory to all. Not till all the scholars were together again could we decide who was to remain throughout the winter at the meteorological station No. 1, and who was to go on with the main caravan. There thus remained nothing else for us but to wait, and the only thing that mattered was to employ the time as profitably as possible.

In this neighbourhood, Etsin-gol flows almost exactly to the north-east and is 140 metres broad. From the camp eleven mud-banks are visible in the bed of the river. The velocity of the current amounts to approximately 1 metre a second. Just below the camp there is a ford; in the channel of the stream itself the river is at most 1 metre in depth and elsewhere only 10 or 20 centimetres. In two places near our promenade along the shore one cannot touch bottom. Naturally all these figures were subject to great changes during the forty-one days that I spent in headquarters. A measurement of the volume of water, which Dr. Haude undertook, gave something over 20 cubic metres a second.

In headquarters we had sixteen tents, whose openings were all to the south-east. The camp has a length of 180 and a maximum breadth of 80 metres. My tent lies at a distance of 40 metres from the glistening river. On the outermost right wing the Mongols have their three tents, and quite near them are the resting-places of the camels. On the outermost left wing stand the two tents for Dr. Haude and Dettmann, and in their neighbourhood the shed for the meteorological observations, the mast for the measurement of the direction and strength of the wind, the sun-dial, and the gauge for the water level of the river. Here one has also constructed a bridge, in order to be able to determine easily the water level and the temperature of the river, as well as the velocity of the current. Near this little quarter of the town, which is known as " the harbour," there rises up one of the antennæ of our wireless receiving-station. " The harbour," as contrasted with the Mongols' quarter, lies free and open, not in the shade of thickly-leaved trees.

The second line of tents lies at the edge of the forest, the third in the forest itself. The crescent-shaped area between the forest and the river is open. Here three things attract our attention: the Swedish flag, which flutters over the wandering town from a high mast on the bank; the long lines of provision and instrument boxes; and the place for the great camp fires in the evening. This place lies not far from my tent. During the afternoon hours, when the cool of evening is approaching, one can observe how all the Mongols who have nothing else to do drag and carry whole tree-trunks to the place for the fire, and how Larson, who makes a hobby of the camp fires, cuts up the dry trunks into suitable lengths and builds them up into a rectangular pyre, which is lighted after supper.

The kitchen with all its boxes, stores, and pots and pans, lies in a poplar wood in the neighbourhood of the club-tent. Here, when he is present in order to buy sheep, cows, and oxen, from our neighbours, the Torgots, Larson can often be seen. Here almost every day one can also see a jolly old woman with fine features, who brings along a jug of cow's milk for the *noiyen*, the " chieftain," y which I am meant.

That is Etsin-gol—one of the pleasantest and most glorious rivers of the earth. How bravely its winding stream battles with the dry desert of summer, how beautiful it is to camp on its bank, after the long march through suffocating sandy desolation ! If one is accustomed to having one's ration of water measured out, if, during the last days, one has only got water which smells of sulphur and contains soda, then one scarcely believes one's eyes, when one suddenly wades across a river whose water reaches right up to the bellies of the tall camels and is as cool and pure as that of a spring. It seemed to us as if we had come into an earthly paradise.

The last day of September began with a somewhat edifying scene. The culprit who had stolen our two best camels was to receive judgement. By the side of the flag in front of my tent stood Professor Hsü and I, and behind us in a semicircle the other principals. The accused was led forward by Mongols, and assumed an aspect of sub-mission and penitence, bending down and holding his cap with both hands. I spoke a few words, which Hsü interpreted.

" We took you into our service fully trusting in your honesty and expecting that you would fulfil your obliga-tions honourably. You have abused our trust, in that you appropriated to yourself two of our best camels, although you knew that we could not spare a single one of our animals. According to Chinese law your offence would take you to prison. It is, indeed, in our power to send you to Mamu and hand you over into the arm of justice. But we have decided to let mercy take the place of justice. You are to be given your freedom again and taken into a forest region 60 *li* away to the south by two Mongols. There you will be set free and can then go where you will. You will get provisions for the first days. Now make yourself ready to leave."

Hsü translated, and also added to it a few suitable admonitions of his own : the thief ought to give up the evil habit of stealing camels, and reflect that he had children to whom he ought to be an example. The malefactor then had to make a kotow, and rendered thanks for the lenient sentence. Then he was led away, and set free in the forest in the south. As the Mongols rode away, he shouted after them : " Look after your camels ; I shall come again." But that was only empty words ; for he knew quite well that in this case the Mongols would simply shoot him down—without any long proceedings.

A task which occupied Larson, von Marschall, Mühlen-weg and several Mongols for a rather considerable time was the arranging, examining, and estimating of all our stores. In spite of the fact that we had been two months on Hutyertu-gol and two months on the march, I could not for my part see that the long rows of provision-boxes, which formed complete walls on the edge of our fixed camp, had grown smaller. But I explained to Larson, that for the camels that were to go with us to Hami, I wanted if possible only half loads, and that we need only take there with us just as much provisions as was necessary for the journey itself. In inhabited country we could quite well live on the same food as the inhabitants—better than on the eternal preserves. On closer examination it turned out, however, that a part of the most necessary stores was beginning to run short, especially wheaten flour, rice, and sugar, and this deficit had to be made good in Mamu before our departure.

The whole of the provisions were unpacked and arranged on straw matting on the ground. Then one saw small mountains of boxes of peas on one mat, boxes of herrings on another, and sardines, corned beef, beans, cocoa, tea, and coffee, on the rest, as well as chocolate, milk, cream, marmalade, syrup, sugar, and then all those things which are not to eat, but yet are for pleasure or necessity, such as cigars, cigarettes, tobacco, stearin candles, petroleum in cylinders, matches, and other things besides.

So long as all these goods lay exposed under the open sky, night watch was kept in the camp. At the same time the boxes were made smaller by our carpenters, and then everything was stowed away afresh, booked, and numbered. Finally the new boxes were mounted with the old iron bands, and were ready again to be shipped across the desert sea.

Hand in hand with this work our stores were divided into different groups. Everything that was needed by Station 1 on Etsin-gol for the space of at least a year, was set aside for it, and the stores that would be consumed by the main caravan on its march to Hami formed a second heap. In a third were set apart the goods that were required for our rest in the fixed camp, reckoned at one month. The boxes of a fourth group contained our collections.

Meanwhile work went vigorously forward on my boat.

On the 30th of September I was asked to come to the "dockyard." Here stood our splendid Mongol Gombo, proud and dignified with an axe over his shoulder, and showed me the canoe that he had made, out of the hewn-out trunk of a newly-cut poplar. The rough, heavy dug-out was released from the stocks, and Mühlenweg took his place in it. But he had not yet gone a distance of 2 metres from the bank, when he overturned and swam to land. Thereupon von Kaull tried it with an out-rigger, but took a sudden bath too. The Mongols and Chinese who were watching the naval manœuvres and diving practice roared with laughter, and Mento could hardly stand with amusement.

"Are you really of the opinion that I shall plough the

View of the " Black Town "

KHARA-KHOTO

[face p. 184

A large *chorten* on the north-west corner of the wall

The breach in the wall made by Koslov

KHARA-KHOTO

[*face p.* 185

waves of Sokho-nor with this cockle-shell here ? " I asked
Larson timidly. " I am not at all entertaining ideas of
suicide."

" Patience, patience, dear Doctor ! " he replied. " We
are going to build a second cockle-shell as well and then
join them together with a common deck."

Thirty kilometres down-stream dwelt the chieftain and
prince of the Torgots, whose friendship and trust we had
to win—not least on account of the station and to get permission to pasture the camels that were to remain here
over the winter. During the very first days we therefore
sent off a courier to him, with orders to present him with
Hsü's and my visiting-card and say that I intended to pay
him my visit shortly. In answer he sent us his visiting-
cards and bid me welcome to his house.

Late in the afternoon I usually inspect the camels, and
after supper Larson lights the enormous pyre. Then, in
a semicircle on the side of the forest, covers are spread,
on which we sit or lie ; and when the Mongols' orchestra
—a flute, a stringed instrument, and a singer—produce
their soulful Asiatic melodies, we find our existence glorious.
The colder it became, the greater was the popularity
enjoyed by this camp fire. The space round the blazing
stack of wood became our club-house, where no-one was
absent who was not kept away on account of observations or the reception of the Nauen time-signals. Here
at the fire from now on I held my conferences with Professor Hsü and the other members of our wandering town,
and here the orders for the next day were given out.

Dr. Hummel and Haslund are zealously engaged in fit-
ting out their small caravan for Gashun-nor and Sokho-
nor. They will be the first of us to see the longed-for
lake on which we are thinking of setting up our first
meteorological station. The reason for their haste is that
Hummel wants to collect plants and insects before the first
night frost arrives. They are taking four camels with
them, which Serat leads, and two riding-horses hired from
the Torgots. Larson is unrelenting, if our camels are to
be used for excursions ; of the first-class animals that are
to travel the long road to Hami, he will not hand over one.

The troop for the excursion to the lakes only gets such as are to remain here over the winter; most of them are out of Andrews' detachment. They are excellent, but somewhat tired and thin, and are in need of rest and pasture.

Early in the afternoon the little caravan was ready to start out. Serat and the four pack-camels had already left when our young doctor and our Danish friend said good-bye. Glowing with youth, health, and *joie de vivre* —a sight to delight the heart—they swung on their lively little white Torgot ponies and disappeared in the forest, stirring up clouds of dust. To their saddles they had fastened their weapons, field-glasses, photographic apparatus, leather bags, and raincoats, and all this rattled in a warlike fashion.

The pyre of our evening camp fire was statelier than usual—in honour of Hindenburg, who to-day, the 2nd of October, was 80 years old, and by the light of the roaring flames I made a short speech.

The next day Larson was ready with his " ship." It consisted of two canoes that had been fixed together by means of two strong cross-bars. Over these he had placed a deck, made of boards which had remained over when the packing-cases had been made smaller. I went on board and invited Professor Hsü to take part in the trial voyage. The crew consisted of von Kaull and Gombo, who were bare-footed and were armed with poles. They pushed off, and we were seized by the current. After a while we ran aground on a hidden sand-bank, but our crew jumped into the water and got us afloat again. The river is only deep on the left bank, where the current flows. A little below the camp the deep channel runs over to the right bank.

Suddenly we ran aground for the second time, now in the middle of the bed of the river. Some Mongols who had followed us on the bank waded out to us, in order to join the vessel. Mento went to the bow, where I sat. By our shore he got into such deep water that he could not touch bottom, and since, the same as the other Mongols, he could not swim, he clung firmly to the stem of one of the canoes and dragged down the much too heavily loaded vessel, so that the water streamed into the canoes. But at the last moment the passengers could jump on land, after they had had a slight foot-bath.

After that, von Kaull and I made a trial voyage alone, with a rudder; then it went better. But the result was that this ship was thrown about. It was too heavy for such a shallow river, and dangerous on an open lake, where, in the event of a storm, the waves would quickly fill the canoes. Quite a different type of ship had to be found, something in the nature of the English collapsible boats that I had employed in Tibet. The problem was ardently discussed. Von Kaull was an expert and soon placed before us the drawings of a boat made of wooden ribs covered over with tent canvas or with the thick cloth of the awning of our club-tent. But, when we made the test, both let the water through, and we thought of employing sheepskins in their place. Meanwhile Larson's ferry-boat was drawn on land near the dockyard, in order thoroughly to dry. To the fixed station it might, indeed, still become useful. So the whole question was left high and dry for a time.

On the 4th of October the archæologist Huang started on an expedition, reckoned to last twenty-five days, to Gashun-nor and into the region to the south-west of this lake, where, according to the annals of the earlier Han, the old town of Kü-yüan is said to lie. He took with him five camels and the necessary servants and stores.

At the same time I sent the Mongol Saran Görel to Borosonch to look for Matte Lama, who had been left behind at Camp XXXVI with the sixteen camels that needed rest, and to show him the way. He also found the missing one; he had saved the camels and their loads; only two had died on the way.

On the 5th of October Hempel and Zimmermann set out on a little excursion along the river to the north-east. We had heard speak of a mud house on the left bank, which had been built originally by a Chinese merchant and was now in the possession of the prince of the Torgots. It might, perhaps, be suitable as a store-house for Station 1, which in this case would have to be moved there. I had also suggested to Professor Hsü that we should leave our collections in camp at the station, until the camels that were left behind here could convey them to Kuei-hua-chêng—instead of now sacrificing camels that we needed for the road to Hami. Hsü approved of my suggestion in every respect, and the collections were to remain behind in the care of the director of the station. The mud house was not suitable, however, and a new excursion to the lakes became necessary, in order to find out if there was a better place there for the station than the one we had chosen for the purpose by Camp XLIX.

In the evening I visited the Chinese students in their large tent. All four were at home working. They are industrious and eager to learn, happy and friendly. Li and Liu are quite excellent. Ma has only a single great disappointment; for he has been chosen to remain at the station. It is just the same with the Europeans : all would like to accompany the others on the journey right to the end; no-one wants to miss the experiences and adventures which await us. If the desires of the staff were fulfilled, then we should only get one station, the last, on the Khotan-darya. But Ma is a reasonable young man and reconciles himself to his fate.

After the experiences that Dr. Haude has had up to now, he regrets very much that we gave up our original intention of setting up a meteorological station in Paotow. From the scientific as from the purely practical point of view, it would be very desirable. We have therefore decided, in agreement with Professor Hsü, to take up our plan again, and have entrusted the student Tsui with the important task of erecting a station in Paotow. He is therefore to return from here to Peking, get into communication with our committee and with the central observatory, and on the 1st of March proceed to Paotow in order to begin his meteorological observations there. When I now informed him of this, he took the news with the greatest calm. For company on the journey he has the laundry-boy and a cook, whom we can well spare, and two Mongols that we are dismissing as idlers.

Meanwhile autumn was advancing; the forest became

more and more yellow, and the leaves began to fall. In the night before the 7th of October the first frost began with 1 degree below zero at a height of 1·6 metres above the ground. At the same time, we had had, the day before, a maximum of 20·9 degrees. At 7 o'clock in the morning on the 7th of October the water of the river had a temperature of 7·6 degrees. In the morning the water in the wash-basin was covered with a thin layer of ice, and one noticed that something of the coldness of the night still remained in the ground and in the air. The brazier of live coals was therefore quite welcome.

XV

A CHINESE FESTIVAL AND A GERMAN COURIER

TIME elapsed, and one beautiful day we learnt, that on the 10th of October 16 years had gone by since the inauguration of the Republic in China and that the Chinese principals of our expedition wanted to celebrate this day of commemoration with a feast, to which the Europeans and Mongols were ceremoniously invited. During the last week before the great day one could well have suspected that something was in the wind. The Chinese students and the Mongols had suddenly begun to practise foot-racing and athletic feats of skill. The students had borrowed colours and brushes from Dettmann, and had asked von Kaull and Zimmermann to help them with certain preparations. Larson had explained to the Mongols that the camp fire on the evening of the 10th of October must be the biggest fire in the history of the world, and its light ought to be seen, perhaps, as far as Peking, which was, indeed, only a paltry 1,500 kilometres away. But for all that, I could never have suspected that it would be such a magnificent festival.

In the night before the 10th of October the temperature went down to 8·3 degrees below zero, and even at 12 o'clock we did not have a higher temperature than 4·9 degrees above zero. At 3 o'clock the river had a temperature of 10·5 degrees, and at 9 o'clock in the evening 5·5 degrees with an air temperature of zero. These figures had a certain significance for those who were taking part in the contests.

The festival began at 10 o'clock in the morning. When I arrived at the place for the festival, all the Europeans and Chinese and all our servants, as many as were in the camp, had assembled in front of the little recess-like arbour which had been arranged between some poplars. In the middle stood a platform, two boxes placed one on top of the other, on which a white cloth had been spread; it was decorated with green sprigs and many-coloured bunches of flowers. Before the entrance to the " banqueting-hall " there hung from a horizontal cord the symbol of the Chinese Republic, a white sun with rays on a blue field. To the right of it a Swedish flag, painted on paper, waved in splendour, and on the left a German flag. At the sides a number of sheets of paper with noteworthy mottoes hung from cords. There, among others, one could read: Forward! Progress day by day.—Liberty, Equality, and Fraternity.—Who has a strong will, always succeeds.—Mutual help.—*Ta-tung* [common weal].—In former days one said, " Knowledge is easy but understanding is difficult " ; but Sun Yat Sen says, " Understanding is not difficult, but knowledge is difficult."

Professor Hsü now stepped forward, declared the festival open, and saluted the three flags. Then followed a two minutes' silence, during which all stood there with bowed and uncovered heads, a sign of reflection on the meaning of the day.

The next number on the festival programme was the singing of the national hymn. This is an innovation introduced after the inauguration of the Republic. In the days of the Tang dynasty there was something that corresponded to the national hymns of later times, but the song really only consisted of a glorification of the great emperor Tang Tai-Tsung, and when it was sung in his presence, even His Majesty had to rise. The present Chinese hymn of the people is peculiar. It does not contain a single word of politics, nationalism, patriotism, or actuality. Its words date from antiquity and are said to be four thousand years old. In all its astounding simplicity it reads : " The clouds are very beautiful ; they are white like cotton. The brightness of the sun and moon continues from day to day." That is all, and this song was now sung on the bank of Etsin-gol.

After a Chinese cheer for the Chinese Republic, Pro-

fessor Hsü mounted the platform and made a speech in
Chinese addressed to his countrymen, which he then
translated into French for us foreigners. I have noted
down its main points :

" Europe believes that it is not going so well with the
Chinese Republic as with the old empire. Even if this is true
at the moment, still it is only appearance and the fault of the
warring generals. But this state of affairs will pass. The
development of China is marching forward to better times,
without civil war, to a united, harmonious, and peaceful
China.

In the 7th century before Christ civilization, not the art
of war, stood high in honour in China. But in the days of
Confucius, a century later, the times had changed. Then the
semi-barbarians invaded China, and China had to defend itself.
There was at that time a small state, Lü, which was not strong
but, when on all sides it was attacked by the barbarians,
defended itself with extreme determination. Confucius himself belonged to Lü, so with his new doctrine he proclaimed
among his countrymen the new spirit of love for the fatherland and defence of one's native soil. Without Confucius
Lü would have been destroyed ; now his new doctrine and
the new culture spread over the whole of China. The
Chin dynasty conquered China with force ; Lü conquered
China by means of its culture and its spirit. Its work was
a peaceful penetration. From Lü originates the Confucian
tradition, to which from that time the Chinese have always
remained faithful ; its aim is to develop Chinese culture as
highly as possible and to use it as a weapon and defence against
foreign enemies.

At the present time the South—Kuo-min-tang or Canton
—is following the principles of the old tradition and wants
to use Chinese culture as a weapon against its foreign enemies,
that is against the foreign powers that treat China almost as
a colony.

We still have much work to do ; we are in many respects
backward. We need all the help we can get, not least from
Sweden and Germany. With the assistance of these excellent
guides we shall make great progress in the civilizing of China,
which will be to the advantage of the whole of humanity.
On that account the Republic is certain to do much for the
world."

In concluding Professor Hsü turned to me personally and said friendly and courteous words of thanks for the time that we had spent together up to now. He thanked all the Europeans for their good comradeship and, in particular, those to whom we owed to-day's festival.

To my surprise I found that the next item on the programme simply read : Dr. Sven Hedin's Speech. Well, I thought, I have been in worse predicaments before, and stepped towards the platform. I expressed my delight with the splendid festival, expressed the sincere good wishes and the warm sympathies and hopes which we, and with us the people whose representatives we are, cherish for the well-being and prosperity of the great Chinese people, and concluded with a fourfold cheer for the Republic of China.

Then, in the name of the guests, Zimmermann, who shortly before had been chosen as director of the station on Etsin-gol, made a really brilliant speech—in French, partly even in verse. After him, Liu spoke to his young countrymen, full of zeal, enthusiastic, republican.

Number 7 on the festival programme bore the heading : " Music and Recitations," and had a whole series of subdivisions.

The poems that were recited and read out, in many cases dated from earlier times. Thus, for example, a strophe of the Tungus (Hsien-pi) Hou Lü-chin, a great general of a Tungus dynasty in northern China living in the 7th century A.D., who could neither read nor write Chinese, but nevertheless gave expression to his poetic feelings :

" The river Chi-lei flows at the foot of the Yin-shan. The sky is like a tent, covering all the four quarters. The sky is grey, the steppe without end. The wind bends the grass, and one can see the pasturing oxen and sheep."

Another song that we now heard deals with Su-wu, who was sent by the emperor Wu Ti of the earlier Han dynasty as emissary to the Huns (Hsiung-nu). The latter tried to persuade him to go over to them. When he refused and remained faithful to the banner of the emperor, he was banished by the Huns to the coast, where for 19 years he tended sheep. At last set free, he was allowed to return to China. Even at the present day, after more than 2,000 years, the following song is sung in honour of the faithful Su-wu :

" Su-wu stays with the Huns and will not be humbled. The ground on which he has spent 19 sad years consists of snow and ice. If he is thirsty he drinks blood ; if he is hungry he eats the wool of sheep. He tends sheep along the coast of the northern sea. He can never forget the territory of the Hans. After the (imperial) emblem had been destroyed, he could not return. He has battled against all kinds of difficulties. His heart is as hard as iron and stone. At night, when he sits awake and listens to the sound of the flutes of the Huns, he suffers pain. Suddenly the north wind rises, and flocks of wild birds return to China. His white-haired mother hopes that her son will return. His beautiful wife sits lonely behind the curtain. In the middle of the night they all three dream of each other. Until the sea dries up and the mountains crumble to dust he will not be humbled. But perhaps the hearts of the Huns are growing faint, and perhaps they will bend under the power of the Hans."

It was, however, not only very ancient classical poetry that our Chinese hosts recited to us. Quite modern songs of freedom, more or less communistic, also resounded among the trees on Etsin-gol.

The literary and musical part of the Feast of the Republic took place on the level surface in front of the tents. Here were spread the covers of the pack-saddles in the form of a square whose sides measured 12 metres, and here there was singing, playing, and reciting, almost without end.

The majority of the participants in the festival, not least the Mongols and Torgots, certainly found greater pleasure in the second half of the programme, however, than in the first. For now they at least understood what it was about, and could enjoy themselves to their hearts' content.

By the side of the track on which our Olympic games were to take place, a stand for spectators had been erected.

It consisted of a line of boxes on which camel-covers had been spread.

It was really only Hsü, Larson, and I who sat here, for almost all the others took part in the contests. Walz, who is a great sportsman, was unfortunately ill and was feverish, but nevertheless wanted to participate. I begged and implored him to take care of himself, but he would not be held back. Lieberenz followed the games with his large cinema-camera, as alert as a setter, and took a fine series of splendid pictures on his strips of film. Hsü, Larson, Zimmermann, and Hempel were umpires. I myself am not a sportsman, and am therefore not in a position to describe in accordance with all the rules of the art the course of the wild contests which on the 10th of October were fought out in front of our peaceful tents.

Shortly before sunset there was an interval, during which the Chinese festive meal took place. It was not only a great success and appetizing, but in addition had also the advantage that no speeches had to be made. Speeches in honour of the Republic had, indeed, already been made for hours—now there was to be eating. The menu read : Wine. Meat-dumplings. Sardines. Stewed apples. Rice. Green pea-soup. Coffee, tea, and cake. Cigars and cigarettes. The " wine " that was provided was Mongolian produce and tasted very doubtful. We were in a very gay and lively mood, and the Chinese were excellent and courteous hosts.

After the meal the distribution of the prizes took place. It was rather complicated, since all the Europeans renounced their prizes in favour of those Mongols who had received none.

As the last item on the programme, there followed Larson's splendid contribution to the festival, a stack of whole tree-trunks piled up in the form of a square, 4 metres high and filled up with branches and logs as dry as tinder. When the darkness had descended on the open country on Etsin-gol, the pyre was lighted ; it was really a fire such as none of us had ever seen before—if one excepts outbreaks of fire in which whole houses burn.

By the light of its high-mounting flames the last contests of our Olympic games were decided. Six Germans and six Mongols measured their strength in a tug of war. The Mongols, who were accustomed to our heavy packing-cases, finally won. When the Germans were exacting revenge the rope broke, and all twelve fell on their backs and stretched their legs in the air—to the endless delight of the spectators.

Then musical recitals followed again—Chinese, Mongolian, and European music, gramophone and mandolin. Tea was served, there was chatting and joking in all possible languages, and as if on wings the hours sped by in gaiety, harmony, and sociability. Without flattery and without in the least exaggerating, I was able to assure Professor Hsü, in the name of the guests, that the Feast of the Republic had really gone off brilliantly and splendidly, that we were glad to have taken part in it, and that this cool autumn day and the sincere homage that the Chinese had offered to the new constitution of their fatherland we should not quickly forget.

After the great political festival, life on Etsin-gol returned again to its ordinary quiet lines. The autumn coolness continued—in the night 8 degrees below zero, at 10 o'clock in the morning 3·1 degrees above zero, and frost again as early as 6 o'clock in the afternoon.

It was now time that the " commissariat column " was started on the march to Mamu, in order to make up the stores before we set out on the long road to Hami. Mamu, the Moching of the Mongols, lies on the right bank of Etsin-gol, the distance away from us amounting to 223 kilometres. Baron von Marschall was entrusted with the leadership of the column, which, with the students Liu and Ma, a Chinese camel-driver, and seven camels, set out after dinner on the 13th of October. The little caravan took quite a list of different tasks with it. More important, almost, than everything else was the fetching of the post that Professor Hsü and the other Chinese expected from Peking. I too looked forward to these letters with a certain eager curiosity ; for the answer to my proposals to the Peking committee was to be expected.

Ski-ing

Prayer-wheel beside a Mongol yourt

PEACE AFTER THE STORM

[face p. 196

Unusual country : the camels fording the river

The camp is pitched on the edge of a wood

We reach Etsin-gol

[face p. 197

A number of letters which Hsü and I had written jointly and which were now to be entrusted to the post in Mamu were, for the future vicissitudes of the expedition, not less momentous. After mature consideration they had been written by Professor Hsü, who in the interests of security gave me a French translation.

The most important letter was addressed to the powerful governor of Sin-kiang in Urumchi, Yang Tsêng-hsin. After we had made, in introduction, a brief report of the scientific aims of our expedition and our journey to Etsingol, we informed him that we had the intention of shortly continuing our journey to Hami and Shan-shan (Pichang) and from there to Turfan and Tihua (Urumchi).

"In Hami we want to establish a station for the observation of meteorological phenomena. We know quite well that you always most energetically support science. We believe too that you will show goodwill towards our undertaking. We should look forward with especial gratitude to the information, that you were pleased to send orders to the authorities along our road, to be at our disposal in case of necessity. After our arrival in Tihua we will pay you our visit, in order to listen to your wise counsel. We wanted to send you this information in advance."

These brief statements contained nothing that was new to Governor Yang. Marshal Chang Tso-lin had already during the winter informed him by telegraph of my expedition, and had in addition given me a friendly signed letter to take to Yang; and our committee in Peking too had informed the authorities of the province of Sin-kiang of our coming and had asked them for their support. Our letter only had the object of informing the governor of the course of our journey and how it had gone with it up to now. He had certainly been expecting us a long time ago. How he would receive us, and how far the political situation in China, of which we had only heard uncertain rumours, would affect his attitude towards us, we naturally did not know in the least. But this uncertainty increased the fascination and suspense of our undertaking. Should we succeed, or would Yang, who has governed his province of Sin-kiang since 1911 with an iron hand, thank the Kuo-min-tang for a scientific invasion of Europeans and Chinese? On the road to Hami this suspense must increase still more; not till we reach the borders of Sin-kiang will all mysterious questions find their answer.

Chinese as well as Europeans make use of the opportunity to send off letters to their relatives at home; so the post became quite bulky. When everything was ready the little troop set out on the march. Upright and calm, Marschall marched out; he led his camel the first part of the way. Liu sat huddled up on his riding-animal and began immediately to draw the route of the march.

One fellow-citizen of our wandering town seemed to be ill-humoured and embarrassed, when von Marschall had disappeared out of our midst—the little antelope Dicky. It jumped about, and looked in vain for Marschall's tent and its owner, and at the camp fire in the evening it was unsettled and puzzled. Only with difficulty did we succeed in capturing it and locking it up in the store-room of the club-tent, where its sleeping-rugs had been taken. But, as the days went by and Marschall was away and remained away, it bore its fate with equanimity. All were persuaded that it could not easily forget its master and protector and friend.

In headquarters scientific work went forward in the usual way, as also practical preparations of every kind. When the weather was favourable, both during the day and in the night, Dettmann made an astronomical determination of the position. On the 12th of October, after a series of observations and after daily checking by means of the Nauen time-signals, he had determined the geographical position of Station 1 on Etsin-gol as 41°53′ 6″ latitude north and 101° 6′ 36″ longitude east of Greenwich. By means of new observations, he intended to get still nearer to the final values. In the meantime, he was painting water-colours.

Several excursion troops had set out in order to find the better position for Station 1 that we desired; but in the end we found that the best was the position which

Larson had chosen for the camp on the 23rd of September and where we still were. Dr. Haude and his European and Chinese co-workers were therefore able, about the middle of October, to begin to set up the observatory, where, during an interval of a year and a half, meteorological observations were to be carried out. A fence was put up on open country near the bank, and inside this there soon rose up the four high posts that were to support the box for the meteorological instruments.

Every day a pilot balloon was let up, and Dr. Haude was quite enthusiastic over the remarkable results that he had already obtained concerning the movements of the higher air currents in summer and autumn. The balloon of the 12th of October rose as high as 14,840 metres above the surface of the earth, that is more than 15,700 metres above sea level. This last-named value will attain a still greater precision, when the daily observations of five weeks are worked out, and we shall later get still nearer to the true absolute height, on the basis of the results of a year and a half.

During the days preceding the 15th of October, most of us, and I above all, had various anxieties. Our travelling-chest began to run short. We could still get to Hami comfortably, but there we needed money. I had had a considerable sum transferred to Urumchi for me, and now wanted to have a part of it in Hami, in order to be able, without inconvenience, to continue our journey from there to the capital of Sin-kiang.

I therefore had much to do during these days. I sat from morning till long past midnight at the writing-table in my tent, and wrote and wrote. Only when the great camp fire burnt before my tent in the evening did I tear myself away for an hour or two and take part in the social life of the other principals or listen to the music. Then I went on with my work, and every two hours Mento had to bring me a large brazier full of red-hot coals. All foreign letters had to be entrusted to the post in Urumchi, in order to reach Stockholm as quickly as possible, on a road which was considered safer than that by Mamu.

On the 8th of October I gave Walz instructions, on the

morning of the 15th of October, to set out for Urumchi as a courier, and he accepted this difficult task with unconcealed delight and gratitude.

Walz is a Bavarian. He is a distinguished sportsman and mountaineer, a picture of concentrated force and energy. He is one of those men who know no difficulties and love wild neck-breaking adventures. In a straight line the distance from Etsin-gol to Hami amounts to 650 kilometres and from Hami to Urumchi 550 kilometres. The courier was, however, again to return from Urumchi to Hami, thus covering a further 550 kilometres, or altogether 1,750 kilometres. But as a matter of fact the road bends, and the stretch covered amounts in consequence to 2,000 kilometres, if not more.

I was almost frightened to give such an unpleasant task to a member of my staff. The courier had to ride through regions which had recently been infested with robber bands, and had only two camel-drivers with him, the Mongol Särche and a congenial young Chinaman. I thus took a very heavy responsibility on myself, but Walz himself laughed about it and declared that he hoped with all his heart to meet with a band of robbers. Larson asserted coolly that in this case it would fare worst with the robbers, for Walz is a brave man and a certain shot. Lieberenz declared himself ready to pay 50 dollars for every robber, if only one could procure a genuine band for him to film. And besides—if one is afraid of everything that is hazardous or dangerous, then one had better not travel to Asia, but should, rather, remain comfortably at home by the well-stocked flesh-pots and at the green tables.

The two Asiatics too were delighted that they were allowed to go with him, and, the same as Walz, regarded the commission as an honour and a great sign of confidence. Walz could only take one tent with him, in which his two companions had also to sleep. Larson had the task of putting eight of our best camels at their disposal. Three of them were riding-camels; the rest carried provisions, winter clothing, sleeping-bags, tent and personal equipment, weapons, ammunition, cooking-utensils, and two small water-containers.

The route of the march that I had outlined led along the great caravan road by Barkul to Guchen. Here Walz was to leave the Mongol Särche and the eight camels behind, in order to continue his journey with the Chinese to Urumchi, either on horseback or in a cart. In the capital he was to pay a visit to Governor Yang, convey our personal greetings, and hand over a letter to him, which was really only a confirmation of the previous one that we had sent by post via Mamu. The letter concluded with the words :

"We are now sending you as special courier a member of our expedition, the German Herr Walz, who is to visit you and inquire after your health. Moreover, a long time ago we sent a sum of money to Tihua, a part of which we need in Hami. Our courier has therefore been given the task of drawing this amount and returning to Hami by Turfan and Pichang. We should be particularly grateful to you if you would give orders to the authorities along the road to afford him the protection that he perhaps needs."

After the visit to Yang, Walz was to draw the money and have handed over to him the letters, newspapers, and books, that had arrived for us. He could arrange the dispatch of these precious things at his discretion, as it seemed best to him, either under an escort, which he must request from the governor, or in a little ordinary horse-vehicle, for which he himself could act as armed guard.

With a daily performance of 30 to 40 kilometres, forty days must suffice for the journey to Urumchi. Walz must thus be at his destination on the 25th of November. Five days would suffice to discharge all his commissions in Urumchi, and in fifteen days he could again ride to Hami, which he must thus reach on the 15th of December, at approximately the same time as we, who were contemplating setting out on the 5th of November and on the 15th of December reaching Hami.

On the evening of the 14th of October all present in the camp had gathered round the fire, which was bigger than usual, in honour of Walz. The orchestra of the

Mongols played, and the noise of the fresh wind that swept along over the expanses of grass-land accompanied its melodious airs. Hummel and Haslund, who had just returned from their botanical excursion to Gashun-nor, put before us a curious and extremely rare liqueur which we have christened Hutyertu. When all our tin drinking-vessels and cups had been filled, I stepped to the fire and made Walz a splendid farewell speech, which I concluded with a fourfold Swedish cheer.

At 7 o'clock in the morning on the 15th of October we were all up and about. Fat and well fed, Walz's eight camels already stood there with their light loads, ready for marching. One of them, a white one, had been with us from the beginning; a few of the others were newly bought, and as yet had no long chafing marches behind them. All were in the best of form. I regarded them with the same feelings of awe that move one, when one is in the harbour to say good-bye to a ship that is about to sail out into the ocean. How many storms these ships of the desert would experience! Would they hold out, or would some of them remain by the side of the road? The black riding-camel that Walz is riding has carried him the whole of the way from Paotow right to where we are now.

Särche and the young Chinese were walking about examining the loads and smoking their cigarettes, as calmly as if it was only a one-day excursion.

Then one last hand-shake, and the little company disappeared between the trees near the tent town of the Mongols.

With them on the road to the west went a large part of my chronicle of the journey. But my letters, it was certain, could not be in Stockholm before the New Year. To reassure all those who were thinking of us at home, I also sent a telegram along with Walz, which must reach Stockholm at the end of November.

We then quite often talked of Walz and his lonely ride and tried to reckon just where he was. He was free to choose his road for himself. We had only imagined that he would take the straight, in part waterless, desert road to Barkul and so leave Hami at least 100 kilometres in the south, on the other side of the range of mountains.

In truth, I was not very concerned about Walz. A German officer who has received the *Pour le Mérite* for distinguished bravery in the field, is not afraid of a journey through the desert, not even one of 2,000 kilometres.

XVI

BY CANOE ON ETSIN-GOL

ON the 15th of October the expedition was scattered at six different points. In the main camp only fourteen of us remained out of twenty-four. But our number was to be reduced still further, for we were just about to equip two new small expeditions. After von Marschall and Walz had set out and had taken all my letters with them, I was free of the wearisome correspondence and could think of an excursion to the lakes. I had scarcely said good-bye to Walz, when I went to the " dockyard " and inspected Larson's wonderful boat, which had now lain long enough on land and was dry. With Haslund I made a new trial voyage. It took us a few *li* down-stream, and when we landed on the left bank after repeatedly being stranded, I could see the state of affairs quite clearly. " *That* boat cannot be used on Etsin-gol," I declared to Haslund : " it is too heavy and sinks too deep in the water. The deck must go, and the canoes must be hollowed out still more, until they are about half as thick and heavy. Then we shall pass over at least half of the shallows on which we now run aground."

Four Mongols, among them Gombo, the shipwright, had followed us along the bank, and helped Haslund to drag the vessel again to the " dockyard." Here Larson received new orders and immediately set to work. There was work on the boat throughout the whole of the day and right into the night by the light of the fires. On the floor of the canoes red-hot coals were placed ; the hollowing out then went easier and quicker. I could hear the blows of the axes and the grating of the saws for still a long time after I had lain down, and I awoke next morning to the same sounds. The canoes were hollowed out still further; all around, there grew up little mountains of chips and splinters. We wanted to set out on the morning of the 17th of October. No time was to be lost. The river had begun to fall. The highest water level that we had had amounted to 59·5 centimetres; now the gauge showed 55·5. That meant running aground still oftener.

Not till 4 o'clock in the afternoon was the vessel ready, and it was then just as I had prescribed. The canoes were, at their broadest part, roughly at the water-line, 45 centimetres across, and, at the breast-rail, 30 centimetres, and were fixed together at a distance of 35 centimetres apart by means of two strong cross-pieces. In the front part a box-cover was placed over them—that was my map and writing table. In the middle part, between the two canoes a small board was fixed, on which I was to sit, one leg in the right canoe, the other in the left, and the rest of my body balanced over the water. Haslund, the crew, had his place on a second small cross-board behind me, from where he worked the paddle. With this scarecrow of a ship we now undertook on the after-noon of the 16th of October a new trial voyage. Now everything went easier. Whenever we came into contact with a mud-bank, Haslund sprang into the water and got us free, and then we glided on with the stream. For more than an hour and a half we let ourselves drift, moving over to the right bank and then being carried again to the left, where we moored in a sheltered bay against a wood of old stately poplars and drew our vessel on land. The trial voyage was an excellent success; the next morning we would travel farther down Etsin-gol.

It was already late, and the sun was just setting, when we set out on our journey back to the camp, through little thickets, over dunes overgrown with tamarisks, and through waving yellow fields of grass as high as a man. After a few minutes a water-course stopped us, a side branch of Etsin-gol. It might be 20 metres broad and 30 centimetres deep, and had a scarcely perceptible flow. Haslund carried me across. and we marched on. Twilight overtook us and it became dark, but soon the fires and lights gleamed between the trees, the dogs began to bark, and we were home.

The plan of the excursion, as I had thought it out, was as follows. The canoes could not be burdened with luggage. For that reason Larson was to accompany us with a little caravan on the left bank, keep in constant communication with us, and in agreement with us fix the camping-places. Professor Hsü and Li were to accompany him, since they both wanted very much to see the two lakes. Hempel and Zimmermann were also to proceed to the lakes with a small caravan of their own and cartographically survey the western arm of Etsin-gol, which is known as Oboen-gol and goes to Gashun-nor, and on the way back that arm of Kundulung-gol which is said to flow farthest to the east and to unite with the middle arm of Etsin-gol, Dondur-gol, before the latter opens into Sokho-nor.

When we set out on the morning of the 17th of October, the personnel of the meteorological station No. 1 had dwindled still more; only Haude, Hummel, Dettmann, Lieberenz, Mühlenweg, and Tsui remained behind here. Of our servants we were accompanied by the Mongols Mento, Banche, and Matte Lama, and the Chinese Ming and Wang. The two Germans had their own servants and camels. We left the camp together, but our roads soon divided, not to meet again till after three days' marches, quite near the headquarters of the prince of the Torgots. To this ruler I intended to make a visit in the company of Professor Hsü, and with this opportunity to introduce to him—or more correctly his eldest son, since he himself is old, blind, and ill—Zimmermann, who, indeed, was to stay for a year and a half in his territory.

Haslund and I rode to the little poplar wood where we had left our double boat on the previous evening, dismounted, and went on board. We only took absolutely necessary things with us : sheaf of maps, compass, watch, pencils, field-glass. Haslund, who had to go again and again into the water, even sent his clothes along with the caravan—except for a woollen vest and bathing-drawers. Larson followed us on the left bank with his rifle in his hand and shot a pheasant and a wild duck. His riding-camel was led by the Mongol Banche.

We pushed off from the land, moved into the stream, and glided at a comfortable speed, neither too fast nor too slow, with the current down Etsin-gol. The banks hurried past us with their autumn-yellow thickets, thick copses of tamarisks, steppes of grass and reeds; now and then also bare or plant-bound dunes, the latter usually showing sharply washed-away vertical bank walls. We soon noticed that the only navigable channel flows just along such sharply cut-out slopes as these, and we therefore, as often as possible, let ourselves drift immediately along the bank.

But the current often goes over from one bank to the other, and then we had to cross the bed of the river. It was just at these stretches that we were accustomed to run aground; for here lay most and the most cunningly hidden of the mud-banks. When the stem pushed into the sand the vessel turned round, and Haslund jumped into the river, to wade in the mud and look for deeper water.

I myself sat at my observation table drawing my map of the lower course of Etsin-gol. One had to be sharp. Just like all other rivers, Etsin-gol winds along in a meandering stream, and only very rarely did one set of bearings hold good for more than a minute. I had, therefore, to observe compass and watch and draw on my map without interruption. The other notes and observations that were necessary had to be attended to as quick as lightning. From time to time I measured the speed of the current, in order to get a value for the length of river we had covered. At 10.15 the temperature of the air amounted to 22·1 degrees above zero and of the water 10·1.

At several places we had lookers-on. Torgots who had their tents not far from the river hurried to the bank, greeted us, and looked at us full of astonishment. When on one occasion we glided along close to the left bank, two men in blue coats and a woman dressed in red came riding to meet us. They were very interested, saluted us courteously, turned back, and accompanied us a short distance. They had heard of our projected river journey, and wanted to see with their own eyes how it went off. At three different places camels were pasturing. They looked at us with staring eyes and seemed to be not less astonished than the Torgots. A big yellow camel was standing on the bank drinking out of the river. We travelled past it without making a sound. It raised its head, looked at us for a moment, turned round, and disappeared in the forest.

Immediately after 1 o'clock Larson appears between the tamarisks, just as we are drifting along by the left bank. He declares it is time to take lunch; besides, we have been carried forward so quickly that he must rest a little while. We moor our boat, go up on land, and spread our simple meal, which consists of a thermos flask of tea, a piece of chocolate, and a few biscuits. But in the thick tamarisk wood we find it very comfortable; the air is warm (23 degrees), and Haslund gets properly dry.

Then we go on. A few times we come past long-stretching islands. One of them separated us from Larson for a considerable time. Soon after 3 o'clock we reach the point where Etsin-gol divides into two branches of apparently about equal size. The left is Oboen-gol, "the obo river," which empties itself into Gashun-nor; the right is called Dondur-gol and goes to Sokho-nor. To judge from the information that we had already obtained from Torgots, Dondur-gol, "the middle river," should be narrower and deeper than its neighbour on the left, and I had therefore decided to cartographically survey the former branch first. Larson must therefore cross Oboen-gol here, and Haslund searches on foot for a suitable ford: I don't like to let Larson go into very deep water; for he cannot swim. Banche is sent on foot to Mären's camp, a good stretch farther down-stream on the left bank of Oboen-gol, where Mären, the chief of the Mongols, has for some time been looking after our camels. Professor Hsü has also gone there with his caravan.

Now we glide into Dondur-gol. On the left bank a little in front of us a flock of wild geese is resting. They

Professor Hsü makes the inaugural speech

The table for the feast

THE FEAST OF THE REPUBLIC

[*face p.* 208

Wrestling among the Europeans . . .

. . . and among the Mongols

"OLYMPIC GAMES"

[*face p.* 209

turn their heads towards us, fly up, and make for the south. One can hear the rustling strokes of their wings and can see them fly away, beautifully lit up by the sun. They hold an animated conversation and cannot understand what a strange monster it is that is coming swimming towards them there on the river. They have no more seen a boat on Etsin-gol and its delta tributaries than have the Torgots and the camels. Soon they have disappeared over the wood.

The further we come, the narrower becomes Dondurgol, and the less frequently do we run aground. The guiding and steering of our vessel becomes easier and easier—Haslund has only, in fact, to sit there and keep watch with his paddle. Indeed, he even gets quite dry between the separate immersions. We are now going forward quickly. Sometimes the current threatens, at a sharp, deep bend, to push us against the bank. But I have a thin pole at hand and can push our boat away.

At 4 o'clock the river bends towards the east and then turns aside to the north-north-west. Larson again appears between the trees. Time passes, and the sun is already low. The caravan must find us, and we must camp, before it gets dark. The river is deep here and only 15 metres broad. It resembles an artificial canal, and its bed has no mud-banks. The slope of the left bank falls away steeply, that of the right more gently. On both sides there grows thick forest. The forest on the right bank is sharply lit up by the setting sun. The trunks of the trees are almost brick red ; their crowns glisten like gold, when the sunshine falls on the yellowing foliage On the left bank out of sandy soil stand old venerable poplars. This place is very attractive and inviting. It is like a royal park. Here we will set up our camp. We land. At 4.45 the thermometer still indicates 22 degrees in the air and 12 degrees in the river. Half an hour later, when the sun has set, in the air it is 7 degrees cooler. Haslund draws the boat on land, Larson collects firewood, and I draw two sketches.

Here the river is so narrow and deep, that at a distance of 20 to 30 metres from the bank one cannot see it. It seems to disappear in the yellow forest. To-day had really been beautiful and auspicious : a pleasant summer's day without wind. The landscape was charming ; one cannot get tired of seeing it. From time to time wild ducks and geese fly up on the bank, while the pheasants sit looking at us from their hiding-places under the tama-risks. A vulture hangs over the river. On the left bank the ground is more even and is overgrown here and there with reeds and grass higher than a man, in which oxen, horses, and camels pasture. On a few occasions we saw the tents of Torgots.

Twilight comes on. In the west the sound of cries and of screaming camels can be heard. It is evidently our caravan, which is just on the point of crossing the near-by Oboen-gol. Now the cries cease; thus they have safely come over. Larson lights his fire, in order to show them the direction. Haslund is standing at the blazing fire in the costume of Adam, drying himself, his woollen vest, and his bathing-drawers. Hsü and Li come and sit down beside us. The camels show up red in the light of the fire. The town of tents quickly grows up beneath the poplars. In a trice the kitchen is set up, and by half-past six we have our dinner, meat-dumplings and green peas, rice, and biscuits, and in addition tea. We sit down to our meal on felt rugs which are spread out round the fire-place. It crackles and seethes in the dry hollow trunks, in which the scorpions must believe that it has become midsummer again—before they are roasted. And it rustles so much like home in the leaves on the ground, when one walks over them or when the light evening breeze invited them to dance.

After the meal I lay myself lengthwise on the mat in my tent and write notes in my diary. Then I go to bed under the canopy of the royal park. So long as I am awake I can hear the flutes of the Mongols at the camp fire, where they have spread their sheepskins, to sleep under the open sky. One scarcely has the heart to go to sleep on such a night.

On the following day we drift down-stream in the same way and admire the charming landscape pictures which glide past us. The further we come on our journey through the enchanted forest in the middle of the desert sea of sand, the more deeply do I regret that Lieberenz and his film-camera are not accompanying us. But it is, indeed, not too late yet, and since Larson, with whom in the night camp in the evening I discuss my idea, agrees with me, I write to Lieberenz and ask him to come after us as quickly as possible. Banche, who is taking this letter to headquarters, is at the same time riding past Mären's camp and calling there for four or five camels. In two days Lieberenz can overtake us at the next camping-place, where we are waiting for him.

In the night before the 19th of October the temperature only fell to 3·3 degrees above zero. In the last nights it had gradually got warmer and warmer—as if we were entering spring, not autumn. At 9 o'clock we had a temperature of 10·6 degrees in the air and 8 degrees in the water. The speed of the current was 90 centimetres a second, and since yesterday the river had fallen by a few centimetres.

We pushed off from the bank and continued our drift on Dondur-gol. The journey was glorious; we glided quietly and smoothly along in the narrow bed, and animals and human beings that caught sight of us stared at us in astonishment.

The breadth of the river often changes. Sometimes it is 70 metres broad, sometimes, in sharp bends, scarcely 10. In general the bed becomes deeper. And now again, here and there, Dondur-gol resembles a canal between steep wharfs or erosion-terraces 2 metres in height. Often we drift past beautiful woods.

About midday we moor our boat. Larson has already made a fire in a cosy place, under poplars which throw their shade on the river. On the bank the marks of a species of cat are to be seen; the animal has been at the water to drink, apparently a lynx or a wild cat.

When we again continue our journey we have a new passenger on board. The river is here so deep that Larson can accompany us on the ship. And that is indeed only right and fair, for he has built this splendid ship. He thoroughly enjoys the river journey and talks without ceasing and cannot manage to keep still; now he is measuring the depth, now aiming at a pheasant or a wild duck, now standing up, one leg in the right canoe and the other in the left, investigating the surroundings with his field-glass. Larson's remarks greatly amuse Haslund. I myself am impossible as a companion, when I am counting the minutes on my watch and the degrees on my compass.

To the left the caravan appears. The camels move along on the edge of the bank and offer a view which is as restful as it is charming.

Suddenly the scenery changes. The forest comes to an end. A few isolated poplars are its last outposts towards the lake. Even the tamarisks become more scattered. On both sides of the river stretches the flat steppe of grass and reeds. The charming perspectives have come to an end, and we notice that we are approaching the flat open basin which surrounds the two sister lakes.

It is 3 o'clock. We have a temperature of 16·1 degrees in the air and 11·1 degrees in the river. Matte Lama comes riding quickly up and reports that Hempel and Zimmermann are camping a little way farther downstream, and that our tents are being set up there. After we have described a few more windings, we catch sight of our caravan and go on land.

Between the two rivers of Dondur-gol and Oboen-gol there stretches, only a few metres in height, a flat plateau of hard rubble. On this plain, to the west of our camp, the prince of the Torgots has his headquarters, his small residence. The place is called Ser-sonche.

The prince lives in a house of unburnt bricks, which has just been newly built and contains about forty rooms. Near it he has his *yamên*, his government palace. Not far from the residence the small monastery of Dagelingompa rises up, whose name, it is worth noting, is formed with the Tibetan word for temple monastery, *gompa*, not with the Mongolian *sumo*.

Reliable information regarding the course of Dondur-gol to Sokho-nor, or of Oboen-gol to Gashun-nor, proved impossible to get. We did not know whether, from the point where we were now camping, at a distance of half a league from the prince's residence, we could continue our journey up to the opening of the river into the lake. Haslund therefore made a reconnaissance and found that immediately below our camp Dondur-gol divides into two branches, the left of which forms a series of swamps, from which its water, in several small tributaries, forming little falls, returns to the right branch. This is itself as narrow as a dike, and it was questionable whether our double canoe could come through at all. We were determined, of course, to make an attempt. That the river was falling did not deter us. In our night camp it was exactly 20 metres broad and had a greatest depth of 0·75 metres. The quantity of water amounted to about 9 cubic metres a second. For a certain stretch half at least of this water might be lost, that is to say, might empty itself into the left branch, to return, however, later.

Since we had heard speak of a quite small delta tributary which was said to flow to the east of Dondur-gol, I directed Hempel and Zimmermann, who from here are going to the fixed camp again, to survey this tributary cartographically.

The population on Etsin-gol and in its delta is Mongolian and belongs to the old tribe of the Torgots. Already when we reached Etsin-gol Professor Hsü and I had notified its prince of our visit. Now we were camping at a distance of scarcely half a league away from his residence.

On the morning of the 20th of October we sent Matte Lama to the *yamên*, to learn when His Highness would receive us. It was 12 o'clock, but our messenger had not yet returned with the answer. Perhaps the prince would not receive us at all. We knew that he was old, blind, and deaf, lay always between his furs, and never received guests. But his eldest son, a man 45 years old, who managed all his father's and the tribe's business, had allowed himself to be seen, when Hummel and Haslund called at his residence two weeks before. There remained nothing else for us to do but to wait. Besides, we had, indeed, also asked Lieberenz to join us with his cinema-camera.

In Matte's locality a small south-west storm appeared on the scene; it began to whistle and howl in the reeds. The river became covered with white crests of foam, and there floated over the horizon, betraying the nearness of the desert, a mist of yellow dust. This veil, however, threw into relief as bright blue contours the mountain chains of moderate height which extend to the north of Gashun-nor and Sokho-nor from west to east. They lie in the territory of the Mongolian Republic. In the north-east there stood out Noyen Bogdo, the " chieftain of the gods," with its two flat peaks.

Early in the afternoon Matte Lama returned at last and brought us a very curious answer from the prince. The latter sent us word that we could not be received to-day, for this day, the 25th of their current month, was not favourable or suitable for visits. On the 28th and 29th of October he would send a messenger to our camp, wherever we then were, and let us know which day would suit him. I immediately called Hsü and Larson into my tent, in order to take counsel with them. Hsü, as I did, found the answer almost insulting. Did the " prince " really believe that four days later, when we should pre-sumably be far away from his fixed camp, we should return to pay him a visit, after he had refused to receive us when we were camping almost in front of his tents ? Hsü thought that a petty chieftain over ninety-seven tents was not higher in rank than the mayor of a Chinese provincial town, and such a man ought to be courteous when the leaders of a large expedition came into his town. But looking at it from the other side, the chieftain could not, indeed, know very exactly what sort of people we were, political agents, spies, or white robbers. Larson was of the opinion, and Hsü agreed with him, that imme-diately on our arrival the chieftain had certainly sent a messenger to the Chinese authorities in Kansu, under whom he was placed, inquiring how he should behave towards us. Now he was waiting for instructions, and must therefore give an evasive answer. If such were the case, then the prince was rather to be praised than to be blamed, for then he showed that he governed his territory with prudence. Perhaps, too, even politics had something to do with it. It was said that half of the Torgot population was sympathetic towards the Mongolian Republic and might declare for it at any moment. But Professor Hsü rejected this idea ; for then the prince himself would, of course, lose his title and his position, without getting the least thing in return. He was certainly conservative and loyal to China, and the little power that he possessed he would not abandon.

Haslund now told us that Hummel and he, when they had come past the prince's residence, had met Huang, who required a guide. They had then all three gone to the prince's house, where, however, they were not received, but were shown to his *yamên*. There they talked with some officials and made known to them Huang's request. Within five minutes they had a mounted guide at their disposal. While they were still talking with the officials, there entered the prince's eldest son, the real holder of power, and in a courteous and friendly manner he bid them welcome. He excused himself for not being able to receive them, and added : " You understand that, in times so unsettled and insecure as the present, one must be cautious. For long ages we have maintained peace in our land, and we also want to have peace in future. We must therefore be on our guard against agents coming from various quarters. Moreover, we cannot tell what sort of people you are and why you come here."

Naturally he had every reason to be cautious, when one beautiful day eighteen well-armed Europeans and ten Chinese with a caravan of several hundred camels settle down on his peaceful territory like a swarm of locusts. There had never been anything of the sort before. In China, of course, there was war, but what could this mean here ? We were strong enough to conquer his territory if we liked. Concerning our caravan extremely disquieting rumours had preceded us along Etsin-gol, rumours which in the mouth of Mongols and Chinese traders had gradually assumed gigantic proportions. A whole army of soldiers, so it was said, was on the way, and we had vast caravans, whole towns of tents, and immense quantities of weapons. And, to be sure, there came the vanguard and got a firm footing on the bank of the river, and a few days later a new large section followed. That was quite manifestly serious preparations of a military character. The prince had every occasion to be on his guard.

We decided to go to work with care and consideration, and in all friendliness to enlighten the chieftain concerning our intentions and our plan to establish a meteorological station in his territory. Professor Hsü undertook to draw up this communication; the Chinese letter—after an opening with the customary titles and compliments— read as follows :

" We have to-day come to your camp for the exclusive purpose of paying you our visit. To our great regret we learn that to-day does not suit you and that we cannot make your acquaintance in person. Our expedition, which is under the protection of the Chinese government and of the ' Federation,' is on a journey through the northern parts of Shansi, Kansu, and Sin-kiang, in order to carry out scientific investigations. We have also the intention of establishing, in the neighbour-hood of Sokho-nor, in Hami, in Tihua, and at other places, meteorological stations for the carrying out, over a period of years, of observations of rainfall, winds, and temperature.

We are now on the western bank of Etsin-gol, and have already set up our station. We therefore regard it as our duty to visit Your Highness and Your Highness's officials, in order to explain to you all our intentions, and to ask you, on behalf of the station, for your protection and for that of your country. Since our expedition is an organization with the object of scientific research, all the members of it are men of scholarship and education. With regard to politics, we do not belong to any particular group or association, and the task of the station is of a purely scientific character. We have not the least intention of concerning ourselves with politics. Dr. Sven Hedin has for twenty years been a good friend of the Panchen Ho Fu (Tashi Lama) and has several times travelled in Tibet to explore the country, and on these occasions has always enjoyed the greatest hospitality of His Holiness. And now, too, on several occasions he has visited His Holiness in Peking and informed him of his plan to visit these countries, in which His Holiness has encouraged him in every way.

Professor Hsü Ping-chang holds the Yellow Religion in very great respect. As far as the staff of the station is concerned, we can both of us give a guarantee that it will in no way violate the manners and customs of the country or be guilty of any sort of encroachment upon temples or *obos*.

We should like to explain now, that we should attach great importance to being received by you. In case this is impossible, we should like hereby to inform you, that at the end of this month or the beginning of next we intend to continue our journey to Sin-kiang.

Even if we, Sven Hedin and Hsü Ping-chang, who bear the whole responsibility for this expedition, are not able to make your acquaintance on this occasion, three members of our expedition are fortunately remaining here, and these will be ready at any time to pay you their visit, so that it will be impossible for a misunderstanding to arise. Moreover, all the members of the expedition here concerned are provided with passports from the Chinese Ministries of Foreign Affairs and Education. If you so desire, we invite you to send to our camp one of your officials, invested with full authority, in order to examine these passports."

This letter we transmitted to the prince by Matte Lama, who after a considerable time came back in the company of a *tushmid*, or secretary, and another official. The secretary informed us that His Highness had, indeed, an interpreter, but not one that could read Chinese. Our clever Mongol Serat therefore translated the document into Mongolian for the gentlemen, and the envoys then went away again. And we had to go on waiting, and heard nothing from the chieftain for the rest of the day.

Towards evening Lieberenz arrived in our camp with five camels, two cameras, and numerous films and plates. He was in the best of spirits, and reported that in headquarters everything was as it should be.

When it got dark we could again light a splendid camp fire; we had, of course, drift-wood. Sitting at the fire, we discussed the questions of the day, and especially, why the chieftain had not been willing to receive us. His secretary had been extremely courteous, to say the least, and had assured us that we were welcome and could go where we wished and do what we liked; the prince sent us word, however, asking us if we would be careful if we wanted to go on the lakes in the boat, for there was much water there!

Still more concerned about me, to be sure, was Professor Hsü. He was positively touching in his anxiety concerning my intention to navigate the lakes. One can be brave and courageous, he declared, but one need not be foolhardy. "What is the object of it? You say you want to measure the depths and investigate the size and configuration of the lakes. But that can be done by Zimmermann without danger, when the lakes are covered with ice, and so geographical science will get the desired new knowledge in any case. Think of your responsibility towards your relatives, your fatherland, and the expedition. During the summers that I spent in St. Malo, I often heard speak of sea accidents that could very easily have been avoided. You speak of your adventures on the lakes in Tibet. But at that time you were younger. You have said that it was a question of von Kaull making a safe and seaworthy vessel out of sheepskins, but that one requires too many sheep for this, and that you must economize. If you will wait until this vessel is ready, I will gladly take upon myself the cost of the sheep. I beg you to desist from your intention. You say the canoes are not dangerous when the weather is beautiful and calm. But a storm can arise when you are right in the middle of the lake, and what will you do then?"

"We shall then hoist the sail and pull for the shore with all our might."

"The danger to which you are exposing yourself is far too great in relation to the results that you can obtain. I hope we shall camp together to-morrow evening too, so that we can again talk things over together, before you set out on foolhardy adventures."

This concern for my welfare was an extremely congenial trait of Professor Hsü's, and it was thoroughly genuine.

Finally I asked him jokingly, "What will you do, if I sail out on the lake and do not return?"

"Don't talk about it," he replied seriously, and went slowly to his tent.

XVII

BY SOKHO-NOR TO GASHUN-NOR

ON the morning of the 21st of October the river had again fallen, now, since our arrival, 5·5 centimetres. The temperature had come down in the night to 0·5 degrees below zero, but the morning was clear, the sky turquoise blue, and the steppe shone with a yellow colour. The Swedish flag waved proudly in front of my tent on the extreme edge of the bank of the river.

Larson woke me with the news that the chieftain of the Torgots had come in person, and was sitting chatting with him in the tent. It was of course not the old chieftain, with whom it seems to be all over, but his son. I was ready in an instant, and the distinguished guest was invited into my tent. He handed me a bright blue band and a red visiting-card of his father's. The latter's title and name reads : Kün Wang Dashi. His province is called Etsina. To the right of the name there is also : Torgot elder.

His son, the real ruler in Etsina, our guest, was a big, powerfully-built man of unusually sympathetic and engaging appearance. He was obliging, courteous, and complaisant, and obviously animated with the best intentions. I had Professor Hsü called in, who also received a blue *haddik* and a red visiting-card. We drank tea, conversed, and exchanged the usual compliments. If, declared our guest, we attached great importance to seeing the old prince, we were welcome ; he was, however, ill, and only the nearest relatives and a few servants were allowed to go in to him. I replied that there could be no question at all of our disturbing His Highness. We only asked for our most respectful greetings and compliments to be conveyed to him.

He had also our letter of yesterday with him, and asked

View of our camp

ETSIN-GOL

[face p. 220

Hedin's Mongolian guide

Representatives of Sweden in the Expedition
(In the tent, from top to bottom, Söderbom, Bergman,
Hummel, Norin, Haslund; by the side, Larson and Hedin)

CAMP LIFE IN THE NEIGHBOURHOOD OF ETSIN-GOL

[face p. 221

to have it translated once more. Hereupon he repeated the assurances that his secretary had already given us yesterday, that we had unrestricted freedom and that the station could remain here as long as we liked.

When he inquired if he could be of service to us in any way, I answered that we should be very grateful if we could hire a bullock-cart which would take our boat from Sokho-nor to Gashun-nor and then up to the enchanted forest, which we should like to film. Yes, with the greatest pleasure. " Provided I learn where the cart is to wait for you, and under the express condition that you will pay nothing for it, for it is my duty to assist you as best I can."

Finally I expressed my determined desire to be allowed to make reparation for the damage that would be done to his pasture-lands by our camels that were remaining here during the winter, and asked him to tell me if I might make him a present of some article or other of European origin, which in this case I would send here and have handed over to him by the director of the station. He immediately replied that he would attach great value to a really good field-glass. And that he shall certainly have, and if, as I believe, he is friendly towards the station and its staff, he shall also receive other presents as well.

Not till 10.45 did the amiable chieftain of the Torgots leave us, and he had scarcely disappeared on the steppe when Haslund and I hurried to the boat, pushed off from the land, and abandoned ourselves to the current. On the left bank grow isolated tamarisks ; on the right we can see flat stretches which a short time before have been under water. After barely half an hour we reach the point where Dondur-gol divides into two branches. The left drains through swamps, against which we have been warned ; the right becomes very narrow and winding. Larson went ahead of us on the right bank, in order to call our attention in time if we were approaching the fall of which we had been told. Soon he had disappeared in the reeds, which here grow quite high and thick.

After a while he came running back, and, waving his arms about, and out of breath, called out to us :

" Stop, stop ! I can hear the fall ; it must be quite

near." We threw a rope to him, and he hauled in the boat, which in the current had quite a fair speed. We went on land and explored the channel. The 4 or 5 cubic metres of water which in a second fell over the little ledge 1 metre in height formed a fall 3 metres high, which reminded me of Niagara, for it had the same form as the Horseshoe Fall. Below the cascade the river forms a foaming whirl-pool, which has hollowed out the soil of the river-bed to form a deep basin. After the foaming flood of water has extricated itself from this turmoil, it flows rapidly away in a furrow, which is at first only 2 and then 3 metres broad. The banks form almost vertical walls, 2 or 2½ metres in height, which are sometimes hollowed out and near tumb-ling in. One must therefore walk warily on the edge of the bank.

After we had reconnoitred the awkward position, we returned to the boat and took out everything that was not a fixture. Larson and Haslund grasped the rope and allowed the boat to glide towards the fall, while I tried with the pole to keep it parallel to the current. It drifted backwards towards the top of the fall, where it turned a somersault and fell down into the boiling cauldron and became three quarters full of water. It kept afloat, how-ever, and was drawn to a place where Haslund could climb down and bail it out.

Then we drifted on. The river is like a narrow canal in a slightly winding corridor. But the descent is consider-able, and we rush at a dizzy speed down a series of small falls. Larson on the bank must run in order to keep pace with us. We have just enough water to allow us to go forward. Anything less, and we should stick fast. In any case it was an amusing and exciting voyage.

Soon, however, we had more water again. From the left a little rill rushed headlong down the slope of the bank in a fall 2 metres high. Several others followed, seven in all, and in addition five tributaries. The water from these was quite clear, for it was filtered in the reedy swamps and came from the left branch of Dondur-gol. The river then increased in breadth, soon became 12 to 20 metres across, and finally just as broad as in our first camp. The depth amounted to 0·75 and 1 metre. The banks are low again; they rise in general half a metre above the water. We catch sight of pasturing horses and cattle and a yourt. But gradually the pasture becomes poorer and the steppe only consists of scattered hillocks of vegetation. Finally the land becomes completely barren, and large surfaces are covered with dry, cracked mud.

After travelling for three hours we rested awhile at the new camp that was just being set up. From here Sokho-nor could be seen quite near, like a turquoise-blue basin in the yellowish grey desert.

After I had taken a few bearings, we pushed off again, in order to cover the last stretch of our journey. Soon the river divided into several small delta-tributaries, these again into still smaller ones, quick-flowing rills between mud-banks and held-up drift-wood. We followed the passages which seemed to us most suitable, but often ran aground.

At last we had all the land behind us, and the lake stretched itself out in front of us. But it was still a long way to pure, blue water; several hundred metres from the bank it was still as thick and yellow as pea-soup. If we had believed we could get out here on the lake, we deceived ourselves. In front of the little delta there lay a mud-bank forming a bar, where the water only stood 5 centimetres deep, and where we could not get along, however much we pushed and shoved. Haslund explored the channel till he suddenly sank into soft, blue-black mud, and had to work vigorously to get out again. Here one could push the rod 1·10 metres into the mud forming the bottom, without needing to exert oneself in the least.

We took the boat back, moored, and then went to a point in the north-west where Larson, Lieberenz, and Mento were engaged in digging out a canal from the bank, on which we could sail out on water of adequate depth. The passage was marked with branches of tamarisks.

But the sun was already low. I took the bearings of the visible outlines of the lake and of the mountains lying in the north. Noyen Bogdo lay north 31° east, Kokshin north 20° east, and Tosto north 25° west. In a direction north 7° east there stood out Boro-obo, a votive sign on a hill, a short distance from the north-west shore of Sokho-nor, which was visible from the whole lake and its immediate neighbourhood. Then we wandered home-wards, sat chatting at the evening camp fire, and went to rest in the knowledge that on the 22nd of October we should experience a memorable day.

The new day dawned with bright clear sky and still air. I was awakened by two rifle-shots ; it was Larson, who had killed in flight three wild-fowl of the steppe. When I stepped out of my tent, only Ming, my Chinese servant, was there. All the others had gone to the boat, to carry it on strong shoulders to the canal which was dug out yesterday. Lieberenz filmed the whole proceeding. When I got there, the boat lay a short distance away from the bank, tied to a stake. Haslund rowed out to ascertain the depth a few hundred metres away, and turned back when he had gone so far that he could row unhindered. In the whole easterly and south-easterly part of the lake, where the water is similarly a dirty yellow, one can see clearly that here the sea-birds can walk and stand on the bottom. From his turning-point Haslund had still a good way to go to reach the pure, blue water. The greatest depth that he reached was 55 centimetres. He drew the boat up to the bank as far as it would go, and then carried me out—a picture which comes out splendidly in the film.

We were very lightly fitted out. In one of the canoes there stood a cake-box full of real Swedish biscuits, which our cook had learnt to bake with Swedish missionaries, and two cakes of chocolate. In the other canoe we had a similar box containing cigarettes, bandages, medicine-chest, and a small bottle of brandy, which our doctor had ordered us, in case we were forced to drink water containing salt ; in addition my large thermos flask of tea. That was all. But the lake seemed very small, and we should probably master it in a few hours, and then be able to row to the point on the north-west shore where Larson had orders to camp to the immediate south of Boro-obo. After the approach of darkness he was to light a fire, in case we did not reach his camp till late in the evening.

Haslund was only wearing a jaeger shirt, a woollen vest,

and bathing-drawers, and also took neither shoes nor socks with him. I wore only my usual travelling-clothes, but no outer clothing. On my writing-desk I had a folded blanket, to prevent map and other things from slipping overboard.

Finally we had with us in addition my stick and the cross-rod of a camel-saddle, so that, if there was a wind, we could erect a mast.

All these preparations took up time, and it was almost 12 o'clock before we put out into the lake, waving good-bye to Hsü, Larson, Lieberenz, and the Mongols. In the air we had a temperature of 15·2 degrees and in the water 9·3. In a depth of 33 centimetres we floated without further running aground, and Haslund began to swing the paddle. When a light breeze from the west rose up we stopped a moment to erect our improvised mast.

We had no other sail to hand but my leather waistcoat. It was stretched out on my stick and secured with two shrouds. This curious sail was an excellent trap for the wind, and rowing and steering with the paddle, we glided along so that it swished round the stems of the canoes.

We approached the blue areas of the lake, where the muddy river-water no longer makes its influence felt. From the open expanses we could hear a strong roaring. It is the wind, which is causing the water to run in surf-crested billows. The motion of the water increases, and the billows become more and more threatening. Soon the boldest of them mounts the edge of our canoes. The wind freshens up ; it begins to get dangerous. I vividly remember my adventurous boat journeys on Lop-nor and the lakes of the Tarim, and knew that it was a dangerous game. Since the canoes are hollowed out of round tree-trunks, their edges are bent inwards and invite the waves straight in to visit us. We could hear more and more often the uncomfortable splashing when a wave came rolling into one of the canoes.

We kept our course towards a mark on the shore in a direction north 80° east ; Haslund rowed strongly, and the wind blew so fiercely that the shrouds were stretched as taut as bowstrings. Soon we had Boro-obo in a direction north two seconds west of us. We rapidly approached the open expanse in the middle of the lake, but still the south shore was nearer to us than the north. Here on the deep, clear water only isolated flocks of sea-birds were to be seen, mandarin ducks, grey and white gulls, swans, and a black bird with a red beak, probably a species of diver. They kept in much larger flocks on the shallow water. They kept on flying over us and settling down splashing on the lake. Whenever we approached a flock of them which were swimming on the water, they flew up with noisy flapping of wings. We did not catch sight of any wild geese. They seem not to like the sustenance which Sokho-nor offers them.

I haven't many minutes to spare. At short distances I measure the depth. Sokho-nor is shallow, and in its flat basin resembles a thin sheet of glass. My pole, which was divided into metres and centimetres and which was only 2·53 metres long, was sufficient for almost the whole of the way, and we did not need to stop to take soundings. Only at some few points in the middle of the lake was the pole not sufficient, and I had to make use of a small plummet. The greatest depth only amounted to 2·90 metres.

I measured just as often our running speed and the temperature of the air and of the water, and wrote down all the observations I could make. I had always the field-glass to hand. In the south-east there could be seen two yourts and pasturing cattle. In the south a herd of horses was standing in the water. The mirage lengthened their legs, and they almost seemed to float above the lake. They were drinking, thus contenting themselves with the water of the lake, in spite of its unpleasant bitter taste of soda. We could drink it too, but our stomachs rose against it.

Out on the lake the water is almost perfectly clear. A little white disk fixed at the end of my pole I could see up to a depth of 1·20 metres. The bottom of the lake is quite hard. Where the water that has a yellow colour from the mud of the river gradually changes to pure blue water, the depth amounts to 1·35 metres. When the wind now increased in strength, it gave us a comforting feeling that in the event of a shipwreck we could here find a secure bottom. But the depth increased, and when the crests of the billows began to wash into the canoes, we had over 2 metres of water beneath us. Now it became exciting. I sat with my feet in the water, which splashed backwards and forwards with the motion of the water of the lake. When I looked down I found to my consternation that the canoes were a third full of water. This unnecessary ballast made them still heavier, and made it easy for the billows to board the side of the ship.

I seized the iron ladle and bailed out as much as I could ; Haslund on the other hand was endeavouring with his paddle to break the crests of the worst billows and to check the force of their blows. Sometimes this bailing out seemed to me quite hopeless, and I questioned whether I was bailing out the canoes faster than they were filling again. And yet in the meantime neither could I forget my taking of bearings, my soundings, and other observations. If the wind had been just a degree stronger, then the lake would have got the upper hand of us, the boat would have filled, and at best just kept afloat. Then the question was, how long one would have endured lying in cold water and clinging to the side, before one's limbs grew numb.

But all went well. The depth decreased and soon amounted to only 1 metre and less ; in case of necessity we should thus have been able to walk to land. The only difficulty was to judge how far it was to the shore. When, as here towards the east, the shore is quite flat, the lake appears very large. For safety we also changed our course and kept exactly east, so that we had the full wind behind us and could land better.

On the southern and south-eastern shore there could be seen plant-bound dunes, hills of vegetation, and dark areas which could only be tamarisks or poplars. The northern bank was, so far as one could see from a distance, completely barren ; a short distance away from the shore there ran away a steep yellow clay terrace, which marked an earlier extension of the lake. In the west Sokho-nor seemed to stretch in the infinite distance.

But now the lake becomes more and more shallow, and the flat ripples of the ground on the bottom stand out clearly. It is a quarter-past four when we ran aground on the east shore. From this point we had still 70 metres to go to reach dry land, and Haslund again carried me across on his strong shoulders. Then he had to make this journey twice more, to fetch our provisions and other things.

Meanwhile I went to look for a suitable camping-place and wandered inland for ten minutes till I found ground that was completely dry. Then I immediately began to collect firewood, and we lighted a fire, which in the violent storm was not very easy. We resigned ourselves to having a bad night; to spend eleven hours in darkness, cold, and wet, is no pleasant outlook, when one is only lightly clad or almost completely unclad, and further, in addition, is half soaked through and has nothing warm to eat and by no means too much firewood. But suddenly we heard a noise in the north, and the next instant Banche came riding towards the fire. On his camel he had our sleeping-sacks, two blankets, my cashmere boots, which Larson had had made for me in Kalgan in 1923, Haslund's clothes, and a large box of pickled herrings.

Thus we were saved, and need neither freeze nor be sparing with our firewood, especially after Banche had dragged new supplies to the camping-place. As he now told us, Larson had sent him out to bring help to us, when late in the afternoon we still did not put in an appearance. Professor Hsü had been uneasy and had thought it terrible that I should have to spend the night in the open without tent and sleeping-sack and without warm food.

At 8 o'clock we all three of us had our supper. When the fresh tea water in my thermos flask had come to an end, we had to content ourselves with water from the lake, and then the little bottle of brandy came in useful.

" Brandy and soda-water—that does go down well," said Haslund.

We joked and chatted and smoked; the fire crackled and fizzled, and the hours quickly flew by.

When we laid the last wood on the fire, I undressed and crept into my sleeping-sack, and the Dane and the Mongol tucked me well in. Then on the other side of the fire

Haslund slipped into his covering, and Banche slept by the camel, to protect it against wolves.

The fire went out; darkness descended upon the camp. I lay awake for still a long time, looking up at the starry heavens and listening to the mysterious voices of the night.

After a delightful night in the open air I awoke to the crackling of a new fire. As soon as we had breakfasted and had taken our bearings, we put out again into the lake and steered towards Larson's camp in a direction north 70° west. Boro-obo, the commanding eminence in the west, towered up in a direction north 52° west. The weather was bright and warm, really like summer, and the sun burnt on our backs. To-day Haslund had to row the whole time.

Just after 2 o'clock we reached our goal. The crossing of the lake had taken scarcely three hours. This second line of soundings, on which I fixed the greatest depth at 4·12 metres, was thus considerably shorter than the first.

Larson, Lieberenz, and the Mongols were waiting for us on the landing-place that they had already constructed for us, and received us with shouts of joy—visibly delighted that we were not drowned. The Mongols have an unconquerable aversion to lakes, rivers, and boats, and considered my journeys by water incomprehensible and senseless. Professor Hsü and Li had in the morning started out on their journey by foot round Sokho-nor. That we had not seen them from the boat was due to the great distance.

The bullock-cart had arrived to time, accompanied by a little withered, friendly Torgot and five black dogs. Owing to the unevenness of the country and to the soft sand, the old man could not, however, travel straight from here towards the west to Oboen-gol, but had to choose a point which lay a few kilometres to the south-south-west. After our meal we set out thither, Haslund and I by water, the caravan and the bullock-cart following the chain of lagoons along the shore.

From our camp, when it became dark, we could see Hsü's and Li's fire at the mouth of the river. We sent

Wang, Hsü's servant, and Matte Lama out with camels, to help them over the river and bring them to us.

This evening I could go to sleep satisfied in the knowledge of having spent two unforgettable days on Sokho-nor and of having conquered a new lake in Asia. It was already well known, I admit, but I am fairly certain that no-one before us has visited it by ship.

When I woke up next morning, the old Torgot had already started out on the way with his bullock-cart and our boat, and we only needed to follow his wheel-tracks. We first of all travelled a short distance along the shore, crossed places which had been flooded shortly before, and a belt of dead tamarisks, and came finally upon the hard, almost barren plateau, where in the south-south-west there appeared the residence of the prince of the Torgots. Then we went down again, through thickets of tamarisks and past a rather large *obo*.

After a ride of something more than 10 kilometres we reached Oboen-gol at a sharp bend, where the ridge of the terrace along the bank was 6·20 metres above the surface of the river. The sandy slope descended at an angle of 35 degrees right down to the water. On this incline we let the boat slide down, and we then drifted down-stream. Gashun-nor was no longer far away. But we did not come far, neither on this day nor on the following, and on this occasion I had to content myself with casting a glance over the lake from the land. On the morning of the 26th of October we wandered up a hill of vegetation in the neighbourhood of the south-east shore. From here we surveyed the whole of Gashun-nor with its glistening surface of water. It seemed to be considerably larger than Sokho-nor. After I had made a sketch of the lake and of the distant mountains in the north, we returned to our camp, took down our tents, and started out on the way back into headquarters, where a new section of our long journey was to begin.

XVIII

PERMANENT STATION NO. 1

IN the night before the 26th of October the temperature had fallen to 8·7 degrees below zero, the lowest we had up to now. Haslund and Lieberenz already before sunrise started out on the march back with the bullock-cart and our boat. They were independent of us and had to see how and where they were advancing. Lieberenz wanted to film the enchanted forest from the boat, which was then to be left behind somewhere or other along the bank and be at the disposal of Station 1.

My column travelled towards the south along Oboen-gol through the forest, and on the 28th of October crossed the river, in part already covered with ice, and after a long ride through woods and bushes, over steppes and barren rubbly ground, at last caught sight of our fixed camp. On the bank of Etsin-gol the Swedish flag waved from a high mast, and near the new meteorological observatory belonging to the station there waved the German flag. All hurried here to welcome us. To me it was an especial pleasure to see again Norin and his companions, Bergman, Heyder, von Massenbach, Söderbom, and Ting, who, indeed, had been separated from us for months. They had reached head-quarters on the 23rd of October, five days before us. Immediately after our meal the principals of the northern column rendered me their report. Norin showed his imposing map in twenty-three large sheets, which embraced 2,650 square kilometres and extended right to Shande-miao, and his map of the route in fourteen sheets right to Etsin-gol. Heyder displayed his beautiful survey of the territory trigonometrically surveyed by him, which similarly reaches right to Shande-miao. Massenbach had carried out a series of topographical measurements of valley ways and river courses which the column crossed, and had thereby furnished an especially valuable appendix to Norin's map.

Bergman, strongly supported by the collector Chin, had from Beli-miao right to Etsin-gol discovered a hundred and twenty settlements belonging to the newer Stone Age, of which only fourteen lie on the way from Shande-miao to Station 1. The number of objects found ran to 17,600, mostly cores, scrapers, splinters, arrow-heads, etc., of flint, as well as splinters, axes, knives, and other implements, of stone.

All the members of the northern column were satisfied with their results, and they had reason to be. Moreover, they had only lost one camel and had bought three new ones. Twelve of their camels were in so good a condition that they could set out on the long march to Hami at any time.

Concerning my column they had on the way heard the strangest rumours. Some asserted that we were a whole army and were moving on Etsin-gol in order to conquer the land of the Torgots. Others had heard that we had entrenched ourselves in Khara-khoto, where we had found enormous quantities of gold, and that large bands of robbers had gathered outside the walls to plunder us when we moved on.

In headquarters everything was just as it was before— except for one small matter: winter was approaching. The Europeans were now wearing felt boots, which von Kaull had made, and in addition fur caps and warm clothes. When we separated in the evenings, no-one forgot to take a brazier of red-hot coals with him into the tent.

The days slipped by as usual, for the most part with consultations and deliberations and the discussion of great new plans, which dealt with the wide territories of Central Asia as if it was a matter of some little province or other of my Swedish fatherland. We also asked ourselves the question where Yüan could have got to. The entire southern column had utterly disappeared. As far as the region to the west of Shande-miao Norin had had communication with it, and he supposed that Yüan had then taken a more southerly route. But since then not even the

Floating ice

On Dondur-gol

[*face p.* 232

Camels at water

By the side of Dondur-gol

least and most attenuated rumour of him had penetrated to us.

Von Marschall, Liu, and Ma, were not yet back from Mamu, and we were without recent news of Huang. But the latter like the others could not be long in coming, and it was not to be feared that they would delay the setting out of the main caravan for Hami. Besides, a loss of time on Etsin-gol would only have regrettable consequences in one respect—namely, that the series of observations at Station 2 in Hami would in that case not be so complete. On this account Dr. Haude made me the proposal that he should set out on the 31st of October with a part of the caravan, in order to reach Hami in forced marches on the shortest desert road, where he should arrive about twenty days before the main caravan. On my arrival in Hami I should then find Station 2 already set up and in full working order.

I was naturally in agreement with this plan, and gave Larson instructions to have twenty-four of the best camels ready on the morning of the 31st of October. Haude's caravan would be the middle section; for now too we were marching in three columns. I myself intended to take a more southerly road; Norin and Bergman a more northerly one. Haslund was designated as caravan-guide of Haude's vanguard, and Hempel had the task of surveying the route of the column's march.

Early in the morning on the 31st of October all gathered round those who were going away, to say good-bye to them. The twenty-four splendid camels already had their light loads on their backs; the riding-camels were carrying shining saddles with rifle-cases, saddle-bags, water-bottles, and other things. The servants consisted only of one Mongol and one Chinese. Dettmann had undertaken to act the part of cook. The putting up and taking down of the tents, the making of beds and tidying up, the packing and loading and unloading, the principals themselves were to attend to, and the two servants had only to attend to and keep watch over the camels, under the orders of Haslund. Hempel and Li measured off their first base-line; for both were to survey the road. The last letters were stuffed into the post-bag, the last hand-shake was exchanged; then the eight men mounted their riding-camels, and the small, but strong caravan disappeared between the leafless trees.

During the last days of October and the first of November the river, on whose friendly banks we had spent unforgettable weeks, went down more and more. A part of its water, it is true, was held up in the form of ice—on the 4th of November, for example, the temperature fell during the night to 10·8 degrees below zero—but the formation of ice was not sufficient to explain a fall in the level of the water of 33·5 centimetres below our maximum. The Torgots told us that the agriculturists in the neighbourhood of Mamu and further up-stream were accustomed to flood their fields, so that during the winter there was formed a protection of ice, and they also told us that, as soon as this had happened, one could expect a new high water in the middle of November. The bed of the river looked strange and unfamiliar. The branch that had flowed along our bank had transformed itself into a long bend with lifeless water. Now only in the middle of the river-bed was a narrow channel of water still to be seen, which wound its way along past nothing but exposed sand-banks.

One day Larson surprised me with a yourt, which he had ordered of a Torgot. It was small, but quite new and clean, and when its dome, resembling a cheese-plate cover, rose up in the middle of this blue town of tents, and the spear with the flag was set up to the left of it, then everyone knew that here the chieftain of the wandering tribe dwelt. The pieces of felt with which the yourt was covered were on the outside white and on the inside grey. The door was red. Inside, in the middle stood a stove, made out of an empty petroleum-container and provided with a pipe, which went out through the chimney. The latter was therefore only half closed, and provided me with a sky-light. In the evening, when I had gone to bed and the fire in the stove had gone out, I could, before I went to sleep, enjoy for a while the moon and the stars. My bed of furs for the night had its place, as always, directly on Asiatic soil. To the left of the door stood my " writing table," the old box, and my chair; to the right the two leather bags with the things which I required at any time. Before them was spread the blue carpet from Paotow. The rest of the ground was covered with white felt covers. With a feeling of great ease and comfort I removed to this warm dwelling just at the time when winter began to show us its teeth.

At the same time another winter dwelling was ready also, which immediately enjoyed the greatest popularity, a combination of tent and dug-out, which was even equipped with a *kang*. Here Söderbom was to spend the winter.

On the 3rd of November a roaring sand-storm swept along over our camp and enveloped the whole neighbourhood in light-grey clouds of dust. Out of this mist there suddenly appeared early in the afternoon von Marschall's tall form. He approached, imperturbably calm and steady as usual, leading his riding-camel, and asked in pure Swedish: "Can I have something to eat?" He had what he wanted, and was besieged with questions. The distance to Mamu amounted to 223 kilometres. They had required nine days for the outward journey and eight for the journey back. One of their six camels they had lost in a curious manner. When they forded Etsin-gol, Liu's riding-animal lay down in the middle of the channel of the stream, and could not be made to stand up again. Liu and Ma, who were not backward whenever there was anything to be done, promptly jumped into the river and helped the others literally to drag the camel to the bank, where they camped in order to dry themselves at a fire. In the morning the animal lay dead by the side of the tents.

The forest had come to an end after 130 kilometres, and the last 25 kilometres led through cultivated land with fields, gardens, and canals. The little town of Mamu lies near the right bank of Etsin-gol and is surrounded by a square wall of at least 200 metres along each side, which on both the east and the west side has a gate. The little town is inhabited by barely three hundred Chinese and has only three shops. The district of Mamu numbers about a thousand families.

Our envoys were exceedingly well received by the friendly mayor, in whose hospitable house they dwelt, and

lived in Spartan simplicity, as became the followers of
Marshal Fêng. A shopkeeper, just as friendly, sold them
flour, sugar, vegetables, potatoes, furs, and other things
that we required, and for a very reasonable sum conveyed
the goods on ten camels to Station 1. The shopkeeper's
brother was just at this time celebrating his wedding, and
Marschall, Liu, and Ma, were invited as guests of honour.
As a wedding-present Marschall gave the bride a few silver
dollars, and she made in thanks the great Chinese obeisance,
the kotow.

On the way back they had picked up Huang and Chuang.
These, with Liu, Ma, the shopkeeper, and the caravan,
reached us late in the evening. Liu told us the latest
political news from Peking, and that the designation
" National University " now comprised all universities and
high schools in Peking. To all the requests and proposals
which Hsü and I had addressed to our committee in Peking,
the latter had answered with its consent in a letter of the
6th of August after a meeting of the 4th.

At the midday meal on the 4th of November, which in
spite of the frosty weather we took in the open, there were
eighteen of us at table, for ten principals of the staff were
absent. When I revealed to the eighteen that the main
caravan under my direction and with Larson as caravan-
guide and likewise Norin's column would start out for Hami
on the 8th of November, there burst forth loud cheering,
for now all were longing to get into " the field " again.
There was packing the whole afternoon. Late in the evening the Swedes, Marschall, and Zimmermann, gathered in
Söderbom's winter dwelling, where we were entertained
with Turkish *shislik* and fried potatoes and a strengthening
draught. What adventures the three who are remaining
behind in the land of the Torgots will experience, and of
what remarkable vicissitudes and adventures they will one
day be able to tell!

The 7th of November was again a day of parting ; for
then the student Tsui left our expedition, in order to found
the new station in Paotow.

During the whole time that we spent on Etsin-gol, from
the 28th of September to the 8th of November, there was

work daily on the setting up of the first permanent meteorological station, and towards the end of our stay it was in fact as good as ready. On one of the last days I had every particular pointed out to me by Zimmermann : the scientific apparatus, the dwellings, the equipment, and the stores.

Here and there there was still something to be done and to be altered. As far as the dwellings were concerned, four large Torgot yourts were to be set up on the edge of the forest. In one of them, which was already set up, Zimmermann was to live, in a second Ma, in the third the servants, and in the fourth Mären and the other Mongolian camel-attendants. In Ma's yourt it was to be possible to accommodate guests as well.

In several exhaustive deliberations I discussed with Zimmermann the various tasks which I expected of him. He was the responsible director of the station, and had to see that the meteorological observations were carried out with the greatest punctuality. At the same time, he himself, however, was not constantly tied to the station, for he had, indeed, Ma and Söderbom as assistants. He could thus undertake excursions into the delta of the river, in the winter on the ice, and, as soon as the spring had come, with our " boat."

Once a month he was to send me a report to Urumchi, and, moreover, by the post via Mamu. Communication with this town he could maintain with the best of our own camels, in accordance with Mären's advice. The greater number of the sixty-four animals needing careful treatment which were remaining behind here came from Roy Chapman Andrews' troop. Before these had rested sufficiently, one must hire Torgot camels. The charge for outward and homeward journey, not quite 450 kilometres, only amounted to 5 dollars.

The money in our chest was for a time at an ebb, and we could therefore only leave behind a hundred odd dollars for the requirements of the station, and in addition a smaller sum for Yüan. Therefore we decided that Haslund, who is an excellent caravan-guide, should ride back to Etsin-gol immediately after my arrival in Hami and take money and letters to Station I. That was, indeed, 700 kilometres, there and back 1,400 kilometres, or rather, if one also further adds to that the outward journey in Haude's column, 2,100 kilometres. But that did not worry him.

The population on the lower course of Etsin-gol belongs to the tribe of the Torgots, and is thus of Mongolian origin. It is thus in keeping with the scope of my description of the journey to say here a few words concerning their history. But our companions remaining behind on the little desert river will come into very close contact with them, and so have opportunity to learn all sorts of things concerning the life and customs of the Torgots of *our* time.

As I have already several times mentioned, our Chinese scholars have with them six boxes containing old works on the history of China. In this gold-mine there is also a work which appeared about a hundred years ago and is called *Mêng-ku yu mu chi*, "The book on the cattle-rearing and pasture-lands of the Mongols." The author, Chang Mu, did not reach the point of finishing his work; another investigator, Hê Yüeh-tao, concluded it. In this description to each Mongol tribe a special volume is devoted. Professor Hsü Ping-chang had the kindness to translate for me the most important part of the contents of the little book. One recognizes there much that famous sinologues have already rendered into the great culture languages. If I remember rightly, Koeppen in his work *Die lamaische Hierarchie und Kirche* (1859) has already given an account of the wonderful vicissitudes of the Torgots. In the following I cannot verify the spelling of the names. I write them phonetically according to Professor Hsü's Chinese forms and pronunciation.

The ancestor of the Torgots bore the name of Wung Han. He was followed by seven generations down to Bego Örlek, who had four sons; the eldest was called Dyo Le Tyakan Örlek. The latter's son Ho Örlek lived in the country of Eishör nola, which was a part of Yar, not far from Tarbagatai. At this time there were four tribes that were under the dominion of the Velats (Ölöts). Or in other words, the Velats embraced the following four sub-divisions: Tyolos or the Zungars, Torgot, Hoshot (in Alashan and on Kuku-nor), and Turbet. Hoshot was the only one of these peoples that was descended from Jenghiz Khan. The Tyolos lived in Ili; Turbet on the Ertis (Irtish ?); Torgot in Yar; and the tribe of Hoshot, which had earlier been domiciled round Tihua (Urumchi), at the end of the period of the Ming dynasty left this place, in order under its chieftain Kushe Han to conquer a part of Alashan, Kuku-nor, and Tibet. Kushe Han's nephew Otyito Han led his tribe to the pasture-lands of Alashan. But in the sixteenth year of the reign of the emperor Kang-hsi, that is to say in the year 1677, Otyito Han was attacked and killed by the Zungars, Tyolos. Thereupon a part of the members of his tribe moved into the region round Ning-hsia and was assigned pasture-grounds by the emperor. Kushe Han's younger son had sixteen sons. Of these, four with the permission and assistance of the Dalai Lama settled down on Kuku-nor and twelve in the region round Alashan. With the approval of the emperor they were allowed to dwell in the regions that they had chosen for themselves and which lay at a distance of 60 *li* from the Chinese border.

At this time there were, just the same as before, four sub-divisions of the Velat or Ölöt tribe. After the chieftain of the Zungars, Batur Huntaiji, had forced his way to greater power than the chieftains of the other tribes, the chieftain of the Torgots, Ho Örlek, who could not tolerate the other, decided to move with his whole tribe to southern Russia. This happened at the end of the Ming period; the Chinese source places the headquarters of the Torgots at a latitude 49 degrees north and at 53 degrees west of Peking. To the south of their new dwelling-places Cossacks had one of their original homes. In the course of time the Torgots became Russian subjects.

Ho Örlek's descendants were accustomed, however, to send presents by messengers every year to the emperor of China. His (Ho Orlek's) son was called Shukor Taiji, whose son Pansuk's son, Aityi, accepted the title of " khan." Up to the fifty-first year of the reign of the emperor Kanghsi, that is to say up to the year 1712, Aityi sent envoys to him. Kang-hsi interested himself very much in the distant people and, in order to obtain

239

reliable information about their country, sent Tu Li Tyen through Russian territory to the homes of the Torgots. Tu Li Tyen has described his three-year journey in a work known as *I-yü-lu*, " The book of foreign countries."

In the middle of the 18th century the Torgots were a considerable tribe ; their prince was called Usiba. At that time the Russians were at war with their neighbours, and, since the Torgots were Russian subjects, they too had to take the field. After Usiba, as a result of the Russian wars, had lost many men of his tribe, he was weary of being under the sceptre of the Czar and decided to seek new pasturelands. One of his relatives, who was domiciled in China, appeared in Usiba's headquarters and advised him to conquer the territory of Ili, which China had taken possession of in the twenty-third year of the reign of Chienlung and the time shortly before.

Usiba wanted to lead the whole tribe of the Torgots with him, and sent to those who lived to the west of the river (Volga) the summons to set out on the march in the winter, whenever they could march across the ice. But just during this winter the river did not get frozen up, and Usiba therefore set out with only 160,000 men and moved towards Ili. The Russians pursued him and his hordes, but he had a start and got away. When the Cossacks too began to molest him, he decided to choose another road, and took the direction towards Bulut, to the west of Sin-kiang and to the north-west of Kashgar. When also the Buluts attacked the wandering tribe and plundered its tents and baggage-carts, Usiba sought his escape in the *gobi*, the " desert," where for ten days' marches they found neither pasture nor water and had to drink the blood of horses and oxen. More than a half of the tribe perished, and the pack-animals were lost.

After they had been seven months on the march, they reached the border of Ili. Usiba then only had 70,000 of the members of his tribe left. When the governor of Ili, General Shu Hei-tei, learnt of the approach of the Torgots, he sent out troops to defend the frontier, and envoys to the Torgots to ask what they wanted. Usiba replied that he was all the more willing to submit, in that he, a lamaist himself and filled with a longing for a lamaist country, wanted to remain no longer under the dominion of the Russians, who had another religion and different manners and customs and different clothing to his and his people's.

In China opinions were divided. Some were of the opinion that they should receive the Torgots well; others that they should drive them away. The emperor Chien-lung decided to receive them hospitably, and summoned their leader to Jehol. There he bestowed upon Usiba the title of "khan," and upon his brother the title of "prince"; the other Torgot chieftains also received high honours.

The tribe received new pasture-grounds. Four territories were assigned to them: the southern lay to the north of Kara-shahr, the northern to the east of Tarbagatai, the eastern between Ili and Urumchi, the western to the east of Kulja. On the leaf "Central Asia" in Stieler's Hand-atlas the name of the Torgots is still found to-day in these places.

The emperor made them a present, besides, of 140,000 horses, oxen, and sheep, after they had already obtained 120,000 animals in Sin-kiang. They received, further, 20,000 *chin* of tea, as well as grain, cotton, cloth, yourts, and other things, to the value of 200,000 taels.

The valuable imperial seals that they had received in the Ming period, they gave back to the emperor, who bestowed upon them new Manchu seals in their stead.

The Chinese work finally gives an account of how fate led one branch of the Torgot tribe to Etsin-gol, and with Old Testament exactitude and dryness follows up the genealogy from generation to generation down to the chieftain who was the first on our river. We learn thus that Ho Örlek's son Shukor Taiji had several sons and that the fourth of them, Namu Tyelung, had a son Natyar Mamot, who was therefore a cousin of the Aityi mentioned earlier. In the forty-third year of the reign of the emperor Kang-hsi, that is to say in the year 1704, Natyar Mamot's son Alapdyur set out through the territories of the Zungars on the road for Tibet, where he intended to visit the Dalai Lama and talk with him, obviously to implore his help.

The chieftain of the Zungars, Tyevang Alabutan (also written Tsevang Araptan), was at that time living in enmity with Aityi. Alapdyur could not, therefore, return in safety, but went into the neighbourhood of the city of Su-chow in Kansu.

From Su-chow he sent messengers to the emperor and declared himself ready to enter into the service of the Son of Heaven. The emperor bestowed upon him the district of Sher-tung, a lake with surrounding country, to the south-west of Su-chow. Without doubt, by that is meant the district of Sirting or Shyr-tung to the south-east of the Anambaruin-ula, which I visited in January 1901, and where one finds two lakes, Bulungin-nor and Sukhain-nor. The Mongols that I met with in this region and who provided me with guides across the desert were certainly descendants of Alapdyur's tribe; for this chieftain gratefully accepted the emperor's offer and settled down on the lakes of Shyr-tung.

In the fifty-fifth year of the reign of Kang-hsi, Alapdyur offered to enter the emperor's army. Since, too, the policy of the great Manchu emperor always aimed at firmly binding the Mongols to China with as many bonds as possible, Alapdyur's request was graciously allowed, and the emperor gave him the task of undertaking an expedition to the west with five hundred men of his tribe, in order to search for the lake of Kas, 200 *li* from Lop-nor.

In reality Kas lies a good 400 *li* to the south-east of Lop-nor. The emperor probably knew of the lake from old Chinese maps. Przhevalsky was the first European who made his way to it; he calls the lake Gas. In the years 1900 and 1901 I had two of my headquarters, Mandarlik and Temirlik, on Gas-nor or in its immediate neighbourhood, and also visited the lake.

Alapdyur remained with his tribe on the banks of Gas and died there. From the emperor he had received the title of " kuhan beidsi." His son and successor, Dantyung, went personally to Peking and there received the title of " dolabeili."

In the ninth year of the reign of the emperor Yung-chêng dissatisfaction and disintegration seems to have spread among the Torgots on Lake Gas. Several chieftains went with their hordes over to the Zungars, and Dantyung no longer felt secure against his neighbours. He wanted to exchange his old pasture-lands for new and turned therefore to the governor of Kansu and Shensi, Chia Lang-a, who made over to him and his Torgots certain territories in the Nan-shan range, to the south of Su-chow. These were known as Alak, Altai, and Taibushi, and thither this tenacious roaming tribe wandered, which could, it seemed, find no permanent abode on the earth.

Neither did they remain long in the mountains to the south of Su-chow. For soon afterwards the emperor granted them the lower course of Etsin-gol as a home, down to the two lakes of Gashun-nor and Sokho-nor. In this way Dantyung Dolabeili was in the year 1729 the first Torgot chieftain on Etsin-gol. When we visited the Torgots and their present chieftain, they had thus not yet been domiciled for two full centuries on the river and the two lakes. It was significant, therefore, that the most northerly Torgots assured us that during the last hundred years Sokho-nor had never been completely dried up.

In olden times all the Mongols within the borders of China were under the emperor personally. With the inauguration of the Republic in the year 1911 this relationship of course changed automatically. The Torgots on Etsin-gol, who now only numbered 97 families, came under the supreme authority of the governor of Kansu, although their prince could in certain matters apply directly to the government in Peking.

The territory of the Etsin-gol Torgots stretched in the east as far as Kurne, a region to the south-east of our Station 1, in the south right to the boundary of Mamu near Bayin Bogdo, in the west right to the Gobi, in the north as far as the Atsi-shan range, and in the south-east up to the Holi-shan hills, which appear to lie near the frontier proper of Kansu.

This short sketch only deals with the old Torgots, whose descendants in our day are to be found on Etsin-gol and in four territories far away in the north-west, near Ili, Kara-shahr, and other previously mentioned parts of Sin-kiang.

In addition, a Torgot tribe lives to the south-west of Kobdo, and another to the south of this town. These two tribes are known as " new Torgots." Altogether there are thus seven Torgot tribes, of which five are old.

After the Mongol dynasty of Yüan, Marco Polo's protectors, the Chinese distinguished three large groups of Mongolian lands : in the north the enormous territories of the Khalkha Mongols, in the west the pasture-lands of the Ölöt tribes, in the south the Tyahar and numerous other tribes and their homes. The Khalkhas and Tyahars were descendants of Jenghiz Khan ; of the Ölöts only the Hoshots.

In this world of Mongolian peoples and tribes we find the brave, hardy Torgots. Of their earlier homes one can say, as it is said in the chant : " Not for ever shalt thou dwell under these huts of Kedar ; thou wanderest upon earth a short while, a stranger and a guest." But on Etsin-gol, where the Torgots have spent the last 200 years of their existence, they probably have their home for ever, and here the last small dying branch of their tribe will also become extinct.

The antelope Dicky and the dog Hami

Carrying the canoe overland

An Idyl

[*face p.* 244

Departure for the survey of the river
(Left, the Torgot chief and Professor Hsü ; in the boat, Hedin and Haslund)
On Dondur-gol

XIX

DESERT MARCHES AND SAND-STORMS

WHEN we awoke on the morning of the 8th of November, a day of especial importance lay before us : now we intended to set out on the second great stage, the difficult winter march across the desert that separates Etsin-gol from Hami.

The first day's march was to be only quite short and really only a trial march, to give the Mongols an opportunity to see if the loads lay properly on the camels.

The greater part of the caravan had already set out, when Larson informed me that we had fifteen loads more than we had camels at our disposal. These, then, we must leave behind at Station 1. All the things and stores that we did not need in the next months were therefore eliminated. Haslund was to bring them with him on the second departure that had been arranged for him. Our present shortage of camels was due to the over-exertion that we had demanded of our pack-animals on the departure from Hutyertu-gol. We possessed at the time altogether 272 ; my main caravan numbered 127. The number we had lost up to now was 28 ; in the barren desert regions that awaited us it would certainly become larger still.

The march to Hami took place, the same as the first stage, in three columns : Haude as vanguard in the middle ; Norin, who set out a day later, in the north ; and myself in the south.

Soon we left the river behind us ; then the forest too came to an end. Near it on barren rubbly ground we set up our camp ; it was No. L.

Of the twenty-eight principals of the staff only eleven were in my column : Larson, Heyder, Hummel, von

Massenbach, Lieberenz, Mühlenweg, Hsü Ping-chang, Huang, Ting, Liu, and myself. Five Chinese were now behind us, three of them in Yüan's column, of which we had heard nothing for two months. As camel-attendants we had nineteen Mongols and Chinese. For the rest, we had with us a cook, five servants, and the archæological collector Chuang. We thus numbered altogether thirty-seven. The provisions were calculated for forty days. For the waterless desert regions we were taking six wooden Mongolian troughs with us, whose contents lasted for three camping-places.

On the same day as we, a Chinese merchant caravan of eight hundred camels left Etsin-gol; it came from Kuei-hua-chêng and was making for Guchen via Hami and Barkul. It had loaded with cloth, tea, groceries, cigarettes, and other goods. I mention it now, because during the first part of the journey we had it at a short distance in front of us. Its leader had asked to be allowed to travel in our company, since our rifles would then also afford them protection against robbers. Nothing came of it, however, for we knew that various springs had not sufficient water for so many camels.

The division of labour in our caravan was the same as before.

How happy we all were to be on the road again at last! But no-one suspected how difficult and trying this desert march was to become.

Whilst on the morning of the 9th of November my yourt was being taken down and packed up, I sat at the fire watching how the caravan moved on in seven strings towards the west-north-west. A short while later I followed in its tracks. Behind us disappeared the forests of Etsin-gol and a number of fallen-in watch-towers dating from the Han period. The ground was hard and covered with fine rubble, on which stood isolated tussocks, little hillocks of clay which were held together by roots of plants. A dry river-bed with dying poplars was certainly an old delta-tributary.

Pushing on towards the west, we reached next day the forest on Möruin-gol and walked across its bed 180 metres broad, whose bottom was damp in a few places but for the rest quite dry. On its left bank there was a spring and in the neighbourhood of the latter a pool with fresh, ice-covered water. Möruin-gol resembled Etsingol, but the forest was here thinner and more stunted; the mountain-ash predominated. Under one of these my yourt was set up, and once again we listened to the rustling in the tops of the trees. It seemed to us as if we were taking leave of the summer, this wonderful, unforgettable summer, on which soon there was to follow one of the hardest winters that I have ever experienced in Asia. Near us lay a Torgot yourt, and we learnt that twenty families lived on this river, which reminded me vividly of the Khotan-darya, not least on account of its pools of water. A Torgot by the name of Jantsang was engaged, who was to conduct us to the next spring. From him we learnt that the region was called Toroi-böruk, " the poplars on the sand-ridge." As he told us, wolves, foxes, wild cats, and antelopes are found in the forests on Möruin-gol, but no lynxes. He himself practises hunting and sells the skins to Chinese traders. For a wolf's skin he receives from 10 to 12 dollars. In the spring and early summer the water in the river is very high. During the drifting of the ice one cannot cross it. After continuous summer rain there usually comes a new high water. Jantsang finally told us that Haude and Haslund had from Toroi-böruk taken the southern road to Hami, and he advised us to choose the northern. We followed his advice, a step which proved fortunate from the geographical point of view, but became disastrous for the caravan.

On the night before the 11th of November there was a temperature of 14·2 degrees below zero, the coolest we had had up to now. It was calm and still, and the moon shone silvery white through the chimney into my yourt. In my stove a blazing fire crackled. In spite of the cold during the night, on the 11th of November the temperature rose at 1 o'clock to 10·4 degrees above zero.

The road leads exactly to the north and crosses several other paths. It is therefore well that we have a guide. The steppe across which we are riding is covered with little bushes and tussocks. Steppe fowl are numerous here; they fly in crowds to the pools in Möruin-gol. The paths made by antelopes and gazelles run in all directions. I ride in front; then follows Larson with the guide, then the staff, and behind them the long caravan. Lieberenz comes riding past, in order to film me from his camel—that is, as if a ship on the open sea is filmed from another ship.

After a march of 24·7 kilometres we camped a good distance away from the spring of Shara-holussun. The place where we erected our tents between withered *saksauls* is called Tsakh Shara Holussun, "the boundary of the yellow reeds." Just here a cross-road between Urga and Su-chow crosses the wilderness. It was provided with sign-posts in the form of wooden boards on which two black hands were painted; it is said, however, never to have been used; but only once, as a test, to have been travelled over by a motor-car. In these flat regions with hard and barren soil one can get along almost everywhere with a motor-car, so that the whole work of road-making consists of pointing out the way by means of sign-posts.

This part of Mongolia, whose eastern border territory we are now in, one could justly call no man's land,—it is not under the dominion of the Mongolian Republic, and there are no nomads here, at least not on the stretch which we covered to Sin-kiang, and here the Chinese have no fixed points, not even a store. On the other hand, we saw in several places the traces of old abandoned opium-fields. Of the road that we had now taken, the Torgot Jantsang told us that it had been used for barely two years, and that the Chinese merchant caravans between Kuei-hua-chêng and Guchen used it, in order to escape the toll-stations on the upper course of Etsin-gol. It passes to the immediate west of Gashun-nor, which, however, cannot be seen from the road. From our Camp LIII we had the western corner of Gashun-nor exactly in the north at a distance of 40 *li*. The mountain-chain whose blue outline stands out in the north has the name of Tosto, and on one of its peaks the *obo* of the province of Balten Jasak has been erected. There every year offerings are made to the guardian spirits of the province. The lower mountain-chain in the north-west is called Unuktein Khara, "the black fox mountain." There black foxes and cross-foxes are said to be found. In this mountainous region the wild camel also has its paradise, and from there it extends its raids, as we heard on Gashun-nor, sometimes as far as this lake. During this year herds of about ten animals have twice been seen on the lower Möruin-gol. Jantsang and several other Torgots had seen the shy and swift-footed visitors, before, with the speed of the wind, they beat their retreat across the desert. The Torgots do not kill wild camels, for fear of the wrath of the gods; only the Mongols of the Republic hunt them occasionally.

Our Torgot informant spoke also of the high mountain of Tsagan Bogdo, "the white god," which lies at a distance of eight days' marches in the north-west. In its valleys plant-growth was abundant, and there were also bears there.

With bright weather but a fierce west wind, and after 9 degrees of frost in the night, we set out on the 12th of November towards the west-north-west and thus slowly moved away from Gashun-nor. The desert borderland consisted of coarse sand or fine rubble on a soft subsoil, and the road was often as good as if it had been made with concrete. The land-waves are imperceptible to the eye. One only notices them in the rate of march of the camels, and suspects their existence when the front sections of the caravan disappear, in order then to emerge again on the crest of a new flat land-wave. To make a sketch of such a landscape is very simple. One only needs to draw a line with the ruler. Above this line the sky supports its turquoise-blue dome; below the line is the desert, dark blue shading into violet—and the landscape is finished. There aren't any details that one could draw in—at most a few small yellowish grey dots, which represent isolated tussocks of grass on the steppe.

On the evening of the 12th of November the west wind freshened up to a half gale; then it roared and howled throughout the whole night, and the next morning about 9 o'clock we had a proper sand-storm over us. Larson

came running to my yourt, and shouted: " Just come
out quick and look westward. There the sand-storm is
coming sweeping towards us like a dark wall." It was
indeed a thrilling, nay, almost a weird sight. The sky was
completely darkened with myriads of flying grains of sand
and particles of dust. Luckily I had already taken the
bearings of the mountains in the north the previous afternoon; for to-day they were as if wiped out of existence
and could not be seen at all. Mento came rushing in to
me, in order to fasten a rope in the interior of my yourt
from the chimney to the floor, which was then secured
outside to a few heavy boxes. If it had flown away, we
should perhaps never have got it again. To say nothing
at all of my personal property, which, of course, would
then have danced away, and probably first made a halt
in the forest on Möruin-gol. To move forward in the
face of such a storm is almost impossible. One must
press forward as if through water. And if one goes with
the storm, one must lean backwards and almost at an
angle of 30 degrees against the pressing wind. But
although men can hold their own against such a storm,
for the camels it is well-nigh killing. The animals themselves, as also their projecting loads, form a powerful target
for the wind, and their task becomes twice as great as it
ordinarily is. A series of such stormy days as this can
lay a caravan low. We therefore decided to remain in
Camp LIV, where we had water, it is true, but where
the pasture was worse than bad. On the other hand, it is
characteristic of the storms that they raise the temperature.
The temperature had even in the night only fallen to 0·3
degrees above zero. That was the last time during this
winter that the mercury column remained above zero
during the night.

This storm was without doubt the fiercest that we had
had up to now; we estimated its strength at 30 metres
a second. We were as if besieged or frozen in. Against
my tent there beat not only sand and dust, but a regular
drum-fire of fine gravel hammered against the stretched
walls of felt. On the weather side the yourt threatened
to be driven in. One lath after another fell down from

the roof. I did not allow myself, however, to be disturbed from my task of writing. In Larson's tent, too, time did not seem to hang heavily; he and Hummel were making desperate efforts to explain the game of bridge to Mühlenweg and von Massenbach—from time to time bursts of roaring laughter could be heard from this direction above the noise of the storm. Professor Hsü and the other Chinese did not show themselves the whole day. After supper—thoroughly peppered with flying dust—in Larson's tent, I invited all the Europeans over to my yourt, where the iron stove glowed and shot out sparks, and where we congregated round the light of my lamp reading or writing. The dogs lay curled up behind my yourt, which afforded better protection against the wind than the tents did.

The storm lasted the whole night, and on the morning of the 14th of November it roared and howled and raged still worse than on the day before. Out in the open not a soul was to be seen. All kept under cover, even the weather-hardened Mongols. The deserted ground looked as if a broom had swept over it. Light-coloured comet-tails of dust and sand wound their way along over the ground with the speed of the wind. Whenever one walked among them, one had a feeling of insecurity; it appeared as if the earth was moving and as if one must sink down in its restless billows. When one returned to the tent, one had to protect one's face, for millions of tiny flying particles lashed one's skin. We asked ourselves how the great caravan could have fared which set out before us yesterday and took with it several travellers riding in covered basket-chairs. These sedan-chairs, indeed, offer the wind far larger surfaces for attack, and one would think that such a storm throws them down from the camels quite simply. The caravan has probably not gone on when it was overtaken by the hurricane in the night.

On such a day one has no real rest from work. It tugs and pulls, tears and shakes, at my yourt, and my airy dwelling is more and more pushed over to the lee. But all movable things are packed away in the leather bags, and I am prepared. One gradually gets accustomed to the deafening noise that fills the air. It sounds as if a downpour of hail is beating down on a closed cart in which one is travelling over rough cobbles. Of course we could not start out, but were obliged again to possess our souls in patience. The sun could only be seen as a diffused light, and in the early afternoon disappeared completely. Larson's and Mühlenweg's tent was blown down, and buried everything that was inside under a thick layer of dust and sand; even a saddle had to be dug out. Suddenly one heard cries for help: a tent was threatening to fly away; the storm had pulled out the tent-pegs. I hurried out and found Lieberenz with his cinema-camera already on the scene of the impending catastrophe. This was not long in coming. The tent collapsed and the occupants who were inside threw themselves on the tent-cloth and their belongings, in order to secure them. A roll of toilet-paper succeeded, however, in getting away: it unrolled in a few seconds to its full length of perhaps 100 metres, and fluttered like an endlessly long streamer in the wind. We half killed ourselves with laughter—over the roll as well as over Lieberenz, who did not let this precious opportunity escape him.

In the night the thermometer fell to 7 degrees below zero. The storm dropped somewhat, but in the morning it was still blowing very strongly. When we now continued our march towards the north-west, we overtook a small caravan whose fire we had seen at some distance from our storm camp. To our general astonishment and satisfaction we found that it was Norin, who with Bergman and von Marschall had come upon our caravan road by a more northerly route. We agreed to march together for a few days. Then I intended to follow the northern or caravan road, while Norin was to push on, further to the south, through unknown country. In this way we could, from two sides, cartographically survey the mountain system that was to separate us, and which the Mongols call Kuku-tumurin-ula, "the blue iron mountains." So we now continued our journey together, over hard ground which now and then is overgrown with scattered hillocks of prickly vegetation, but is often completely barren. Here and there a terrace of clay is to be seen, and betrays a former greater extension of Gashun-nor. To our left we leave the " Black Fox Mountain," whose eminences in the west—as a result of the mirage—resemble dark strings of pearls floating above the horizon.

After we had covered 30·6 kilometres in a direction north 8° west, in a terribly desolate region we set up our camp.

On the morning of the 16th of November we received no water for washing, for we had to be sparing with our store in the water-tanks. To-day even the braziers of red-hot coals that were brought into our tents every night and morning failed, on account of shortage of fuel. There was therefore no-one who complained of not being able to wash to-day—with almost 10 degrees of frost.

The air was almost calm when we marched off and travelled exactly to the north across the cheerless desert. The path resembles a bright ribbon which winds its way along over dark grey earth. The mounted Mongols chat, sing, whistle, and shout. It is always pleasant to have happy people round one. In the north-east the blue mountains stand out which form a continuation of the Tosto chain.

The skeletons of camels are very rare here. To-day we caught sight of only two ; the other day not a single one. One receives the impression that the traffic on this road cannot be particularly brisk. Still rarer are the votive heaps of stones which the Mongols erect to the spirits. They gradually came completely to an end, and one noticed that one was leaving the Mongol world behind. To the west of the great desert we come into lands over whose hills there waves the green flag of the Prophet. On the other hand, we once travelled past a sign-post, a small pyramid of stones that had been set up by Chinese caravan men.

The region in which Camp LVI was set up was just as desolate as at the last camp, but our men were able to scrape together some fuel. For places where there was no wood, we had a few sacks of fuel on a camel, for the kitchen and the yourt. The yourt therefore served as club-house, where all our frozen wanderers were welcome.

On the 17th of November Larson set out at half-past six, and I at half-past seven. The road went to the north. We asked ourselves why it did not bend off to the west; we are getting no nearer to Hami in this way. There blows an icy north-west wind, sharp and biting. Everything on the camels that is movable flutters and bangs about. To draw a map in such windy weather is not exactly easy; the hands are soon senseless, and it becomes more and more difficult to get a little warmth into them again in the intervals between taking bearings. The path leads along between hills, again and again crossing a dry erosion-bed. But finally the hills come to an end, and we are again on a level plain. On a last mountain-top a heap of stones rises up; it reminds one of a sea-mark along the coast. We are approaching the Mongolian Republic. It would, indeed, be still worse for us, I thought, if unawares, since we had not been able to get hold of a guide, we overstepped the border of Mongolia and were molested by its frontier riders.

The north-west wind catches us. The camels reel, and I too on my enormous riding-camel fall into a rocking motion. With a feeling of relief, therefore, I see rising up in the distance the smoke of our new camp. When I reach it, I am frozen stiff, and after the rocking and swaying on the camel, the ground under my feet seems to me to be rocking and heaving. But sitting at the crackling fire, one soon thaws, and the ground becomes still again.

Far in the west the " Mountain of the White God " lifted up its light-blue pyramid above the horizon. There the bears were sleeping in undisturbed peace.

The thermometer fell during the night to 8·2 degrees below zero. On the 18th of November the sun rose brilliantly clear. A light breeze blew from the east; in the north-west the sky was covered with clouds. After a heart-felt parting with Norin, Bergman, and von Marschall, and the little antelope, which we here saw for the last time, we continued our journey in a north-westerly direction, while Norin with his column made farther to the south round the Tsagan Bogdo massif. To our right we now had the mountains which form a continuation of the Tosto chain ; to our left the mountain system to which the " Black Fox Mountain " belongs, and which we had crossed the day before. The vegetation is, as usual, poor, hard, withered, and shrunken. To offer the camels such pasture is inhuman. One might just as well work up our packing-cases into sawdust and set that before the animals as fodder. But after we had crossed a belt of *saksauls* on sandy country, and had left the spring of Sebistei behind us, a creeping bush presented itself, in part still green, which was to the camels' taste, and which caused us to change over to a rest. From the storm camp right to the spring of Sebistei we had found no water for three days. When it became dark, over the hills in the south a pale reflection of Norin's camp fire was to be seen. The blazing fire that we were maintaining, they, on the other hand, will certainly have seen clearly.

In the evening the sky in the north-west became still more overcast—had we another storm to expect ?

XX

WINTER HARDENS

I WAS awakened in the middle of the night by the howling of the storm, and when I dressed at dawn I heard someone shouting, " A snowstorm! " which was answered with a cheer by Mühlenweg, who, original enough, has brought snow-shoes along with him. Outside, the snow lay in small white patches in all the tracks made by the camels, and in every depression in the ground, as also in those places that were protected by the low hills and erosion ridges of the steppe, and even now fine snow crystals were drifting in the north-west, where the storm was raging. Streaks of a yellowish-red colour in the east revealed the presence of the sun; elsewhere the sky was dark, and, in the north-west, black, irregular clouds resembled tattered banners. It was gloomy, overcast, and foreboding, and it was as if an impenetrable vaulted roof had descended over the bounds of the desert.

The Siberian winter had suddenly paid us its visit. The previous night we had had a temperature of 5·1 degrees below freezing-point. Now, a very unusual thing during stormy weather, the temperature had fallen, since half-past four in the afternoon, right down to 7 degrees of frost. This was the first day on which the temperature did not rise above freezing-point. The air pressure had in the last forty-eight hours fallen almost by 26 mm., from 656 to 630·5, in spite of the fact that we had been the whole time at about the same altitude. When morning broke the storm ceased, and the morning of Sunday, the 20th of November, was calm and bright.

In a direction south 82° west the summit of Tsagan Bogdo was to be seen. One of our camels had to be left behind at Camp No. LVIII. It would no longer

Student Tsui returns to Paotow
(In the background, Permanent Station No. 1)

Departure for Hami of the column of Haude, Hempel, Haslund, von Kaull, and Dettmann

LEAVE-TAKING

Thousands of minute particles of sand fill the air
(Left, Hedin's yourt)

A tent after the storm

A SAND-STORM

eat its food, and could no longer be made to stand up.

We set out towards the north-west along a valley that was partially interrupted by two sandy hills, overgrown with tamarisk bushes, that ran across it. The view was picturesque and beautiful : winding narrow valleys between threatening precipitous mountains. Then we came out again on open country. On the 21st of November we were surrounded by monotonous desolation and solitude. But on that day there was no wind and the sun had regained its strength, so that it was warm. Riding was therefore a pleasure and not, as during wind or storm, a torment. In the afternoon of the following day there was snow for a change.

The 23rd of November was calm and almost warm. To the north there stretched out an almost endless plain. Here the eye took in a really immense area of the earth's surface. Our march was short as usual. We had in the last five days put exactly 100 kilometres behind us, and now we were at a distance of 256 kilometres from Etsin-gol and 480 from Hami.

To-day we inscribe the 24th of November. It is a month to Christmas Eve. Where shall we celebrate it ? We are optimistic enough to hope that then the whole caravan will have assembled in Hami. Everything depends on our camels. If they hold out we shall arrive to time. But already many of them are exhausted and weary.

We have seen no human beings since leaving Möruin-gol. The great caravan that left Etsin-gol at the same time as ourselves is in front of us at so short a distance that sometimes its camp fires are still glowing under the ashes when we ride past them. But where are all the great caravans from west and east, which, so we had been told, took this northern desert road ? Our informants had assured us that this road was new, at the most two years old. The more southerly, taken by Haude's column, was, on the other hand, six years old. Before us there may be the best road in the territory of the Mongolian Republic. Here we have the land of Death and Silence ; here there is neither man nor beast.

But now there rises up before us at a distance of a few kilometres a brightly-shining yellow belt. Mento, whom I question, says that it is grass, beyond all possibility of doubt. Thank Heaven! So our camels will at last have something to eat. A little later we recognize distinct tracts, with waving grass or sedge, small woods of poplar, and thickets of tamarisk. We cross a murmuring brook, coming from a spring and lower down forming floating ice glistening with a bluish light. On an old opium field stand our tents. The camels are already at pasture. It was a pleasure to see with what a relish they ate, and how their eyes sparkled when they drank the fresh sweet water. A strong westerly wind had set in, but the thick tamarisk bushes sheltered us. We had to rest here for a few days, for this spot, known by the name of Ikhen-gol, was the first oasis since Möruin-gol. It seemed to us, after our march through the barren places of the desert, like a paradise on earth.

Our hunters killed several gazelles and various kinds of wildfowl, and we had fresh meat again. The stores of provisions for the Europeans were still large enough to suffice until Hami was reached, but the Mongols, unable to economize, had only enough flour to last another four days. It was therefore necessary for a messenger to be sent on in advance to buy flour, either from the large caravan in front of us, if it had anything to spare, or else in the small Chinese town of Ta-shih-to, which was said to be on the frontier of Sin-kiang, and to boast of a store. Therefore, to replenish our stores as quickly as possible, I commissioned Mühlenweg, with Camel-Driver Chang and the Mongols Banche and Singhi, on four of our best riding-camels and with an extra pack-camel, to hurry forward in forced marches. He was also told to purchase peas as a restorative for our feeble camels. The sum of money that I was able to hand over to him only amounted to 400 dollars from my own cash-box and 200 that Professor Hsü kindly placed at my disposal. As soon as Mühlenweg had made his purchases he was to hurry back with all speed, and rejoin our party at the earliest possible moment. I gave him the option, as he thought fit in

view of the circumstances, either to hire or to buy fresh
camels for the journey back. From Ta-shih-to he was
to send Chang on to Hami with a letter for Haude and
Haslund, informing them of our position and of the steps
and measures that he had taken to relieve us. My commission to Mühlenweg was admittedly somewhat indefinite,
but no other course was possible. For not one of us
had any idea of the position and possibilities of Ta-shih-to.
We did not even know for certain if one could make the
necessary purchases there, let alone whether the place had
camels for sale. Everything depended on circumstances,
but Mühlenweg is an able man, who can be relied upon,
and he accepted the difficult task joyfully. Besides, he
speaks fluent Mongolian. From the uncertain information we had received he should be able to reach Ta-shih-to
within a week, and, since we too were moving on towards
the west at the same time, we hoped to see him again
within a space of two weeks. Mühlenweg himself was
convinced that he would be with us again by full moon
on the 8th of December.

Whilst Mühlenweg was starting out on his hurried
march on the 25th of November, the remainder of us
with our camels allowed ourselves a few days' rest in the
oasis of Ikhen-gol. Then on the 28th of November—
after a drop in the night to 22·7 degrees below zero—we
set off again. The road led towards the south-west. On
our right we had a small mountain ridge and three flat
dome-shaped elevations. In south 13° west, Tsagan
Bogdo raised up its blue pyramid. We rode past a curious
Chinese inscription. The black rubble on the surface of
the pasturage had been removed, showing Chinese ideographs 2 metres high in the bright underlying loam.
The inscription was translated for us by Hsü :

" When we are united we receive the assistance of the gods.
This road is not often used, but we had to travel along it again
to avoid the toll-stations."

We could see Mühlenweg's footsteps all along the road.
He had obviously wished to spare his riding-camel. On
the bushes along the path hung white flocks of sheep's

wool, a thing we were used to seeing. They are left whenever the bales of wool carried by the camels brush against the thorny bushes, and betray one of the most important articles of trade carried along these lonely roads.

On the march to-day we had to leave two camels behind, and a third only reached the camp with toil and exertion ; already we asked ourselves the question, how many of them would reach Hami. The caravan road that we were following had been dreadfully poor as regards everything. Of fifteen camping-places only one was good. With such losses as we had suffered to-day our position must before long become critical. The Mongols had obtained beans, lard, and a certain amount of flour, which we could do without. We still had everything in sufficient quantity for the staff, and, of course, we would share with the Mongols and Chinese servants when their stocks came to an end.

The following day the wind came from the south, where Tsagan Bogdo now rose up in a direction south 14° east. We still travelled to the south-west, between dark hills. Then we turned into a valley, 40 metres broad, that went to the south. It became ever narrower and more winding, by degrees swung round to the south-west and west, and finally led us to an open valley, shaped like a basin, which was surrounded by the summits of small dark mountains, and whose soil was in places completely barren and in others overgrown with scattered tufts of grass. Here and there still larger patches of snow were lying. In a gully we found a spring, 60 centimetres deep, with sweet frozen water, which invited us to set up the camp, particularly as the pasture was rather better than usual.

A strong westerly gale on the 30th of November forced us to halt. In the morning the tufts of grass were white with frost, which disappeared when the sun had risen. I sat for an hour or two with Hsü, in whose tent a fire was now burning. We took meals in my yourt, where we then remained together for some time and kept up a lively conversation. We slaughtered a camel that we could use no longer, since the Mongols and the dogs were in need of meat. The moon had a halo more than usually beautiful; silent and gloomy the mountains enclosed our camp, where the camels were ruminating over the poor fodder that we had offered them.

In the night the thermometer fell to 24·7 degrees below freezing-point.

On the 1st of December we rode through a flat valley between the mountains and crossed innumerable small gullies. In the north were the outlines of more chains of mountains in ever lighter shades of blue. In the south we had only a low ridge close to us. The broken country tired the camels and made them move at an uneven pace. One of the animals could get along no longer and had to be left behind. A troop of sixteen wild asses appeared and our hunters pursued them in vain. In the middle of the road we found a letter from Mühlenweg and a figure " two " arranged in small stones, which indicated that this was his second communication. The note was very short and simply informed us that all was well.

During the night we had snow. The temperature only fell to 14·1 degrees below freezing-point. On the morning of the 2nd of December it was still snowing, and the snowflakes, which came dancing into my tent through the opening for the smoke, spluttered on the stove. When I went outside I found the ground covered with a layer of snow two centimetres thick. The sun rose bright, however, and the small, fine snow crystals sparkled like the diamonds in a jeweller's shop.

We continued our journey towards the south-west, the snow crushing under the horny feet of the camels and reminding us of home.

We again rode past a camel that had collapsed. It followed us with listless eyes, probably surprised that we did not help it. Maybe it believed, too, that we were not the last, but that others were coming after us and would look after it. Thinking of the abandoned camels caused me pain. Neither Larson nor the Mongols can bring themselves to killing them. When I speak of it, they always answer that an abandoned camel may possibly regain its strength at pasture, after it has had a rest, even when this is poor, and may then be rescued by some caravan or other following later. I do not believe it; for when a camel refuses to stand up, its end is near. Then there remains nothing else but to hope that the poor animal has not too long to lie and wait, but that Death the Deliverer has released it before the moon rises upon the white fields of snow.

We pitched our camp in the middle of the snow at the entrance to a small valley belonging to the mountains to the south of us. The Mongols had forgotten to fill the six water-containers at the last spring, in consequence of which Europeans, Chinese, and Mongols, now went round with spoons, plates, and scoops, and collected snow, which was melted over the fire. The more serious did our position gradually become, the stronger was Professor Hsü's confidence and calm of mind. In the hard times that we had to put up with he showed himself quite equal to the position.

Following the valley at whose entrance we had encamped, on the 3rd of December we went up the incline towards the south-west. We soon came upon Mühlenweg's third report, in which he only stated that he had not yet reached the large Chinese caravan. Then from a poplar near a spring hung the fourth letter, dated the 27th of November, and informed us that Mühlenweg had come up with the rear section of the Chinese and had learned that they reckoned it five long days' journey to the Chinese shops in Ta-shih-to. Neither flour nor peas had he been able to buy from the caravan.

Camp LXVIII we set up at the entrance of an inhospitable valley. In vain did our hunters roam the neighbourhood in quest of game, but not once were fresh tracks of wild sheep or gazelles to be seen.

The 4th of December our way led to the north-west through a maze of small winding valleys. Now and then we had to cross a ridge, only to descend upon another road through the valley on the other side, but finally the country opened out a little, and at some distance we could see, hemmed in by the mountains, a new oasis, where more springs arose and gave the water of life to poplars, tamarisks, and fields of reeds. Our tents were erected in a wood of rustling poplars.

In this excellent Camp LXIX near Tsagan Burgusun we spent two days in which we rested. The spot was picturesque and charming, closed in between black mountains, and with a wealth of old poplars, which raised up their entangled upper branches, divested of leaves, over yellow fields of thickly-growing rushes and over floating ice glistening with a bluish light. To the north one had a splendid view. There the endless plain stretched away in bright light-blue colours like the sea.

In the night before the 6th of December the temperature fell to 21·4 degrees below freezing-point. I woke up at half-past two, since our dogs began to bark and dashed off towards the south. When they paused for an instant from their loud barking, I heard in the far distance the sound of caravan bells. It came nearer and nearer; a caravan was approaching. On such a desert road as this the arrival of a merchant caravan is, as it were, a connexion with the outer world. We hope to get news of China, and question whether the merchants have anything to sell. We could clearly see the column encamped due south of us in the valley.

In the morning we learned that it was a merchant caravan of 1,200 camels and 90 men, which was travelling from Kuei-hua-chêng to Barkul and Guchen; two of its divisions were bound for Hami. Some fifty different businesses were represented in this great caravan. First among them was the Tei-ching-ho, a large firm in Kuei-hua. They had bound themselves together and were forwarding their goods on hired camels, whose owners, seven in all, had provided from 150 to 200 animals each. The goods for the most part consisted of textiles, tea, cigarettes, and various provisions. Only three of the party had travelled this road before and were acquainted with it. A few of the camel-owners were *Hui-hui*, Mohammedans. They have the reputation of being smarter business men than the Chinese.

Between the two camps there immediately sprang up a brisk business. Several members of the merchant caravan came to our fire, and Professor Hsü and Dr. Hummel visited the strangers in the morning. Chuang and Serat had been there already, and had succeeded in buying 80 *chin* (catties) of flour, which they presumably intended to keep for themselves. But when Massenbach got to hear of it, he placed an embargo on the provisions, for which he paid, and explained that the flour would be divided out among all equally. There was, in fact, only 50 *chin* over.

Later in the day, I too, accompanied by Professor Hsü, went over to our neighbours. We visited a tent whose Mohammedan owner provided us with a succession of interesting items of information, and we then roamed about in the huge camp and could not see enough of the picturesque scenes that were being enacted everywhere.

The two rest-days were beneficial to both men and animals. Heyder and Lieberenz again went hunting, and brought home two gazelles, a hare, and several partridges. The addition to our meat supply of course could not go far, and an exhausted camel had therefore to be killed for the Mongols.

XXI

DAYS OF ANXIETY

WHEN on the morning of the 7th of December we continued our march towards the north-west, two of the last sections of the great caravan were still camping. We had not yet come far, when we rode past a camel that had refused to follow us further. It stood by the road on unsteady legs and looked at us with listless eyes.

The road leads down through a valley, and we again cross the mountain-chain that we have crossed a few days ago. The landscape is incomparable in its endless expanse.

From the black mountains in the south, there juts out a great precipitous rocky spur to the north, which seems to obstruct our free passage to the west. Before we have reached it, however, we find ourselves quite near the edge of a strongly cut-out drainage-furrow coming from a valley in the south. There where the furrow spreads in the opening of the valley, grow thick fields of reeds. Here the great Chinese caravan has now set up its tents, while our camp lies a short distance further below. The place is called Shara-holussun, " the yellow reeds." A brook with a spring of fresh murmuring water flows along between broad ice-floes. In the north there stretches now as ever the endless sea of the desert, and the landscape is one of the most imposing that we have seen since we left Paotow.

Major Heyder is a good shot and hunter. He comes to our rescue from day to day, by keeping us constantly supplied with fresh meat. Near Shara-holussun he killed two splendid buck gazelles. Two of our men succeeded in purchasing a small quantity of millet and sugar from the Chinese. In contradistinction to us, the Chinese have taken stores of provisions with them which suffice not only for themselves, but also for others. But they have, indeed, an experience which extends over a few thousands of years.

Liu visited a Chinese who knew the road, who gave him particulars of the whole of the way to Ta-shih-to. He learnt from him all camping-places, springs, pasturages, and distances, and from these drew a little sketch-map. According to this information, we should have eleven days' journey, 240 kilometres, to Ta-shih-to. A Chinese map which Liu had with him gave the distance from Ta-shih-to to Tash-bulak as 58 kilometres, and from Tash-bulak to Hami as 120. We should thus have, in round numbers, another 420 kilometres to Hami—that was impossible, for the distance according to our own routes of march could not exceed 300 kilometres.

On the 8th of December the road ran first of all to the south and south-west. At a bend there rose up an isolated pyramid-shaped small mountain-top with a heap of stones at its foot. All at once the thick plant-growth came to an end and we rode through a peculiar valley, rising in a straight line, which was scarcely 100 metres broad. Black towering mountains descended steeply on both sides to the flat bottom of the valley. The landscape was magnificent, but gloomy.

The valley then broadened out, and we travelled through a natural portal of two small eminences crowned with stone landmarks, and reached a very inhospitable camping-place, where there was neither water nor pasturage and fuel was scanty. The consumption of water for washing of any kind was therefore forbidden, and even the kitchen was asked to economize. The dogs had to be content with the washing-up water, but could hold out without harm on the snow which still lay in patches here and there.

In the evening a scene presented itself to us that I shall never forget. In the east one could hear in the distance the old well-known tinkling of caravan-bells, which in measured, solemn rhythm were approaching nearer and ncarer to us. Hsü, Hummel, and I went out to see the nocturnal procession march by. The full moon poured its silvery-white cold light over the desert. Already at 8 o'clock we had 12 degrees of frost, but the wind had abated. Like shadows the first camels appeared. Powerful and majestic they strode along with their calm, dignified gait, and their loads were well and evenly distributed on their pack-saddles. All the caravan men went on foot.

The feeling was enchanting. Innumerable times already had I seen this spectacle, but I could see it again and again. I could not tear myself away before the long procession was over. No, it was not over; far away in the east there sounded a new ringing of bells. But I was cold, for I had not put on my fur, and I gladly yielded to the benevolent authority of our doctor, who ordered me a crackling fire in the stove. That I had quite unprofitably defied the spirits of the cold and of the darkness, I learnt in the night, when pains and restlessness disturbed my sleep. Not till towards morning did I fall asleep, and when I was awakened by Mento, who was making a fire in the stove at the accustomed time, Larson and the others had already set out, and only Heyder was still there to accompany myself and Mento. Since I believed that my indisposition was only temporary, I had not said a word about it to Dr. Hummel. My breakfast, however, remained untouched. Whilst my yourt was being taken down I sat outside at the fire while the sun was rising, and looked at the rose-coloured clouds on the eastern horizon.

Then we continued our journey on the *via dolorosa* of the camels. A terrible west wind chilled me to the bone, and I longed for Camp LXXII. Fortunately we had only 14 kilometres to go to an open spring, whose ice-floes were surrounded by passable pasturage. At the fire, which was already burning between the tents, Dr. Hummel gave me a first examination, and immediately fixed the diagnosis with unmistakable certainty: a new attack of gall-stones. He ordered me rest—in the first instance for to-day and to-morrow, and Hsü sided with him and implored me to keep to my bed until the attack was over.

My protests were of no avail. I did not feel so bad as not to be able quite well to continue the journey. Under no circumstances did I want to hold up the march of the caravan, especially as our position was critical, our camels were tired, and our provisions were running low. To remain a day in Camp LXXII did us no harm; water and pasturage were better than usual. I was therefore immediately put to bed and nursed and cared for like a little child.

During the rest-day a Mongolian caravan from An-hsi reached the spring. It was carrying barley and flour to Jasaktu-khan. Two days previously they had come across Norin's column, and they told us that the latter intended to camp to-day, the 10th of December, near the spring of Sebistei, three days' journey to the south-west of here. Norin's camels had marched well and had appeared well and active. This news was comforting, for I had been rather anxious concerning the column, which was travelling through unknown regions. The Mongols themselves were thirteen days on the journey since leaving An-hsi and reckoned six days to reach home.

The great question now was: should we overtake Norin, Bergman, and von Marschall, near Sebistei, or would only our roads cross near the spring?

For several days the whole staff had gone on foot, even the Chinese. Since the strength of our camels decreased more and more and almost daily a new martyr remained behind, we had to conserve their carrying power and even employ the riding-camels as pack-animals. The Mongols, who are not used to walking, still rode, and I was seated as usual in my " crow's-nest."

Dr. Hummel walked by my side when we set out at half-past eight on the 11th of December. The air was still and the sky covered with clouds.

After a march of two hours he ordered a halt, lit a crackling fire, and put me to bed in furs on the soft sand. I had such gall-stone pains that he gave me an injection of morphia and caffeine, which acted as a relief. For a full two hours we remained lying at the fire, and then when we continued our journey in the tracks of the others,

Full moon

Hoar-frost

WINTER IN THE GOBI

With difficulty the famished camels drag themselves forward. Many remain by the wayside, others are slaughtered because of shortness of meat

Hedin ill and carried on a stretcher

WINTER IN THE GOBI

I did not exactly sit very firm on my high, swaying riding-animal. Never have I longed so much for camp. We covered 20·6 kilometres, and, as hitherto, I drew the route of the march. At last we caught sight of the smoke of a camp-fire in the distance and finally landed among our party. My yourt was already standing there ready, and I moved into my " field-hospital."

In the evening Dr. Hummel brought his sleeping-sack, his furs, and other things, into my yourt, in order to be able to attend to me, if it became necessary.

When the following day we moved along in the accustomed way behind our caravan, and were at a distance of only another 2 kilometres from our camp, which was No. LXXIV, against the sun we caught sight of two forms that came hurrying to meet us. One was Larson; the other Norin. It was a great joy to us to see Norin safe and sound and to hear that Bergman and von Marschall were camping at the spring of Sebistei scarcely 50 *li* to the north-west.

In Camp LXXIV, where there was no water and the pasturage was bad, Norin remained the night with us. It was now a question of in some way or other conveying my poor body to the spring of Sebistei, where everything—water, pasture, and fuel—was to hand, and where the doctor with inflexible firmness ordered two weeks' rest for his patient. Just as definitely did he forbid me to ride, since the rolling gait of the camel was obviously not beneficial to my disturbed gall-stones.

But how in the world was I to get to Sebistei, if I could not walk and was not allowed to ride? Naturally there wasn't any vehicle here, and one could not be made with the small store of wood we had with us.

Shortage of water forced us already next morning to continue our journey to the spring of Sebistei. Professor Hsü made the suggestion of making a sledge out of tent-poles and boards from boxes. That could be drawn either by camels or by men. But Larson explained that, owing to the stony ground, such a conveyance would come to an end after 2 kilometres. He himself was for a litter, which might be carried by four mounted Mongols on quiet camels. I protested, however, that I had no liking at all for mounting such a flying-machine, which ran the risk any minute of being either crushed between the four camels, or torn to pieces if the shying animals pulled in four different directions.

Then the 13th of December dawned, a day which in the chronicle of my life shall be marked with three stars. It is one of my most cherished memories, for it gave me one of the greatest and finest proofs of friendship and devotion that I have ever met. I believe too that my companions will remember the 13th of December—one thing is certain in any case, that they will never forget how terribly heavy I was and how strange it looked carrying a living man across the deathly silent Gobi Desert.

At half-past nine we started out. Outside there waited an iron bedstead. Along the two sides two tent-poles tied together were fastened. The bed consisted of the sleeping-sack and a few cushions. In cashmere boots, cat's-skin fur, and cap, I lay upon it, and was covered over with the large sheep-skin. The litter with all its appliances weighed at least as much as I myself. A good forty kilos weighed on each of the shoulders that carried me. As soon as I was wrapped up like a mummy, the first bearers stepped into their places; on a given signal, Heyder and Hummel, Norin and von Massenbach, lifted the litter on their shoulders and started in motion. After eight minutes Matte Lama stepped into Heyder's place, while the other three men only changed shoulders. Then new bearers gave a hand: Lieberenz and his servant Charlie and also the Mongol Jangsun. The rate of marching and the weight made it necessary that there should be a change every seven minutes. We thus had two sets of bearers, which relieved each other, so that each bearer carried for seven minutes and for the next seven minutes went free. I had my watch in my hand and called a halt when the time was up. I also made observations in my note-book just as usual. The Mongolian bearers did not understand marching in step. On their shoulders the movements were in irregular jerks. I had a feeling of greater rest and security whenever the four Europeans stepped under the litter again.

After about an hour and a half a rest of half an hour was made and the litter was set down by the side of a glorious warming fire. I was probably the only one who needed it, for those who carried me were warm enough with their work. Whilst we halted Heyder rode on ahead on Norin's camel and took instructions to Larson to send immediately at least eight Mongols to meet us, to relieve our first two sets of bearers. They were to ride, so that they might be here as quickly as possible.

After the rest the procession moved on through the wilderness. Lieberenz took films and photographs, and I confess I was quite curious about the plates, which could not be developed until we reached Hami.

At 1 o'clock we halted at a point where *saksauls* provided us with fuel, again lit a blazing fire, and had a sumptuous luncheon: roasted antelope's kidney and green peas, cakes and butter, tea and cream.

After we have thus refreshed and rested ourselves we continue our journey, and my litter swings over new stretches of the endless Gobi. Mento, Bonk, Matte Lama, and Jangsun are my bearers. Relieving now takes place every five minutes. It is half-past three and the sun is nearing the horizon. I have it straight in front of me. We enter a labyrinth of low dark hills. Here the ground is undulating, but that is more noticeable to the bearers than to me.

Another half hour goes by and in front of us there shows up a picturesque quickly-moving troop of riders as dark silhouettes against the setting sun. They are ten of our Mongols and Chinese, who have been sent from Sebistei to meet us. They are riding in a quick trot. We halt. They dismount, and four of them immediately step towards the litter and bear a hand with new strength. Their steps are short but quick, and the hills to the side of the road disappear at a quicker rate than hitherto. Their walking does not, however, keep an even step—it is as if one is rowing through a ground-swell.

271

Suddenly Bergman approaches me, youthful, robust, and sunburnt; in passing by we exchange a hearty handshake. A few minutes later von Marschall appears beside me, as calm and cheerful as usual. I express to him my condolence on the loss that he and all of us have suffered by the pretty little antelope Dicky having finished the part it played on our peaceful campaign. The misfortune had happened a few days before, when Norin's column was on the march and Bergman, at a distance of a few kilometres from the road, had shot a wild ass. Von Marschall had gone to it, and his faithful pet Dicky had accompanied him as usual. About half-way the antelope had turned back and its master had supposed that it would find its way back to the caravan just as easily as usual. But in the evening, when Bergman and von Marschall came into the new camp, Dicky was missed. Early next morning they had set out to look for him, but all their search was in vain. They called and whistled, but the desert lay still and silent and did not give back its prey. It is probable that Dicky had strayed into the hilly country. He was too light to leave footprints behind in the hard ground. Dicky was lost and remained lost, and we missed him very much. We tried to console ourselves with the hope that he has found relations and has been hospitably received into a herd.

Our procession had now assumed imposing proportions. Before me rode three Mongols, of whom first one then another covered up for me the red ball of the sun on the horizon. On both sides of the litter rode the Europeans on the camels of the Mongols, a guard of honour as it were, and behind me rode the first body of Mongols. Now we advanced more quickly. The sun went down and twilight came on.

It gets gradually darker. It is cold, and the cold penetrates through my furs. In front of us the light of a fire is to be seen. When we reach the first tent—it is Norin's, Bergman's, and von Marschall's—I call a halt, although Larson has set up our own camp 200 metres farther on. But I can get no further; I have had enough. The litter is set down in the opening of the tent, and Dr.

Hummel finds shelter for me in the heated tent while my yourt is being set up.

It was glorious to come into a heated tent out of the increasing cold of evening. Here I now lay like a pasha and received the envoys of the neighbouring peoples. Hsü was the first. He sat a long while by my bed and was most concerned, as ever, in his anxiety and his friendly and wise counsel. Then Larson's tall form appeared in the opening of the tent; he gave me a report on the state of the caravan. Huang, Ting, and Liu came, in order to inquire after my health, and several of our servants, too, gave expression to their affection and sympathy.

But the evening advanced, and my yourt was ready. Those who were living in the other camp went their way, and finally it became calm and still with us. Norin told me that first three, and then two more, doubtful-looking Mongols, all armed with Russian army-rifles of 1886 pattern, had come to his camp and had talked with our camel-attendants. They were camping at some distance from us and were in possession of about fifty splendid camels. How they had come by these one could imagine. Without doubt we had a small band of robbers for neighbours, and now they had cautiously approached in order to ascertain our strength and the prospects of a sudden attack.

Norin suggested that we should forestall them and make a sudden attack on their camp with all men capable of bearing arms. I entirely agreed with him, and when I lay awake in the evening, I meditated on the plan of operations that we must then follow. Our military forces would take the band of robbers prisoners and hand the scoundrels over in ropes to the authorities in Hami; their fifty camels would enter the service of our tired caravan, in order later to be delivered up likewise to the authorities. After such a victorious campaign against the pest of the peaceful trade caravans, we should enter Hami in triumph and be received as heroes throughout the whole of Sin-kiang.

In the interests of safety we decided to keep watch by our tents during the night. At 2 o'clock I heard firm steps before my yourt. I knew that it was Bergman, who was now on guard, and called him in to me. He came and made the stove up ; with this Hummel woke up, and we talked until 4 o'clock and forged plans for the future.

In the morning it was reported that the band of robbers had gone away ; they had probably found us too strong. So our proud scheme went up in smoke.

Camp LXXV, which we had reached in such strange circumstances, became the most momentous of our whole journey. Here at the spring of Sebistei we entered upon a new stage of our adventures, and here the history of our expedition began to get troubled and dramatic.

Well wrapped up in my sleeping-sack, I spent the whole of the following day in a series of important con-sultations. I had long talks with Professor Hsü, Norin, and Heyder, von Marschall and von Massenbach, Larson, Bergman, and Lieberenz, and, when it was necessary, Dr. Hummel drew up minutes.

Before I was taken ill, it had been our intention to leave Larson and a number of Mongols behind at the spring of Sebistei with the heavy baggage, while the whole staff with the necessary baggage and provisions and the whole of the hundred and thirteen camels proceeded to Ta-shih-to. At the shops of the merchants there the camels were to be fed up with strengthening food and left behind in the charge of the rest of the Mongols. A caravan of hired camels was to go to Sebistei, in order to fetch the large baggage and Larson and his Mongols. I myself and the whole staff together with the Chinese servants, on either hired camels or the best of our own, would have continued our journey by Tash-bulak to Hami, which we should have reached by Christmas.

In consequence of my illness our plan was altered so that Dr. Hummel and I were also remaining behind at Sebistei. The doctor firmly persisted in his opposition to my continuing the journey on a camel, and ordered me complete rest in all circumstances. Meanwhile, it should be possible for our party that was riding on towards the west to get hold of a cart with a team of mules and horses, on which, without needing to be apprehensive of a relapse, I could journey to Hami. When Larson heard of the band of robbers near Sebistei, he considered the danger to the heavy baggage much too great, and proposed to take it to Ta-shih-to with our own animals. He wanted to march by night, so that the camels could pasture throughout the whole of the day. I approved his plan the more readily as I had always had a dislike of leaving valuable baggage behind—one indeed never knows for certain when one will be able to fetch it later.

Norin now made the proposal that he and Bergman should stay with me and Hummel, especially as they would then have an opportunity to make an extensive and thorough geological and topographical investigation of the neighbourhood of Sebistei, which was in many respects interesting. For that they required from one to two weeks. Moreover, they would both have more than enough of notes and the working-out of their results to deal with. I probably scarcely need particularly to emphasize, that to both Hummel and me the time of waiting at Sebistei appeared in quite different and much brighter colours, when it was decided that during these days of uncertainty Norin's and Bergman's tent should stand at a distance of scarcely 5 metres from our yourt. On the whole of the long journey from Paotow we had enjoyed all too rarely the company of our two splendid countrymen, and now we should share joy and sorrow together for who knows how long, and should then experience in common the deliverance from a camp which, whatever would be the end of it, would certainly not leave anything of dramatic suspense to be desired. For reality is often more wonderful and more romantic than fancy, and although, at the moment I am writing this, I know no more of our future vicissitudes than the reader does, I nevertheless have a presentiment that they will confirm the truth of this statement.

When all the various consultations had been brought to an end and twilight had fallen, probably for the last time, over our common camp, I summoned the whole staff into my yourt, where Chinese, Germans, and Swedes grouped themselves round my bed. We consisted of five

Swedes, four Germans, and four Chinese. Now, after mature consideration, and in agreement particularly with Hsü Ping-chang, I issued the following orders:

1. Larson is taking the main caravan and almost the whole of the baggage to Ta-shih-to. With him are going the German and Chinese members of the staff. In order to make his caravan more efficient, Larson asked for seven of Norin's camels, which were always better than his own, for they were looked after according to Chinese, not Mongolian, principles. In place of these he was leaving behind at Sebistei four discarded camels out of his own troop. What steps could be taken for our relief in Ta-shih-to depended on circumstances. We indeed knew nothing certain about this place. When we sent Mühlenweg out from Ikhen-gol, we had believed he would join us again by the 8th of December. The information that we later obtained proved that the distance to the Chinese store was considerably greater. But now it was already the 14th of December. If Mühlenweg had obtained what he sought, he should already have been back again. But perhaps there was nothing at all to be got in Ta-shih-to. I therefore had to leave it to Larson and his companions, themselves to judge the situation and act accordingly.

2. Von Marschall and Liu, accompanied by the collector Chin and the Mongol Ottehong, who besides was half Chinese, are going in forced marches towards the west on the road to Hami, in order, in the first place where a relief caravan can be got together, in Ör-ja-hutung, Ta-shih-to, or, at the worst, Tash-bulak, to hire camels for the baggage left behind at Sebistei, to buy the provisions that we required there, and, if possible, to hire or to buy a cart and three mules for me. Von Marschall and Liu were also lent seven of Norin's splendid camels. They were to carry out the march back to Sebistei as quickly as possible and could, according to circumstances, leave Norin's camels behind at the turning-point, so that they could rest and pasture. After Marschall had taken over Norin's travelling-chest, we had at Sebistei only 7 dollars left.

3. Liu is returning here with Marschall, in order on his second journey to the west to draw a map of the route of march; for that was not possible on the forced marches during the night.

4. Haslund is waiting for us in the village of Tash-bulak, 100 kilometres to the east of Hami, with money and Norin's and Bergman's post. For the two were planning a little excursion and would probably not reach Hami till a fortnight after me, but, just like us others, were longing for news from home.

Concerning Mühlenweg we were alarmed and anxious. He had completely disappeared; it was as if he had been swallowed up by an abyss. On the last days' marches we had neither seen his track nor found letters from him. We asked ourselves if he had turned off on the more southerly and more direct road to Hami and had abandoned Ta-shih-to, which lies on the road to Barkul. When he parted from us on Ikhen-gol, he had provisions for barely a week. But he had his rifle with him and could shoot antelopes. He scarcely ran a risk of starving, for in case of extreme necessity he could kill the worst of his four camels. He was, moreover, a regular dare-devil; and a man who right in broad daylight and amid a thousand dangers had fled out of French captivity does not get lost on the road to Hami. The help which we had expected from him had not appeared, of course, and it was not impossible that our large caravan would pick him up on the way and bring help to the helper—instead of the reverse.

When the issuing of orders was over, I began to draft the enormous telegram, which comprised eight hundred words and, in case this was possible, was to be sent from Hami to Stockholm. It gave an account of our stay on Etsin-gol, of the establishment of Station 1, of our plans to extend the expedition, and of our advance towards Hami as far as the spring of Sebistei. In the second draft the message was condensed to five hundred and sixty words and was translated by Hummel into French for Professor Hsü and into German for the Germans. Hummel made a clean copy of the telegram in the third

277

and last draft and read it out at 3 o'clock in the night. As agreed upon, it was then put down at the entrance in my yourt, where Heyder was to fetch it in the morning.

Most of us did not get much sleep this night. The stores of provisions had also been looked over and distributed, and we who were remaining here received our share. At the last minute Hummel took possession of the large gramophone, which in large measure sweetened the time of waiting for us, while those who were leaving would scarcely have had an opportunity to listen to its notes.

Late in the evening those who were leaving gathered in my yourt to say good-bye. I said a sincere good-bye to each one separately and expressed the hope that they would soon succeed in raising the relief that we needed —camels, cart, and provisions. Last of all Professor Hsü sat on alone with me. He was fighting a hard battle with himself: ought he to remain with me or accompany the large caravan to Hami? His desire was to remain. On the other hand, he believed that by his position and his authority he could be of service, if it was necessary, in equipping the relief caravan. In this I most positively agreed with him. Since he and I according to the agreement of the 26th of April had equal rank in the expedition, I regarded it as absolutely necessary that one of the two should be with the main caravan when this crossed the border of Sin-kiang. The political situation might have changed, and one might demand guarantees and declarations from us. So Hsü and I also took heart-felt leave of each other, and during the exciting adventures that I afterwards experienced, it was a great comfort to me to know that Professor Hsü was with the main caravan, which was making for the far west.

Hummel and I had scarcely fallen asleep, when at half-past three on the 15th of December there sounded the reveille so pregnant with fate. At a quarter-past five the caravan started out in pitch-dark night, after Heyder had fetched the telegram from our yourt. An hour later von Marschall, Liu, Chin, and Ottehong started out on the march with Norin's seven best camels. Finally at

7 o'clock Professor Hsü with Huang and the servant Wang followed them. Meanwhile, Norin had found in the careful examination of our provisions, that of certain things we had only insufficient stores. He therefore wrote to Larson, that it would be best if they hurried with all possible speed, since we had flour, rice, sugar, salt, and other things, only for ten days. This letter he sent with Professor Hsü.

XXII

CHRISTMAS IN THE GOBI

NOW all our connexions with the outer world were severed, and an impenetrable silence descended upon us. There were nine of us: four Swedes, Norin, Bergman, Hummel, and myself, two Mongols, my camel-attendant Mento and Lama from Alashan, and Norin's three Chinese, the cook Wang, the servant Chang, and the camel-driver, old Lao Wang—all, both Chinese and Mongols, splendid men. Hummel's, Marschall's, and my baggage amounted to eleven camel-loads; that of Norin, Bergman, and our servants, to fourteen. Apart from the riding-camels, we should thus have required twenty-five camels, in order, after my complete recovery, to be able to think of continuing our journey to the west without first waiting for help. But in point of fact we had only eight of Norin's camels and the four that Larson had discarded and which were so exhausted that they did not count at all. We were thus bound here to the spring of Sebistei for an indefinite period and could not stir from the spot until, from somewhere or other, we were joined by reinforcements in pack or draught animals.

Our camp, No. LXXV, lay in open country. In the north the horizon was marked off by a chain of black hills with short valleys. In the east and north-east stretched the hilly landscape over whose expanses two days before I had been carried on the litter. To the immediate south of the camp there rose up very low hills. On the top of the highest there waved from its stayed mast the Swedish flag, visible far away to gazelles, wild camels, and wild asses; for other neighbours we did not have, and even the two last-named species of animals were extremely rare in this region. From the "Flag Height" one had a

Received with surprise in Hsiao-pu, . . .

. . . the first settlement on the other side of the mountains

THE DESERT IS VANQUISHED

[face p. 280

Larson has to stay behind with the loads, which the animals can drag along
no longer

Larson's emergency quarters

WINTER IN THE GOBI

wonderful view, towards the south reeling away over land-waves and low ridges of hills changing into light shades of blue, towards the west-north-west and west charming and stupendous, where the steep-rising white pyramid of the Emir-tag and the Karlik-tag, similarly crowned with eternal snow, formed as it were the propylæa of the High Alpine world of mighty mountain chains which bears the name of the Tien-shan, " the Mountains of Heaven."

In these surroundings of desert country, endless spaces, and a high distant mountain range, we had set up our tents. Here stood my yourt, in which Hummel and I lived, and directly to the south of us the blue tent which was Norin's and Bergman's airy dwelling. Fifteen metres east of us there rose up the kitchen tent, in which our servants lived. Round the tents stood our packing-cases, and near them the twelve camels had their places for resting. Not quite 100 metres north of us the spring of Sebistei came to the surface, to form among yellow and eaten-down reeds blue glistening ice-floes.

When we saw our great caravan move away, it seemed to us, not without reason, as if we had been landed on an uninhabited island in the middle of the ocean, whilst the ship continued its voyage. But he who would therefore believe that our position appeared tragic to us would make a mistake. Naturally it was certainly of little satisfaction that our camels had been overworked, and that their number had therefore been reduced. But no catastrophe had occurred; we were equal to the position and had firmly resolved to extend the scope and the tasks of our expedition, not restrict them.

Thus began our period of waiting; raging westerly storms roared round our tents, and day by day we climbed up on the heights where the Swedish flag fluttered defiantly over the silent, mysterious desert, and looked out towards the west.

With constant westerly storm and alternate frost, the days passed by for us quicker than we had thought. In spite of all the smaller and greater anxieties, we were cheerful and confident. We worked and read and forged new plans, and in the evenings cultivated a comradeship as stimulating as it was happy, with joint scientific reading and discussions or with joking and chatting and gramophone music. Bergman, as a certain shot, supplied us daily with fresh gazelle meat. My condition quickly improved, thanks to Dr. Hummel's care and skill, and already on the 18th of December I was allowed to get up for a few hours, and the next day I could even take a little walk and climb up to the Flag Height.

Almost before we expected it, Christmas was upon us. Dr. Hummel, who on account of my improvement had now of course more free time, had already for several days been very busy and reserved. He made all sorts of preparations, cut out coloured paper or sat in front of a board and kneaded dough and made little Christmas cakes. On the 24th of December he was unapproachable. I had scarcely slipped into my clothes, when he courteously but resolutely drove me out of my dwelling and sent me to Norin and Bergman, in whose tent a small fire was crackling and giving out warmth. Whilst Norin was drawing his latest map of the neighbourhood, and I was writing in my diary, Hummel and Bergman were getting ready the Christmas feast in my yourt.

All at once we were interrupted in the middle of our work. Unaccustomed whining sounds were heard in the entrance to the tent, and Chang entered, holding in his hand a tiny new-born puppy, no larger than a rat. And behind came the mother, the black bitch Snappy, which had joined Norin's column in Shande-miao. Her concern for her new-born puppy disappeared when we had arranged with blankets a real bird's nest in a corner of the tent, which she and the little creature occupied. But she was not satisfied with the one puppy. In the course of a few hours one after another made its entrance into this wicked world of barren deserts and raging storms. Our little community was increased in the afternoon by seven new members, and each of us four Swedes received a Christmas present and a memory of this day that we shall never forget. The three most weakly animals would probably be sacrificed to frailty. In any case it was wise of Snappy to arrange the happy event whilst we were remaining in camp. Norin and I watched the course of events with close attention and asked ourselves what would become of these Christmas children and along what paths in the heart of Asia they would wander. We gave Snappy blankets, meat, and water, and were amused at the little whining creatures, which, awkward and helpless in their blindness, crawled round their mother's coat.

Now came Dr. Hummel with new delicacies, which were to be roasted, fried, or baked, and the steam of sugar-cakes and saddle of antelope mingled in barbaric harmony with the smell of new-born dogs and the fumes of a smoking fire.

Then Christmas eve came upon us. It was already quite late, when Dr. Hummel announced: " The guests may now come into the Christmas room." An arch smile played round his lips as he said this, with the thought of the surprise and astonishment with which we should be filled the next instant. The door of my yourt was opened wide. A sea of light flowed towards us. But what was that ? Was it an apparition or a dream ? I could scarcely recognize my old everyday yourt. That was indeed a drawing-room, furnished with billowy divans and decorated with oriental splendour. And in the middle stood the Christmas table, laid with plates and glasses and innumerable good things, and over all this overflowing abundance there poured a flood of light from the seven-armed candlestick, which, wound round with paper of all colours of the rainbow and provided with artistic little candle-holders, supplied the Christmas-tree.

How had Hummel accomplished all this here in one of the greatest and most desolate deserts of the earth ? Could he work magic ? Norin and I were so overwhelmed, when we took our places at the further side of the table, that for the moment we gave ourselves up to deep reflection over Hummel's relations with spirits, angels, or trolls.

Bergman seated himself at the right end of the table, Hummel at the left, and the nearer side remained free. There were indeed only four of us. In front of the table stood the stove, which was so hot that it glowed.

Now we could look rather more closely at the festive

283

attire of my yourt. The divans had been made quite
simply out of piled-up sleeping-sacks and sheepskins,
which had been covered with finer furs. Round the
vertical walls of the yourt hung many-coloured carpets
from Kuei-hua, Paotow, Ning-hsia, and Hami, and above
them, as a transition to the dome, ran a frieze of blue silk,
made out of the " haddiks " which I had received on
various occasions from the chieftain of the Torgots and
from the cousin of the Tashi Lama in Shande-miao.

Sitting on our warm and comfortable divans, we believed
ourselves set down in the circle of a saloon on a small
steamer, an illusion which was intensified still more by
the stove and its chimney, which rose up vertically to the
skylight, the flue. Above the door, which Norin and I
had directly opposite us, a round white medallion bore the
inscription " A Happy Christmas." To the right and left
of the door stood two boxes, which served as sideboards.
The section of the yourt nearest the door was separated
from the drawing-room proper by two Swedish flags which
hung down. Above the left flag there hovered from the
dome an angel with outstretched wings, which held in its
hands a long white band with the words : " *Gloria Deo
in excelsis, pax in terra, hominibus bona voluntas.*" (Glory to
God in the highest, and on earth peace, good will toward
men.) Such an angel had always hung over the Christmas-
tree in my old home. Over the right flag hung a grey
tomte, a Swedish goblin, with a red night-cap on his head
and three-armed candlesticks in his hands. Bergman was
the artist who had made it, and he had also put up in the
middle of the dome a copy of the " wheel of life " of the
Buddhists, which turned round in the hot air which rose.

The Christmas table was a miracle of ingenuity and
taste. I hardly believe that a poor child who stands
astonished in front of a brilliant Christmas show-window
can devour with covetous eyes all the delightful things
that he sees. On the inner side there stood up the seven-
armed candlestick in all its blinding splendour. Before
each one of us there stood the portraits of our loved ones
at home. Hummel could, whenever he wished, meet
the glances of his respected mother. In front of Norin

there shone in glass and frame a picture of his clever and charming wife, and before Bergman the portrait of a young girl, glowing with Nordic beauty and sparkling life. From the hallowed stillness of the grave and in a flood of light my beloved parents looked towards me, and between them stood a group of my beloved brother and sisters. We talked about our loved ones in the distant homeland, and followed in thought from hour to hour their Christmas festivities and knew that they were thinking of us at least as much, and were asking themselves how it fared with us to-day. They were certainly wondering that they had received no telegram from us. Had we been swallowed up by the desert? Had we to battle with stern tasks and freezing cold? When would all vague questions find their answers?

The white cloth on the Christmas table and the table-runner of blue silk were covered after the custom at home with a great number of comic pictures. Adam and Eve, glowing with red, wandered arm in arm between plates and cups, little goblins tripped around, and fat Christmas pigs practised rolling on a ball. And in the middle of the Mongolian winter there bloomed a whole spring-time of red paper roses, the masterly achievement of Dr. Hummel.

Now Norin blew a fanfare on his whistle, and Chang brought the soup in, boiling hot, *Consommé à la Gobi.* It tasted simply magnificent, and the little slices of antelope's tongue which floated in it strongly reminded one of turtle. A bottle of spirits, which Norin had kept concealed at the bottom of a box, stood in proud isolation on our table, and now the glasses were filled. I said a few words about Christmas, the Christmas feasts of our youth, and Christmas Eve in the desert, and drank to the health of our loved ones at home and to the prosperity of our great expedition.

But I should indeed almost have forgotten one of the most important and most home-recalling items on our romantic festive menu—to the spirits we had a real Swedish dish: caviare, sardines, Swedish Christmas ham, ox-tongue, cheese, and butter, and in addition real Swedish hard-bread, a last remnant of the store that Norin, Hummel, and Bergman had once taken with them on the journey across Siberia.

There followed as the next dish *selle d'antilope*, saddle of antelope. Splendid! When I returned to Stockholm, I was resolved to recommend our doctor as *chef* to the Grand Hotel Royal. Such a saddle of antelope as we had here in the middle of the desert has never yet been equalled in the Grand Hotel. To the roast we had green peas and salted cucumbers.

The sweet consisted of vanilla ice with pine-apple, *glace aux glaciers de Tien-chan*, also very excellent, and accompanied with cream-buns and pagodas made of sugar. Then followed cakes and cheese, and Brie and Holländer too, and finally coffee and cognac and good cigars. On the table there stood the whole time a plate of sweets, lemon drops, and chocolate, and between the various courses, after the Russian fashion, we smoked a cigarette or two.

Finally Dr. Hummel made a speech. He spoke beautifully, in a lovable manner, touchingly, and Norin and Bergman supported him in his remarks. We were all agreed that we should never forget this Christmas that we four Swedes had spent under Swedish flags in the greatest desert, at a distance of 400 kilometres from Etsin-gol and 300 from Hami. We swore a sacred oath to put forth our strength to the utmost, in order by our work to serve science, solve several of the great problems, and bring honour to the Swedish name.

The Christmas festival had passed away, the last week of the year went by, the new year, 1928, commenced, and still we were stuck fast here in the middle of the desert like ice-bound polar explorers, waiting for relief. The Swedish flag on the Flag Height sent its call for help, its SOS, towards the west across the sea of sand, but the longed-for help did not come. Throughout the whole day there was a wild storm, which went like ice through our airy dwellings; it was dark and gloomy, but we were in radiant spirits.

On the 3rd of January it was reported to us by Wang, our cook, that flaked oats, sugar, salt, pepper, coffee, and green peas, were at an end, that the next day it was for the last time that we should be able to bake bread, and that we had only a few handfuls of rice left. But we still had pea-soup powder, cocoa, and tea, and our servants a quantity of millet. Water we had, and Bergman shot each day at least one gazelle.

Early next day Mento woke us with the words: " Two riders are coming from the west." We sprang up as if stung by tarantulas. " How far away are they ? "— " Three *li*." On the Flag Height the large telescope had already been set up. One could see that they were Mongols. They were riding quickly towards us on their camels. Now they were quite near, and we recognized Bonk and Sanje Gipche. They sat weather-tanned and secure on their riding-animals, were wrapped in baggy sheepskin furs, which were held together by body-straps, and had red fur-lined *bashliks* on their heads. In five nights they had rode here from Ta-shih-to, bringing for us with them 50 catties of flour and several exciting letters from our party. Marschall informed me that he had heard that Hempel, Haslund, and Mühlenweg had reached Hami, and that Walz under military protection had been seen on the road to Urumchi. " The soldiers here look wild, but are friendly. Beware of believing that they are robbers. A happy new year ! "

In another letter Hsü Ping-chang told of his and Heyder's journey to Ta-shih-to. Of this Heyder himself gave an arresting report :

On the first day he had shot six gazelles and seen a wild camel. On the 17th of December no water ; a strong west wind. Two camels dead. The 18th : a fierce snow-storm. One camel was shot so that they might have meat. The 20th : the storm increases in strength. They remain still. The 21st : a raging snow-storm. Impossible to start out. The 22nd : two camels frozen to death. All the others exhausted. It was decided to leave Larson and two Mongols behind with the whole baggage, while the rest continued the march with the camels and the most indispensable things. The 23rd : started out with a hundred and two camels, of which two died on the way. No water, but

snow. The 24th: a fierce snow-storm; only a march
of 3 kilometres; no water. The 25th: a storm; two
camels collapse. The Mongols receive flour for the last
time; will then live simply on camel's flesh. The 26th:
a fierce wind; one camel dead, another is shot for meat.
The 27th: another camel collapses. The 28th: they
reach four yourts, the first since Etsin-gol, and buy flour,
sugar, and five sheep. The 29th: they reach Ta-shih-to.
A camel dies. They hope to reach Hami in seven days.
The two Mongols are sent off to us.

Finally, Larson reports that he was situated 160 *li* to
the west of us, that a four days' snow-storm had broken
the camels' power of resistance, and that he himself could
make do with the store of flour that he had.

With this we had received the first news, although not
of the outer world, yet of our own forward detachments,
and we had learnt of one and another of the hard times
which they had had to encounter. Then when we returned
to our accustomed occupations again, our longing for the
relief was greater than ever.

When the 5th of January dawned, we four Swedes had
been at the spring of Sebistei for twenty-four days. The
hours went their accustomed course. But only until
7.20 p.m.; for then a change took place which, at one
stroke, transferred us from the realm of plans and dreams
into the world of hard reality.

We were all four sitting at the "writing-table" in
my yourt. Hummel and I were writing, Bergman was
studying Asiatic archæology, and Norin was working on
his latest chart. There was a crackling in the stove, otherwise all was quiet—except for the wind, which roared
round the yourt. Then there was a knock at the door!
Our servants never knocked, but simply entered. The
dogs had not barked.

"It is Marschall!" I cried, fully convinced.

"Yes, it's Marschall," he answered in pure Swedish,
and added, "Have you anything to drink, lads?"

I doubt if ever in his life Marschall has been so affec-
tionately tended and cared for as on this evening. We
fairly dragged him into a corner and made him a bed

288

between cushions and furs and poured him out a good drink. He was frozen stiff right to the marrow of his bones. Mento had to make the stove up, so that it glowed and shot out sparks. Meanwhile, in his accustomed calm and easy manner, Marschall answered the storm of questions that buzzed about his ears.

" Are you alone ? "

" No, I have Ottehong and three Chinese with me, twenty-five hired and five of our own camels, a sedan-chair, and several letters from our party."

" Yes, but tell me how your own journey has gone off."

" Splendid. After a trying forced ride I reached the little village of Mu-öhr-go, where, among wild, turbulent soldiers, I felt something like Hildebrand in the camp of the Huns. I joked and drank with them, we became friends, and they helped me to hire camels, buy provisions, and procure the wood for the sedan-chair, which we cut into shape in a twinkle. Then I hurried back here and have been seven days on the way and have had to remain still for three days on account of a snow-storm, and then froze terribly. The day before yesterday I spent the night with Larson and gave him a supply of mutton. To-day the road seemed as if it would never come to an end. We covered kilometre after kilometre; sometimes I rode, sometimes I went on foot, in order to keep my blood in circulation. I was about half an hour's journey in front of my caravan. At last I could see the glittering ice-floes by the spring of Sebistei and shortly afterwards the tents and the flag-mast. And now here I am."

We thanked Marschall for having carried out his difficult task in so excellent a manner. He had had, it is true, the student Liu with him as interpreter, but he would never have succeeded in his commission if he had not possessed his excellent humour and the ability to get on well with both Chinese and Mongols. Everybody liked him, and all competed against each other in helping him. As a sign of our gratitude we now elected him a Swedish fellow-citizen.

In conclusion, Marschall also told us, as a secondary matter of little importance, that certain difficulties had placed themselves in our way. He believed, however, that these could be overcome, as soon as I was in Hami. Wild rumours had been in circulation concerning us. We were, it was said, the vanguard of an invading army, which had evil designs against Sin-kiang. Troops had been called out and the caravan traffic towards the east had been stopped, in order to rob us of the possibility of buying provisions in the desert. Except for two hundred letters which had been sent to Hami, our whole European post had been sent to Peking, so that there it could be thoroughly examined and scrutinized. Already now it could clearly be seen that we were under very great suspicion, and that the fears were perhaps justified which prophesied for us that we should be compelled to go back again from Hami on the roads that we had come. Perhaps we should not be allowed to enter Sin-kiang at all, which was the true object of our great plans. Were all our hardships and sacrifices really to be in vain?

Under strong military protection . . .

. . . the caravan at last sets out for Hami

WE ARE UNDER SUSPICION

A stream near the Mohammedan town

HAMI

[*face p.* 291

XXIII

SIN-KIANG WILL HAVE NOTHING TO DO
WITH US

NOW the hour of our deliverance had arrived. In a fierce north-west storm and with 12 degrees of frost, the baggage was packed, and the sedan-chair was fastened to its long poles, covered with a tilt, and padded soft with blankets. The new Chinese caravan men had set up a tent for themselves out of poles and covers, which resembled a Lapp hut; when the wind blew it down, they built a hut for themselves out of boxes, in which they kept a small fire burning. During the storm the gazelles were more careless than usual, and Bergman shot four—a welcome addition to our larder.

Oh, these eternal icy winter storms! On the 7th of January too we still had to remain. With their bulky loads the camels cannot start out against the wind. The next day the storm had abated, and immediately after sunrise Norin was ready for marching with his section. One of his strings, five camels, mutinied and threw off its loads. But the rest could be held in check, and a short time later Norin's caravan disappeared in the west. Then we others followed and resigned the spring of Sebistei to the great lonely desert. The young puppies that were born on Christmas Eve lay in a padded box on the load of one of the camels. Their mother, Snappy, ran about, whining, among the camels, looking for her offspring. I myself, wrapped up by Dr. Hummel like a baby in long clothes, took my place between cushions and furs in the sedan-chair. I had, of course, not quite recovered yet, and had to take care of myself. The two camels which carried me were tied one behind the other. The extreme ends of the poles of my sedan-chair were placed through the loops of strong ropes which were fixed crosswise between the humps of the camels. Mento mounted the front camel and the curious conveyance started in motion. I had never travelled in this way before, although I had travelled in a sedan-chair carried by mules, in March, 1897, when I came to Peking for the first time. The camels went quietly and steadily, and the vertical swaying motion was pleasant and increased still more when the two animals were in step. Marschall and Hummel went in front of the litter on foot.

To the right and left of the road there rose up low black hills, between which stretched flat plains, sometimes hard rubble, sometimes piled-up sand. Usually the ground was thinly covered with dry tufts of steppe grass, now and then with *saksauls* or tamarisks. At the "red spring," Ulan-bulak, gazelles and partridges could be seen in the reeds.

In the night the temperature fell to 26·7 degrees below zero, and on the morning of the 10th it was bitterly cold. Our march went on towards the south-west between dark low ridges of sedimentary schist and agglomerate. The snow increased; it lay in the hollows from 1 to 2 feet deep. When it became evening, we at last caught sight of the light of a fire, and soon afterwards I was sitting in Norin's tent. The camp was bad, fuel was scanty; to get water we had to melt snow. Bergman's and Marschall's riding-camels had broken down on the way.

Fortunately we had only 8 kilometres to march the next day, for the wind was terrible and the cold biting. We were therefore glad when, on coming round a hill, we caught sight of Larson's fixed camp. Wrapped up in his great red Mongolian fur, my splendid caravan guide came to meet me. He cried out, as happy as a sandboy, "Welcome and best wishes for the New Year." He had made for himself out of boxes a hut with a forecourt, which protected the entrance against drifting snow. The interior of his dwelling had a floor space of 2·3 by 2·1 metres, the walls were hung with camel-covers, and the roof, which rested on saddle-poles, consisted of the same building-material. Under a four-cornered flue the fire burnt in its iron *tolga*, and here the tea-kettles were boiling and antelope meat was sizzling in a frying-pan. Five Swedes, a German, and two Mongols, Serat and Matte Lama, took their positions round the fire-place, and we guests, hungry and frozen through as we were, did all justice to the breakfast.

So here was the place where the great caravan had suffered shipwreck after a four days' storm, and from here, under the command of Heyder and Professor Hsü, with a hundred and two camels, of which thirty animals carried riders and the most necessary baggage, it had then continued its journey to Hami, while about a hundred boxes remained behind with Larson and his two Mongols. The little colony consisted, for the rest, of only four tired camels and three half-wild Chinese dogs with bells round their necks, which were to strike terror in intruding wolves. Unfortunately they also understood how to hunt dark argali sheep and shy wild asses which from time to time strayed into the neighbourhood of the camp.

In my yourt I had a long talk with Larson. We were approaching a country which, for the most part, was inhabited by Eastern Turkish peoples, and the great caravan had to undergo a sweeping change. We decided to dismiss all the Mongols in Hami and send them home; on the other hand, Norin's and Bergman's four Chinese were to remain if they wished. Larson was therefore of the opinion that in Hami his task would be finished and that he would have to return home on the desert road with the Mongols. Since, however, he regretted that in this case he would miss becoming acquainted with Urumchi and its trade possibilities, I suggested to him that he should accompany us as far as there and then return to Kalgan across Siberia. He was, moreover, then as now to remain a member of our expedition, particularly as I had an important commission for him in the Far East and in Mongolia.

On the 12th of January we again took leave of Larson and continued our journey towards the west, between black clean-swept hills, which towered up out of the white covering of snow. Slowly and monotonously my sedan-chair swung along over quartz rubble and snow which gave under foot, until a quite unusual picture suddenly rose up in the distance. There numerous camels were pasturing, and there smoke rose up from a tent at the foot of a hill. Was this a merchant caravan, or were they some of our party ? When we reached the place, Saran Görel and three hired Chinese came hurrying up to my sedan-chair and saluted me. They had been sent with fifty camels to bring help to Larson, and were glad that they had met me and learnt that they had only another 22 kilometres to their goal.

Saran Görel handed me a packet of letters. They were from members of my staff and were read out aloud in Norin's and Bergman's tent. Very bad news ! We had fallen between the millstones of the internal politics of China. Would they grind us to pieces ? Would everything be lost ?

As one will remember, I had already sent Walz on ahead from Etsin-gol to Urumchi, to report our coming to Yang, the governor of the province, and to fetch our post and the money which, thanks to the accommodating spirit of the postal authorities in Peking, had been directed for us to the capital of Sin-kiang.

Under the date of the 25th of November Walz wrote from Hami that he and his servants with their eight camels had crossed the desert in night marches, often without a road and without water. A camel had died; a second they had had to leave behind in a village in the neighbourhood of Hami. When on the 11th of November he reached the frontier of Sin-kiang, he was encircled by twenty frontier-riders, who, in order to instil respect into him, loaded their rifles before his eyes. In spite of vigorous protests he was kept as a prisoner for six days. In the meantime a *noyen*, chieftain, arrived, accompanied by two mounted squadrons, four flags, and four trumpeters.

At last Walz received permission to continue his journey to Hami under military protection. They took a short cut along the foot of the mountain range, through ice and snow. For the camels the road was very difficult. During one dark night three of them together with a rider slipped down an incline, without, however, coming to any harm. When Walz reached Hami on the 21st of November, he had covered 733 kilometres.

In Hami he was led into a house with a court-yard, at the door of which two officers and twenty men kept guard. The following day he received a visit from the brigadier-general, Liu Darin, who subjected him to an examination.

"I must get to Urumchi as quickly as possible, in order to carry out important commissions, and I am provided with passport and arms licence," Walz explained.

"You must wait here until I get instructions from Urumchi," replied the general.

Walz was disarmed and his whole baggage investigated. Everything was made off with and gone through for money and opium. A metal tin box belonging to Lieberenz, which contained films, was broken open, as the key wasn't with it. Nothing was damaged, however. The young postmaster Chên, who speaks English, acted as interpreter. Then one day after another went by, and letters went to and fro between Walz and Liu Darin. The Bavarian major, who won't be played with, demanded that the general, who had detained him for twelve days against his will, should pay all expenses for him, his men, and his camels. If he did not receive a definite reply next day, declared Walz, he would himself telegraph to the governor in Urumchi. Finally, Liu Darin gave the major permission to proceed to the capital on the 27th of November, but not on horseback, but in a cart, and accompanied by a mounted "bodyguard." So much for Walz's letter.

In a second report Mühlenweg, whom I had sent out to Ta-shih-to on the 25th of November from the camp of Ikhen-gol, described his adventures. Unfortunately, as a result of his hurried and adventurous journey, which he mostly had to undertake in the night-time, he had not been able to make a sketch-map of his road, and it is therefore not always easy to follow his tracks. Only a dare-devil such as he could carry out such a march.

After eight days he had reached the spring of Sebistei, which I reached with the large caravan a week later. The three men then continued their journey by night, and on the 5th of December came across a solitary camel-rider, a lama, who came from Lhasa and during the last twenty-five days had only seen a single Mongol. He gave them information as well as he could about the neighbourhood. Then they had flour and antelope meat for only one day more.

On the 6th of December they wandered towards the south and after long search found a path which might run in the direction of Hami. When, however, they noticed on the following day that no flocks of cotton from the camel-packs had been caught on the thorn bushes, it became clear to them that this road did not come from Hami; for it is from there that the cotton caravans start out. The next day they found a caravan road with flocks of cotton, and knew that they were on the right track. At midnight they camped at a spring, at which Hempel, Haude, and Haslund, had also rested with their caravan, which was clearly to be seen from empty preserve-tins and thrown-away scraps of paper.

On the 9th of December they came past a ruin to the side of the road. Mühlenweg and Banche rode up to it, whilst Lo Chang went on with the pack-camels. They could see how he made straight for a second ruin, in which a troop of unknown men were stopping. Their horses were tethered in the neighbourhood. The strange men looked at each other and began to speak to Lo Chang. Mühlenweg immediately hurried up to them, holding his revolver ready, and Banche came pale and frightened behind. Lo Chang declared that the ten men armed with rifles were soldiers. Mühlenweg ordered his two men to go on and himself led the camels down into the valley. But then the leader of the troop rode after him and ordered him to stop, at the same time loading his rifle.

" Show me your passport," he said roughly.

" First show me your own," answered Mühlenweg.

" I don't need a passport. But here is my chief's visiting-card."

" Well then, here is my passport and my arms licence."

" If you want to continue your journey to the west, you must hand over your arms to us. Otherwise you must go back on the road you have come."

Meanwhile the whole troop had mounted their horses and surrounded the pair.

" Our road goes to Sin-kiang and we have no intention of allowing ourselves to be held up," declared Mühlenweg.

" All right, but then first hand over your arms to us."

After this had taken place, they all travelled together towards the west and late in the evening set up the camp. To Mühlenweg's question, whether other Europeans had come through the neighbourhood, the leader replied: " Yes, first one man and then five. They are now all prisoners."

On the following day they continued their journey. Near the road some antelopes were grazing. Mühlenweg asked for his rifle. His request was also granted him, but the antelopes had made off in time. For some time they followed the road to Hami, but afterwards left it again and rode across country. Our party found their position uncomfortable. The soldiers were not wearing proper uniforms and gave rather the impression of robbers.

After a while they rode into a gorge-like valley and halted finally in darkness in front of a cave, in which, so they said, their chief dwelt and two fires were burning. Spring water and reeds were in the neighbourhood, but no chief was there. He had obviously gone on the An-hsi road to Hsing-hsing-hsia, they said, and thither they must also take Mühlenweg. Since, however, the latter stubbornly refused to go anywhere other than to his destination of Hami, the men declared they would have the chief fetched by a messenger, and until he arrived, Mühlenweg and his servants would be their prisoners. They received permission, however, to set up their tent before the entrance to the cave.

Mühlenweg went into the cave and was well received. Inside he noticed nothing other than riding-saddles and on that account doubted that the mysterious companions were robbers. Banche, full of fright, stuck to his opinion that they had fallen into the hands of a robber band, whilst Lo Chang was convinced that they were really soldiers. In the middle of the night Mühlenweg was awakened by Banche, down on his knees, reciting lamaist prayers. When he asked him what the matter was, the Mongol answered that they were in the hands of robbers and would certainly have to give up their lives. The rider who had been sent out after the chief had returned alone after half an hour. In Banche's opinion the whole thing was only done to deceive them. The robbers only wanted to draw them deeper into the desert, in order then to be able to plunder and murder them unhindered.

The following day they really went on with their prisoners. Towards evening the troop rode on ahead, in order to light a fire and set up the camp. Only the leader, who likewise was riding on a camel, remained with the three prisoners. Mühlenweg felt a strong temptation within him to fall on the fellow, tear the rifle out of his hand, and fly. But then Lo Chang reported that a caravan was to be seen to the right.

" I want to know what sort of caravan that is," Mühlenweg explained to the Chinese leader; " it may be one of our own sections." The Chinese had no objection, but made in a quick trot towards the caravan. Lo Chang went on in the tracks of the troop of riders, but Mühlenweg and Banche remained still. It was already beginning to get dark.

" Now our hour has come," said Mühlenweg to his companion; " they are in fact robbers. We must escape to-night."

Banche was nervous : " We have nothing to eat."

" That makes no difference. Here we can escape. The night is dark. We must hurry to the north and then sharply to the west."

" We must sacrifice the camels," suggested Banche, who had allowed himself to be persuaded; " otherwise they will find the tracks, and in the mountains the camels will make bad progress."

" All right, we will leave the camels behind. If they are robbers, then they will steal the animals; if they are soldiers, we shall get them back."

Banche had a piece of fat, which was the entire provisions, and Mühlenweg took half of the travelling-chest, 350 dollars, which he could conveniently carry. The other half remained in the saddle-bag of one of the camels and was lost for ever. Then, on foot, they left their pasturing camels and soon came into a mountain valley. Where the ground was composed of soft dust or sand, Banche trailed his fur behind him, in order to obliterate their tracks. He soon got tired, however, and suggested that they should walk on their toes, so that their footprints resembled those of the wild asses.

They marched half the night, then, tired as they were, rested, but did not risk lighting a fire, so as not to give their probable pursuers any indication of their whereabouts. What shall we do if they come? they thought. But no-one came. They marched the whole of the next day up to 4 o'clock; then they were completely exhausted and had to take a rest. Now the fat came to an end and at a spring they found water covered with ice. After a new march they slept in the night from 11 to 1 o'clock, when the cold roused them. The following day they discovered good drinking-water but had nothing to eat. They lighted a small fire, and then the wild pursuit went on. On the 12th of December they wandered throughout the whole day and the whole night. When day dawned they could hear the roar of flowing water. A brook at last! On its bank they lighted a fire. Then they threw sand over the glowing cinders and so got a warm bed to sleep on. After two hours Banche woke his master, saying:

" To-day we shall see heaven."

" What do you mean ? "

" Yes, I can hear a cock crowing."

They immediately started out and came to a simple house, in which a Chinese lived. Here they ate their fill and drank tea, bought flour and meat and an ass, and in the afternoon went on with their journey on the great road to Hami.

After they had marched for an hour, they met two mounted soldiers of Mongolian race, who put a number of questions to them and then rode away again in a gallop. After ten minutes a whole troop of riders appeared, whose leader instituted a new minute examination. Mühlenweg was master of the Mongolian language and answered all questions clearly and plainly. The two were now led to a court-yard with several yourts, soldiers, and horses. The " commander-in-chief " of the troop lived in a mud house, on whose *kang* they sat down and conversed. He had heard that two foreign prisoners had escaped, and now knew that they were the two that had been arrested here. They would, however, get their camels back the following day, he assured Mühlenweg. But neither on the 14th nor on the 15th of December did the animals come. There had been rumours that a great caravan of Europeans was approaching, and that late in the autumn twelve hundred men in eighty tents had camped on Etsin-gol. Now he wanted to know if we belonged to Fêng Yü-hsiang's army. The whole of the eastern part of Sin-kiang had been mobilized on our account.

On the 16th, Mühlenweg made the plain declaration : " If I haven't my camels back to-morrow and we are not given two horses, we shall go on foot to Hami." They got horses. In the village of I-kwai-shu they met Walz's Mongol Särche, and on the 18th they continued their ride and reached Hami, where General Liu took them in charge and conducted a new cross-examination. On the 22nd, Lo Chang arrived with the two camels for which he was responsible. Mühlenweg immediately sent us help and on this occasion too showed what a splendid man he is.

From Haslund, who had been Hempel's and Haude's caravan-guide, I received a letter dated Hami, the 18th of December. In the village of Miao-go his column had been intercepted by Mongolian and Mohammedan soldiers, disarmed, and held prisoners for eleven days. On the march across the desert they had lost only three of their twenty-four camels, from which it is clear how well Haslund has carried out his commission. That in Hami they were anything other than welcome, was only too clear. " One can see that something is wrong there." His request to be allowed to hurry to meet my column in the east had been refused.

Dr. Haude gave a more detailed account of the march of the column across the Gobi Desert from the 31st of October to the 27th of November, when they reached

A gate of honour

A peep-show

HAMI

[*face p.* 300

The citadel of the Mohammedan king Shah Maksut

HAMI

Miao-go and were forced to make a halt. They were strongly guarded—on the 3rd of December they counted eight hundred riders, and this force was afterwards strengthened still more. On the following day the column received a communication from Governor Yang, saying he did not wish the expedition to come to Sin-kiang. " He had already previously telegraphed to Peking that he did not wish to see the expedition in his province." [1]

Hempel, Haude, and Haslund, who also had von Kaull, Dettmann, and the student Li in their column, therefore drafted the following telegram in English to Governor Yang, which was dispatched to Hami and handed in at the telegraph station there :

" We have to-day been informed that the members of the scientific expedition of Dr. Sven Hedin have not the permission of Your Excellency to cross the frontier of Sin-kiang, and that you demand our return to Peking. In reply we inform Your Excellency that our march back across the desert is impossible, for the following reasons : Our expedition left Peking without sufficient winter equipment, since we had the intention of procuring this for ourselves in Sin-kiang. Since the journey here has taken much more time than we had reckoned, our entire provisions and the whole of the rest of our equipment have moreover been used up, and we lack the necessary things for a journey back at this time of the year. All our money is in Tihua (Urumchi) or was to be sent there from Peking after our arrival. A large number of our camels have been lost in the desert, and the rest are in such an exhausted condition that they cannot stand a desert journey of many days. We have been told that we are suspected of being communists. This we most positively deny, and we remind Your Excellency of the fact that the Swedish Legation and the German Legation in Peking have given a guarantee to His Excellency Marshal Chang Tso-lin that not one of us has the intention of meddling with politics of any kind and that not one of us is a communist.

[1] In October Governor Yang had got into communication with the Ministry of Education in Peking and in this had exchanged detailed telegrams concerning our expedition. With skill and energy the Swedish Minister, O. Ewerlöf, made himself responsible for us as ever and gave my relatives in Stockholm a faithful account of the changing state of affairs in Peking and in Sin-kiang.

We ask Your Excellency to take the foregoing into consideration and on that account permit us to journey to Hami. We take the opportunity to express our most excellent respects to Your Excellency."

On the 6th of December the leader of the column, Major Hempel, received a favourable answer from Governor Yang, who allowed twenty-six members of the expedition, that is to say the whole staff, to continue their journey to Sin-kiang, subject to the three conditions : disarmament, examination of the baggage, and the leaving behind of all servants and camels at the frontier.

On the 9th of December the section again set out on its march and in three days reached Hami, where all arms were immediately handed over and the whole baggage was carefully examined. Not until towards the end of the month did the members of the column receive a part of the money that we had had transferred from Peking to Urumchi, and on the 29th they at last set out thither in three carts.

In a letter of the 24th of December Haude further reported that it had been forbidden them to take photographs and draw maps and to set up a meteorological station in Hami.

But—all's well that ends well, and so I must further mention in conclusion a letter written by Professor Hsü from Ta-shih-to on the 31st of December. It is calm and dignified and expresses the hope that all the difficulties that we encountered on the frontier will be solved.

All these letters were very carefully read in Camp LXXX, and then for several hours we discussed the threatening situation. It was of course not to be wondered at that we were unwelcome guests, if we had been looked on as so suspicious that the whole district of Hami was put in a state of war and the caravan traffic going towards the east was interrupted, in order to deprive us of the possibility of supplementing our stores. Already at the beginning of the year Marshal Chang Tso-lin had at my request informed Governor Yang in a long telegram of our expedition. We were therefore very surprised at the cool reception on the frontier of Sin-kiang. What grieved me not least was that our entire post from May to September, 1927, had been sent to Peking, so that there it might be thoroughly examined ; for in Urumchi there was no-one who could read Swedish and German.   For this important post we had in consequence of this to wait until the end of March, 1928.

It would seem to us already now, however, as if a change was in process in the view of our persons and intentions.   Thus von Marschall had been received quite friendly by the officers and soldiers that he met on the frontier.

However much we hoped for better weather, the atmosphere in Sin-kiang was in any case charged, and it was necessary for us to play our cards well.   In the evening I wrote therefore to Larson, gave him a view of the situation, and asked him to hasten his march, so that we could perhaps enter Hami together.

XXIV

IN HAMI AT LAST

ON the 13th of January we continued our march towards the west. The thermometer had fallen in the night right to 21·7 degrees below zero. The country that we were crossing was monotonous, and was completely dominated by the Emir-tag and the Karlik-tag, which belong to the outermost spurs of the Tien-shan towards the desert. From time to time we came past the stiff-frozen body of a camel—the section under Heyder and Hsü Ping-chang had had heavy losses.

From the 15th we marched close together, for now we might at any moment encounter the first reconnoitring troops of Sin-kiang. We kept towards the south-west, while we looked for the road between Ming-shui and Mu-öhr-go which is found on Stein's map, and in the course of the day crossed the road which leads from Ming-shui to Barkul.

Travelling across the plain, white with winter, on the 18th we caught sight of the first stone sign-posts, and the following day our long solitude came to an end. After we had reached a brook, which flowed along in a furrow cut out 3 metres deep, we could see, below a spur in the west, an oasis of willows and pyramid-like poplars. We followed the valley of the stream upwards and left a small Buddhist temple to our left, whose sole serving sister was a large black sow. On one of the dark hills in the neighbourhood there rose up a *masar*, the tomb of a Mohammedan saint, with cupola and wall. We saw grass and wild-rose bushes, farmyards, yellow mud houses, and walled enclosures. Here we camped near a little wood of willows. The place is called Mu-öhr-go. Of the two hundred soldiers who had been stopping here on Marschall's visit, no longer was a single one there. Only five Chinese peasants and three Eastern Turks were we able to find. One of the latter, the seventy-two-year-old Khodayer, was village elder, *durga*, of the neighbouring village of Tal and the owner of twenty-five of the fifty camels that had rescued Larson's baggage. Concerning us he had heard that we were a whole army of two thousand men. It was a pleasure to me to be able to speak Eastern Turkish again, which I had not made use of for 19 years. But it still remained to some extent and was soon brushed up again.

In Mu-öhr-go a sheep cost 5 silver dollars and thirty steppe fowls cost 4. Here we obtained excellent wheaten bread, eggs, onions, and cabbages, and imagined ourselves, after we had furrowed the waves of the desert sea for two months and ten days, landed on a coast of civilization. Towards evening we could hear Hummel shouting: "There comes Larson." And truly, there in his red fur Larson came riding up at the head of the fifty hired camels, and glowing with health in the glare of the setting sun.

Late in the evening there was heard the ringing of bells from the west. It was a caravan of a thousand camels and twenty-five tents, which was travelling to Paotow. The prohibition of traffic had thus been raised.

We remained a day in the shelter of the shrine of Khojam Yagus and in the course of this received a visit from the chieftain Chang Darin, the commander of the troops that had to keep a look-out for us and watch over our roads. He told us that Yüan and his column, which had been missing for so long, had passed through a week before. That was joyful news, which freed us of a great anxiety.

When we continued our journey on the 21st of January, Hummel, Bergman, and I employed a new means of conveyance, a broad cart with two wheels 4·65 metres in circumference. Hummel had softly padded the vehicle with the felt covers of the yourt, our mattresses, sleeping-sacks, and furs, and we sat in ease and comfort. The driver and the horse-boy were Mongols. They took their places well in front when we went forward quickly; otherwise they walked by the side. One horse goes between the shafts ; the other three are tied in front to long ropes. The driver drives his team without reins, merely by means of cries like *oa, oa, ih, ih,* and the horses understand him. Occasionally he makes use of the whip. Should the animals bolt, that matters nothing—the steppe is big enough and the cart is strong and secure.

Near the village of Huang-lung-kang, where we spent the night of the 22nd, our way joined the great caravan road to An-hsi. The 23rd was the Chinese new year's day, and in the morning we were therefore visited by all our servants and the village elder. The wooden pillars in front of the shops in the main street were decorated with the customary red placards, but the businesses themselves were closed.

We did not allow ourselves to be stopped, however, by the Chinese day of celebration, but continued our journey and soon came past the camels of our three sections, which, a hundred and thirty-eight in number, were here pasturing. Then from the south-east the telegraph-line from Peking via An-hsi ran into our road with its two wires. We travelled at times between dunes held together by vegetation, at times over flat, hard desert country. Here and there there rose up the ruins of an old watch-tower. Now and then we rumbled through a little village with woods or avenues of poplars and willows. Here holiday-making Chinese were philosophizing over the new-year's feast, here children were playing, here dogs old and young were basking in the sun, here crows and jackdaws were making a noise, and here a burial-ground reminded one of transitory things. At an open pond in the village of Ching-dongtse asses and cows were drinking, and by the side stood a cart drawn by a horse and an ox.

We had already crossed the frontier of Sin-kiang to the east of Mu-öhr-go. Now we were approaching the first town of this province. Enveloped in dust a dark troop of riders came to meet us. In front rode a chief, *bek,* thick-set and commanding in fur-edged *chapan.* He accompanied us and we conversed about the state of affairs in Hami. The road gradually changed into an avenue with canals and old round willows at the sides.

306

We went through streets between grey walls and over bridges with carved railings, rumbled through the double gate of the Chinese town, and finally reached the *yamên* of Brigadier-General Liu. In the outer court-yard we were courteously received by the general's suite, and went between double ranks of saluting soldiers into the inner court-yard, over the gate of which there hung two red flags, and into the reception-room, where we were awaited by several officials, the mayor, and Yolbars Khan, an influential man of Eastern Turkish race.

While tea was being served General Liu entered, a man of fine breeding and gentlemanly manners, thin and pale, and immediately started a lively conversation. As interpreter we were attended in this by the English-speaking postmaster Chên, a friendly and courteous little man, who had been of service in various ways to our vanguard. Liu asked about our journey and our privations, our roads and our losses of camels, my illness in the desert, and many other things. To my question, when we could continue our journey to Urumchi, he replied that we could start out at any time. I had hoped to be able to send Norin and Bergman direct from here to Lop-nor, but Liu regretted that only Governor Yang in Urumchi could decide this matter, and declared he would send a telegram regarding it immediately. He knew of my earlier expeditions in Central Asia and assured me that now I should travel with much greater security in Sin-kiang than then.

Then Liu came to the subject of Yang's three conditions for the continuation of our journey to Urumchi : disarmament, examination of our baggage, and the leaving behind of the Mongols. He excused these steps on the ground that for 3 years a state of war had been declared in the province. I was able to inform him for his comfort that the Mongols would in any case have been sent back home, since they were strange to this land and did not understand its language. Our baggage was at his disposal, and Larson, who was just on his way, would receive instructions to unload his camels in the court-yard of the *yamên*. Liu asked if he might examine the things which I had in my cart. " Yes, with the greatest pleasure."—" But then you yourself must be present."—"That is not at all necessary. I will leave the matter to you and your officials." Hummel, Norin, and Bergman were present, however, at the inspection. The whole matter was disposed of in a few minutes, and nothing was touched.

In the court-yard Liu introduced to me twelve of his officers, who over long grey tunics were wearing black silk waistcoats, and then we left the *yamên*, while the soldiers again saluted.

We had not far to go to the farm that had been placed at our disposal, where all our party received me. The soldiers that had to guard us stayed in the arched gateway. None of us were allowed to go into the town, unless accompanied by two armed troopers.

Hsü Ping-chang and Yüan told me that at least a part of the misunderstandings that had arisen was to be ascribed to an unhappily or impishly worded letter which a student in Peking had sent to one of our students. In it it read : " I congratulate you on the two hundred warlike men which you have in your caravan." Presumably the writer of the letter had only wished to say by this that there were many of us and that we were well armed against sudden attacks. The authorities in Urumchi, however, read this letter, and the consequence was that *all* letters, both to the Chinese and to the Europeans of the expedition, were sent to Peking, so that they might be examined there. Probably the censor's office had thereupon informed the authorities of Sin-kiang that our post contained nothing prohibited or suspicious, and therefore the post from August to November had been kept back in Tihua (Urumchi) and now had been sent to Hami. On the very first evening Postmaster Chên delivered to me a few hundred joyfully-welcomed letters.

In spite of all dark rumours and threatening clouds we had reached Hami, the little Mohammedan town on the edge of the desert and at the foot of the Mountains of Heaven, the Tien-shan, one of the most continental towns of the earth, far from every ocean, forgotten, hidden away, very rarely visited by Europeans, in the heart of Asia. Hami has its Chinese town and its Turkish town, its

Mohammedan bazaars and Chinese shops, its mosques and temples. As a frontier town it is a garrison for troops, and several generals have their headquarters here. The district of Hami is reckoned a war area, and so long as civil war prevails in China proper between the various generals, the rulers responsible for the security of the province of Sin-kiang are of the opinion that an invasion from the east might not be impossible.

"Hami is famous for its melons, Turfan for its grapes, Kulja for its horses, and Kucha for its women," says a proverb. Round the town there stretch gardens, in which fruits of every kind are cultivated. The water necessary for irrigation comes from the Tien-shan in the north. Great caravan roads start from Hami : via An-hsi to Su-chow, Lan-chow, and Ning-hsia, and—the road that we ourselves had tested in part—across the desert.

Already on the first day it seemed to me as if our position had improved. We were still prisoners as it were, it is true, but for all that we were treated with the greatest consideration. New occasion for worry, on the other hand, was given us by a telegram from Su-chow sent by the student Ma. Ma, whom we had left behind with Zimmermann and Söderbom at our first meteorological station on Etsin-gol, telegraphed :

"Station No. 1 has been prohibited by the authorities of Kansu and has been ordered to leave the province ; we have no money."

With the help of the postal authorities we gave telegraphic instructions for 100 dollars to be paid over to Ma.

Professor Yüan, whom I now saw again after a separation of four months, had behind him an adventurous desert journey rich in results, and had discovered among other things three old towns in the neighbourhood of Chên-fan. All his men and animals were in good health, and he had, moreover, managed with an incredibly small sum of money. He had also visited the station on Etsingol, and he delivered over to me a letter from Zimmermann of the 1st of December, in which it says :

" Yüan was exceedingly friendly and courteous and, as also those with him, in every way most companionable. We have worked and lived together in the greatest harmony. The station is in full working order, the observations go on like clock-work from 7 o'clock in the morning to 9 o'clock at night, everything is first rate, and we ourselves are well and contented."

Söderbom had added : " Best greetings to all. Here everything is peaceful, and we are enjoying the quietness in our little colony."

Thus on the 1st of December. Since then almost two months had gone by, and now we received this disturbing telegram from Ma. Professor Hsü telegraphed and wrote in detail to the civil and military authorities in Su-chow, and for the rest we had to wait for the development of events.

We remained in Hami till the 4th of February, and during this time of resting our relations with the authorities improved step by step. The whole baggage under Larson's command was loaded and examined in Liu's presence. During this there came to light from one of my boxes a huge portrait of Chang Tso-lin with dedication and signature in his own hand, which made a visibly deep impression on the general.

A Chinese caravan-guide who wanted about this time to return to Kuei-hua-chêng with a large number of unloaded camels undertook to take our twenty-one Mongols back to their homes. Each Mongol, apart from the payment due to him, which was to be drawn in Kalgan, received 90 dollars, sufficient supplies of flour, tea, and mutton, and two hired camels. They were also to take with them 500 dollars for Zimmermann and his companions. The departure of the Mongols was, however, postponed, since thirty of the camels of the owners of the caravan had to perform transport services for twelve days for the military. No merchant caravan receives permission to travel to the east without a tax of this kind. With the assistance of the authorities we succeeded, however, in hammering out better conditions.

In a telegram I informed Governor Yang of the arrival

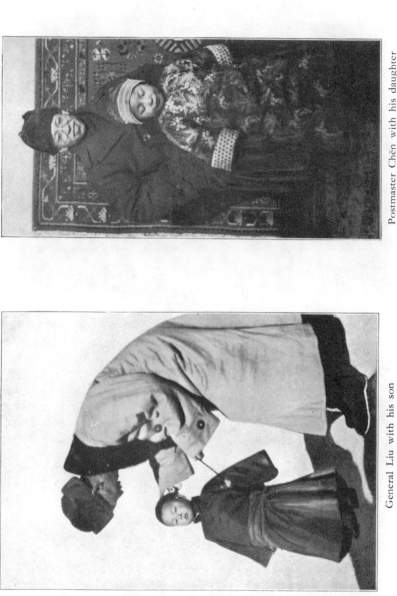

[face p. 310

Postmaster Chên with his daughter

General Liu with his son

HAMI

Ceremonial reception at the banquet in the house of Yolbars Khan

The Mongol prince makes a return visit

THE FEELING HAS CHANGED

[face p. 311

of the last column in Hami, thanked him for his hospitality and his friendly concern, and expressed my pleasure of soon being able to make his personal acquaintance. I also asked for permission for Norin and Bergman to go straight to Lop-nor. In his answer Yang bid us welcome to Sin-kiang. So far as the Lop-nor expeditions were concerned, this question must be decided in Tihua. Obviously the governor wanted first to see us himself, before further steps could be undertaken. Therefore the whole staff, both Europeans and Chinese, had to present themselves for inspection in his capital.

On one of the first days, our friend the postmaster Chên gave us a dinner. The thirty-eight courses were brought into our own house and served one after the other. While we were still sitting at table, music was heard in front of our door. It was General Liu Darin, who, accompanied by riders and banners, was coming to pay his new-year's visit. We did not receive him. It is considered a sign of ill manners to be at home when a high mandarin makes his new-year's visits. If all received him the day would not be long enough.

The next day Hsü and I drove out to make visits. Led by six soldiers in sheepskin furs, we rolled along over dusty roads and streets between walls, trees, and canals, and finally reached the residence of the Mohammedan " king." His palace is built in Chinese style and is surrounded by a high mud wall, through the arched gateway of which asses were just being driven, loaded with the dry bundles of grass from the steppe which serve as fuel and with water in wooden tubs covered with hoar-frost.

We enter a spacious drawing-room with carpets, tables, and rows of red-covered chairs. On the walls hang four huge scrolls, on which one recognizes the characters for happiness and long life. They were manifestations of favour and honour from the Empress Dowager, which the prince had received on his four visits to Peking.

We had scarcely been led into a smaller audience-room, when the prince, Shah Maksut, known to the Chinese as Sa Ching Wang, appeared and greeted us in the most courteous manner. He is a portly little man of 70

years, with a reddish complexion, friendly eyes, aquiline
nose, and snow-white beard, and wears Chinese clothes.
His dynasty has had Hami as its capital and town of
residence since the sixteenth year of the reign of Kang-hsi.
The power which Shah Maksut exercises is, however, only
a fiction; strictly speaking he is only tolerated by the
Chinese. In Turfan also, where his son-in-law resides, and
in Kucha, there are other Mohammedan shadow princes of
the same kind. From the true believers he raises a tax
which is said to be bigger than the taxes of the Chinese, and
he is said therefore not to be particularly popular even
with those professing Islam.

Shah Maksut, whom his men addressed as " Padishah "
(king), was a lively, jovial, and entertaining man. We did
not require an interpreter in order to make ourselves understood; we conversed in his own mother tongue, Eastern
Turkish. His first question concerned Professor A. v. Le
Coq of Berlin, who is famous on account of his epoch-
making expeditions in the region of Turfan and other sites
in Central Asia. " Do I know v. Le Coq! He is one of
my very best friends," I was able to reply, whereupon the
prince told of his recollections of that time and asked me
to convey his greetings to v. Le Coq.

Concerning my fatherland, Sweden, and its position, he
had very confused notions. " How far away from Istambul
does your country lie ? "—" Four days' journey by the
railway."—" Oh, then you are indeed neighbours of the
Turks."—He himself requires three months to travel to
Peking. Then he inquired about our journey across Asia,
and could not understand why we had been eight months
on the way, when the caravans only need three months for it.
I explained to him that we had worked, taken observations,
and made collections, and I asked him why they had been
afraid of us and had entertained the suspicion that we had
something evil in view. He answered : " When so many
well-armed Europeans approach our frontiers, it is really
not astonishing if we have the suspicion that they are the
front detachment of a hostile army. In China there is war,
and we must be careful. But afraid of you we have not
been, especially as we knew that the son of your king has

spoken well of you, and that you have been recommended by the government in Peking. We could, however, not know whether you were the right ones or were others. Now we understand the matter."

We took our leave and continued our round. General Liu was now kindness itself and invited the whole staff to a banquet, at which he himself, the town authorities, and Shah Maksut would be the hosts. The feast would take place in the house of Yolbars Khan, the only one in which the king could go, for there he was secure against the danger of being given a dish to eat that had been prepared with the fat of the pig.

Finally with our visit we also honoured the mayor, a stately, affable man, also the amiable General A, who had served for 30 years in Sin-kiang, particularly in Ili and Tarbagatai, and the postmaster Chên, who entertained us with candied walnuts and gave us good advice.

On the 29th of January our faithful Mongols came from their camp into the town to buy clothes and provisions. They filled our court-yard with their large tents, themselves, and their baggy furs. Just then we received various return visits, whereby the crowd became still more mixed up. Among others General Liu appeared, who, accompanied by riders, drove in his elegant little carriage into our court-yard. Our club-tent had been transformed into an operating-theatre, since Chên's little daughter had been badly bitten by a dog and now was to be treated by Dr. Hummel.

As a result of this the general was received in my more than simple work-room, and the tea-cups were placed on the writing-table. He made me a present of a beautiful panther-skin as a return gift for a present that he himself had received the day before and which Norin had presented to him, a large telescope on a stand. He was thoroughly delighted with the valuable present and paid us quite a number of choice Chinese compliments. In Nan-yang near Shanghai he had lived for several years and had come into contact with many Europeans, but never with such fine men as we were! Professor Hsü and the other Chinese he could not congratulate enough on their being granted the opportunity of travelling with us the whole of the long road from Peking to this town and farther. He even rose to the bold comparison of calling the province of Sin-kiang a money-chest which is kept in a family—no-one can open it until the one comes who has charge of the key. And now we had come and had the key to all the treasures of Sin-kiang. Our work, he assured us, would be to the advantage not only of the province but of the whole of China.

The Mohammedan king had at the same time invited us to be present at a hunt with falcons. A few friends of the noble chase therefore rode out with the hunters. They were very satisfied with what they saw—the bag consisted of three hares. The hunting-falcons are caught in the autumn. With the help of pigeons or hens under stretched nets the falcon is enticed into the snare, gets entangled in the meshes, and is captured. It is tamed in fifteen days and learns how to sit on the leather glove and wear the hood and, above all, hunt foxes and hares. In this hunting it is employed during the winter, and in the early summer it regains its liberty. When the autumn comes new birds are caught. Then perhaps there are caught in the nets even such birds as have already before been forced to enter the service of man.

Now the great day dawned when the feast took place in the house of Yolbars Khan. Yolbars Khan, the " Tiger Prince," is a very influential man. He is the right hand of the Mohammedan king and is also on a particularly good footing with the Chinese authorities. To us he was of great use; he helped us to settle our affairs, took charge of our camels and got pasturage and shepherding for them, procured provisions and carts for us for the journey to Urumchi, and, in a word, assisted us in everything.

His house was built of wood in the Turkish style and had two storeys. Even the Chinese were accustomed to borrow it on festive occasions. When we reached the porch, over which there waved two five-coloured flags, we found the street crowded with sightseers, while the military band in the arched gateway blew a resounding fanfare. Between soldiers at attention Yolbars Khan led us to the stairway which goes up from the court-yard to the inner gallery.

In the large room we were awaited by our hosts, two of whom first of all took us round the wonderful palace. In the winter garden roses were blooming and pelargoniums and oleanders were showing their array of colour. From the gallery lying towards the street one had a splendid view over the Turkish town and the Chinese town with its wall, and the range of mountains in the north, the Tien-shan, with its blinding white snow-fields.

Then hosts and guests took their places at three round tables in the room. I sat at the middle table, at which His Majesty the King of Hami acted as host. In accordance with old Chinese custom he stepped towards my place, took hold of the drinking-cup and the ivory chopsticks and raised them to his forehead, whereupon he passed his right hand over my chair, as if to convince me that it was dusted. At the second table General Liu was the host and Hsü Ping-chang the honoured guest; at the third the mayor presided and Larson occupied the place of honour.

Shark's fins, bamboo shoots, and seaweeds and other wonderful delicacies were served, and the king invited us to drink. While he, as a true believing professor of the Koran, does not drink himself, he held that it does one good to drink, so far as one is allowed. His conversation was very entertaining.

"Why do you shave, when your young countrymen (Norin and Bergman) have respectable beards? In order to look younger? The beard is an ornament of man; it is unnatural to shave it off."

"Are you married?" he inquired.

"No, not yet."

"How strange! And why not?"

"I haven't had any time for it."

"Oh, there is nothing that is more important. One must at least have a wife and a good crowd of children. You must marry a Russian woman when you get to Urumchi."

The sun touched the horizon, and the old king went out to perform his evening prayer. When he came back, he immediately came out with new funny questions. He had noticed that Larson left the Chinese wine untouched.

" Why doesn't he drink ? " he asked. " Is he a priest or scribe ? "

" A priest," I answered. That was, indeed, not quite true, but in his youth at least, Larson had been a missionary.

" No, our priests don't drink either, but they eat all the more to make up for it and have enormous stomachs."

At the conclusion of the feast Lieberenz took a flashlight photograph. For this the king hurried out again ; for a true believing Moslem may not show his face in a picture.

The feast was a real success, original, full of colour. A reflection of times long passed away hung over the affair. We took our leave, came again past the noisy oriental band, and journeyed back to our court-yard. Over us there streamed the light of a Turkish crescent in a dark-blue field, and the lacquered wooden pillars of the shops shone blood-red through the dust of the streets. We felt positively elated with victory. As criminals or at least as suspicious characters whom one might think capable of who knows what evil intentions, we had a short time before first crossed the frontier, been arrested and disarmed, and led along the road like prisoners. And now princes and generals honour us with splendid feasts ; trumpets and drums resound out of respect for us. We are honoured in all imaginable ways : we are sent eatables, rice, sheep, and melons ; one seems to want to keep us here as long as possible. But there will, indeed, probably be few towns on the earth, where life runs along such uniform lines as in Hami, and our arrival meant an extremely unaccustomed change.

We did the proper thing of course, and on the following day gave our feast. It resembled the first in every respect, with the difference that the hosts of yesterday were the guests of to-day and the guests of yesterday to-day were hosts, and that now the Mongol prince, the thirty-eight-year-old Kara-shahruin Gigen, " the incarnation in Kara-shahr," was also present. To be exact it is his nephew who is prince of the Kara-shahr Torgots, but Gigen represents the real prince during the latter's minority. At one table von Marschall was the host. He excited the boundless admiration and the loud cheers of the Chinese by his ability to toss off a bumper, or as the Chinese say, *kan-pei* (drink the glass empty). For they played a drinking-game, which consists in two opponents stretching out towards each other a certain number of fingers of one hand and both at the same time calling a number between naught and ten. If now one stretches out three fingers and the other five and one of the contracting parties calls eight, then the opponent, who has perhaps called six, must empty his full cup. Sometimes the penalty was three cups, nay, at Marschall's table once even nine bumpers. Marschall lost, and drank his nine *kan-pei* without turning a hair. The Chinese cheered lustily.

In the evening there arrived via Su-chow a letter from Zimmermann of the 18th of December. It confirmed that the station on Etsin-gol had been prohibited by the authorities of Kansu. The previous day he had received a visit from a committee of inquiry consisting of four Chinese, who with courtesy and consideration asked to be allowed to take note of the activities and observations of the station. When after conducting the inquiry they returned to Su-chow, Ma accompanied them in order to explain everything by word of mouth and in writing. Zimmermann had then only 15 dollars left, but he soon received assistance both from Hami and from Peking, and he had eleven large boxes of preserves, flour, and rice. He was afraid that if we met with an unfriendly reception on the frontier of Sin-kiang, this would have an injurious effect on the station on Etsin-gol.

On the 1st of February the Mongol prince honoured us with a visit and received as a return present Heyder's target-rifle, which with General Liu's permission was unpacked from the sealed box. The prince had given us to understand that he dreamt of possessing such a weapon, and that it might be of advantage to us to have him as a friend. For reason of his position he was a certain powerful factor in the province. As a return present he gave to each of Professor Hsü and me a bearskin from the Tien-shan, and later in Urumchi he presented me with a first-class riding-horse of Mongolian stock. When he now visited us he travelled in a little Russian droshky, which was drawn by a big black trotter. His escort, strong young Torgots,

317

made an extremely good impression. They were wearing yellowish-grey uniforms of faultless European cut and were all riding on cream-coloured horses.

In order to make acquaintance with the objects of interests in Hami, I made a tour with my friends Hsü, Huang, and Kung. This took us first of all to the temple erected to the memory of Tso Tsung-tang. Tso Tsung-tang, who in his day with Li Hung-chang and Tsêng Kuo-fan formed in China a triple constellation of great men, was about the year 1880 largely instrumental in making an end of the Tai-ping Rebellion in the interior of the country. After he had cleared Shansi, he marched to Sin-kiang, which Li Hung-chang had intended to give up, suppressed the rebellion, and saved these enormous territories for the Chinese Empire. Therefore the temple in Hami has been erected in his honour. We went along through gateways, between red-lacquered pillars, and under curved roofs, and, after we had crossed two court-yards, made a halt before the front of the temple, the centre of which is occupied by a room resembling a miniature stage. Here in the middle there is found in a sort of small sentry-box or cupboard a picture of the general, a little more than a foot in height. He is dressed in yellow clothes and mandarin's cap, wears a black moustache, and looks determined. In front of him there stands a metal vessel with sticks of incense, which are burning in his honour. On a tablet all his titles of honour are recorded, and on other tablets at the sides there can be read the names of the leaders of his army.

Tsêng Kuo-fan was the father of the famous Marquis Tsêng, who in the year 1881 by diplomatic skill brought Ili and Kulja to China, after these towns and their surrounding country had been under the dominion of Russia for ten years. Kulja now as then is one of the pearls of the desert province of Sin-kiang. The name Sin-kiang, "the New Province," was introduced when Tso Tsung-tang had again restored peace and order in the country. Previously these regions were usually known as Hsi-yü, the "Western Countries."

Another temple in Hami is dedicated to the god of the

province of Honan; for Tso Tsung-tang and most of his generals were from Honan.

On the edge of the town there rises a burial mosque, under whose dome Shah Maksut's grandfather and several other members of the dynasty rest. It is a cubiform structure, with plain faience, and its front is ornamented with *pishtak*, recesses, everything in straight lines and points, not in round curves as is usual elsewhere in Islamic architecture.

We rolled through bottomless dust and met walkers and riders, whole lines of bullock-carts, which are loaded with fuel or timber, and small caravans of stately camels. At the sides run canals, which along the road give water to willows, pyramid-shaped poplars, and mulberry trees.

When the time came, the third feast took place. We were honoured like princes. This time the corps of officers of Hami were the hosts, and the participants were the same as at the two earlier arrangements, the persons of rank in the town and ourselves.

Already in Hami we became acquainted with the strange coinage of Sin-kiang. The usual means of payment is, as good as exclusively, money certificates, "Sin-kiang-liang," which are printed in Urumchi and are only met with in 1-*liang* certificates. The little bronze coin, "ta-chien," with a square hole in the middle is also current, and sometimes one also sees "yambaus," boat-shaped ingots of silver with the stamp of a town in the middle. The Mexican silver dollars that may be in circulation are greatly sought after by shopkeepers, who buy opium from Tun-huang, and many hide them in their boxes, as the paper money does not inspire particularly great confidence. When we sold Mexican dollars we received only two and a half *liang* for them; whenever we bought them on the other hand, we had to pay three and a half *liang*. Sin-kiang is thus suffering from a slowly progressive inflation. Our Mongols who were returning home we could only give silver dollars, since the *liang* is worthless outside the frontiers of Sin-kiang. We required 2,000 dollars. A Western Turkestan merchant from Verni, Ahun Bai, offered me his services. He hardly believed that there were 2,000 silver dollars in the whole

of Hami. But he would try to buy 50 dollars here and
50 dollars there. But 4 *liang* was now wanted for a dollar,
and if it became known that we needed dollars, the price
would then rise to 5 and 6 *liang*. Finally we got assistance
from Yolbars Khan, who obtained the whole amount for
us at the usual price.

During our stay in Hami no one of us had so much to
do as Dr. Hummel. Day in and day out there came to him
sick persons in order to be treated and given medicine.
He had also many patients whom he visited and treated in
their houses, as the son of Shah Maksut, the mayor, General
Liu, and various others.

On the evening of the 2nd of February our Mongols said
good-bye to us. I thanked each one separately for his
watchfulness and good services and wished them a happy
journey. They had played their parts and were leaving
the scene of our expedition. They now went into their
camp outside the town, but did not set out on their homeward journey until the 12th of February. On the 5th of
June, when Larson sent me a letter from Kalgan, they had
still not been heard of in their home province. I hope that
on their long road across the Gobi Desert they have not
fallen into the hands of robbers.

Of our camels the seventy best were sent to Turfan,
where they are to rest and pasture, in order later to be
enlisted in the Swedish and Chinese caravans in Sin-
kiang.

The following day a crowd of fellows celebrating the
new-year's feast came marching into our court-yard with
noisy music. The display was opened by two men, dressed
and made up like women, walking in two wooden frames,
which were to represent boats. They performed a comical
dance and made their boats rock as if on a heavy sea.
Behind them came the music with cymbals and hard pieces
of wood, which resounded whenever they were struck one
against the other. They formed a semicircle in front of
us and struck up a song in our honour, which concluded
with the request not to make fun of their display.

For the rest we utilized this day for the purpose of paying
farewell visits. When I was informed that a military escort

Msi-yeng-tse

The tomb of a saint near Chiktam

THROUGH THE LAND OF ROCK TOWNS

The carts often get fast in the mud

Once again the road goes over high mountain passes

THROUGH SIN-KIANG

would accompany us to Urumchi, I asked if they believed that we were robbers, that they surrounded us with so many soldiers. " No, not in the least. They are a guard of honour and only highly-placed persons are deemed worthy of such a distinction."

XXV

TO URUMCHI VIA PICHANG AND TURFAN

AT last the 4th of February dawned, the day of our departure. In our court-yard there was picturesque disorder—eight of the large carts with two high wheels were standing ready to be loaded, and between them were the boxes, trunks, sacks, and all the belongings that we were taking with us. Our servants and drivers ran hastily hither and thither, the loads were packed on the carts and bound secure with ropes, each of the members of the staff made his cart as soft and comfortable as possible ; Hummel, who was travelling with me, understood particularly well how to pad our travelling-coach. The yellow Mongolian horses stood tied to a wall ; the escort, too, which the Mongol prince sent along with us, had already put in an appearance, together with its leader, Lao Tung. Messengers came and went, and our new friends, Chinese, Mohammedans, and Mongols, sent us farewell presents : mutton, live poultry, eggs, pastry, sweets, fruits, and similar things.

In the midst of the worst confusion there appeared Shah Maksut in a little covered carriage, who was taken into our club-tent and entertained with tea. He had heard of a sort of telescope that was said to be so constituted, that with it one could see right through the mightiest mountains, and it was impossible to shake his belief that there was such an instrument.

After His Majesty had finally taken his leave and the horses had been put into the carts, we were able to take our places in our simple vehicles. We said good-bye to Ming and a few other servants who had been dismissed, likewise to the Mongols who were still in Hami, Serat, Bonk, Seran Görel, Särche, and Gombo. Larson, Marschall, v. Massenbach and Mühlenweg, Yüan, Huang, Chen, Liu, and Kung were not to follow with the whole of the heavy baggage until after a week. We were travelling in two sections, in order not to be so cramped in the Chinese inns.

It was already 4 o'clock in the afternoon before my cart, followed by the other seven, moved creaking out by the arched gateway. We went through the bazaar and—in at the east gate and out at the south—through the Chinese town, in order then to bend off towards the west. At my side rode Yolbars Khan's stately son, Yüan, and Kung, in order with a whole crowd of curious people to give us a bit of a send-off.

Soon we left the town behind us. Beneath willows and mulberry trees we rolled along, over high-arched rumbling wooden bridges which led over the irrigation-canals. The evening was glorious ; the sun was already touching the horizon, glowing with shades of red and yellow. The long line of heavily-laden carts presented a picturesque scene. One already travelled here thus thousands of years ago. It was as in the days of the Thirty Years War, when the commander of an army had sacked a town and marched away with the booty.

Hsü Ping-chang's cart and mine had roofs of straw matting and white cotton material and were provided with three small glass windows, one on each side and one at the back. In front of Hummel and me, the constantly singing Ibrahim Arabakesh, the driver Abraham, sat on a nose-bag and urged on the horses. He had no reins, only a whip, but his horses obeyed his every sound. We sat comfortably upon hay, blankets, sleeping-sacks, furs, and cushions. But that, indeed, was necessary ; for the road was deplorable and one was thrown wildly hither and thither—one can become seasick with a very slight " sea."

Our state-coach led the procession ; then there followed, two in each cart, Hsü and Ting, Norin and Bergman, Heyder and Lieberenz. In the fifth Chin and Wang were seated, in the sixth Chang and Hsü's servant Wang, in the seventh Lieberenz's servant and assistant Charlie. The eighth and last cart carried only baggage.

Indeed, our rolling caravan was really an enjoyable

spectacle, for which the setting sun provided gay colours, and our Mongolian bodyguard fitted in with this painting. In the background there faded away the still purple snow-fields of the Karlik-tag, and the full moon shone into our cart, in which Dr. Hummel was already snoring—vying with the creaking of the wheels and the hollow sound of the three large bronze bells which had been screwed on the under side of the axle. We went slowly and heavily forward. The dust whirled round the column. Near a village we made a halt of half an hour, so that the escort and the drivers could consume their evening meal.

At 9 o'clock we had 12 degrees of frost. We were now in the desert again ; the stillness of the solitude surrounded us. Now and then we were met by little caravans of asses, mules, or horses, and carts loaded with cotton. One could hear the tinkling of their bells throughout the night. At 3 o'clock in the morning we drove into the village of To-po and stopped in front of a well-built house, which belonged to the Mongol prince. Here we were invited into a room whose table threatened almost to give way under the load of dishes containing sweets, butter, bread, eggs, preserved fruits, and honey. After these Mongolian first dishes there was meat-broth, mutton with vegetables, macaroni, and mushrooms and hash cooked in dough. It was already a quarter to seven before we went to rest.

When we continued our journey on the 5th of February, we were given a send-off by fifteen Mongolian riders in a cloud of dust. The road led across steppe ; the ruts had been cut as much as 30 centimetres deep in the soft ground. We met a caravan of two hundred splendid camels, which were carrying huge white bales of cotton. Near the village of Astani, which had a bazaar, a pond, and a small waterfall, the desert began afresh. It extended right to the village of San-po, where in three miserable huts we spent the night on the *kang*. The *kang* occupied almost half the floor space of each one of the rooms ; in front of it there was an altar-shaped elevation for the fire, which filled the room with suffocating smoke. Provisions we ourselves had with us, and Norin's cook, Chang, prepared for us the most glorious dishes.

On the 6th of February we travelled mostly across barren desert. A few times we came, however, past gardens in which peaches, apricots, melons, and apples were grown. In this region we also saw the curious subterranean canals, " kares," which at a depth of about 4 metres carry the water for irrigation to the villages lying further to the south, which could not be seen from our road. These canals betray their presence by the openings of the vertical shafts which at a distance of 20 to 30 metres connect the surface of the ground with the canal.

In the village of Taranchi, where we spent the night, there lived two Chinese families, one Zungarian family, and one Eastern Turkish. As on every evening, Adil Ahun, the foreman of our drivers, came to my quarters to receive my orders and give me particulars of the section for the next day. Our drivers told us that they had a month's pay of 15 *liang* (approximately 10 shillings), but that they received in addition from their employer, Yolbars Khan, 2 *chin* of flour every day and 10 *chin* of fuel.

The next day we again rolled across desert, over hard rubbly ground and now and again through little furrows in which scattered tufts of steppe grass were growing. The western horizon disappeared in a haze. In the north there towered up the snow-capped ridges of the Tien-shan. In a village, Shutte-bulak, a wedding was being celebrated. The country was uniform, but nevertheless impressive in its majestic grandeur and solitude. In the evening we rested for two hours near the little village of Ördeklik, where our horses received maize, whilst we took our simple evening meal in a ruin. Our group presented a romantic picture in the double light : the reddish-yellow reflection of our fire, and the moon, which poured down its silvery white light over the desert.

It was already late in the night when we made a halt in the village of Lo-tung. Here we gave our horses a day's rest, and were surprised by a courier, who, however, only brought us illustrated journals and books.

On the 9th of February our road led through the region which is known as Tokus-davan, " the Nine Passes," sometimes in windings and bends, sometimes straight over little steep risings before passes through red ravines and past heaps of stones. The village of I-wan-chuan, consisting of two small Chinese farms, where we spent the night, had at disposal an inn of the simplest kind ; its miserable dark rooms had holes for smoke in the roof, a hole in the mud wall, and a door-opening without a door. The region from this place to the town of Pichang is known as " the Desert of the Winds," for here in spring there is a storm which is said to be able to overthrow carts and pack-camels.

On the following morning the wind came from the north-west and the sky was covered with clouds. The storm howled round the carts, and the dust rose up behind horses and wheels. Our Mongolian escort rode a good distance in front. After we had crossed two rather steep passes, we came into barren mountains and halted finally in a narrow valley near the village of Chi-ku-lu-chuan, " the Spring of the Cart-wheel."

Under the radiant morning sun, which marvellously lit up the valley, we travelled down the winding ravine, sometimes only 20 metres broad, which is squeezed in between hills 40 to 50 metres high. It opened on the endless plain between the mountain chains of the Tien-shan. In the village of Chi-ko-chin, where we made a halt, there is a telegraph-station. Here we received a telegram from Yüan, who informed us that his section under Larson was to start out on the 12th of February.

Our next day's journey was of 49 kilometres and the following of even 53. We got up therefore at half-past two and crept by the light of a lantern into our furs in the cart, where we soon fell asleep again.

Not till 9 o'clock in the morning did we wake up, when the cart stopped for some time near Tung-yen-cha, " the Eastern Salt Lake." A lake, indeed, was not to be seen, but instead of it there was here the tomb of a saint, a little round structure with a dome, and a temple in Chinese style with turrets and the sacrificed horns of ibexes and argali sheep. On the inner walls hung strips of red fabric with Chinese writing, and the sarcophagus-like tomb was covered with white material. In the shrine our Mohammedan drivers tarried over their devotions ; they poured some of the oil that they carried with them on the lamps of the altar, which they lit. Most of the pilgrims, however, are said to be Zungars.

After a long wearisome journey between mountain chains of medium height, we came into a narrow, romantic ravine, where towards evening we made a halt, so that the horses might be given their maize. The region was completely barren, but a splintered telegraph-pole that was no longer fit for service offered us firewood, and a few remaining patches of snow in a crevice in the ground provided us with water. Over the fire pea-soup and tea were got ready, and we spent a pleasant evening hour in the open.

When we continued our journey, the valley became so narrow that two carts meeting would hardly get past each other. At 9 o'clock in the evening we crossed a pass 1,160 metres high; in the course of the day we had ascended 800 metres. After a journey of twenty hours we took up our quarters for the night in the little village of Hsi-yen-cha.

When on the 13th of February we stepped into the open, we found ourselves surrounded by dark, romantic mountains. Between these in the afternoon we rolled on— despite the setting sun. The wheels creaked and rumbled in the rubbly ground; the drivers were singing. Gradually it became dark; we dozed, and finally nodded off to sleep, not to wake until the next morning in the village of Tu-tung-tse, where we rested for two hours on account of the horses. Then we went on as far as the village of Chi-ko-tai, a little fort. On the last stretch we had descended 500 metres again.

On the 15th we started out at daybreak. A short distance in front of the village the ground was covered with sheets of ice and was crossed by a spiteful ditch. The horses took a leap, slipped, fell, and got up again, the cart sank in up to the axle, but came luckily across, only we and our things were thoroughly shaken up. Ibrahim understood his business. His comrades did not have it so easy. One cart stuck so badly that eight horses were required to pull it out again.

Red sandstone mountains surrounded the low country in which near the village of Bir-bulak, " One Spring," three Mohammedan families were cultivating wheat, maize, and melons. We travelled past a *masar*, the tomb of a saint, and the ruins of a watch-tower. Soon we noticed that we were approaching a town. A large camel caravan, which was carrying cotton to Kuei-hua-chêng, came towards us ; carts and little caravans of asses were to be seen ; against the setting sun there showed up the outlines of gardens and high poplars—it was the oasis of Pichang. The road changed to an avenue with willows, poplars, and mulberry trees, riders and farm-wagons appeared out of the clouds of dust, and on both sides lay isolated farms. We rumbled into a bazaar street, in parts covered over with straw matting, with Chinese shops and tea-houses, shopkeepers, and customers, travelled over a bridge which arched a deep canal and past a burial-place, and then came into a new bazaar street, in which our inn was situated. Adil Ahun asked for a rest-day, as we had lost one horse and needed four new ones.

Pichang has four gates and a main street between the north gate and the south gate. Only three hundred families are said to inhabit the town, a great part of them Chinese. The country is almost exclusively inhabited by Eastern Turks. A *chien-chang*, or mayor, and three officers are the only officials that have their residence here.

After Tso Tsung-tang had restored peace in Sin-kiang, the present administrative districts were set up. Names like Tien-shan-pei-lu, " the road to the north of the Tien-shan," and Tien-shan-nan-lu, " the road to the south of the Tien-shan," which are geographical rather than administrative concepts, lost their significance. Pichang received the name of Shan-shan, since it was believed that the town and its surrounding country corresponded to the old Shan-shan. That was not correct ; for in reality the town of Lou-lan which was discovered by me in the year 1900 lay in the country of Shan-shan. But of course one could not know that two decades before my discovery. It would be better to abolish the name of Shan-shan and to put a new one in its place.

Dr. Hummel did not get much rest in Pichang. In the morning a dense crowd of sick people was standing in front of his clinic. People afflicted with consumption, leprosy, eye complaints, and other terrible diseases sought his advice, and he helped them, so far as time and circumstances permitted.

Pichang was number a hundred, C, among the camping-places of the route which my column had covered from Paotow, and on the road to Lieh-mo-chin we began the second hundred. While in the court-yard the doves were cooing and the sparrows were twittering, the long procession of carts started in motion. After an hour we found ourselves in completely barren desert and had quite near to the left the belt of sand-dunes that is known as Kum-tag, " the Sand Mountains." To our right some small oases were to be seen, from which the water sometimes came right down to the road. Lieh-mo-chin had a picturesque village street with grey walls and bare trees and a tavern with a veranda and a view over a little river-valley.

On the 18th of February at 7 o'clock in the morning we had 7·2 degrees below zero and at 2 o'clock in the afternoon 8·4 degrees above. We travelled along in a thick haze of dust between low mountains and came finally into the romantic wild valley of the Sängim, which led us to the north-west. Here to our right we had a river containing a fair amount of water. Its channel has cut itself out 25 metres deep, and the erosion terrace falls vertically to the narrow band of vegetation along the bank. The road ran sometimes on the extreme edge, and one questioned whether the loose material would sustain the weight of the cart or would hurl it into the depths. A little bridge crossed the watercourse where the road led up, by a side valley coming from the right, to the rock-caves of Bäzäklik, described in so masterly a fashion by Professor von Le Coq. At our side there could be seen caves and galleries with simple paintings. Along the river lay a few farms and a mill. The scenery was magnificent; on both sides of us there towered up rocks of red sandstone. The waterfalls were roaring in the river. We rolled along over a very low bridge and reached the village of Sängim-agis, in which there was a small garrison.

On the morning of the 19th of February all except Norin

and me rode up to the grottoes of Bäzäklik and returned towards midday quite enthusiastic with what they had seen.
They had been in a great number of cells, which showed
clear signs of the work of the German Turfan Expeditions.
Here and there decorative paintings could still be seen,
some of them covered over with a sort of plaster, in order
to protect them against destruction.   On some of our party
the antiquities and the glorious scenery had made such an
impression, that they competed eagerly for von Le Coq's
book, although all of them had read it.

Soon we were again out in the desert and were only
30 metres above the level of the sea.   We were approaching
the remarkable depression near Lukchun, to the south of
Turfan, whose deepest part, according to the statement
of Sir Aurel Stein, lies 980 feet (298 metres) below the
level of the sea, a figure which, however, requires veri-
fication.

Out of the turbid air a little burial mosque appeared.
The sun was setting and became pale in the haze ; the glow
of sunset did not appear.   Towards midnight we rolled
into the court-yard of an inn in Turfan.

In this town we rested a day.   Hsü Ping-chang and I
visited the mayor and the commandant, General Huang
Darin.   The general had been in Kashgar and knew Sir
George Macartney ; he had also been present when the
motor-car road between Urumchi and Chuguchak was
being constructed.   Hsü celebrated my birthday with a
brilliant feast in a Chinese inn, in which also the mayor
took part.   In the evening fireworks were even let off.

During my stay in Turfan I received a geographical report
just as unexpected as it was interesting.   My informants
were two inhabitants of the town : Tokta Ahun, who
for 18 years had gone three or four times a year via
Ying-pen along the dry river-bed of the Kuruk-darya to
Tikkenlik on the Konche-darya, in order to buy sheep,
which he sells in Turfan ; the other, Khoja Abdul, the owner
of the house in which we were staying.

Tokta Ahun now reported, and Khoja Abdul confirmed
his words, that 7 years previously the water of the
Konche-darya had gone over into the bed of the Kuruk-

Pichang
(The streets are roofed over as a protection against the rays of the sun)

Turfan
(Here the cotton trade flourishes)

Town Life in Sin-kiang

[face p. 330

A thaw

URUMCHI

[face p. 331

darya and since then had flowed in the latter. The place of bifurcation was situated near Kuslik, a day's march above Tikkenlik. The new river in the old bed thus flows past Ying-pen, where there was a ferry, for one could not wade across the river. On its way further to the east it gradually shrunk, for the volume of its water was drawn away by side branches, which led to swamps and small lakes. Three days' journey to the north of Dunkhan (Tun-huang) it dried up, without having formed a terminal lake. Abd-ur-Rahim was the only person who had been there. This Abd-ur-Rahim in the year 1900 was my guide. Anyone who desires further information concerning this problem is referred to my book *Central Asia and Tibet*, London, 1903, vols. i and ii, and elsewhere. New vegetation, especially reeds, had shot up on the banks of the Kuruk-darya, and seeds of poplar had taken root. Even the fish followed the water on its new way to the east.

One will be able to understand with what joy and satisfaction I received this news, for I had predicted this event, above all during my long periods of stay on Lop-nor and in its delta in the years 1900 and 1901. I had likened the branches of the Tarim to a pendulum and Lop-nor to the weight at its lower end, which swings now to the south, now to the northern part of the desert. The desert is almost completely flat and the water is therefore very sensitive to all changes of elevation. When the bed of the present lake, which is usually known as Kara-koshun, and that of the river itself have filled in the course of time with sand and decaying animal and vegetable matter, the water flows over into the northern basin, which in the meantime has been complete desert and has been hollowed out by the fierce east-north-east storms of spring and summer.

The river which ages ago flowed to the immediate north of Lou-lan has thus returned to its old bed—just as I predicted in the year 1905—and although the period of the " swing of the pendulum " amounts to almost 1,600 years, it has been granted me to live to see the correctness of my theory and establish it myself.

The information which I received in Turfan might, however—it was not quite unthinkable—be pure fancy or rest upon misunderstandings.   Norin, like me, was therefore burning to establish the fact by a visit to the spot.   No European had been there since the water had changed its course.   An immediate visit was not possible, for Governor-General Yang had demanded that I should present myself with the whole staff in Urumchi.   But as soon as we had received permission there to explore the Lop-nor desert, at the beginning of March I sent Norin on a first investigation along the Kuruk-darya.   Among other things I gave him instructions to investigate whether the restored waterway would be navigable for a small vessel, for I cherished the desire to cartographically survey the river later myself and plunge once more into this hydrographic problem which had taken up so much of my time in my youth.

In the middle of July in Stockholm I had the pleasure of receiving from Norin a report of the 20th of May, in which it says :

"Concerning your plan to travel down the new river in a boat, I should advise you not to undertake it, unless you can be sure of the journey back up the river again.   The region to the north of Lou-lan, through which the river flows, has changed into a real swamp with innumerable small lakes, and it is impossible with camels to approach the main channel of the delta.   Even 50 kilometres to the east of Yardang-bulak you will not be able in the north to reach ground that will bear you.   How it looks to the south of the river I do not know, but our guides say that there several arms of water go to the south and that it is impossible for camels to cross them.   The journey down the river can easily be accomplished with a boat, but once at the end, it will be difficult to return."

Norin has thus not only established the truth of the statements that our informants made to us in Turfan, but has also found that the new river has a sufficient volume of water to permit a journey in a boat.   My plan is therefore clear.   In the winter, when the river and all the swamps and lakes are frozen up, I intend to travel over the ice and cartographically survey the whole area.   But the carrying out of this plan depends on the political situation in Sin-kiang, and the future will show whether and how my project can be put into operation. Thanks to Norin's investigation the main lines of the problem are now already clear, however, and we have made a geographical conquest of really great importance.[1]

The mayor and the commandant of Turfan have their offices in the "Old Town," Kona-shahr, which is inhabited by only a hundred families and has four gates, the northern of which is almost never used.

After we had travelled on the 21st of February in through the east gate of Kona-shahr and out again at the west gate, where we were held up for a short time by a few friendly customs officers, we made our entry into the "New Town," Yangi-shahr, which was established 58 years ago by Yakub Bek and is inhabited by six hundred and sixty families. Only a tenth of the population of Turfan is said to be Chinese.

We rolled through an endlessly long bazaar street, which was covered over with a sun-roof made of poles and straw matting. On both sides ranged Chinese shops with red sign-boards and strips of blue, green, or red material with written characters along the frieze of the roof. This line was only interrupted by the mosque with grey dome which rose up on the south side of the street. In the narrow thoroughfare, through which also the great highway to Urumchi runs, there was a life and bustle without parallel. We had great difficulty in getting forward between riders and carts, camels and asses, purchasers and people walking, dervishes and beggars, women with white kerchiefs over their heads, who walked on foot, rode on asses, or travelled in little blue carts. Two-wheeled *arabas* were conveying coal, jostling asses were carrying water in wooden tubs, a string of camels were loaded with bales of cotton. In their stands sat the shopkeepers, selling fruits, sweets, tobacco, woven materials, and all kinds of small articles. For an instant a Chinese temple was to be seen. Here and there a beam of sunlight penetrated through the pro-

[1] Vide below: *Lop-nor, the Wandering Lake*, pp. 360 et seqq.

tecting roof and formed a pleasing patch of light and colour on a Chinese sign-board. A roaring din of shouts and noises, voices and ringing bells, filled the tunnel, in which half dusk prevailed. Our escort, a third of which was remaining in Turfan, rode much intoxicated in front of my cart, in order to make a way for us, and our vehicle forced its way forward slow and creaking through the crowd. At last we reached a canal, at which the asses' water-tanks were filled; snow-white geese were cackling, and there were pigeons which, when they flew, produced curious sounds with little whistles that were tied to their wings. To the left there lay, surrounded by many other graves, the tomb of a saint, a *masar*.

After an hour and a half the last groups of trees and fields disappeared behind us and we were in the desert again. Between barren hills, with red mountains on our right, we turned off towards the north-west and followed a valley upwards, where a little village lay by a brook. The road then left the valley again and crossed the hills on the left. They consisted of sandstone and, filed and eaten into by winds and storms, showed curious forms, which in the glow of the setting sun resembled red ruins. At last we arrived in the village of Kang-kang, in the Eastern Turkish language Kindik, where we spent the night.

Our next day's journey led along the mountains. The country was completely barren. Beyond the village of Togra-su the sun set, and darkness came on. Armed with an electric lamp, Norin went on foot in front of our cart and showed us the way, which here could easily be lost. Hummel and Bergman had ridden on in front, and when we finally reached the village of Kovurga, which the Chinese call San-kou-chuantse, "the Three Springs," they had already put our poor lodging in order and prepared an excellent chicken-soup.

On the road to Kugolo or Ho-kow, which led through a reddish-coloured rocky region, limestone traversed by sandstone, with flat spurs and valleys, we crossed the frontier of the districts of Turfan and Urumchi. This spot was marked by a boundary-stone.

When on the morning of the 24th of February we stepped

into the open from the dark holes of our lodging, we admired the magnificent landscape which surrounded us : a narrow valley with a rushing stream hemmed in between mountains, shaded at the bottom by young willows. A caravan of asses was just being loaded with large white bales of cotton, in order to set out for Urumchi. In the north-west there rose up a mighty group of brownish-red mountains.

We got up into our carts, and a very fatiguing journey began. First we rolled heavy and rumbling across the rubble on the river-bed and along in its rushing water. Then the horses had to exert their strength to the utmost, in order to get the heavy carts up on a path on the bank to the right, where we had to cross several outcrops of primary rock, were thrown to and fro, and had to hold tight in order not to receive too severe blows.

Then we went down to the stream again ; we pushed our way through thick willow bushes, whose branches and twigs struck against the roof and windows. After we had finally left the brook for good and had got past a new steep slope, the incline became rather less steep, but was yet still so sharp that the horses could never make more than ten to twenty steps and then had to recover their breath. Behind us we could hear stirring shouts and cries. An *araba* had stuck fast and all the drivers were pushing and helping. We longed for the pass, but the road twisted in ever new turns and opened ever new prospects. With the sharp incline we came only slowly forwards. But at last we had the sharply-defined saddle of the pass in front of us. The deeply cut-out ravine which runs across the ridge was so narrow that an *araba* could just get through. In the north we were now offered a splendid view of snow-covered mountains. It was the south slope of the Bogdo-ola that we could see.

The road down from the pass was steeper still. Here the three front horses were untackled, and the horse that went in the shafts took over by itself the labour and responsibility. It set its straightened front legs to the ground and lay back so far on its bent hind-legs, that it sometimes almost sat on the ground. One wondered whether the heavy load would not overwhelm the animal. But everything went well, and we safely reached the farm of Ho-go.

Still a second pass rising we had to cross. The road up to the ridge was short but very steep, and each cart required eight horses. At the north foot of the pass we turned off to the west and crossed the river which breaks through the chain with the two passes, and which we had already seen from our night quarters of the day before. In the north we had a mountain chain glistening with shades of red and violet with beautifully sparkling snow-fields, on the right swamps and sheets of ice, which was very difficult to cross. In the large village of Daban-tien we spent the night.

Between high chains of the " Mountains of Heaven " we travelled next day further to the west and left a little lake to our left. When it was already dark night, Ibrahim got off the road and might almost have thrown us into a treacherous pit. Our camping-place was called Chai-wo-pu.

The next day's journey led us in a whirling south-east storm to the village of I-i-tsantse, and then when we started out on the morning of the 27th to cover the last stretch to Urumchi, there was a snow-storm, the ground was white, and the air was raw and gloomy. Carts and horses were covered with wintry snow. But in the course of the morning the snow became wet and squashy and water ran down on the window-panes. The country was hilly, and we crossed several risings. Heyder and Lieberenz preferred to go on foot after one wheel of their cart had become damaged.

A short distance in front of us we caught sight of two new droshkies which were stopping, and by the side of them a little group of men. Soon we recognized Hempel and Walz ; the third man bore the name of Schirmer and was the representative of the German firm of Faust & Co. in Urumchi.

We took our seats in the droshkies, so far as there was room, and now travelled along at a quick pace. It was still early in the afternoon, when we came into a street with bottomless mud and stopped in front of a one-storeyed house in the usual Russo-Asiatic style. The house had belonged to the Russo-Asiatic Bank, which in the past autumn had gone bankrupt, and had now been placed at our disposal by Governor-General Yang. Those of our comrades who had reached Urumchi before us, von Kaull, Dettmann, Haslund, and the student Li, received us and immediately led us to dinner, at which the Tartar Burkhan, the interpreter of the governor-general and head of his park of motor-cars, also took part. Burkhan and the Russian Gmirkin had been attached to us as waiting and communication officers, in order to be at our service so long as we stayed in Urumchi, while to our Chinese two Chinese officials, Wu and Li, had been attached.

In the wide court-yard Dr. Haude's meteorological observatory was already in full working order; the observations were carried out by Dettmann and Li. Haude himself had gone to the Bogdo-ola, where he had set up a mountain station at an altitude of 2,700 metres.

After the meal I was visited by among others two Catholic missionaries, the German, Father Hilbrenner, and the Dutchman, Father Feldmann, who initiated me into the situation there. Both were cheerful and happy as well as scholarly men, and during the time which I spent in Urumchi, it was always a pleasure to me to be with them.

Since now the whole staff was gradually assembling in our new headquarters, the building of the Russo-Asiatic Bank was not sufficient, and Major Hempel, the leader of the German troop, had therefore hired a dwelling a short distance further on in the same street, which belonged to an old Sart from Tashkent, Isakh Jan. To this house, which was similarly built in Russian style and was clean and comfortable, I now went with the members of the staff who were to be my fellow-lodgers there, Norin, Hummel, Bergman, Hsü Ping-chang, and Ting. Each one received his room and had plenty to do until the evening in arranging it. From the street one came through a large gateway, which was kept shut at night, into an oblong court-yard. Immediately to the left a few steps of a staircase led up to the main passage, which opened into a room in the front. To the left of this was my room, in which I worked and slept, to the right the common dining-room with a long table, which was decorated with little flags of Sweden, Germany, and China.

Adjoining the dining-room was Dr. Hummel's room, which looked more like a medical laboratory, and the simple rooms of the rest of the members of the staff. Just opposite this suite of apartments, in a low building the kitchen and the Chinese servants were accommodated.

Already on the first evening we felt completely at home here, and the great Yang Tsêng-hsin had the kindness to extend to us a cordial welcome through Mr. Burkhan. Already now it was quite different from the position in January, when we crossed the frontier of Sin-kiang and were suspected of evil intentions.

XXVI

MARSHAL YANG, THE GOVERNOR OF SIN-KIANG

SO now we were in Urumchi, the Tihua of the Chinese, the capital of the powerful Yang Tsêng-hsin, and the two whole months that I and some of the members of the staff spent here became of great importance for the further development of the expedition. Larson and his column did not reach us until the 8th of March.

After we had fulfilled the usual obligations of travelling guests, had given notice of our arrival and presented our visiting-cards, I was requested to present myself at 12 o'clock on the 29th of February, with the members of the staff of the expedition that were already present, at the house of the governor-general. So now we were to be thoroughly tested.

Through the bottomless mud of the streets, in which during our stay two horses were drowned and even children are said to have perished, we travelled in a line of little blue carts, the droshkies of China, through the main street of the White Russian settlement, through Turkish quarters and the great gates in the wall of the Chinese town, to the *yamên*, a group of red houses with intervening court-yards, from whose holy of holies the enormous province is governed. We had two rectangular court-yards to cross before we reached the audience hall. At the porch sentries were standing and presented arms. In the vestibule we were received by the ruler of Sin-kiang, surrounded by several officers and his ministers Fan Darin and Liu Darin, as well as the soldiers of his bodyguard.

Here we now stood face to face with the autocratic ruler who had set himself against us with such icy coldness on the eastern frontier of his province, and who could, if it had occurred to him, have frustrated our plans and

339

forced us to turn back. He wanted to see what we looked like, whether we were gentlemen or bandits. Without moving a feature of his stern face, he inspected us one after the other with penetrating glances and greeted each one separately with a soft warm shake of the hand and a scarcely perceptible bow.

If Yang Tsêng-hsin measured us searchingly from head to foot, we on our part regarded him with no less attention. We had heard so much of this extraordinary man, this last great mandarin of the period of the Empire. We knew that he was born in Yünnan, had held a number of different appointments in Kansu, and had climbed higher and higher up the ladder, until he was finally chosen as the military governor of Sin-kiang. Then he had suppressed the insurrections of the Dungans, Kirghiz, and Mongols in the Altai and Ili area, and already in the first year of his governorship had brought peace and order to his great province. His high office he had now held since the year of the Revolution, 1911. With an iron hand he has for 17 years suppressed all attempts to rebel against his power. He has promoted trade, improved the roads, introduced the motor-car, founded an electric power-station and an engineering-works, and constantly busied himself with further schemes of improvement. We knew that this man, since the beginning of the civil war, had protected Sin-kiang against all conflicts. The eastern frontier of his province near Hami was garrisoned with strong bodies of Mongolian and Mohammedan riders under the command of Brigadier-General Liu Darin. Their task was to parry the first blow of a possible attack of the " Christian General," Fêng Yü-hsiang, the only one for whom Yang really has respect. He ruled over a territory which from north to south measures 2,000 and from west to east 1,500 kilometres and comprises almost 3,000,000 square kilometres. Sin-kiang is thus six times as large as Sweden; its area corresponds to Germany, Italy, France, Spain, Portugal, Great Britain, Holland, Belgium, Norway, and Sweden thrown in together, but in consequence of its immense deserts there live there only about three million people : Eastern Turks, Mongols,

Street life

Governor Yang comes on a visit

URUMCHI

[face p. 340

A mother's joy

A Kirghiz with a hunting-eagle

ANIMAL LIFE

Kirghiz, Dungans, Taranchis, Tajiks, Dolons, and Chinese. According to Yang's own statement, one can, indeed, according to the tax rolls put the population of the province at eight millions.

Yang was looked upon as just, and demanded absolute discipline in his small army of scarcely two thousand men. When, shortly before our arrival, he was once taking his usual walk through the streets of the town accompanied by two of his soldiers, he noticed that one of his soldiers, and moreover in uniform, was standing in front of a boot-shop and was stealing one pair of shoes after another with his iron-tipped stick. Yang stopped and looked on. Then he gave a sign to his bodyguard. They stepped forward and shot the thief on the spot. While one procured a little wooden lattice cage, the other cut the thief's head off, which was placed in the cage and hung up by the side of the shop. There it remained hanging for several weeks as a warning to thieves.

After the marshal had concluded his first inspection he gave me his hand and asked me and the rest of the guests to follow him. We crossed two smaller rooms and entered the dining-room, a longish white-plastered room, which for the greater part was taken up by a long table. Here he sat down in the middle of one side and offered me the place opposite. On his right sat his Russian interpreter and confidant of many years, the Tartar Burkhan from Kazan, and on his left his best friend and highest dignitary, the commissioner of education, Liu Darin. Behind him stood a corpulent major with a black moustache and friendly appearance, who accompanied him in and out of the house like a life-guardsman and was never absent from his immediate neighbourhood. On my left sat Professor Hsü Ping-chang.

On the table there was an array of tarts, cakes, sweet-meats—all baked by the White Russian confectioner—cigarettes, and bottles. Serving-men helped us to cognac and white wine. In front of Yang there lay a thick port-folio full of papers, letters, and telegrams, that concerned our expedition. He turned over the documents, took out a letter, and handed it to Professor Hsü. He said as he did so : " This letter from a Nationalist student in Peking arrived here some months ago and is addressed to a student Li. The censor's office handed it over to me as very suspicious. Since it speaks in it of troops which are pushing forward towards the eastern frontier of Sin-kiang, you will understand that I had to be cautious. For that reason I gave orders for you to be closely examined when you approached Hami."

Hsü read the letter and handed it to me. In the text there occurred the phrase : " I congratulate you on your having two hundred soldiers with you in your caravan "— a joke, which was not meant so bad as it sounded. Military escort we had, indeed, only during the first week on the march through the robber districts.

Now the champagne-glasses were filled. Yang rose to his full height and made a speech, which Burkhan interpreted. He bid us welcome in Tihua, a town whose dirty streets were a picture of the present political situation in China. " It is a blessing for science, for Sin-kiang, and for the whole of China, that you, gentlemen, have come here. You will extract the secrets of our great province, find valuable metals and coal, and be our teachers in our attempts to increase the well-being of Sin-kiang. I shall look upon it as a privilege to facilitate your efforts in every way."

In my reply I thanked the governor for the splendid hospitality that he had already shown us, and for his promise to give us his powerful assistance. The reputation of his excellent rule and of the order and security which he maintained had already penetrated to us in Peking, and on the journey here from Hami we had received a deep impression that this reputation was well founded. During a time when the whole world was in a ferment, when a world war was raging, and when now in China civil war still prevailed, he had maintained peace and order in his province and thereby presented an example to the whole world. We hoped by our work to be able to be of service to him, to science, and to Sin-kiang, and we should consider it a gain to us if we could in any way contribute to the well-being of the province.

There was a buoyant, happy feeling at the table. Professor Hsü spoke in the name of our Chinese, cast an historical retrospective glance over the position in China 2,000 years ago, and expressed the hope that his country might now experience a new prosperity and, above all, unity and harmony between all the provinces.

Yang Tsêng-hsin then in conversation revealed with surprising candour his views concerning the civil war between the various generals. I handed him Marshal Chang Tso-lin's autograph letter, which was now more than a year old. He read it without moving a feature, but afterwards expressed himself not exactly favourably concerning the marshal, who, in Yang's opinion, only fought for the sake of his own advantage. "He does not think of peace and the people's happiness, which on the other hand are my sole object here in Sin-kiang." Now, as I write this, both have fallen by the hand of the murderer.

We knew that Yang was a scholarly and well-informed man. His reminiscences he had printed in thirty volumes, and he still made daily observations concerning his life and the administration of his province. He had therefore great respect for all who write books, and in order to pay me a compliment, he explained to me that he knew that I had published several works, not least on the geography of Sin-kiang.

Yang had obviously received a favourable impression of us, for on the 4th of March we were invited to a real Chinese state dinner in the same room. There we were entertained with an endless succession of Chinese dishes, with shark's fins, seaweeds, bamboo shoots, roast ducks, and all the other things that belong to a princely table in China.

At this he brought the conversation to our plans and desires, and I asked that Norin might be allowed to undertake a geological journey in the Lop Desert and Bergman and Haslund an archæological exploration journey in approximately the same regions. "Yes, with pleasure; they can start out when you like; they need no special passes, for I will give orders to the local authorities that they shall be well received." I further asked him for the permission to establish permanent meteorological stations in Charkhlik and Kucha, where Germans and Chinese would take up their residence and carry out observations. " Of course. There too I will send the necessary orders. It grieves me not to be able to allow you a station in Hami, for this town lies in the war zone. But you can in place of this choose Turfan, Guchen, Chuguchak, or Kulja."

To all that I asked for, he answered yes without reservation. We received a perfectly free hand to do what we wished. Although all our Chinese were Nationalists and belonged to the Kuo-min-tang, he gave Yüan, Huang, and Ting permission to undertake the exploration journeys which they had planned.

In spite of his stern exterior Yang could also joke. He asked me : " Why do you go to the trouble of riding about in the deserts looking for old ruins ? Here in my *yamên* you have abundant opportunity to study archæology, for, as you see, everything is near tumbling down and the plaster in this room falls off in great pieces."

He would hardly believe that I was only three years younger than he was himself. " Is it possible that your teeth are genuine ? " I seized them strongly with both hands and showed him plain enough that they were firm. He laughed and showed me a few bad stumps which he still had. And one of them, moreover, still gave him pain. I recommended him to apply to Dr. Hummel. When, however, the latter was called two weeks later, he was not allowed to draw the aching tooth, but could only give something to deaden the pain.

Such a Chinese feast lasts a full four hours, and the whole time one sits at the table. When we finally rose to go home, our host accompanied us courteously across both court-yards, bowed, and waited until we had taken our seats in our cart.

In Urumchi it was universally said that never before had Yang received European travellers with such friendliness and courtesy as he received us.

It had been a risky enterprise, in the midst of the civil war, to march into the interior of China, but we had succeeded. At the frontier of Sin-kiang we had been treated with distrust, but in the capital, already during the first days, we were received with great hospitality, and as far as our plans were concerned, the future lay clear in front of us. For this favourable turn we had Marshal Yang's acuteness and discernment to thank. He was a psychologist and a judge of human nature. He only needed to see us, to recognize that we were far removed from anything that can be called politics, and that our scientific intentions were independent of the political winds of the day. For men who worked he had the greatest respect, for he himself was a diligent worker, who, after a few hours' sleep, got up at 4 o'clock and was occupied throughout the whole day.

We who came into close contact with him during the last period of his life treasure a deep, enduring impression of his great personality and his powerful form. He was, perhaps, the last representative of an age gone by, and possessed in high degree the great virtues of Old China : pride, and love of fatherland. His only dream was of a united China, and he once declared to me that on the day when the southern troops marched into Peking, he would not hesitate to recognize the new order. To us he was a benefactor ; he helped our expedition across a gulf which could have become dangerous for us.

For that reason we remember him with veneration and gratitude.

On the 7th of March the two ministers with whom, on account of their departments, foreign affairs and education, we were in constant contact, Fan Darin and Liu Darin, gave a magnificent European dinner for the members of the expedition. At that dinner innumerable speeches were made, and the reception was overflowing with food and drink. It was evident that the Chinese really wanted to honour us in every conceivable way.

The visits and return visits that I had to make took up valuable time. On the 12th I was woke up early with the news that Liu and Fan had come on a visit, and I had to throw myself into my clothes with all haste to receive the distinguished guests. They asked in their own and

Yang's name to be allowed to inspect our meteorological station, and the students Li and Liu showed and explained to them the instruments. The next day Liu set out with Major Hempel for the Bogdo-ola, in order to replace Dr. Haude at the mountain observatory. On the same day Bergman and Haslund started out on their exploration journey to the Lop Desert. They had three carts for their baggage and looked very stately on their lively horses. They were getting in Turfan about thirty of our own camels, veterans from the Gobi. Norin with thirty-five camels and his Chinese servants had moved towards the south four days before.

The part of the town in which both our houses are situated is known as the " Russian Settlement " ; for this, the most southerly part of the town, has been assigned by Yang to the three hundred White Russian fugitives who sought a refuge in Urumchi. Most of them live in conditions of poverty and support themselves by a trade, baking, washing, sewing, and the like. The former White Russian consul general, Jakov, a scholarly, sympathetic man, has remained in Urumchi since the Revolution. He receives a pension from Yang, but lives poor, since he sends most of it to his family in Russia. There are also a few Russian doctors and druggists here. Gmirkin and his relatives, who live in the finest private house in the town, are in quite a good economic position. He has been Liu Darin's interpreter and business correspondent.

We were under a strict censorship. One evening Burkhan came to me on behalf of Yang and brought me a telegram in cipher from Peking. Yang wanted to know what it contained. Unfortunately we had forgotten to take a code with us and therefore could not decipher the dispatch. Thus Yang at least received a proof that we had no secrets from him.

On the 18th of March I again had to get up quite early, since it was reported to me that the governor himself was on his way to us and in a short time would make his entry into my court-yard. But it was some hours before we heard the flourish of trumpets in the distance. We thus had time to procure cakes, sweetmeats, fruit, and champagne and to lay the table in our dining-room. Then fifty riders in bright yellow uniforms, Yang's escort, filled the street. Some of them rode into our court-yard, while the rest made a halt before the entrance. The loud blare of trumpets echoed from the nearest houses, the little blue cart drove up in front of our steps, and the great Yang got out and was received by Hsü and me. We escorted him into our dining-room, and I greeted him in a ceremonious speech.

After two hours Yang rose, and we accompanied him out to his carriage. As the troop of riders disappeared down the street, it suddenly shot through my head : I only hope now that nothing happens to him after he has just been on a visit to us.

Later, Burkhan came back to us, and I expounded to him my plan to fly over those desert regions which are inaccessible to camels. He was very interested and promised to back up my request, which would have to go through the hands of the director of foreign affairs.

After Burkhan had himself explained my wish in detail to the governor, I was requested on the 20th of March to present myself in the company of Hsü before the commissioner for foreign affairs, Fan Darin. His *yamên* is built in Russian style, but has in front the usual court-yards. We went through a passage, where a parrot, which spoke Chinese, was sitting, and entered a bright, pleasant reception-room, at the green table of which we sat down. Burkhan was also present and acted as interpreter. Hsü did not take part in the conversation.

Fan said friendly and complimentary words concerning the great importance of our expedition for Sin-kiang, and I explained to him that it would be a pleasure if I could, by means of deeds, show my gratitude to a province in whose forests, mountains, and deserts I had spent so many happy years of my youth. But there were here still regions which I had never been able to reach, and therefore I had thought that one could only extract from them their secrets with the flying-machine.

With his soft refined voice Fan answered, with continual bowing, that to-day he had had a long talk with

Yang and had received instructions from him. Almost a year ago the Ministry of Foreign Affairs in Peking had communicated my wishes to the governor and informed him that the Government itself met the flying plans with a refusal ; it left it, however, to Yang to make his decision, in the way that he considered best in the interests of Sin-kiang. For political reasons the governor saw himself compelled, unfortunately, to give a refusal to my request. The internal situation in China would have to clear first. He offered a thousand apologies, but one would have for the present to wait for the development of events.

Our flying plans we could therefore shelve for the present, and it was a small consolation that Fan had been commissioned to invite me in Yang's name to draw in local money the whole 60,000 Mexican dollars which we needed for our stations and expeditions. Hereby he conferred upon me a great trust, since we had not yet been in a position to pay the counter-sum to Yang's son-in-law in Peking.

In the evening a raging storm burst forth. It howled over the roofs and moaned and shrieked round the corners of the houses. On the next day there was a heavy fall of snow, and the dirty town became white again—leaving out the seas of mud in the streets, which became worse than ever. I was awakened with the shout : " Peking has fallen ; China is united." Two days later Fan Darin was able to refute the rumour. It was only a premonition.

We were without reliable news, although there was a connexion by wireless with Mukden and Tientsin, but the antenna was not in order whenever it was most needed. There was also a telegraph-line via Su-chow and Lan-chow, but it was unreliable and slow. A second line ran via Chuguchak to Semipalatinsk. On the Russian side it was excellent ; on the Chinese, on the other hand, it was past redemption. The state of the road was also such that for the time being neither motor-cars nor carts could come and go between Urumchi and Semipalatinsk, and therefore we were a long time without news.

That, however, did not bother us. We had plenty to do, made preparations for the new expeditions, thought things over and held consultations, wrote and worked. I had, moreover, often to serve as interpreter for Russian and Eastern Turkish.

From time to time I received a letter from this or that member of the staff. From Turfan wrote Norin, that there on the 17th of March at 9 o'clock in the evening there had been 17·5 degrees above zero and during the whole day tropical heat had prevailed, while here in Urumchi it had been white winter. From the threshold of the Lop Desert he says :

> " I have never looked forward so much to a journey as to that before which I now stand. What is all up to now—and still it was a great experience—against that which now awaits me ? I have no idea, and therefore I can allow my fancy unhindered to make the wildest leaps and can imagine what I will. The great desert, which lies before me with its roadless expanses, is like a piece of eternity."

In a letter of the 13th of March from Su-chow, Söderbom reported to me that Ma had gone to Lan-chow in order to explain the object of our station on Etsin-gol to the authorities of Kansu. He was of the opinion that no danger threatened. We were kept, however, in constant anxiety concerning Major Zimmermann, who was alone at the station. He could speak no Asiatic language, but he was a capable and fearless man.

As Mrs. Larson informed her husband, the student Tsui, whom we had sent to Peking from Etsin-gol, had reached his goal safely, after having lost three of his ten camels in a snow-storm. I always felt relieved whenever I received good news of the travelling members of my staff.

Apart from the White Russians who had fled from their homeland, there were only a few Europeans in Urumchi, missionaries or merchants. The English missionaries Ridley and Hunter, whose acquaintance I had made more than 30 years before (*Through Asia*, London, 1898, vol. ii), I again met to my great joy. They were living in a simple house, teaching and preaching as before. Mrs. Ridley in the meantime had died, and we talked of the old times in Kansu. The young German merchant Mr. Schirmer, who here represented the firm of Faust & Co., was of the greatest use to us in everything that concerned practical life, in the engaging of servants and the buying of horses and provisions as well as in the forwarding of our parcel post from Europe.

The head of the post-office in Urumchi was the Irishman McLorn, who lived with his young wife in a splendid stone house in the neighbourhood of the official dwellings of the high Chinese dignitaries. This representative of the British Empire performed many invaluable services for us ; he was untiring in his care of our out-going and in-coming post.

Across the street we had as nearest neighbours the Russian consulate-general, an extensive plot of land with several white houses, club, theatre, tennis-court, and garden. Here the white Russian church lifted its green spire, and here the bells were rung for divine service. The former consul-general, who had left Urumchi a year before, had forbidden the White Russians to perform devotions in its church, but Governor Yang, who was a pious man himself and also had respect for foreign creeds, ordered that the church should be kept open for divine service and assemblies of the community.

To the new consul-general, Mr. Gavro, I made my visit in the company of Larson and Lieberenz. Both of these, and later also von Kaull, wanted to return to their homes and required passports and information. In order to be allowed to travel to Russian territory from Sin-kiang, one must have a special permit from Moscow. All these formalities were settled by Mr. Gavro with the greatest willingness, just as, generally speaking, we always experienced goodwill and a spirit of accommodation on the part of the Russian consulate-general and its personnel.

On the 5th of April we gave a big dinner to Governor Yang and also invited to it Fan Darin, Liu Darin, the Mongol prince, Pan Tse Lu, and a few Europeans. Hummel had converted my room into a tasteful drawing-room, and in his own room we had laid the table for the personal attendants of the gentlemen of high rank. The walls of the dining-room were decorated with flags of Sweden,

Yang, governor general of the province of Sin-kiang

THE MAN ON WHOM DEPENDED THE FATE OF THE EXPEDITION

[face p. 350

Governor Yang and his foreign minister, Fan Darin (the first to the right of the left pillar), among the members of the Expedition

PEACE IS CONCLUDED

Germany, and China, and above the door of our house there waved two Chinese banners. Burkhan acted as interpreter for all speeches and conversations. The feast was magnificent; Yang felt at ease with us and was in the best humour. When one gives a dinner to the governor-general and the latter appears with his bodyguard of fifty men, one must of course entertain this whole company too. We had therefore spread tables for his escort in the court-yard and food and drink was ordered from the bazaar.

On Easter Sunday I had a two hours' conference with Yang in his private study, a more than simple room with one large window, two tables covered with books and papers, a comfortable easy chair, and a smaller table in the middle of the room, at which we sat. Burkhan was also present, but Professor Hsü interpreted. We talked once more about my flying plans, and Yang expounded to me logically and calmly the political reasons for his refusal.

Just as the bells of the Russian church were announcing the Russian Easter festival, Ting and Chên were starting out for their long journey along the south foot of the Tien-shan.

The Chinese feasts in Tihua took up, it is true, a dreadful lot of time, but they were inevitable and had a certain importance. Only then did one meet in intimate companionship and get to know each other. Dr. Hummel was usually absent from the feasts. He had plenty to do with his patients: the governor of Aksu; Liu Darin's sister-in-law, who had malaria; a mandarin with dysentery; and several others. One day he was called to Yang, who now as before wanted to keep his bad tooth, but allowed himself to be thoroughly examined from head to foot, and asked the doctor whether he could give him five more years of health. Hummel gave him ten years. Afterwards Yang invited him to a motor-car journey to the public garden, in whose memorial hall he allowed himself a short leisure hour, after which he drove him back to his yamên and invited him to dinner. Dr. Hummel had better opportunity than we others to get to know the life and death of the Chinese. Once when he was leaving the governor of Aksu, he received an urgent message from another mandarin, asking if Dr. Hummel would come to him immediately. In the house of the mandarin he found a servant stretched out on the floor and apparently dead. The Chinese had taken so large a dose of hashish that he was near dying. He had been dismissed the same day, and had considered it so unjust that he decided to take his life in the house of his master. Such a revenge is not uncommon in China. The servant takes his life, not perhaps out of sorrow and grief, but because his master loses face by his death—if the death has taken place in the house of the master. Hummel made a diagnosis and ordered him a good douche of cold water on his naked body. That helped—the man recovered his senses, got up, and was even able to go his way. When, however, everything was quiet, he returned and took a dose perhaps twice as strong. Then he had more luck and could no longer be restored to life.

When Marschall and Liu returned from the Bogdo-ola on the 20th of April, it came Hummel's turn, with his assistant and teacher of the Russian language, Vorotnikov, to take over the station on the "Sacred Mountain." With his patients it was now going so well that they could spare him for a little while. On the same day Yüan started out for Guchen (Ku-chan-tse) and the Altai. Professor Hsü received a telegram from a celebrated member of the government in Nanking, Tsai, the former rector of the National University in Peking, who informed him that he had vouched for the fact that the station on Etsingol had only scientific objects and therefore would remain unmolested.

On the 25th of April Hsü and I again paid a visit to the governor-general. I wanted to inform him that at the beginning of May I was travelling to Europe for a few months, and to talk to him about the position of the expedition and the organization of its work during my absence. To all my requests he answered yes as before. He asked me to get him two pistols with ammunition and a fairly large telescope. We should receive passports, papers, and motor-cars to go to Chuguchak. When I told him that

I had the intention of writing a description of him and his activities in Sin-kiang and handing it to the world's press, he said modestly that he was far too small and insignificant a man to merit such a notice, but if nevertheless I wrote anything about him, I must not forget that his first and most important object was the welfare of the people.

The reason for my journey to Europe was the necessity of detailed discussions in Berlin and Stockholm. The guidance of the expedition I could all the more easily entrust to Professor Hsü and Major Hempel, as the stations were already secured and the various sections were working in the provinces allotted to them. Since the Chinese had not allowed us to fly, I had no reason for keeping all the German flying men in Sin-kiang, but was taking four of them to Berlin with me. The five Germans who were remaining among the members of my staff were all occupied at the stations. Thus the expedition now still numbered eight Swedes, five Germans, and ten Chinese. It was my dream to utilize the excellent position that we had gained, for the purpose of reinforcing the Swedish natural-scientific staff, and this was not the least reason why my journey to Sweden was necessary.

Of the last busy days in Urumchi, when all preparations for my departure were being made and all the obligations were discharged which Chinese etiquette demanded, I will mention only a few episodes.

At the end of April it rained heavily, the rain turned to snow, and the country became white again. But the 29th was a beautiful day. I had invited Governor Yang, Fan Darin, Liu Darin, several other eminent persons who had been helpful to us, and the heads of the Russian consulate-general, who had procured for us permits, passports, and letters of recommendation for the journey across the frontier and through Kasakstan—all these gentlemen I had invited to a farewell feast in the large memorial hall of the public garden.

The public park of Urumchi has been provided by Governor Yang, and, indeed, not only for the enjoyment of the people, but also for his own glorification. In a wood of fine trees the property lies along the bank of the little river which flows along the west side of the town. The main building is erected in an unusual style, a confused mixture of Chinese and Mohammedan architecture, here and there with a touch of Russian influence. The large rooms lie on the first floor and are in immediate connexion with a balcony, a sort of gallery on wooden pillars. The memorial hall proper is a room along one of whose sides there is a Chinese altar with all its decoration and sacrificial vessels, and, forming an altar-piece as it were, a life-size portrait of Yang in full-dress uniform. Without doubt he has had this curious temple built in order thereby to hand down to posterity the memory of his name and of his work in Sin-kiang. In the court-yard in front of the entrance, under a pavilion supported by pillars, there is also erected a statue of the governor, resplendent in rich gilding. That is almost like a warning. He is indeed not dead yet. We are awaiting him for the feast in his own memorial hall!

Exactly opposite the entrance to the main building there stands a pavilion, the roof of which rests on wooden pillars and from whose parapet one has a wonderful view over a small lake surrounded by thickly-leaved trees. At one end of the veranda there has been erected a little summer-house with the usual high seats, and a little table.

Here our guests assembled. To keep to appointed times is a thing that one does not pay especial heed to in China. But we had scarcely stepped upon the platform of the pavilion, when the horn of Yang's motor-car was heard on the bridge and the bright yellow troop of riders galloped into the court-yard and arranged themselves in two ranks between the pavilion and the main building. We hurried down and received the ruler of Sin-kiang. He greeted us in a friendly manner and walked with firm steps up into the summer-house. Here we sat a good hour talking, before the rest of the guests came.

When all had presented themselves, I led Yang up into the room for the banquet, in which three round tables were laid. There were only Chinese dishes served. We were in a merry mood, and several speeches were made.

During the speeches one stands, and afterwards **one** goes

round to all three tables and comes into contact with each one present. When after such a stroll I returned to my place, I found Yang sitting in my chair and engaged in a lively conversation with Hsü. I therefore sat in Yang's seat of honour. But then he came back and whispered to me : " Ask Hsü what I have said to him."

As Hsü now told me, Yang had asked him to put before me his request, that during my visit to Sweden I might buy ten motor-cars for him which were suitable for the roads of Sin-kiang. He would pay for them on my return, but I could use as many of them as I wanted, as long as my expedition lasted.

I then talked with Yang and Burkhan in still greater detail regarding this matter and made the proposal, first of all only to bring four cars with me. To this the governor had agreed.

On the 5th of May I drove up in front of the government palace of the governor-general in order to say good-bye to him. From the guard I learnt that he was at dinner with the Russian consul-general, and I therefore handed in my card. Scarcely, however, had I again taken my seat in my carriage, when Yang's motor-car rolled into the court-yard. He himself and Burkhan got out and beckoned me to them. Yang stretched out his hand to me, and we went in and sat down in the first room. Here we sat at the round table and talked about my journey and my return. The conversation came also to the question of the motor-cars, and Yang asked me to bring two Swedish mechanics with me to Tihua, who spoke Russian and could keep his motor-cars in order. I promised to do my best.

The old governor was tired and I took my leave after a quarter of an hour. He accompanied me across the court-yards right up to my cart and once again wished me a safe journey. Finally he said : " Come back soon." Now the driver cracked his whip, and we rolled away. I had seen Yang Tsêng-hsin for the last time.

Then came the 6th of May. I had hoped to be able to start out in all quietness, but not even now were we left in peace, when Heyder, Marschall, Massenbach,

Mühlenweg, and I had still a thousand small things to think of. It had been ordered by the highest authorities that our start out should take place from the pavilion of the public garden, where Fan Darin, Liu Darin, and the rest of our friends were to be present at our departure. We therefore assembled at the long table, and were entertained with cakes, sweets, cigarettes, and wine, and again long speeches were made. Old Yang had commissioned Fan to convey to me his greetings and his large red visiting-card, and I asked Fan to transmit my greetings and my thanks to the governor. Liu Darin, who was to leave Urumchi three days after us, in order to travel to Tientsin via Siberia and Harbin and there to represent his own and Yang's interests, had been so kind as to take in his retinue three of our men, the collector Chuang and the servants Chang and Charlie, who had asked for their discharge. I had thought of sending them back on the great caravan road via Su-chow, but since Yang did not wish them to travel through Kansu, only the way via Siberia stood open to them, and now, thanks to Liu's accommodating spirit, they had obtained an excellent opportunity to return to their homes.

But time went by, the two motor-cars were standing in front of the steps, I rose, we took a heart-felt leave of all, and rolled away and left the garden and the town behind us, in order to travel through the northern part of Sin-kiang, Kasakstan, Russia, and Poland, for Berlin and Stockholm.

I had scarcely reached Berlin on the 2nd of June when the news of significant historical events in China sped round the earth. Chang Tso-lin murdered, Peking fallen. The Nationalists of the south had been victorious, and one might at last hope that China, at least for a time, would become united. Naturally I wondered how these events would react on Sin-kiang and on my expedition. At the end of June I received in Stockholm a letter from Hummel; but this had already been sent off in Urumchi on the 27th of May and spoke only of the situation in Urumchi, where up to then everything was still quiet. Hummel reported that on the 10th of May Haude, Dettmann, and Li, had set out for Charkhlik in order to set up the meteorological station there, and that Walz and Li had on the 22nd of May gone with the same object to Kucha. On the 11th of May Hummel had visited the governor and had asked for permission to make a botanical excursion to the Bogdo-ola. Yang had willingly complied with his request and had asked him to sound the depth of the little lake near the temple known as the Fu-shou-sze and to test whether the climate there in the mountains would be beneficial to his health, for in this case Yang intended to spend a part of the summer on the " Sacred Mountain."

For the rest Hummel spent his whole time with botanical excursions in the country surrounding the town, with sick-visits, and a growing practice.

Professor Hsü Ping-chang and Major Hempel, who was my representative during my absence, occupied themselves among other things with instructing a few new students in the art of taking meteorological observations. When Hempel petitioned for approval to send a caravan to our station on Etsin-gol in order to fetch the fifteen camel-loads which we had left behind there in November, Yang declared that he did not wish it. This again was an out-come of his aversion to any connexion with Kansu. At the end of his letter Hummel congratulated me on the pleasing news which had come from Etsin-gol and proved that " the Etsin-gol problem is solved at last." It was a great pleasure to me, at last to know for certain that the station and its staff, Zimmermann, Söderbom, and Ma, were out of danger.

Then came the days when even Urumchi was to become the scene of dramatic events. On the 2nd of July the Ministry of Foreign Affairs in Stockholm received a tele-gram for me from the Swedish Legation in Peking : General Ma Fu-hsiang has been appointed " Pacification Com-missioner " of Sin-kiang, " which probably means that Yang will be removed from his post."

To my inquiry whether this step could be regarded as prejudicial to the continuance of the expedition, one of my Chinese friends in Peking gave me the answer : " No cause for anxiety ; Yang will become a member of the Provincial Committee."

This comforting assurance was substantiated by a letter of the Swedish Legation in Peking which arrived on the 2nd of August, in which it said that the Chinese news bureau " Kuo Wên " had published the report " that Governor Yang has informed the government in Nanking in a telegram that he has hoisted the Kuo-min-tang flag and has reorganized the government of the province in accordance with the principles of the Kuo-min-tang. He will fully submit to the orders of the government in Nanking."

But already on the 7th of July an event had taken place in Urumchi which knocked all the decisions of the National-ist Government on the head. On the 16th of July the following news was to be read in both Swedish and foreign newspapers :

" Shanghai. Reuter reports : The Nationalist Government has received information that Yang Tsêng-hsin, the military governor of Chinese Turkestan, has been shot at a prize-distribution in a Russian school in Urumchi by the escort of the commissioner for foreign affairs. The murderers were arrested. The Chinese population is greatly stirred by this news. One fears new disturbances in Chinese Turkestan, where the influence of Soviet Russia has spread.

The commissioner for foreign affairs and twenty men of his escort, by which, as it is reported, the fatal shots were fired, have been executed by order of the civil governor."

There is no Russian school in Urumchi, although there is a law school and a physics school, the latter for the training of telegraphists. Both institutions are purely Chinese. In the law school there is also given instruction in Russian, and at an examination in Russian the governor-general appears to have been murdered. According to reports from Russia, the commissioner for foreign affairs mentioned is no other than our friend Fan Darin, whose full name is Fan Yao-nan. The story was told in Urumchi, that this Fan Darin some years ago had been sent to Tihua in order to overthrow Yang and himself occupy his position. Yang had seen through this intention and had managed to retain Fan ever since in Urumchi and had made him director of foreign affairs. How little did we suspect, when we sat together with Yang and Fan round the cheerful table, that these two men, who at least to outward appearance seemed to stand on a friendly footing with each other, would become the principal figures in a bloody drama, a drama in which both lost their lives!

After the murderous attack, as Russian telegrams reported, a provisional commission is said to have appointed the so-called "civil governor" as executor of the highest power in Sin-kiang, until the government in Nanking shall have nominated a new governor. There is no civil governor in Urumchi, since Yang governed alone with absolute despotic power. Probably the governor of the district of Tihua is intended, who had his seat of government in Tihua.

In what way have the events in Tihua influenced the position of the expedition in Sin-kiang? I do not know; for since the 14th of June I have received no letter from Hempel, Hummel, or Hsü Ping-chang—probably after the murder a stricter censorship has been introduced.

But I hope soon to hear that in headquarters, at the stations, and with the sections working in the field, all is well. For now, a month after the death of old Yang, I am again thinking of returning to my post in the heart of Asia and continuing and completing the great journey.

LOP-NOR, THE WANDERING LAKE

I

WRAPPED in winter mist and the dusty haze of the easterly storms of spring, steaming in the blazing heat of the sun during summer, and at the times of migration in spring and autumn the haunt of myriads of swimming-birds, there lies in darkest Asia the mysterious desert lake of Lop-nor, half forgotten, difficult of access, at a greater distance from all seas than any other lake of the earth, and, moreover, shut in by some of the mightiest systems of mountain ranges of the earth, the Tien-shan, the Pamirs, the Kun-lun, and the mountains of Tibet.

To the Chinese this lake has been well known for 2,000 years, and in their geographical literature it appears under various names. As a result of the false interpretation of an ancient text, the Chinese have believed throughout long ages that the Tarim is the source of the Hwang Ho, which is swallowed up by Lop-nor, to appear again, after a long subterranean course, in the Hsing-su-hai, the sea of stars, in north-eastern Tibet, where the real source of the Yellow River is situated. In the imagination of the Chinese the lake has been surrounded therefore with an air of mysticism.

To Europeans too Lop-nor was and remained a mysterious phenomenon. About 200 years ago the lake appears on European maps of Asia. In the year 1733 the Swedish officer Lieutenant Johan Gustaf Renat brought home a Zungarian map of Central Asia, on which Lop-nor, under the name of Läp, is rendered extremely true to nature, while d'Anville's map of the same year does not come so near the truth. For the rest, Europeans drew their knowledge concerning Lop-nor from Chinese sources. Even in the year 1875 Lop-nor is found in

Stieler's Hand-atlas on the sheet India and Central Asia in the northern part of the Lop Desert, in a latitude 40° 40′ north, exactly as on old and recent Chinese maps.

But no European had ever been there ; no-one had seen the remarkable lake. Marco Polo had in 1273 travelled along the road to the south of Lop-nor, but does not mention the *lake* in his immortal description of his travels, but only the desert of Lop, in which he has heard voices of ghosts speaking and out of whose depth there seemed to him to come the beating of drums—the howling of the sand-storms. Benedict Goes has been in the neighbour-hood of the lake of Lop on his journey in 1603–7, but after his death his notes were burnt. In the sixties of the eighteenth century the Emperor Chien-lung sent out the Jesuits d'Espinha, d'Arrocha, and Hallerstein, that they might determine astronomically the position of important places in the newly-acquired territory in the west, but these too have nothing to report of the mysterious lake.

On all Chinese maps the Tarim flows exactly towards the east and receives on its left the tributary known as Khaidu-gol, the Konche-darya, before it empties itself in a latitude 40° 40′ north into Lop-nor or Pu-chang-hai, Yen-tsê or Lou-lan-hai, the sea of Lou-lan.

It awakened therefore the greatest astonishment in the geographical world, when the Russian colonel, N. M. Przhevalsky, on his famous journey in 1876–7, *Von Kuldscha über den Tienschan und den Lop-nor zum Altin-tag*, made the discovery that the Tarim turned off towards the south-east and south and Lop-nor lay in the southern part of the desert, a geographical degree further south than the Chinese maps had given. Dr. August Petermann wrote in his *Mitteilungen*: "This discovery has the same geographical importance as the reaching of the North Pole or the crossing of Africa."

The famous China explorer Baron von Richthofen pub-lished at the same time in the *Zeitschrift der Geographischen Gesellschaft in Berlin* a discriminating paper in which he proved that Przhevalsky had not discovered the old his-torical lake of Lop-nor, but another lake, which had formed at a later time as a result of a wandering of the

water only allowed us a stay of twenty hours, we crossed the desert, in whose northern part I found numerous proofs of the existence of earlier basins of lakes, for many centuries dried up.

Since I saw that the discovery of the old town was of extraordinary importance—both geographically and historically—at the beginning of March, 1901, I returned there and unearthed in one of the houses about 150 manuscripts on wood and paper, many of which were provided with the date and revealed that the old town was called Lou-lan and was flourishing at about A.D. 260–270.

Then I undertook a levelling of the desert from north to south, in order to determine in figures the position and depth of the old basin of the lake. Against the levelled line the depression of the old basin of the lake showed itself with the greatest clearness. The whole desert proved almost horizontal, and the starting-point near Lou-lan was only a little over 2 metres higher than the surface of Kara-koshun.

I now formulated the theory that, in a desert whose surface, practically speaking, is just as level as that of the sea, the flowing water must be extremely sensitive to even the most insignificant changes in the surface. The southern lake, Kara-koshun, whose mean depth, as I found, amounted to 0·81 metres, fills with mud which the Tarim carries with it, with decaying animal and vegetable matter, and with shifting sand, while the dried-up northern parts of the desert are hollowed out by the mighty force of the strong east-north-east storms and sink in the course of the centuries. Sooner or later this action will lead to the lake having to wander again into its northern basin, and the Tarim to flow again in the channel of the Kuruk-darya. Kara-koshun must dry up, and the lake of the Chinese maps in the northern part of the desert must fill with water again. In my work *Central Asia and Tibet*, vol. ii (London, 1903), on page 174 there is found the following prediction:

" I am convinced that in a few years' time the lake will be found in the locality where it was formerly placed by the

Chinese cartographers, and where Baron von Richthofen proved by an ingenious deduction that it must once have been."

In my work *Scientific Results of a Journey in Central Asia 1899–1902*, vol. ii (Stockholm, 1905), on page 355 I wrote the following words:

". . . And in the light of the knowledge we now possess, as to the relations of level that obtain in the Desert of Lop, it is not too bold a thing to say, that some time the river [Tarim and its tributary the Konche-darya] *must* go back to the Kuruk-darja. . . . It is merely a question of time, but the country hereabouts [i.e. the Kara-koshun] will become so choked with alluvia that the river will be forced to return to its northern bed. The lowermost limb of the river thus oscillates backwards and forwards like a pendulum, and even though the periodic time of each oscillation does amount to 1500 years, yet that, counted by the clock of geologic time, is relatively of no longer duration than one of our seconds."

I predicted exactly 30 years ago that both the river and the lake in a few years *must* return to their old beds in the north.

The geographers presumably attached little importance to my apparently much too venturesome predictions, and Sir Aurel Stein declared that *one* levelled line only was not sufficient " to place the town of Lou-lan on the shore of the old lake." Concerning my conviction that both the Tarim and the Konche-darya once flowed into the old lake, he wrote that it was impossible to reconcile this theory with his own observations of an archæological as well as of a natural-historical nature, and in the very least with the description which a Chinese geographer, Li Tao-yüan, has given about A.D. 500.

In the spring of 1927 our expedition left Peking and travelled westward across the Gobi Desert by Etsin-gol to Hami. A new investigation of the Lop-nor problem was the first item on my programme, and, as I have told above, I therefore sent a telegram to the Governor-General of Sin-kiang, Marshal Yang Tsêng-hsin, asking him to allow my geologist, Dr. Erik Norin, to undertake a three months' journey in the northern part of the Lop Desert. Marshal

Yang answered no. We must first all present ourselves in Urumchi. Old Yang did not trust us very much, for warlike rumours had hurried before our great caravan. For that reason the autocratic ruler of the province wanted to see us with his own eyes, before he let us tread the desert paths.

On the 19th of February, 1928, we entered the old town of Turfan, where we remained over the 20th, living in the house of Khoja Abdul. On the morning of the rest-day a merchant, Tokta Ahun, came on a visit. As usual I questioned him about everything possible, not least about trade and his roads. He told me, among other things, that he went every year to the village of Tikkenlik on the Konche-darya in order to buy sheep, which he then sold again in the bazaars of Turfan. I asked him to tell me what road he used and at what places he spent the night. When in his description he had reached Ying-pen, he said :

" Here travellers and their goods are carried across the river on a ferry, since the water is too deep to wade across."

" What do you say ? " I exclaimed. " A river near Ying-pen ! On my visit 28 years ago there was desert there."

" Yes," continued Tokta Ahun, " but 7 years ago (1921) the Konche-darya went over into the bed of the Kuruk-darya."

" Is that true ? " I asked, greatly astonished. " Have you seen this change with your own eyes ? "

" Of course," he answered smiling; " I cross the new river several times a year, and often have great trouble in getting the sheep across on the ferry."

" How far to the east does the river flow ? "

" Oh, it goes a long way to the east; some say three days' journey to the north-west of Tun-huang. No-one else has seen its end but Abd-ur-Rahim, the camel-hunter."

One hour after another went by. Never have I cross-examined a native more thoroughly, not even at the time when as the first European I was conducted by road-experienced Tibetans to the sources of the Brahmaputra and the Indus. Tokta Ahun gave me a very clear and authentic description of the Kuruk-darya that had filled up with water again, and of the return of animal life and plants to the formerly so dreary desert.

It became evening, and when Tokta Ahun said good-bye, I asked him to come again next morning, which he also promised. He did not put in an appearance, however. I sent a messenger to his dwelling : he was not at home ; to the bazaar : he was not there either. Was he afraid ? Had he betrayed things that ought to remain secret ? Did he fear that his information might have unpleasant consequences for him ? It almost appears so. In any case he brought me to a problem of gigantic dimensions. Its geographical range I knew only too well, but here there opened prospects of world-historical significance and of a span in time of more than 2,000 years. It was a romantic history, which had been dormant for centuries, and which now on the 20th of February, 1928, came to life again, and it was reserved for our expedition to connect together again in one whole the separate pieces of the chain. If our expedition had made no other geographical discoveries than the final solution of the Lop-nor problem, it would nevertheless have secured for itself a prominent place in the history of discovery in Central Asia, and the heavy expense that it had occasioned would have more than amply repaid itself. Lop-nor was the lock of the chain, and the information that I obtained in Turfan had brought us to the final solution of the riddle of the waywardly wandering lake. Behind us lay 2,000 years, the time during which Lop-nor had been known in the history of China, and before us innumerable years wrapped in mist.

In Chapter XXV of this book I devoted only two whole pages to Lop-nor and the hydrographic changes that had taken place since 1921. My intention was only to settle in print once for all that it was our expedition that had received the very first knowledge of the last pulsation in the history of the lake of Lop, and that I, who almost 30 years before had predicted the shortly imminent wandering of the famous lake and river to the north, was of all men in the world the one who received the first news that my prediction had been fulfilled. That I, after I had not visited this part of Asia since 1901, found myself in the neighbourhood of Lop-nor only a very few years after the great change and, before all others, learnt what had taken place, was an event so wonderful and improbable that it would have miscarried and appeared far-fetched in a work of *fiction*.

But I kept silence, and contented myself for the time being with the short notice which is to be found in the Swedish edition of this book (Stockholm, 1928). And concerning the historical significance of the problem I have kept silence up to this day. I had also good reasons for this. First of all, one or more of us had to establish that Tokta Ahun had told the truth, that is, that the Tarim and the Konche-darya had again occupied their old course in the bed of the Kuruk-darya, and that Lop-nor had returned again to the place where according to Chinese maps the lake had been situated in olden times.

In truth, I could scarcely sleep for impatience. I lived and breathed in an atmosphere of history—history of the earth as of men. I was thinking of this remarkable lake, which soon would become the most famous of all the lakes of the earth. That its wanderings were periodic I had proved, and the single period extended probably over one and a half thousand years. Now one such period had ended. My theories had proved correct, and it had been granted me, not only to live to see this event, but also myself to receive the first news of it.

I thought of the long, laborious marches in the river-bed of the Kuruk-darya 28 years before. How well I remembered the broad, deep, dried-up river-bed with the dead forest on its banks! There stood the trunks like the gravestones of a churchyard, grey, split, dried, and as brittle as glass. Nothing living was to be found, nor a drop of water; a more God-forsaken region one could not imagine on the whole earth. More than fifteen hundred years ago a great stream had flowed through this furrow. Its life-giving water had flowed past a town, Lou-lan, that had been flourishing in the centuries just before and after Christ, a town with walls and towers, caravanserais, market-places, trade, and garrison, a town that had been an outer fort on the ancient silk route between China and the West. Rolled up in bales and sewn in sacking, there was carried on camels the precious silk with which the hetæræ in Rome at the time of the Empire adorned themselves for the dance.

And this endlessly long trade route led along the shore of Lop-nor. From this blessed lake or from river-tributaries and little lakes that are closely connected with their hydrographic system, merchants, their servants and animals, marching troops, and the members of embassies, could quench their thirst.

At the beginning of the fourth century Lou-lan perished, after it had been attacked and plundered by the barbarians living in the north. The threatening wars are spoken of by several of the documents that I found in the deserted town in 1901, and which have been translated and published by Professor Conrady in Leipzig. But other places too, fortifications and villages, completely disappeared, when at approximately the same time or a little later the lake of Lop-nor dried up and wandered to the southern edge of the desert, after the Tarim, the Ho of the Chinese, had changed its course and dug out for itself a new bed towards the south-east and south. Men and animals fled towards the west and south, where the water flowed along ; millions of fishes and molluses perished, and their dry bones and shells break now under our steps in the old watercourses like fallen leaves in autumn. Death and oblivion lay like a shroud over the remains of the high culture of Lou-lan. When, not far to the south of this region, Marco Polo travelled along on his famous journey to the court of Kublai Khan, Lou-lan had been slumbering in its desert nearly a thousand years, and the great Venetian had no idea of the former existence of this town. When I crossed the Lop Desert 625 years after Marco Polo, my lucky star led me to the old houses. Impenetrable silence of death lay there over the sleeping town, and for more than one and a half thousand years the great silk route had been cut off. Long centuries had passed away since the last caravan travelled along between Tun-huang and Lou-lan to the tinkling of its bells. Since this time the waterless desert had lain there still and deserted. When in February, 1901, I risked the attempt to push on to Lou-lan from the region to the west of Tun-huang, I had on one occasion to cover eleven days' march without finding a drop of water, and what finally saved my caravan from perishing was the tracks of the wild camels, which led to the salt springs at the foot of the Kuruk-tag.

Now I had learnt that the hour of resurrection had struck for Lou-lan and for the whole region which up to the beginning of the fourth century had been watered by Lop-nor and its river-tributaries. Now the water had returned to its old beds, and had brought with it fishes and molluscs, steppe animals and plants, tamarisks and poplars, and now it would not be many years more before the spring storms again sang their old melodies in the tops of the trees as in the first centuries after the birth of Christ.

It was only a question of time of a very few years before men would follow afresh the returned water on their journeys towards the east. Perhaps, too, one day the day of resurrection would break—not for those who for 2,000 years had been sleeping in the darkness of their graves, but for the town itself, ancient Lou-lan, which it had fallen to my lot to awaken out of its sleep of death. In time fishing villages and stations would doubtless grow up again on the banks of these waterways. Although 30 years have since passed away, I still remember as if it were yesterday the strange feeling that came over me, when in March, 1901, I stepped through the open door in one of the old houses in Lou-lan, a door which the last Chinese had forgotten to shut when some time or other at the beginning of the fourth century he left his dwelling for ever. For more than one and a half thousand years the sand-storms had rushed on over the forsaken town, and certainly no man had set his foot there during this long period. It was curious to know that one was the first to step again over the threshold of the door that had been open for so long.

Our geologist, Dr. Erik Norin, was inspired with the same burning desire as I, to make a journey without delay into the Lop Desert and investigate the new phase into which the Lop-nor question had entered since 1921. A second telegram to Marshal Yang was answered just as negatively as the first from Hami. We must first present ourselves in Urumchi and show ourselves before the searching eyes of the governor-general.

As quickly as ever we could go, we hurried to the capital of the province. On one of the first days, we received the message to appear in the marshal's *yamên*. In smart field-grey sports clothing we stood in a semicircle—twenty-four men, Swedes, Germans, and Chinese—in the innermost court of the *yamên*. The old marshal walked up to us upright and commanding. He presented a stately appearance : well made and strongly built, with high forehead, serious, penetrating eyes, arched nose, snow-white moustache and pointed beard—one could see he was a man of the old stock, one of the last representatives of the vanished Chinese Empire of the Golden Dragon Throne.

This old man of sixty-six years it was, who had now for 18 years governed with an iron hand the greatest province of the earth, Sin-kiang, six times as big as Sweden, it was *he*, Yang Tsêng-hsin, who could with sovereign power decide our fate, at his own discretion send us back to Peking, or open to our inquiry all the doors of his province, *he* it was who held the key of Lop-nor in his hand.

With a scarcely perceptible bow he stretched out to me this strong hand of his and then, one by one, greeted each of the members of my staff. It went slowly, for with a searching glance he measured each one of us from head to foot. His face brightened up, and when he had greeted the whole circle, with a courteous smile he invited us to step in and then led me by the hand to the table that was spread. The inspection had evidently turned out in our favour, and Yang had seen that we were no highwaymen, but honest people.

Then began a magnificent feast, which lasted for several hours. Yang seized his glass, filled with sparkling champagne, stood up, bid us welcome, called us his guests and friends, and declared that by our investigations we should become tutors to both him and his officials and his whole province.

I replied, and thanked him for the hospitality that he had

accorded our expedition from the first hour. Professor Hsü Ping-chang returned thanks in the name of his Chinese companions, and before the meal was over I asked the Governor-General of Sin-kiang for his permission for Dr. Norin to journey to the northern part of the desert.

" With pleasure," he replied ; " a passport is not necessary ; I will myself give the order that Dr. Norin shall everywhere be well received."

Now lay open to us the road into the land of my desire and of my prophecies, and now it was to be granted to the members of our expedition to feel the pulse of the wandering lake and of the wandering rivers.

IN the previous chapter I have given a brief account of the recent history of Lop-nor: from 1877, when Przhevalsky discovered that the wandering lake, contrary to the evidence of the Chinese maps, lay in the southern part of the desert, to the 20th of February, 1928, when in Turfan I obtained the first information that the famous lake had returned to its old bed in the north. I have also told how the Governor-General of Sin-kiang, Marshal Yang Tsêng-hsin, gave us unlimited freedom to move about in the Lop Desert and solve the riddles of the much-discussed problem.

Now began again the hunt after Lop-nor. I gave Dr. Norin instructions to assemble his first caravan as quickly as possible and, via the little village of Singer in the Kuruk-tag, to go straight down from the mountain range to the river-bed which I had cartographically surveyed in the year 1900 and which was then known as Kuruk-darya, the " dry river," or Kum-darya, the " sand river." The Tarim and the Konche-darya had now returned to this bed after 1,600 years, and the chief task that I gave Norin was to survey cartographically the course of the river that had come to life again, so far as the advanced season of the year permitted the stay in the desert. I readily admit that this order was dictated not a little by national and personal ambition. I had, of course, surveyed the river-bed in my youth, while it still lay dry ; I was the first European who crossed the Lop Desert, in 1900 and 1901 ; I discovered on that occasion the ruins of the old military colony of Lou-lan, and formulated the hypothesis that Lou-lan had been situated on the northern shore of the Lop-nor of the Chinese maps ; I found watch-towers on the military road of the older Han dynasty across Asia, and established by means of levelling the existence of a flat depression in the northern

The Kum-darya
(Bergman photograph, 15th November, 1928)

The Konche-darya to the north-east of Tikkenlik
(Haude photograph, November, 1928)

THE CHANGED RIVERS

[*face p.* 372

The Konche-darya below Yü-li-hsien

(Bergman photograph, 8th October, 1928)

The ferry over the Konche-darya

(Bergman photograph, 8th October, 1928)

THE CHANGED RIVERS

[*face p.* 373

half of the desert, from which I assumed that long ages ago it had contained a part of the old lake of Lop-nor. Finally, I predicted in two of my books almost 30 years ago, that in a short while both the Tarim and Lop-nor would return to their old beds in the north. Whether the physico-geographical facts on which I built this theory have now been correctly stated or not, in any case my prediction had now been fulfilled, and one will pardon me if I was filled with a burning desire to secure for Swedish research and my own expedition the credit for having solved the Lop-nor problem in its last phase. Dr. Norin fully shared my desire, and it was only a very few days before he was ready to march with his caravan, and began the spring and summer campaign.

On the 11th of April he left Singer. Soon he had the mountain range behind him and could see in the south at a distance of scarcely 10 kilometres the Kum-darya river that had returned to life winding along like a blue ribbon through the white desert. He followed the river 220 kilometres to the east up to a point which lay about 20 kilometres north-north-east of Lou-lan, cartographically surveyed its course, the lakes along its banks, and its swamps, and determined that the mighty stream followed for the most part the same furrow that I had sketched 28 years before. The river was 100 to 150 metres broad and several metres deep and had a rate of flow of approximately 1 metre a second. The flow of its water must thus amount to at least 200 cubic metres a second. To the north of Lou-lan the Kum-darya had split up into an inland delta, and 20 kilometres to the north-north-east of the old town there flowed a tributary 50 metres broad with clear fresh water. Considerable volumes of water lay still further to the east. Norin could not push on to Lou-lan, for the greater part of the desert to the north of the old town was inundated by lakes and swamps.

Vast fields of reeds grew rank along the banks of the Kum-darya. New tamarisks were taking root, and the seeds of plants were being carried by the stream deeper and deeper into this desert, which in my youth was as barren and desolate as the moon. Now wild pigs were rooting

373

up the ground here in impenetrable thickets of reeds, wolves hunted antelopes and hares, ducks and geese swarmed on blue lakes, and storks and cranes sought their food in the swamps.

Life had returned to the desert; plants and animals had again settled and taken control of these regions which had been sleeping for sixteen hundred years. How long would it be before man too returned to people the banks of the Sand River anew, and before the once flourishing Lou-lan again woke up out of its long sleep of death?

Summer begins very early in the Lop Desert, and Norin and his caravan animals were tormented by whole clouds of gnats and gadflies. He had to content himself with this first reconnaissance of the Sand River along its whole length, and in this he secured for us the first claim. Thus for the present he left Lop-nor to its fate, and devoted the work of the summer to geological studies in the Kuruk-tag, where among other things he made a remarkable discovery in establishing traces of a permo-carboniferous ice-age.

In February, 1930, Norin undertook his second expedition to the Sand River, and on this occasion in a more suitable season extended further the investigations that he had begun on his first reconnaissance. As on the previous occasion, now too he had an excellent support in my old friend and guide the camel-hunter Abd-ur-Rahim in Singer, and the latter's house was his base and headquarters. By Norin I had sent a present to Abd-ur-Rahim, and later I received a letter from him, in which he invited me to come to Singer and be his guest and recall common memories of the time 30 years before.

In this second journey of Norin's our young astronomer Dr. Nils Ambolt from Lund took part. On the 19th of February they set out from the spring of Kurbanchik in the Kuruk-tag and went directly to the south to the Kum-darya, on whose northern or left bank they set up their Camp XXXV. This point became in their work a station of the first order. Here Ambolt carried out extraordinarily exact astronomical observations, and by means of wireless obtained time-determinations for the geographical longitude. In Camp XXXV he also carried out complete series of pendulum-observations for the determination of gravity, as well as earth-magnetic observations, trigonometric surveys, the determination of the terrestrial and astronomical refraction, and, finally, complete meteorological observations, which were always carried out at two stations simultaneously, by means of which one obtained exact absolute altitudes. Especially in the last-mentioned series of observations, the young Russian Vorotnikov was an invaluable assistance to Dr. Ambolt.

Norin's masterly exact topographical-geological map of this whole little-known, in part completely unknown, territory, where I had once travelled as a simple pioneer of the way, obtained through Ambolt's various labours a reliability previously unthought of, both in the network of co-ordinates and in the verticals. The map of the Kuruk-tag and the Kum-darya that Norin and Ambolt have produced by their joint work surpasses all the leading achievements for the *whole* of Central Asia, and is drawn with an exactitude that no map of another similar desert region of the earth can show.

On the 5th of March they moved to Ying-pen, an outer fort with watch-towers on the old military road dating from the period of the older Han. This important point too became a station of the first order, at which all the series of observations mentioned were carried out.

Then the two Swedish explorers continued their work along the Kum-darya up to a longitude of 90 degrees east, that is to say, a point 40 kilometres to the north-east of Lou-lan. Norin was in no way satisfied with his present map, but devoted an attention at least as great to late quaternary chronology. In the report dated Kashgar, 29th September, 1930, which I received a short while ago in Peking, Norin gives a summary of the results of his labours during the past year. From his extreme point in the east mentioned above he has followed the line of the northern shore of the late glacial Tarim lake right into the regions to the east of Kashgar, and has given us extensive and extraordinarily valuable information concerning the late quaternary history of Eastern Turkestan. His distant view has even taken in the world of the gigantic system of mountain ranges which surround the Tarim basin, the Tien-shan and the Kun-lun, and I can already now disclose that he will in time present us with an unexpectedly magnificent picture of the formation of the mountain ranges and the geological genesis of High Asia.

But here for the present we are concerned with Lop-nor.

In late glacial times, according to Norin, the whole Tarim basin was filled in by an enormous lake or inland sea, a Mediterranean Sea, of whose great volumes of water the historical lake of Lop-nor is the last disappearing survival. At the southern foot of the Kuruk-tag, Norin found the line of the northern shore of the Tarim lake, as he names the inland sea, extraordinarily sharply and clearly defined, and entered it on his map. The shore-line forms a terrace-shaped bank. The lacustrine deposits decrease towards the east ; to the north and north-east of Lou-lan there are no deposits. Norin established that the north-eastern shore of the Tarim lake has in late glacial times been situated to the north and east of Lou-lan, and that the mighty lake, which together with its continuation towards the east has probably been as large as the Caspian Sea, has sent out long inlets towards the north-east. In this region the lake has been shallow and swampy.

Further to the west the northern shore-line is often interrupted ; the gaps have been caused by great rivers which in late glacial times flowed from the Tien-shan to the Tarim lake. Along the Masar-tag to the east of Kashgar the old shore-line disappears in the direction towards the south-south-east under the sea of sand of the Takla-makan Desert. At the turn of the year Norin was occupied with following up the southern shore-line of the Tarim lake towards the east, and it is his intention to connect up its entire winding course.

As Norin was able to determine by means of extremely accurate measurements of altitudes, the crust of the earth has undergone age-long changes of level since the Tarim lake disappeared ; for the northern shore-line shows a very pronounced fall from west to east. If Norin marks a point on the shore-line to the north of Lou-lan with the value zero, then the same shore-line near Aksu has a relative height of 300 metres. Further to the west the difference of altitude recedes again to 250 metres.

Through this movement of the earth's crust, which in the west was expressed in a relatively stronger elevation —or less strong depression—than in the east, the waters of the Tarim lake were thrown towards the east and formed in the eastern part of the basin a lake which Norin calls Great Lop-nor. On a few tracts he has been able to draw the outlines of this lake—namely, at those places where it has stretched its waters north of the deposits of the old Tarim lake. The almost complete absence of mechanical deposits in the northern part of this new sea-bed indicates that the period of strongest melting of the ice-age had at that time already come to an end; for during the previous period enormous masses of deposits had been laid down in the Tarim lake and had completely filled up its western part.

Now the lake had entered a period in the history of its development when the peripheral inflow was not sufficient to replace the loss of water that it experienced through the evaporation at the surface of the Great Lop-nor. Owing to this the lake shrank further and further back and was transformed into a constantly diminishing salt lake. The last 2,000 years of this period, during which the lake changed almost into an island delta with a wandering freshwater lake as its final recipient, belong to the historical period. But Norin supposes that men have already dwelt on the shore of the Great Lop-nor; for on the north and west shores of the old lake he has found roughly-fashioned arrow-heads of jasper. The men, who have perhaps lived on the shores of the Great Lop-nor in the palæolithic age, had an abundant quantity of drinking-water at their disposal, for that lake, just like its predecessor, the Tarim lake, was fresh.

For many thousands of years the Tarim river, the Ho (" river ") of the Chinese, which right till late times was regarded as the upper course of the Hwang Ho, has wound its way along over the dried-up lacustrine deposits of the Tarim lake. As a result of the evenness of the country

377

and the softness of its material the river has been constantly subject to great changes, has moved from one bed to another, and has every year, sometimes here and sometimes there, cut new channels for itself.

One of the most remarkable changes that have taken place in the past—we really know nothing *more* about it than that it has really taken place—was that particular change which at the beginning of the fourth century, probably in the year A.D. 330, gave to the map of the eastern part of Eastern Turkestan an entirely different appearance from what it had had since the time of the older Han dynasty or probably much longer still. At that time the Tarim with its tributary the Konche-darya left its old course towards the east—the furrow that was known as the Kuruk-darya, the " dry river," when I surveyed it cartographically in the year 1900, and in which for centuries it had flowed to the east past Lou-lan to the Lop-nor of the Chinese maps —turned off towards the south-east and south, and at the north foot of the Astin-tag in the southern part of the Lop Desert formed the lake which at a later time was known as Kara-koshun and which Przhevalsky discovered in 1877 and established as the Lop-nor of the Chinese. In the year 1901 I proved that the days of the Kara-koshun were numbered and that the lake *must* return to its former basin in the north.

Twenty years later, that is to say in the year 1921, the most noteworthy of all the changes in the river-bed of the Tarim took place—most noteworthy because it has taken place in our time and before our eyes, and so can be examined and investigated. In its time, that is to say the year 330, the earlier change in the bed had of course a much greater importance than that which took place now, for with it there faded away and disappeared a whole culture-area in the heart of Asia, which for centuries had been watered by the most important artery of the Tarim system. Towns became deserted and were transformed into ruins, men went away, communication and roads became cut off, lakes dried up, and the plant and animal worlds became extinct.

The last change in the course of the Tarim and the posi-

378

tion of Lop-nor is not of very great political and historical consequence; for, when it took place, there were living on the lowermost course of the river and on the lake of Kara-koshun only a few hundred poor fisher families of the tribe of the Lopliks, and these migrated to the nearest oases at the foot of the mountain range in the south. If the wandering back of the lake to the north is of duration, then the plant growth in the south is sentenced to become extinct, and likewise also millions of fishes, molluscs, and insects, while the birds and four-footed animals have probably been able to save themselves.

In the world of geographical science this hydrographic change can probably reckon on great attention, and it is not impossible that its significance to politics and trade in the future may become greater than we now suspect.

According to the information that I obtained in Turfan, it happened in the year 1921 that the Tarim 15 kilometres to the south of the little town of Yü-li-hsien or Kara-kum left its old bed, made for itself a new channel towards the east, and on its way to the dried-up bed of the Kuruk-darya took the Konche-darya with it. It is very difficult to cartographically survey this area, partly in consequence of the new changes that arise every year, partly in consequence of the extensive inundations, and finally because of the desperate attempts of the natives to force the water back with the help of canals to the villages in the south, which are now suffering from a shortage of water.

On his second journey in February and March, 1930, Norin completed the observations that he had made on his reconnaissance two years previously. Five kilometres to the south-south-west of Kurgan the river flowed between erosion terraces 1 to 2 metres in height, carried water brown with clay, and was shut in by vast fields of reeds. Where the road from Turfan crosses the new river quite close to Ying-pen, a ferry had been established, as Tokta Ahun had informed me.

Further to the east there is a forest of dead, withered poplars, as I have seen and described in 1900; new poplars had not yet taken root. Shut in by extensive, reed-overgrown bank-lakes and swamps, the river becomes unapproachable. In general it flows along the foot of the heap of rubble of the Kuruk-tag, on the border between this and the lacustrine deposits. Soon it is divided into several tributaries; soon these unite, but only to divide again in the form of a delta. After the water has flowed through lakes and swamps, it flows on perfectly clear in a single furrow, which is 150 metres broad and up to 8 metres deep and has a rate of flow of 1 metre a second. A short distance further on to the east the river divides into three arms, which lose themselves in a number of small and large lakes.

Approximately 30 kilometres to the west-north-west of Lou-lan the stream has united again in a single furrow a hundred metres broad. Its speed is here so great that the clay-coloured water roars. Then it divides again into a labyrinth of lakes, the largest that Norin has seen in the Lop country. In the east one can see new lakes as blue streaks as far as the eye can reach. In them there usually lie elongated islands of reeds. To the north-east of Lou-lan the vegetation that has immigrated since 1921 gets thinner and thinner and finally ceases altogether, possibly because the water is still engaged in spreading. Moreover, the ground there contains many salts, so that the water becomes saline. A river-tributary 40 kilometres to the north-east of Lou-lan had clear but slightly salt water.

On the shore of one of the newly-formed lakes to the south of Altmish-bulak Norin found to his great astonishment the fresh tracks of a caravan of horses, asses, and a cow, which with their guides had travelled from east to west. He could imagine nothing else than that the tracks were to be attributed to fugitives from Kansu who had come from the town of Tun-huang.

My friend the camel-hunter Abd-ur-Rahim told Norin that in 1929 he had undertaken a reconnaissance excursion along the Kum-darya and had travelled about 10 kilometres further to the east than Norin. There he had reached the outermost lakes in this direction, had gone round them in a south-westerly direction, and had finally pushed right on to the ruins of Lou-lan. To the direct south of Lou-lan he saw a considerable river-tributary flowing towards the east. Norin believes, therefore, that the true Lop lake of the present time is situated to the east of Lou-lan in the central part of the Lop Desert, where he supposes the deepest depression to be. Probably the depression whose existence I established by means of levelling is a western offshoot of this area of deepest depression. When one speaks of depressions in the Lop Desert, one must not forget that these depressions in the flat country are imperceptible to the eye and only reveal themselves by the spreading of newly-arisen water or can only be discovered by measurements with instruments.

Norin mentions in his report that he is not in a position to decide whether the distribution of water is the same now as at the time when Lou-lan was still flourishing in the third century. This question will quite possibly never be decided. Norin believes, however, that at that time too, 1,600 to 1,700 years ago, lakes and swamps stretched between the foot of the mountain range and Lou-lan and offered the Chinese military colony a natural protection against the barbarians living in the north.

By his thorough and conscientious investigations Norin introduces a new epoch in the history of Lop-nor. He treats the problem geologically, while we others who have occupied ourselves with it have only considered the vicissitudes of the wandering lake in the historical period. He goes right back to the ice-age and draws the shore-line of the lake at that time when the Tarim lake filled the whole of Eastern Turkestan and probably extended far to the east past Kara-nor and the Sulo-ho. As a result of the desiccation or gradual drying-up which began towards the end of the ice-age, when the ice retreated and the quantity of water in the rivers decreased, the once so enormous lake shrank and entered the wandering stage, whose last part we know. If this drying-up process continues longer and the climate of Eastern Turkestan becomes drier and drier, then Lop-nor will disappear and the Tarim will experience the same course of development as the Cherchen-darya, the Khotan-darya, and the Keria-darya.

Norin's researches on the Kum-darya were supplemented in the spring of 1930 a short distance to the east of Lou-lan

by the Chinese member of our expedition Mr. Huang
Wên-pi, who there performed an extremely valuable and
conscientious work, and placed at my disposal his whole
material, an explanatory sketch-map, and two essays showing learning and discrimination, one on Lop-nor, the other
on Lou-lan.   In another connexion I shall have occasion to
publish these essays, full of original and new ideas and
points of view, in a translation by Professor Ferdinand
Lessing.   The views that Huang expresses concerning the
historical significance of Lou-lan are especially interesting.
Seeing that the old town had until then only been visited
by two Europeans, an American, and a Japanese, it is of
great value to hear the opinion of an unusually well-read
and well-informed Chinese on this question.

To Lou-lan itself Huang did not, indeed, succeed in
pushing on.   Just as with Norin, he too was hindered by
newly-formed tributaries and swampy ground, in which
the animals sank hopelessly.   He started out from Lukchin
and went from Altmish-bulak towards the old town,
and to the south could see two of its towers in the
distance.

Then he travelled on towards the east-north-east, and
thereby always had water on his right—to the south and
east of Lou-lan stretch great lakes.   He followed a river-
tributary, which had a breadth of 30 metres and a depth
of 4 metres and a very slow current.   A camel-hunter told
him that the water, which came from the Konche-darya,
had reached this point five years before, that is to say in
the year 1925.   After a wandering of 44 kilometres along
the new watercourse, Huang came to a watch-tower on the
bank of a lake which is undoubtedly a part of the old
Lop-nor.   Since the town lies quite near Sir Aurel Stein's
route, it is probable that it is one of the towers that Stein
has entered in his map.   Huang believes, however, that his
watch-tower was not visited by Stein.   He found in the
interior of the tower about eighty inscribed pieces of wood
dating from the time about 80 B.C.   The place was called
To-kin 2,000 years ago.

As far as Huang could see towards the east through the
misty air, a distance of approximately 5 kilometres, he could

382

see nothing but lakes and swamps. From To-kin he turned round towards the north.

Huang's guide shot a wild camel that had come to the bank of the lake in order to drink. For these roaming inhabitants of the desert and their conditions of life, the last change in the hydrography of the lower Tarim has been of the greatest importance. While the " fish-eaters " near Abdal and on Kara-koshun had to migrate to Charkhlik and Miran when the water disappeared, the wild camels needed no longer to search for water. I had seen them like ghosts wandering about in the desert between the little scanty islands of vegetation that are miles away from each other, and their tracks had led us to the three little meagre salt springs which lay to the east of Altmish-bulak. There, where the tracks ran together from all directions towards the opening of a little valley between hills, one could be sure of finding a salt spring. The wild camels have known for centuries where the springs have lain, and have gone there at least once a week to drink.

Now, after the water has returned to its old beds in the north, the camels no longer require to make mile-long wanderings in order to quench their thirst. Wherever they may find themselves at the south foot of the Kuruk-tag or in the eastern valleys of this desolate system of mountain ranges, they need only turn straight towards the south and are always certain to arrive on the shore of a lake or on the bank of a river-tributary. And they need no longer be satisfied with the salt water of the springs. The water which the desert has now quite unexpectedly presented them with is fresh and, where it has gone through reed-overgrown swamps or shallow lakes, quite clear. Just as little need they search for pasturage. Wherever they turn their fleet steps towards the south, they find extensive fields of reeds and fresh tamarisks. Only to the east of Lou-lan does the desert get poorer and poorer ; but if the water stays in its old beds, it will not be many years before the vegetation will have spread right to the outermost lakes.

With the changes that have taken place since 1921 in the

hydrographic distribution of the Lop Desert, a golden age has set in for the wild camels. But dark clouds also hang threatening over their future. If the Tarim and the Konche-darya remain in the bed of the Kum-darya, it will not be long before man follows the path towards the east of the water, the plants, and the wild animals, and along the river establishes settlements and farms. Perhaps, too, the day will come when the town of Lou-lan, which has been slumbering for seventeen hundred years, will wake up out of its sleep and rise up to new life. Then the hour of the wild camels will have struck. Then they must migrate into the inviolable expanses of the desert, where man does not disturb their rest.

When I travelled along the dry bed of the Kuruk-darya 31 years ago, it seemed to me as if I was carrying out a court medical examination on the body of a geographical object. Since then 28 years had passed by, when I sent Dr. Erik Norin out to examine the patient, which, as had been shown, had only been in a trance. I had myself, after my cartographic survey of the dry bed, expressed the following view : " I am of the opinion that the Kuruk-darya was the main artery of the whole Tarim system and that the lake into which the Kuruk-darya opened only lay in the northern part of the desert." At the beginning of the historical period the terminal lake or rather lakes have changed year by year, and so it has also been since Przhevalsky's time. But since then the lake has been in the southern part of the desert. For a certain interval of time, which, as I suppose, is before the historical period, the lake has been triangular or crescent-shaped. When the water of the Tarim left its northern bed and flowed to the south, the northern wing of the triangle dried up and the water collected in the southern corner. When the Tarim in 1921 returned to its northern bed, the southern lake dried up and the basin in the northern part of the desert filled again.

Between these wanderings lie innumerable intermediate stages, which one cannot possibly follow up. Parasitic lakes and new lake formations have arisen here and there, but only soon to disappear again. Avullu-köl, Kara-köl, Tayek-köl, and Arka-köl, which I found in 1896, were just

The Kum-darya to the south of Ying-pen
(Haude photograph, November, 1928)

The Konche-darya near Sai-cheke, Camp 255
(Bergman photograph, 23rd October, 1928)

THE CHANGED RIVERS

[face p. 384

Pools of water in the otherwise dry bed of the Tarim at Camp 233
(Bergman photograph, 29th September, 1928)

The bed of the Tarim with isolated pools and slowly dying bushes along
the bank in the neighbourhood of Tukum

(Haude photograph)

THE CHANGED RIVERS

[*face p.* 385

such ephemeral formations as all other watercourses and collections of water in this changeable land.

It was of great interest to me to compare my own description of the Kuruk-darya of 1900 with Norin's description of the new river in the years 1928 and 1930. Between the two there exists one striking agreement. Norin says himself in his reports, that the new water for the most part follows the furrow that I cartographically surveyed. I expressed the supposition that, at the place where the bed came to an end, the river, just like the lower Tarim, had passed through shallow lakes. Several of these passage lakes Norin has now found. At one place which I formerly visited, the bed had a breadth of 75 metres and a depth of 5–6 metres and sharply-defined bank-terraces with a dead forest. At another place the breadth amounted to 94·5 metres and the depth to 6·5. The old river, as the new, winds immediately along the heap of rubble at the south foot of the Kuruk-tag. I believed, however, that the river came to an end to the immediate west of Lou-lan and there emptied itself into the first lakes of Lop-nor, but Norin, Ambolt, and Huang determined that it flowed on about 40 kilometres past Lou-lan towards the east-north-east. On my journeys from Altmish-bulak to Lou-lan I saw no river-bed, and now Norin reports that just here there extend lakes and swamps. In the year 1901 it seemed obvious to me that the lake had sent out a considerable offshoot to the north-east; for in February, 1901, I crossed in that region the floor of the old basin of a lake. Similar expanses of ancient lake-bottoms with encrustations of salt over them were crossed several years later by Stein and Huntington. But this lake-bottom may have already lain dry before the beginning of the historical period.

According to Norin's estimate of the capacity of the new river, the Kum-darya, in the spring of 1928 and in the first months of the year 1930 at least 200 cubic metres a second flowed along its bed. This statement already gives one reason for the suspicion that the new river not only receives the Konche-darya, but also the greater part of the Tarim water. For near Korla I had found that the Konche-darya carries 72 cubic metres a second and that this value remains

about the same throughout the whole year, since the lake
of Bagrash-köl acts as an equalizing and distributive factor.
Absolute certainty, however, could not be obtained until the
beds of the two rivers pointing towards the south-east and
south had been investigated.

Five members of my expedition travelled in the year 1928
across or along the dried-up beds of the mysterious delta-
land, and two of them, the archæologist Folke Bergman
and the meteorologist Dr. Waldemar Haude, have given
me all the information that I desired. They found the
lowermost sections of the Tarim and of the Konche-darya
almost dried up. Flowing water could at most stream
along the beds in the form of a tidal wave during the period
of high water. As far as Argan, in the years before 1928
but after 1921, not a single drop of flowing water had found
its way. Only pools with stagnant water could still be
found in the deepest parts of the Tarim bed. From that
it clearly follows, that in 1928 both the Tarim and the
Konche-darya had taken their course through the Kuruk-
darya, which in 1900 I had found completely dry and
lifeless.

It only remains further to search for Lop-nor in its
present form and cartographically survey it. I have reason
to suppose that this lake is considerably larger than Kara-
koshun was in 1901, so far as the development of the oases
and the increased tribute that the irrigation of the new
fields demands of the rivers of Eastern Turkestan has not
impaired the quantity of water.

As I have calculated, throughout the whole year at the
end of the century on an average 64 cubic metres of water
a second have flowed past the fishing village of Yurt-
chapgan and into Kara-koshun. Already 30 years ago I
formulated the theory that, if the lakes along the shore near
Yangi-köl and the chain of lakes from Avullu-köl to Arka-
köl suddenly dried up, 18 cubic metres a second from the
former and 19 from the latter would benefit the Tarim and
would empty into Kara-koshun. The terminal lake would
then receive, instead of 64 cubic metres a second, 101 cubic
metres throughout the whole year, and the lake would swell
in capacity from 2,000 to 3,000 million cubic metres.

Since 1921 both Kara-koshun and the two chains of lakes have disappeared, and the water, which now flows to Lou-lan, has not to part with anything on the way and is therefore of much greater volume than was the Tarim near Yurt-chapgan. It is true that new lakes along the bank, parasitic lakes which draw away the strength of the Tarim, have arisen along the new course of the river to the east of Ying-pen, but in any case considerably greater volumes of water are now flowing into the terminal basin in the northern part of the desert than into the southern basin before 1921.

LOP-NOR, THE WANDERING LAKE

III

IN conclusion I should like to say a few words more concerning the *historical* significance of the remarkable hydrographic changes that have taken place since 1921 in the waterways of the lowest part of the Tarim and in its final recipient, the famous wandering lake of Lop-nor.

Dr. Albert Herrmann has already in 1910 in his work *Die alten Seidenstrassen zwischen China und Syrien* drawn with admirable clearness and learning the course of the principal ancient thoroughfares on which 2,000 years ago the noble silk was brought from China to Rome. On his outline-map of Central Asia he has shown how the great road ran from China proper along the north foot of the Nan-shan or Richthofen range, touched the towns of Tun-huang and Yü-mên-kuan, and to the immediate west of the latter town divided into two branches, the northern of which went by Hami, Turfan, Kucha, and Kashgar, and the southern by Lou-lan, Khotan, and Kashgar. The southern road is in its eastern part also a *limes*, a military road protected by defence-works, which Sir Aurel Stein has described in so meritorious a manner.

Up to the beginning of the fourth century the lake system of Lop-nor, as we have seen, had been situated in the northern part of the Lop Desert, and the above-mentioned southern military road ran therefore from Tun-huang to Lou-lan along the north shore of Lop-nor. Near Lou-lan it divided into two branches : the northern followed the Kum-darya as far as the region where now the town of Korla is situated, and the southern went in a south-westerly direction to Khotan.

It is thus only to be ascribed to the position of the waterways and the existence of Lop-nor in the northern part of the desert, that the road from Tun-huang by Lou-lan and along the Kum-darya was available for traffic and formed an easy road for the invasion of China.

When at the beginning of the fourth century the Tarim with its tributary the Konche-darya changed its course and turned off towards the south-east and south and the terminal lake wandered into the southern part of the desert, and when, as a result of this, the northern waterways and lakes near Lou-lan dried up, the old trade route and military road between Tun-huang, Lou-lan, and Kucha, lost its importance, and communication with the West along this line was cut off and came to an end.

Now, as I have explained, a new and mighty swing of the pendulum has carried the flowing, as also the stationary waters back to the north again into their old beds in the Kum-darya and the lakes near Lou-lan. Thereby there have been produced anew the same conditions as prevailed 2,000 years ago, and the old intimate connexion between Tun-huang and Lou-lan has at the same time been restored.

What these incisive changes mean to the great republic of China it is easy to understand. A remarkable event in the province of physical geography and hydrography has put a means in the hand of the Government to open the old line of communication to traffic again. Just as in the days of the Han dynasty, now too will it be possible to construct a through-going high road which leads from China proper by Tun-huang, Lou-lan, and Kucha, to Kashgar. But while the camel caravans in olden times required four months, one would now with motor-cars be able to cover the stretch between Peking in the east and Kashgar in the extreme west in two weeks. By this means the distance between the most westerly Chinese province and China proper would be cut down to a fraction of the time it takes at present, and Sin-kiang would approach nearer to Nanking. By means of a wisely-organized traffic with goods motor-cars, the products of the province of Sin-kiang could be conveyed to the coast, and in the reverse direction foreign groceries could be conveyed to Sin-kiang ; officials and other travellers could cover the 4,000 kilometres quickly and conveniently. The large traffic between Sin-kiang and China would move entirely on Chinese soil, as also the traffic in the northern part of the province, which would have to be directed to the great thoroughfare by Turfan and Hami. In this way the trade would make use of roads that lie within the borders of China and would become independent of the Siberian Railway.

Perhaps André Citroen's great plan of a motor-car journey across the whole of Asia will provide the impetus for awakening the two-thousand-year-old thoroughfare to life again. This great expedition, which is under the leadership of M. Georges-Marie Haadt, and to whose scientific staff Father Teilhard de Jardin belongs, will in a short time set out on its journey across the whole of the Old World. Without doubt their experiences and observations will become of the greatest practical use to China, and one can only wish the French undertaking all the success that it deserves.

At a meeting of the Chinese committee in Peking that represents the interests of our expedition, and of which all the members are Chinese scholars, I made known our discoveries in the hydrography of the lower Tarim and submitted the plan of constructing a motor-car road between Peking or Nanking and Kashgar. My proposal to deliver a communication to that effect to the Government was favourably received, and the committee declared itself ready to support such a proposal with its own expert opinion.

Asia is to at least as great an extent as America the land of great possibilities, and one can be certain that within a short time events will take place in the heart of Asia that have not been dreamed of.

PEKING, *December* 28th, 1930.

LOP-NOR, THE WANDERING LAKE

IV

WHEN I wrote the last chapters of this book dealing with the changes that had taken place in the course of the lower Tarim River, I was, unfortunately, unable to give the exact situation of the new Lake Lop-nor. As several members of our expedition, both Europeans and Chinese, in the summer and autumn of 1928, had travelled along the dry bed of lowermost Tarim, and had found Przhevalsky's Lake Kara-koshun completely dry, it was obvious that the new Lake Lop-nor must be situated somewhere further north in the Lop Desert. In the late autumn of 1928 I approached the Governor of Sin-kiang for permission to go down to the river Kum-darya and to the lakes into which it flowed, but permission could not be given, as the region was said to belong to the war zone where fugitives from Kansu entered the territory of Sin-kiang.

In the summer of 1930, when I was in Peking, and Dr. Nils Hörner and his assistant, Mr. Parker C. Chen, were working in the Nan-shan mountains, I sent them instructions to go and find the new Lake Lop-nor which, according to information given me by natives of Turfan, had been formed in 1921.

Very soon after the Lop-nor chapters of this volume were sent to press, I received the following telegram from Dr. Nils Hörner. The telegram was sent by special courier on camel-back from one of Hörner's and Chen's camps at 40° 20′ North lat. and 91° 40′ East long., on April 20th, 1931, to the telegraph station of An-hsi. From there it was dispatched to the Swedish Legation, Peking, and finally reached Stockholm on May 9th, 1931. As this telegram contains the final and definite solution of the Lop-nor problem, at least for the time being, and as this problem has been much discussed ever since Przhevalsky's discovery of the southern lake in 1877, I quote Dr. Hörner's message here as an addition to the Lop-nor chapters of this book. It runs as follows :

"Latitude forty twenty longitude ninetyone forty April twentieth stop topographical Lopnor survey ordered by you completed stop Mr. Chen and I started from Tunhwang oasis December seventh with four men twenty three camels for desert work and small hired caravan to depot last of dry salt crust of ancient Lop sea stop December thirtieth reached new Lopnor big open saltwater lake causing serious detour stop found fresh water and grazing at new river January eight camels near breakdown after fourteen hard days without drinkable water or grazing stop single river branches north of ruined city of Loulan discovered by you nineteen hundred stop east of Loulan longitude we have mapped whole lake system except small island area temporarily inaccessible stop as Doctor Norin has already surveyed river to beginning of delta whole new phase of Lopnor problem solved by our expedition stop we have measured volume of water in different river courses and mapped considerable way of ancient shore line stop connecting to Norin's previous work studied geological development of land and lake stop neolithic and later finds plentiful all way west of lake stop returned safely to depot April second met nobody for four months stop remain in desert for additional work as long as heat permits stop expect to call for telegrams Anhsi before June first mail Tunhwang stop except camels all splendid Hoerner."

This message is the most important I have had from any member of my staff during the $4\frac{1}{2}$ years of our exploring work. Every student of geography will understand the great importance of the new geographical facts and discoveries it contains. A discussion of these facts would take us too far here and must be left to another occasion. This is so much the more necessary as, two weeks ago, I received both the scientific and personal reports of Dr. Hörner's and Mr. Chen's exploration together with three sketch-maps and many photos.

The material secured by the geographical, geological, and topographical survey made by members of our expedition will make it possible to write a more detailed and correct study of Lake Lop-nor than has ever been the case during the last two thousand years.

STOCKHOLM, *July 14th*, 1931.

INDEX